D0761079

A HISTORY OF
Beaver County

A HISTORY OF

Beaver County

Martha Sonntag Bradley

1999
Utah State Historical Society
Beaver County Commission

ISBN 0-913738-17-4
Library of Congress Catalog Card Number 98-61325
Map by Automated Geographic Reference Center—State of Utah
Printed in the United States of America

Utah State Historical Society
300 Rio Grande
Salt Lake City, Utah 84101-1182

Contents

Acknowledgments

$\mathbf{M}$y earliest memories of Beaver County were formed when my family made our annual trek to the beach at Southern California. Part of the ritual, from which we never deviated, was to stop at Beaver for dinner. It became our refuge, our rest stop at least, a time when we could finally pile out of the car and come up for air. Each year my mother patiently pulled into the covered parking lot of a restaurant on Main Street carefully parking between two poles that held up a metal covering, not unlike a carport. Each year after we were fed and were acting like human beings again, we got back in the car and she pulled out. As if it were part of the ritual, each year she scraped the side of our station wagon on the metal pole to one side or the other of the car, something bending it slightly. I have always considered that our family's unique contribution to Beaver.

My parents, however, inadvertently instilled in me a great love of rural Utah on those trips for I would watch the miles and miles of changing terrain and skies so much bigger than at home and believe this was the backdrop of the story of the Mormon pioneers. To me that meant it was sacred turf. The land, the beautiful rock and adobe buildings we explored, and the stretch of mountains and plateaus became a part of me as a youth and I still carry that great regard and respect for Utah that I learned from my parents as a child.

Now, my experience of Utah is in a car filled with different children, with a fresh vision of the land and its beauties. My children help me see Utah with new eyes, and have supported me in my endless search for greater understanding of it. Better than the finest cut sandstone foundations of Utah's beautiful pioneer buildings, my children are the rock I rest on and the backdrop of every story I write and live and I am always grateful for what they give me so generously. Jason, Elizabeth, Rachael, Emily, Katelyn, Patrick, and now Mark and Aspen make my life rich and beautiful.

I am grateful for the enthusiastic support of Betty Miller, the Director of the Beaver County Travel Council and the chair of the Beaver County Centennial Committee who organized this project. Newcomer herself to this place (more than a decade ago) she saw its beauties and the value of its history with an enthusiasm and newness that was always inspiring. Her committee, which included Dell Hollingshead, Ann Messer, Gladys Whittaker, J. D. Osborne, Glenna Osborne, and Richard Albrecht, have been enormously helpful in providing ideas for improving the manuscript, identifying photographs, and have been incredibly patient with the pace of the work. This series, and certainly this book, would never have happened without the untiring efforts of Allan Kent Powell and Craig Fuller— being a part of this unique effort to chronicle the histories of counties of Utah has been a privilege.

Allen D. Robert's work on the architecture and landscape of Beaver County is a part of this manuscript and as always Allen has mentored me through my efforts to better understand the built environment and I recognize his important contribution. What a fitting conclusion to the project to have my friend Gary Bergera copy edit the manuscript. His careful eye and meticulous attention to detail has strengthened my efforts.

General Introduction

When Utah was granted statehood on 4 January 1896, twenty-seven counties comprised the nation's new forty-fifth state. Subsequently two counties, Duchesne in 1914 and Daggett in 1917, were created. These twenty-nine counties have been the stage on which much of the history of Utah has been played.

Recognizing the importance of Utah's counties, the Utah State Legislature established in 1991 a Centennial History Project to write and publish county histories as part of Utah's statehood centennial commemoration. The Division of State History was given the assignment to administer the project. The county commissioners, or their designees, were responsible for selecting the author or authors for their individual histories, and funds were provided by the state legislature to cover most research and writing costs as well as to provide each public school and library with a copy of each history. Writers worked under general guidelines provided by the Division of State History and in cooperation with county history committees. The counties also established a Utah Centennial County History Council

ix

to help develop policies for distribution of state-appropriated funds and plans for publication.

Each volume in the series reflects the scholarship and interpretation of the individual author. The general guidelines provided by the Utah State Legislature included coverage of five broad themes encompassing the economic, religious, educational, social, and political history of the county. Authors were encouraged to cover a vast period of time stretching from geologic and prehistoric times to the present. Since Utah's statehood centennial celebration falls just four years before the arrival of the twenty-first century, authors were encouraged to give particular attention to the history of their respective counties during the twentieth century.

Still, each history is at best a brief synopsis of what has transpired within the political boundaries of each county. No history can do justice to every theme or event or individual that is part of an area's past. Readers are asked to consider these volumes as an introduction to the history of the county, for it is expected that other researchers and writers will extend beyond the limits of time, space, and detail imposed on this volume to add to the wealth of knowledge about the county and its people. In understanding the history of our counties, we come to understand better the history of our state, our nation, our world, and ourselves.

In addition to the authors, local history committee members, and county commissioners, who deserve praise for their outstanding efforts and important contributions, special recognition is given to Joseph Francis, chairman of the Morgan County Historical Society, for his role in conceiving the idea of the centennial county history project and for his energetic efforts in working with the Utah State Legislature and State of Utah officials to make the project a reality. Mr. Francis is proof that one person does make a difference.

ALLAN KENT POWELL
CRAIG FULLER
GENERAL EDITORS

BEAVER COUNTY

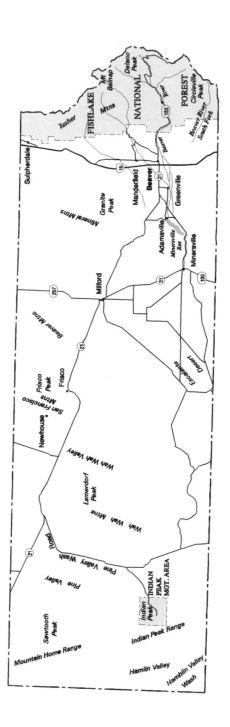

INDEX MAP

CHAPTER 1

Introduction

BEAVER COUNTY:
THE PLACES THAT SHAPE US

In part, my love of Beaver's countryside motivated me to write this book. It is easy to find many attractions in rural Utah, and in Beaver County these natural features abound—mountains to hike and explore, fertile farm fields and grazing land to the west, and small historic towns to investigate and learn from. For those of us who live outside the county, rural Utah has been home for significant periods of our lives, and it is where the stories of our ancestors play out. I feel privileged to have been able to help tell their stories.

As have many of you, I have become increasingly concerned about the many threats to Beaver County's historically rural atmosphere. It is possible that our state will undergo overwhelming changes that will alter the whole landscape irretrievably in the next generation. In some places change is accelerating beyond our ability to imagine its impact by the end of the century. Therefore, places like Beaver County that hang onto some vestige of the hundred years of rural life are important to preserve.

Technically a rural environment is sparsely populated, lies well beyond the metropolis or the suburbs, and is a place where natural

1

resources are the basis for at least some of the residents' livelihoods. Here farmers, ranchers, miners, and individuals who enjoy the forests and mountains abound. Rural environments are always more directly tied to nature, the weather, the changing seasons mark their days, and therefore a rural environment is deceptively stable.

In Beaver County natural resources abound. The mineral wealth of the varied mountain ranges, the fertile soil of the fields, and stretches of land perfect for grazing of stock offer numerous opportunities for employment and extraction of raw materials for use. Perhaps, more importantly, we must also embrace the idea of the community as a resource, from individual farms or landholdings, to social institutions, to the local economy as a whole. This rural community, built first by the Mormon pioneers in the 1850s and later by their progenitors and newcomers, has used both the natural resources at hand and their own talents and traditions—a substantial investment in this place. Their collective investment deserves our respect and justifies this attempt to better understand and define the dimensions of that effort at protecting and building upon the land, enhancing natural and scenic resources, preserving buildings, traditions and institutions of cultural significance, and enhancing the local economy and social institutions.

The colonization of Beaver County can be characterized as the settlement of dichotomy. When white settlers first came to the area, they chose to locate their homes by the proximity of their land to water, the mountains, and natural resources. The county is marked by geographic dispersion across an area that stretched to the western border between Utah and Nevada, and soon towns were built at the base of mountain ranges across the county. Beyond these basic settlement motifs, Beaver County is distinguished by contradictory but complimentary patterns of settlement: agricultural vs. mining communities; theologically based towns vs. secular communities; cooperative economies vs. traditional capitalist economic organization; orderly superimposed grid plans vs. unplanned geographically determined town settlements, and finally the confrontation between Mormons and gentiles.

As early as 1860 Beaver County was at the center of a colonization network that stretched north into Idaho, south to San

Bernardino and west into central Nevada. As such, efforts at settlement mirrored those in numerous other places. Attempts at building irrigation systems, platting towns, building homes, schoolhouses, and churches reflected community values—the larger community of the Mormon empire. But in many important ways, Salt Lake City set the model.

By 1860 Salt Lake City had streets stretching from the town's center in every direction—straight, wide streets, some close into town lined with dry goods stores, blacksmith's shops, drugstores or hotels, others with houses at even intervals. Salt Lake City's cultural life afforded amenities available in Eastern cities—theatrical presentations, dances, philosophical and literary societies, and numerous clubs formed around the interests of locals. This then set the model. Both physically and culturally, Salt Lake City was quickly an established town with a stratified society, relatively sophisticated repertoire of activities, and a thriving economy.

During the first three decades after settlement, Beaver built a community that mirrored Salt Lake City. Virtually all services, cultural events, and educational facilities were available in this fledgling community in southern Utah to a lesser degree. Beaver had a theatrical company, literary associations, suffrage unions, and other social and cultural groups. Mormon men gathered together a School of the Prophets for religious instruction independent of their church activities. Cooperative and communal activities reflected the churchwide movement for self-sufficiency. On the other hand, the county's mining towns—Frisco and Milford—rivaled Park City in both size and activity and had populations that were markedly diverse. Clearly, in the nineteenth century Beaver County had established itself as a place with potential and most certainly a place to be watched.

The Mormons came to Utah in the effort to escape religious discrimination and persecution. After the death of their church president and prophet, Joseph Smith, in Nauvoo, Illinois plans began for a mass exodus into the isolated Great Basin region. Mormonism had always invited controversy, and the Mormon people had moved several times in the wake of harassment, first to Kirtland, Ohio, then to Missouri, and on to Illinois.

Although Beaver County was one of many centers of settlement of the Mormon pioneers, its history is unique. It isn't just another place, but a place with a difference. What distinguishes Beaver County? Is it the clean water, the rich farmland, the dramatic mountain ranges, the beautiful historic rock buildings, opportunities to hike and fish? Is it the willingness of neighbors to help one another? The unique combination of rich mineral resources and the mining industry alongside stock raising and farming? The resources seem endless, and yet it is the unique combination that forms the answer. Identifying community values and concerns such as these seems like a good place to start to answer this question. Certainly, each county has its own particular character and needs. This sense of place is shaped in part by the natural environment, by its place, but also by the interaction of this particular group of people with that place, the way they have collectively and individually responded to the unique challenges and joys it provided.

One artist and author, Alan Gussow, suggests a list of six questions in attempting to identify the unique character of a place.

1. If you took a visitor around your community, what places would you be certain to include?

2. Where would you get out of the car and walk around? Why those places?

3. What are the recurring events, both natural and human, in your environment? Are they marked or observed? How?

4. Small towns and their surrounding countryside interact with each other. What indicators, if any, do you find in your town which reveal the beneficial effects of being in a rural setting? Can you think of any good qualities in the countryside which result from the nearness to a town?

5. What part of the environment in which you live is most likely to change? Is this change for the better? If not, why not; and what could you do to prevent or lessen the impact of this change?

6. If you could change one thing about your community, what would it be? Most importantly, what would be the first step to take in order to work toward that change?[1]

Like many rural counties, Beaver County faces key issues during the next century. While some urban counties in Utah are facing the problems associated with inordinant growth, Beaver County must struggle to escape the grip of economic stagnation and decline. Future decline might be caused by local problems, as was true when the county reacted to the interstate freeway that bypassed Beaver's communities, or a national trend such as a drop in prices of certain commodities. As one business goes out of business, so do the businesses they patronize. The interrelatedness of a county comes into focus with the rise and decline in fortunes. Everyone suffers with the failure of a major county business or entity. Vacant stores, abandoned gas stations, and gaping holes on streets where buildings once stood are visual evidence of the major impact that economic change has already had.

Much of this has played out on the town level. Small towns form the backbone of this county. They are the economic, social, cultural, and political centers of action in Beaver County. Here, stores, schools, doctors, farm-equipment dealers, and most customers are located. Few of these towns are the diverse, largely self-sufficient communities they were when they were settled. More county residents are traveling the distance to malls and shopping centers in Cedar City or St. George to the south. As a result, many of these towns have suffered. Not only have businesses faltered, or closed down altogether, but also key social institutions such as local schools, churches, or restaurants have changed. No longer the scene of critical social interaction, these important community functions are being displaced or replaced by new ways of interacting. It is important to remember the interconnectedness of community institutions.

Beaver County's people are its most important asset. As each community was settled during the nineteenth century, as they grew and developed over the next several decades, their residents created a unique character based on their ethnic, religious, and occupational backgrounds. Their commitment and energy created this place, colored it with a special dedication to taming a wild environment and bringing it into usefulness.

In part, recognized for its indigenous buildings and landscapes, Beaver County's physical environment evokes familiar and comforting associations of family and community, an interesting and evocative juxtaposition of traditional spaces on the natural environment. These buildings and the historic landscape conserve tangible and visible links with the community's past, preserve places that are important parts of the community's identity, and retain important resources that teach us about the past, about how this place was settled, developed and changed over time.

This juxtaposition of building shapes and forms, the rich mixture of architectural styles and building types and materials, the color, texture, and shape of the physical environment create a diversified landscape. The physical landscape is particularly rich in historic resources—houses, barns, granaries, windmills, fences, and out buildings teach us how farmers laid out their fields, how the people joined together for irrigation projects for cooperative businesses or community wide projects.

This centennial history seeks to find answers to the question: What is Beaver County about? It looks at government and community institutions, the built environment and settlement patterns, cultural and social life. It attempts to identify the way these disparate elements weave together to create a design filled with meaning and memory, history, and a sense of future direction.

ENDNOTE

1. Alan Gussow, *Saving America's Countryside* (Baltimore: The Johns Hopkins University Press, 1989), 8.

CHAPTER 2

THE LAND AND ITS PEOPLE

Named for the abundant beaver that inhabited the Beaver River when settlers first came into the area, Beaver County is located in southwestern Utah. The county seat, Beaver City, is located 210 miles south of Salt Lake City, 520 miles northeast of Los Angeles, California, and halfway between Salt Lake City and Las Vegas, Nevada, on U.S. Highway 91 and Interstate 15.A number of short mountain ranges oriented for the most part on a north-south axis cross the county. The highest is the Tushar Mountains in eastern Beaver County whose peaks are over 12,000 feet in height. The Beaver River originates in the Tushar Mountains and flows in a northwest-erly direction into Millard County at the southern end of the Great Basin drainage area.

Beaver Valley reaches an elevation of 5,970 feet, and Milford Valley 4,962 feet.

Slightly more than three times longer than wide, Beaver County is rectangular in shape, with the exception of its irregular eastern boundary, formed by the ridgeline of the Tushar Mountains. The 94-mile length of the county runs east-to-west, while its short 30-mile width is its north-south dimension. The county is bounded on the north by Millard County, on the east by Piute County and a small section of Sevier County, on the south by Iron County and a small portion of Garfield County, and on the west by the state of Nevada's Lincoln County. Only the third county north of the Arizona-Utah state line, Beaver County is thus considered part of Utah's southwestern geologic region. It is part of "Color Country," a five-county travel region designated by the Utah Travel Council which also includes Iron, Washington, Kane, and Garfield counties.

The thirteenth largest of Utah's twenty-nine counties, Beaver County contains an area of 2,587 miles, or 3.15 percent of the area of the state. Roughly half of the county is mountainous, with the other half in valleys. Most of the major mountains are in the east, while the deserts are in the west. Roughly 20 percent of the area is farmed, while another 40 percent is grazed by livestock. Seventy-five percent of the county's area is federally owned, about 9 percent is owned by the state, and only 16 percent of the land is privately owned. These statistics reflect the high percentage of government-owned land statewide.

The lowest point in Beaver County, located near the Murdock Siding north of Milford, is 4,700 feet above sea level. The highest point is the peak of Mount Delano at 12,168 feet. The height difference of 7,468 feet is similar to that found between the valley floors and tallest mountains to the east in Weber, Salt Lake, and Utah counties.

Tushar Mountains

The tallest and most resource rich range in Beaver County is the Tushar Mountain Range, the entire western slope of which falls within the county. True mountains rather than rolling hills or plateaus, the tallest Tushar summit is Mount Delano (12,168). However, because it is steeper and features the intact remains of an old heliograph station on its peak, slightly lower Mount Belknap (12,136) is the more interesting peak to climb. Other major peaks include Mt. Baldy (12,082), City Creek Peak (11,165), Circleville Mountain (11,332) Birch Creek Mountain (10,824) and Mt. Holly (10,029). The latter is the home to Elk Meadows Ski Resort. This

Mt. Belknap. (J.D. Osborn)

group of peaks forms the third tallest mountain range in Utah, with only the peaks of the Uinta and LaSal mountains higher.

By virtue of their size and wealth of natural resources, the Tushars are the dominant range in Beaver County. These mountains are composed primarily of volcanic rocks from the Miocene period. Some of the area is classified as Mt. Belknap rhyolite, while in the more southern Birch Creek Peak region, rock is from the Muddy Creek formation. In the northern Tushars, several old mines may be found in the intrusive rocks around Bullion, Brigham and Bluebell peaks.

Because of their remarkable height, length (thirty miles), and width (twenty miles), the massive Tushars are the source of important stands of trees, wildlife habitats, canyons, and creeks which allow for the flourishing of the city of Beaver and other communities to the west.

Mineral Mountains

Situated between Milford and Beaver valleys, the Mineral Mountains extend from just above the Millard County line on the north and the Minersville reservoir on the south. The range is about twenty-eight miles long and averages roughly five miles in width. Its major prominences are Granite Peak (9,578) in the center of the range, Bearskin Mountain (9,095) to the north and Bradshaw Mountain (8,011) to the south. Like most of the other ranges in the county, it runs north-south. Geologically, the Mineral Mountains are dominated by Tertiary intrusive rocks on its eastern slopes and older, Quaternary alluvial deposits on its west face. Its tallest peaks are rhyolite outcroppings, while the southern end of the range is a mixture of at least eight different periods of rock formation. As the name suggests, the Mineral Mountains have been a source of metal-bearing ore extracted from such mines as the Blue Star. The range is of sufficient size to produce small, seasonal streams which feed the tributaries running to the Beaver River. Several small springs also emanate from the Mineral Mountains.

Black Mountains

Across Minersville Canyon south of the Mineral Mountains are the Black Mountains, most of which lie in Iron County. The only east-west oriented range in the county, its highest peaks, Chipman (7,966) and Baboon (7,310), are a short distance south of the Iron County line. The range consists primarily of basalts and Miocene volcanic rock. Aside from providing some watershed to Minersville reservoir, the uninhabited Black Mountains play a minor role in Beaver County's economy and recreational picture.

San Francisco Mountains

This small range is located about fifteen miles due west of Milford and features Frisco Peak (9,660), one of the county's most popular hiking mountains. At the southern end of the range are the ruined remains of old Frisco, a nineteenth-century mining town which produced silver, gold, lead, and zinc from its mines. The north-south trending range is roughly twenty miles long and four miles wide. The north half of the range extends into Millard County where it connects with the south extremity of the Cricket Mountains. The rolling San Franciscos are formed mostly of Precambrian rock, except for the southern end of the range which includes Ordovician sedimentary stone, Tertiary intrusive rock, and, on the west slope, Cambrian rock.

Frisco Peak consists mostly of metamorphic and quartzite rock from the Precambrian period. On the peak one finds twisting, weathered bristlecone pine and a fine panoramic view of the Great Basin. The range is marked by numerous nineteenth-century mines, kilns, and railroad grades. The Indian Queen and Imperial mines are on the west and south faces, while the King David, Golden Reef, and Horn Silver mines are found on the eastern slopes. A few springs have their sources in the San Francisco Mountains, among them Pitchfork, Horse, Crystal, Morehouse and Tub springs. Small, seasonal creeks run down Morehouse, Sawmill and other numerous canyons. While the undeveloped range contains neither hiking trails nor campgrounds, good campsites and hikable mining roads exist in many locations.

Shauntee Hills

These "hills" are a small, relatively low mountainous area surrounded by the Wah Wahs on the west, the San Franciscos on the north, the Star Range on the east, and the Escalante Desert on the south. Geologically, the Shauntie Hills are an extension of the San Francisco Mountains' Tertiary volcanic rocks. White Mountain (6,781) is the major peak in this little sub-range.

Star Range

Only six miles long and not very wide, the Star Range is the smallest of the county's mountain groups to be designated a range. Its highest prominence is 6,088 at the north end, while Topache Peak rises near the south tip of the range, about five miles due west of the Upton Siding. The north end of the range begins six miles due west of Milford. The nominal importance of this little north-south running range may be due to its proximity to Milford, its geological complexity, and the fact that it has attracted mining activity. No one type or period of rock dominates the Star Range, which features rock formations from at least seven major geological periods.

Wah Wah Mountains

About twenty-four miles east of the Nevada border, the fifty-mile long Wah Wah range runs north-south the entire width of Beaver County. Its highest section, including Wah Wah Peak (9,393) and

Lamerdorf Peak (8,425), is near its southern end. In the same area are Tasso, Lou, and other mines, some of which have been recently active. Geologically complex, the Wah Wahs have Cambrian quartzite to the west, with middle and upper Cambrian rocks, mostly limestone, in the center and peak areas. Wah Wah Peak is one of the highest summits in this part of the Great Basin. Its height allows for a few streams whose waters are collected in a series of reservoirs along the south foot of the range. Good stands of bristlecone pine are an attraction in the highest climes. Hikers must depend solely on animal trails and exploratory mining tracks for access.

Needle Range

The first mountains encountered in Beaver County east of the Nevada state line are in the north-south trending Needle Range. What on some maps is identified as a single range is considered on others as two separate ranges—the Mountain Home and Indian Peak mountains. The smaller, two-mile long Mountain Home range is the northernmost of the two. Its principal prominence is a somewhat isolated peak called the Toad (7,543). Across a four-mile wide plain to the south begins the Indian Peak Mountains, a taller, twenty-five-mile long range. Its major summit is Indian Peak (9,790), a popular climb for hikers. Although it appears to be a volcanic cone, it is not. Yet it is composed of rhyolite, basalt, and tuff, various volcanic rocks from the Tertiary period. To the south and northwest of this peak are intrusive formations which have been exploited for their mining potential. The Holt Bluebell and Cougar Spar mines are located south of the Indian Peak State Game Management Area, a four-by-four mile square reserve due east of Indian Peak. The Needle range is a remote, nearly unpopulated area except for a few scattered ranches. Its canyons generate several small, seasonal creeks which drain to washes in the surrounding valleys during the wet periods.

Valleys

As if the fingers of a giant hand had been drawn across its ancient surface, Beaver County is divided into five north-south running valleys by several small, parallel mountain ranges. Hamblin Valley, the westernmost in the county, is bounded on the west by

The "B" on the mountain east of Beaver as seen from the fairgrounds race track. (J.D. Osborn)

Nevada's Limestone Hill (to the north) and White Rock Mountains (to the south), and on the east both the Mountain Home Range (to the north) and the Indian Peak Range (to the south). East of these two ranges is Pine Valley, also the drainage area of the Wah Wah Mountains to the east. Wah Wah Valley is bounded on its east by both the San Francisco Mountains (to the north) and the White Mountains (to the south). These ranges in turn form the west mountain enclosure of Milford Valley which contains Milford and the railroad sidings of Upton, Murdock, and Thermo, as well as Minersville. This narrow, east-west-running canyon cuts through the Mineral Mountains, the western boundary of Beaver Valley, in which the county seat, Beaver, Manderfield, Greenville, and Adamsville were established.

Beaver Valley

Cradled between the looming Tushar Mountains to the east and the less imposing Mineral Mountains to the west, Beaver Valley is one of the county's two most fertile and populated flatland areas. About twelve miles wide and twenty miles long, and very roughly oval-shaped, the northern part of the valley begins at the narrow saddle separating the two surrounding mountain ranges. The east and west boundaries of the valley are created by the irregular forms of the mountain foothills. Likewise, the bottom or south edge of the valley runs along the north foothills of the east-west oriented Black Mountains.

The City of Beaver, the namesake of the county, valley, and primary river, sits approximately in the center of the valley. More than any other populated locality in the county, Beaver Valley is blessed with streams to feed its agricultural-based economy. The five largest waterways—Beaver River, North and South creeks, Indian Creek, and Wildcat Creek—all originate high in the Tushars. Each of the five settlements—Beaver, Adamsville, North Creek, Manderfield, and Greenville—was located along or near one of these streams.

Milford Valley

Beaver County's largest flatland plain is Milford Valley, the northernmost portion of the Escalante Desert. With the city of Milford in its center and Minersville at its southeast corner, the valley is one of only two in the county supporting sizable populations. Eight to sixteen miles in width, Milford Valley runs north-south the entire thirty-mile width of the county. Like Beaver Valley and the desert valleys to the west, Milford Valley is the result of ancient Quaternary alluvium and colluvium deposits. Watered by the Beaver River and the Minersville Reservoir from the south, and small creeks and washes from the Mineral Mountains to the east and the San Franciscos, Star Range, and Shauntie Hills to the west, Milford Valley is sufficiently fertile and moist to support an agricultural economy. Its relative flatness and proximity to several nineteenth-century mining districts made it the valley of choice for the Union Pacific railroad lines which pass north-to-southwest through the area connecting Salt Lake City with southern California.

Wah Wah Valley

Between the Wah Wah Mountains to the west and the San Francisco Mountains and Shauntie Hills to the east lies the largely unpopulated Wah Wah Valley. It runs north-south through the height of the county and into Millard County to the north. The valley is two to ten miles wide. The Quaternary deposits on the valley floor are not fertile and moist enough to support substantial farming, although a few ranches exist at the stream-fed mouths of nearby canyons. During the wet seasons, Wah Wah Wash collects small quantities of water from Willow Creek, Grover Wash, and lesser tributaries. A few small reservoirs and aqueducts north of Highway 21 allow for some limited farming. The northeast edge of the valley once supported Newhouse, a mining town now reduced to ruins.

Pine Valley

Like its neighboring parallel valleys, Pine Valley runs north-south the thirty-mile width of the county. It lies between the Needle Range to the west and the Wah Wahs to the east. It too consists of Quaternary alluvium and colluvium, with the exception of an area of ancient Lake Bonneville deposits on its north end. Isolated ranches are situated along the seasonal creeks that drain into the valley. The waters of some of these are collected by Chamisa, Woods, and the CCC reservoirs. Pine Valley Wash Road runs nearly the length of the valley, and Highway 21 cuts across the northern end on the way to and from Nevada.

Hamlin Valley

The southeast portion of Hamlin Valley runs through the southwest corner of Beaver County. Only six miles wide where it passes through the county, Hamlin Valley widens to twenty miles as it moves north into Nevada. Unpopulated and containing few natural resources, the valley carries Hamlin Valley Wash, a waterway of some consequence both north and south of Beaver County.

Geological History

Geologists divide the more than 4.5 billion years of the earth's geologic history into four eras: Precambrian, Cambrian, Mesozoic, and Cenozoic. These last three eras are subdivided into several periods and some of the periods into epochs.[1]

The longest of the eras—comprising more than 85 percent of the earth's geologic history—is the Precambrian which began with the origin of the earth and ended about 570 million years ago with the appearance of fossils. The best examples of Precambrian exposed rock are in the Grand Canyon; however, examples of outcrops of Precambrian rocks can be found at several Utah locations including the Uinta Mountains, Wasatch Mountains, Tintic Mountains, and along the western base of the Mineral Mountains in Beaver County.

With the advent of the Cambrian Era, which lasted for over 325 million years beginning 570 million years ago and ending 245 million years ago, water covered the western part of North America. Primitive marine life developed in various forms such as invertebrate shellfish, trilobites, corals, and brachiopods whose remains left extensive limestone deposits on the ocean floor. These deposits, along with shale and sandstone sediments, accumulated to depths of several thousand feet. During this era Beaver County was covered by warm seas, although some land surface may have emerged from time to time.

The Mesozoic Era lasted about 180 million years from 245 million years ago to 66 million years ago and included three major periods—the Triassic, Jurassic, and Cretaceous. During the Triassic period, most of Beaver County remained under water. Animal life continued to develop as the evidence of large reptiles and amphibians attests. However, the land also began to rise and the sea retreated westward. Volcanos erupted covering large areas with volcanic ash which preserved many trees through fossilization. The Moenkopi Formation followed by the Chinle Formation were laid down during this period, with most of the petrified wood found in the Chinle Formation.

At the beginning of the Jurrasic period, most of Utah became a vast desert and blowing sands created the light-colored Navajo Sandstone Formation, which is known as the source of Rainbow Natural Bridge, the great monoliths in Zion and Capitol Reef national parks, and other locations throughout southern Utah. Later the Mesocordilleran Highlands emerged on the western side of Utah—including most of Beaver County—and a series of rivers flowed out of the highlands eastward into seas that had formed. This river action gave rise to the Morrison formation of the late Jurrasic period—the location of dinosaur footprints and bone deposits that are approximately 150 million years old.

During the Cretaceous period, the last of the Mesozoic Era, the last large sea covered much of Utah—dividing North America into two large islands. The western shoreline of the sea followed the foothills of the Mesocordilleran High. About 100 to 80 million years ago, the mountains were thrust upwards during what geologists call the Sevier Orogeny—named for the Sevier Desert—the area just north of Beaver County where the mountains reached their greatest heights. While the ancient mountains covered what is now Beaver County throughout the Cretaceous period, to the east the sea, rivers, and swamps produced a series of shale, coal, and mudstone deposits between 66 and 144 million years ago.

The most recent geologic era, the Cenozoic Era, began about 66 million years ago and continues to the present. It is divided into two major periods, the Tertiary, which includes all but the last two million years covered by the Quaternary, the most recent period. The Tertiary period is subdivided into five epochs: Paleocene 66 to 58 million years ago; Eocene, 58 to 37 million years ago; Oligocene, 37 to 24 million years ago; the Miocene, 24 to 5 million years ago and the Pliocene, 5 to 1.6 million years ago.

The land in Beaver County during the first two epochs of the Cenozoic Era remained mountainous, although continuous erosion of the mountains commenced. Outcroppings of Paleocene and Eocene rocks are evident in the Tushar Mountains in the northeastern corner of the county. Other examples of these two epochs area found in the strata of Cedar Breaks National Monument to the south and Bryce Canyon National Park to the southeast.

As erosion of the Mesocordilleran High continued during the Oligocene and Miocene epochs, the area became very active for a period of twenty-five million years. Igneous rocks pushed up causing bulges in the earth's surface and broke out in numerous places to spew the black lava rock that can be found in Beaver County and throughout much of the western half of southern Utah. This activity produced three major mineral belts in Utah which have been the location for most of copper, gold, silver and other metal mining in the state: the Oquirrh-Uintah Belt, the Deep Creek-Tintic Belt, and the southern most belt the Wah Wah-Tushar Belt, which runs from west to east through Beaver County into Piute County. The dean of

Beaver Canyon. (Don O. Thorpe)

Utah geologists, William Lee Stokes writes of the Tushar Mountains, "Here is the most concentrated and varied assemblage of igneous rocks known in the state and a record of volcanic action longer than that of any other center."[2] The largest exposure of intrusive igneous rocks in Utah, according to Stokes, is found in Beaver County's Mineral Mountains.[3] The rocks of the Oligocene and Miocene epochs were especially important to Beaver County in the nineteenth century for the extensive metal mining that occurred and the use of the black basalt rock for the construction of many of the substantial buildings and pioneer homes that remain in Beaver.

Volcanic activity continued until the end of the Cenozoic Epoch, leaving the most recent evidence of volcanic activity in two major fields—one near St. George and the other known as the Sevier Desert Volcanic Field which stretches from northern Beaver County through Millard into Juab County. The igneous rock from this field indicates that the last volcanic activity in Utah occurred less than a million years ago. The black rock used in the construction of Cove Fort was produced during this most recent time of activity.

The Quaternary period includes two epochs, the Pleistocene,

which lasted approximately 1.6 million years, and the Holocene, which covers the last 11,000 years—approximately the period of human occupation of the region. One of the major features of the period was Lake Bonneville, the southern tip of which stretched into Beaver County. Glaciers formed during the Ice Age east of the Lake Bonneville in the Tushar Mountains as well as other mountain ranges in Utah leaving evidence of their action during the Pleistocene era. Evidence of Pleistocene animals—the mammoth, native horse, deer, camels, mountain sheep, and musk-oxen—has been found. About 11,000 years ago, as the Ice Age came to an end and the last or modern epoch—the Holocene—began, Beaver County emerged with its land forms and features that are recognizable today.

Collectible Minerals and Fossils

Rich in diverse geological resources, Beaver County features a score of popular rockhounding sites which produce a remarkable variety of collectible minerals. In the west are two sites in the Needle Range—one below Sawtooth Peak and one near the contact of the intrusive and surrounding limestones in Wah Wah Pass in the northern Wah Wah Mountains. In the old townsite of Newhouse, collectible specimens of pyrite, chalcoprite, pyrite, and quartz crystals can be found on the mining dumps. At least twenty types of minerals, including galena, pyrite, and sphalerite, are located in the Horn Silver mine area. Northwest of Milford, iron (ludwigite), azurite, malachite, brochantite, and chrysocolla may be found on the mine dump at West Springs in the Beaver Lake Mountains, while these minerals plus copper and quartz are found in the open pit of the OK Mine in the same mountains. Several other abandoned mines in the same vicinity host these and other minerals such as chalcopyrite and galena. Chalcopyrite and several other minerals are available near the Old Hickory Mine and others in the Rocky District area a few miles northwest of Milford. Lead sulfide is located in mines of the Star and North Star districts southwest of Milford. Five major rockhounding localities in the Mineral Mountains northwest of Beaver produce other varieties of collectible minerals such as beryllium, aquamarine, blue beryl, lead and zinc-wulferite, smoky quartz, feldspar, and garnet. Garnet and a dozen other minerals may be found in the Granite and North Granite mining districts on the north side of East Pass Canyon in the Mineral Mountains. Agates are the prize in the South Creek area south of Kane Canyon about six miles south of Beaver. Sheeprock Canyon in the Tushar Mountains produces alunite, amethyst, argentite, limonite, quartz, and tellurium minerals. Clearly statewide and local members of numerous gem societies, rock clubs, mineralogical, geological, and archaeological groups find Beaver County a favorite location for discovering valuable mineral specimens.

Climate

Beaver County's climate is generally temperate and has limited extremes in terms of heat or cold in four well-defined seasons. Sunshine on an average of 320 days a year is unobstructed by urban pollutants, and precipitation is limited to 11.65 inches annually in the Beaver Valley and 8.5 inches in the Milford area.

Beaver City is located at the 5,860 foot level in a broad, gently sloping valley between the Mineral Mountains ten miles to the west and the Tushar Range more than five miles to the east. While the 9,000 foot tall Mineral peaks shelter Beaver from storms, the even taller Tushars impede storm movement, causing air condensation and the dumping of heavy moisture on Beaver. The city's climate is semi-arid and sunny, with low precipitation and humidity, and wide swings in daily and annual temperature. Beaver enjoys four well-defined seasons with below zero but not severely cold winters, and generally light snowfalls which account for one third of the area's annual precipitation. The greatest snowfalls occur in December, January, and February.

Because of its mile-high elevation, Beaver's summers are pleasantly cool, only rarely exceeding 100 degrees Fahrenheit. Maximum temperatures typically range in the 80s, with night-time maximums dipping to the 40s or high 50s. Unlike some other areas in the Great Basin, Beaver's greatest rainfall occurs in the months of July and August, mostly as a result of thunderstorms. March, April, and December receive the next highest amounts of precipitation due to storms moving through the area from the Pacific Ocean. In contrast, June is by far the driest month, followed by November and January.

Aside from the strong winds that accompany storms, Beaver's winds are typically light to moderate. The area's growing season is only 106 days, generally beginning in early June and ending with the first frosts in mid-September. Farmers usually identify 10 June as the end of the late frosts until 25 September which marks the first of the early frosts. Breezes from Minersville Canyon to the east protects Minersville from late and early frosts and supports longer growing seasons.

As a result of the relatively short growing season, beef production and dairying are more profitable than most agricultural pursuits, although the climate is conducive to potato-growing. Weather observations have been made in Beaver since 1889, giving us a fairly comprehensive idea of the area's weather during the historic period.

Milford is situated in the middle of the county along the usually dry lower Beaver River in a gently sloping valley about fifteen miles long. Directly to the west is the small Star Range, and ten miles farther northwest the San Francisco Mountains which rise more than 4,600 feet above Milford's elevation of 5,028. Although 800 feet lower than Beaver, Milford's growing season of 131 days is still relatively short. This is in part due to the steppe climate in which nighttime temperatures are quite cool. The average date of the last frost is 18 May, while the average date of the first killing frost is 26 September. Growing seasons have been as long as 179 days but as short as 80 days. The unpredictability of growing season length, together with the low annual precipitation of eight to nine inches, makes many types of agriculture problematic. Only in March and July does the precipitation average as much as one inch annually. Crop success is mostly dependent on irrigation water obtained from several deep wells and from controlled runoff from Minersville Reservoir.

The average snowfall of thirty-eight inches a year is fairly evenly distributed during the winter months. The snow is light and powdery, however, and has below average moisture content. Local humidity is lower in the summer than winter, making for hot, dry summer days and cold, more humid, somewhat uncomfortable winter days. Most years the temperature will drop to 10 degrees below zero or lower, while temperatures will exceed 100 degrees Fahrenheit in about half the years. July is the hottest, wettest month. January is the coldest and among the most dry with respect to precipitation.

Temperature extremes have reached 105 degrees on the hot end and
-34 degrees on the cold side. Strong southerly winds travel through
the area in the spring and summer, while cold winters cause hazardous snow drifts which endanger local stock and transportation.
Summer thunderstorms and atmospheric disturbances in the beginning of winter and spring contribute to the area's variable climate.

Vegetation and Life Zones

Distinctive communities of vegetation exist throughout Beaver
County, each identified by one or more dominant types of plants.
The characteristics of these zones are determined by latitude, altitude,
temperature, moisture, and soil conditions. Because it contains
mountains, high plains, and lower valleys, Beaver County features
four distinct Vegetation Zones. In the Mountane Zone are the highest
regions of the Mountain Home and Indian Peak mountains, the Wah
Wah Range, and the Tushar Mountains. In the Pinyon-Juniper Zone
are the lower slopes of these same mountains, plus all of the San
Francisco, Mineral and Black Mountain ranges. The Hamblin, Pine,
Wah Wah, Milford, and Beaver valleys are found, somewhat pre-
dictably, in the Sagebrush Zone. The county's lowest areas in northern Wah Wah Valley and the long valley bottom through Milford
Valley are in the Shadscale Vegetation Zone.

Each Vegetation Zone can be defined by its corresponding Life
Zones, each differentiated by the verticality and slopes of their terrain, functions of ancient orographic (mountain-related) lifting.
Again contrasts in precipitation and temperature related to elevations
and slope are responsible for the variations in plant life which mark
each Life Zone. The Montane Zone, which occupies about 15 percent
of the county's land area, includes the Transition, Canadian,
Hudsonia, and Arctic-Tundra Life Zones. The rare Arctic-Tundra
Zone includes the county's few areas located at elevations greater
than 11,000 feet above sea level. Situated only in the highest peaks of
the Tushar Range, this Life Zone has sparse vegetation due to poorly
developed soils. It contains hardy complexes of grasses, sedges,
mosses, and annuals.

The Hudsonian Life Zone includes mountainous areas between
10,000 and 11,000 feet in elevation. The dominant plants in this zone

are Englemann Spruce, which generally prevails, and subalpine fir. Other trees associated with this zone include timber and bristlecone pine. Complexes of grasses, forbes, sedges, and annuals also are found near subalpine meadows and lakes. In the Canadian Life Zone, between 8,000 and 10,000 feet, are found Douglas and White Firs, Lodgepole Pine, and Aspen. Blue Spruce and Ponderosa Pine also typically exist within this plant community and may even dominate in some areas. Above the 5,500 foot level are located mountain brush and Ponderosa Pine in the Transition Life Zone. The underlying brush consists of a chaparral association of oak, maple, mahogany, and sagebrush.

Many of the valley areas of Beaver County are located in the Sagebrush Vegetation Zone, a general classification which includes the Upper Sonoran Life Zone. As its name implies, the Sagebrush Zone is dominated by the most common shrub in the Great Basin—sagebrush. Sometimes crowding out most other plant life, sagebrush prefers gravelly, non-alkaline soils and is at other times associated with various types of grasses. In addition, the Upper Sonoran Life Zone features oak, juniper, shadscale (a salt-tolerant, drought-resistant plant), with juniper, pinyon, greasewood, and saltgrass growing in other areas. The Pinyon-Juniper Association located in the county's lower mountains is also related to the Upper Sonoran Life Zone in which sagebrush merges into the pinyon-juniper community. This condition generally occurs below the 7,500 foot level and accounts for continuous expanses of forest across some of the lower mountain ranges. Where a boundary exists between sagebrush and pinyon-juniper growth, such delineation are sometimes referred to as the "arid timberline." A lack of moisture limits the flourishing of pinyon-juniper species where precipitation is less than twelve inches annually.

Wildlife

Among the large mammals in Utah made extinct in historic times over all or most of their former ranges are the grizzly bear and the wolf, both hunted out of existence or chased away. No moose or mink exist in the county, even though the high mountain terrain would seem to provide habitat for these species.

Kents Lake. (Don O. Thorpe)

Several carnivorous species of various sizes live in Beaver County. With the exception of bears and raccoons, which are omnivorous, the carnivores are mainly flesh-eaters. The dog-like coyote ranges county-wide, much to the dismay of livestock raisers. The smaller kit fox, however, ranges from the Mineral Mountains to the west county line. While the grizzly is gone, the black bear can still be found in small numbers in the high regions of the Tushar Range.

Several varieties of shrews have been documented in Beaver County, including the water and vagrant shrews in the eastern part of the county. The dusky shrew is found only in the high, mountainous southeast corner of the county. Many of the state's nineteen species and subspecies of bats and myotis flourish in Beaver County, among them the big myotis, hairy-winged and long-eared myotis, small-footed myotis, silvery-haired bat, western pipistrelle, big brown bat, hoary and long-eared bats, the pallid bat, and Mexican free-tailed bats. Although rarely seen, most of these range widely throughout Beaver and its neighboring counties.

One of Utah's five kinds of pika, a small, rabbit-like mammal with small, round ears, fore and hind legs of about the same size, and no visible tail, lives in the high Tushars along the county's eastern edge. Among the mountain-dwelling rabbits in the Tushars are the white-tailed jack rabbit and snowshoe rabbit. Virtually the entire county is inhabited by the black-tailed jack rabbit and the Audubon cottontail. The Nuttall cottontail ranges in the eastern quarter of the county, while the pygmy rabbit lives in the western area of the county.

The red squirrel or chickaree, a tree squirrel, lives in the Tushar Mountain Range, as does the yellow-bellied marmot. The eastern two-thirds of the county provides a habitat for the white-tailed prairie dog and the Townsend ground squirrel. There is some occurrence of the rock squirrel in the eastern mountains, while the antelope squirrel dwells county-wide, as do the golden-mantled ground squirrel and the least chipmunk. The say chipmunk resides only in the Tushars, while the cliff chipmunk is also confined to the county's eastern regions.

A few varities of northern pocket gopher and botta pocket gopher occupy minor areas of the county. In the far western areas, the Baird pocket mouse and the little pocket mouse live. The Great Basin pocket mouse ranges widely from the Mineral Mountains west, but the dark kangaroo mouse, Ord kangaroo rat, and chisel-toothed kangaroo rat are restricted to the western areas. Numerous other varieties of mice inhabit Utah, and several of them flourish throughout Beaver County, among them the western harvest mouse, canyon, deer, pinon, northern grasshopper, and red-backed, montane meadow, long-tailed, and big jumping mice. The desert wood rat shares their habitats in many areas.

Intensively hunted for their pelts in the nineteenth century, the county's namesake, the beaver, lives only from the Beaver Valley eastward into the Tushar Mountains. The less sought-after porcupine ranges widely through the county.

Several varieties of snakes live in Beaver County. Racer snakes live in open fields, near streams with grassy borders, in mountain meadows and thin brush in the Upper Sonoran and Transition Life Zones. Reaching over four feet in length, the fast, aggressive racer feeds on frogs, toads, reptiles, small mammals, and insects. It is brown/blue, green/blue, dark gray, or black. The desert striped whipsnake can be seen in warm, rocky, brush-covered foothills and grasslands. It is

The water pipeline crosses at the base of this mountain in Beaver Canyon. (J.D. Osborn)

three to five feet long and feeds on lizards, small rodents, and snakes. The gopher snake measures 2-1/2 to 6 feet long, and is ground colored with light brown, clay, buff, or whitish rows of squarish or oval blotches. It feeds primarily on rodents. Among the garter snakes found in the county are the common western varieties. The main poisonous snake found locally is the western rattlesnake which inhabits the Lower Sonoran to Boreal Life Zones in chaparral, grassland, sagebrush plains, and mountains into the pine zone up to 11,000. It hides in rock outcrops where it preys on rabbits, mice, gophers, lizards, and other mammals. Reaching over four feet long, the western rattler varies in color and pattern but features the blotched patterns on its back common to most rattlesnakes.

As many as ten types of lizards live in the inviting desert climes of Beaver County. Among the most widely distributed are western whiptail, side-blotched lizard, western skink, western fence lizard, sagebrush lizard, collared, and leopard lizards. Also found in some localities are the short-horned, desert-horned, and tree lizards, and the spotted whiptail.

Ancient and Native Peoples

Anthropologists divide Utah's prehistoric peoples into three groups. The Paleo-Indians, which included the Clovis and Folsom cultures, were hunters and gatherers who appeared in North America after the last ice age and probably made their way from Asia in small groups over a thousand-year period across the thousand-mile wide Bering Strait land bridge while it was above the waters of the ocean. The Paleo-Indian occupation stretches back at least 12,000 years and lasted approximately 5,000 years. The Paleo-Indians were big game hunters, and it was likely that their pursuit of mammoths drew them out of Siberia and across the Bering Strait to North America. The plentiful supply of mammoths made hunting relatively easy, and the Paleo-Indian population grew rapidly. Within a period of a thousand years, the pursuit of game took the Paleo-Indian people throughout the North and South American continents. Anthropologists postulate that at their peak population level the Paleo-Indians numbered close to one million individuals.

The presence of Paleo-Indians is confirmed by the discovery of Clovis points—a distinctively shaped spearhead made by the Paleo-Indians and named for the town in New Mexico near which the first spearheads were observed. Another distinctive type of spear point—known as the Folsom point—developed later, but is also used to confirm the presence of the Paleo-Indians. While neither Clovis nor Folsom points have been identified in Beaver County, both types of artifacts have been found in nearby locations suggesting that America's earliest inhabitants found their way into what is now Beaver County 10,000 to 12,000 thousand years ago.

The Archaic Culture began to develop about 8,000 to 10,000 years ago. The big game animals hunted by the Paleo-Indians became extinct about 11,000 years ago. The warming climate, as the ice age came to an end, to which the mammoth was unable to adapt and perhaps the extensive hunting by the Paleo-Indians led to its demise. The Paleo-Indians adapted by hunting the smaller animals which did not become extinct and by giving more attention to the collection of plant foods including roots, seeds, nuts, fruits, and berries. The production of Clovis points ceased and the Paleo-Indians began to adapt to much greater varieties in the natural environment than their pre-decessors had known. These changes and adaptations led to the emergence of many different hunting and gathering cultures identi-fied by anthropologists as Archaic hunters and gatherers to distin-guish them from their Paleo-Indian ancestors.

Perhaps the best known and most recent of the prehistoric peo-ples in Utah are the Anasazi and Fremont Cultures which emerged about 2,000 years ago and lasted until about 700 years ago. These cul-tures are distinguished from the Paleo-Indian and Archaic peoples primarily because of their cultivation of crops such as corn, beans, and squash, and domestication of turkeys and other animals. They also began to construct underground shelters instead of living in caves and natural shelters. The Anasazi especially began to build with adobe and stone and are well-known for the multi-storied dwellings found at Mesa Verde National Park, Chaco Canyon, Canyon de Chelly, and other locations throughout the southwest.

While the Anasazi peoples did not extend as far north and west as Beaver County, the Virgin River or Western Anasazi lived in pre-sent-day Kane and Washington counties. The Fremont people, named for the Fremont River in South-Central Utah, occupied an area from the Bear River, the Great Salt Lake, and Uintah Basin on the north to Beaver and Iron counties on the south.

While the reasons for the demise of the Anasazi and the Fremont have not been precisely determined, climatic changes, internal con-flicts, and the arrival of new groups, such as the Navajo, Ute, and Paiute peoples have all been offered as possible reasons.

The prehistoric peoples of the Beaver County area left countless artifacts at hundreds of sites as a record of their occupation stretching back perhaps as much as 12,000 years into the distant past. While no written record recounts the generations of the area's prehistoric resi-dents, a treasure of pottery, tools, projectile points, weapons, bone remains, and stone tapestries of painted and carved rock art and other physical evidence indicate that the area's early peoples were scattered throughout the county over the millennia since the end of the last ice age.

Important prehistoric sites surround the county and suggest con-siderable traffic through the area, especially as ancient peoples moved in search of game and other resources important to their way of life. Approximately twenty miles south of Minersville, the mysterious Parowan Gap is one of the world's best known rock art sites and displays both Archaic and Fremont styles. Thirty miles south of the Beaver-Iron County line, Evans Mound and Median Village near Summit have been excavated to reveal important information about inhabitants of the region over a thousand years ago. A dozen miles from the northeastern corner of Beaver County, Fremont Indian State Park, located along the route of Interstate 70 through Clear Creek Canyon, is one of Utah's most popular state parks with its intriguing rock art panels and excavated village sites.

Clear Creek Canyon was an important transportation corridor for prehistoric peoples, many of whom were en route to the west slope of the Mineral Mountains to obtain obsidian for arrow and spear points. The Wildhorse Canyon Obsidian Quarry, located approximately ten miles east of Milford and listed in the National Register of Historic Places, is the only known obsidian flow in Utah that was used by historic peoples as a source of raw materials. Because of the large number of "chipping stations" near the quarry, archaeologists conclude that the prehistoric visitors to the quarry remained near the quarry to work the obsidian into points which could be easily transported. Artifacts made of obsidian from the quarry have been found in excavations as far north as Danger Cave near Wendover in Tooele County and Hogup Cave northeast of the Great Salt Lake in Box Elder County. Closer to the source, obsidian artifacts from the Wildhorse Quarry have also been found at Median Village and Evans Mound in Iron County. Ongoing research is likely to uncover Wildhorse Canyon obsidian artifacts in other prehistoric sites throughout the area.[4]

It is likely that obsidian points or tools from the Wildhorse Quarry were used to carve many of the petroglyphs throughout the Great Basin. While there is much to be learned about the rock art left by the area's ancient inhabitants, anthropologists believe that the Archaic, Anasazi, and Fremont peoples are responsible for the geometric designs, abstract figures, footprints, bird tracks, sunbursts, mountain sheep, stick figures, and anthropomorphs which have been pecked into the boulders and cliffs in the area. One site west of

Manderfield consists of thirty boulders with petroglyphs, the largest of which has anthropomorphs with hands and feet pecked deeply into the basalt rock. Another site located on a small hill in Pine Valley in western Beaver County has several hundred squares, spirals, circles, mountain sheep, snakes, and other designs carved into the ledges of the hill.[5]

Contemporary with the end of the Anasazi and Fremont cultures about 700 years ago is the arrival of Utah's Numic peoples—the Goshute, Ute, Paiute, and Shoshoni peoples. They carved few if any petroglyphs but inhabited the valleys and deserts of the Great Basin when the first Euro-Americans arrived during the eighteenth century.

Beaver County was part of a border area where the Southern Paiute merged with the Western and Southern Ute. Anthropologists Isabel T. Kelly and Catherine S. Fowler find that there was little to distinguish the Western Utes from the Paiutes and that the Beaver, Cedar, Kaiparowits, and Antarianuts (located near the Henry Mountains and Colorado River) Indian groups " . . . should be considered transitional Southern Paiute. . . . the Cedar group was called Ute by some of its Paiute neighbors, and to one person from the Cedar area, the Beaver group was Pahvant, who are usually considered to be Western Ute."[6]

William R. Palmer, Cedar City resident and long-time student of the Paiute Indians, concludes that the Beaver County Indians were Paiute. He identifies thirty-five distinct nineteenth-century Paiute bands in southwestern Utah—five of which were located within the borders of present-day Beaver County and are part of the larger Beaver subgroup identified by other anthropologists. The five bands include the Tu-roon-quints band in the northeast corner of the county; the Qui-ump-uts band around Beaver and Adamsville; the Pa-moki-abs band in the vicinity of Minersville; the Toy-ehe-its band in the Milford area; and the Indian Peak band in the western part of the county and into Nevada.[7] Within the bands there were usually several individual camps often headed by relatives. Leadership tended to remain within one family, but did not necessarily pass from father to son. A brother, brother-in-law, nephew, or grandson might become the new leader after the elder men of a group conferred usually in lengthy deliberations that might involve input from neighboring camps and groups.[8]

The Indians relied on small game for food, including rabbits, which were often hunted in drives, and other animals such as rats, mice, gophers, squirrels, chipmunks, and birds. Pine nuts, roots, and berries were also important, and the Indian Peak area of western Beaver County was said to produce the best pine nuts.[9] As early as the eighteenth century, some Paiute groups began to cultivate crops of corn and squash using irrigation ditches. By the early decades of the nineteenth century, the Indian Peak group in Beaver County had begun to cultivate fields.[10] Paiutes lived under shade trees in warm weather and conical brush shelters with a smoke hole and opening facing east during cold weather. Tents of skin and canvas were introduced by the Ute Indians in the 1850s.

Their unique ways of gathering food and surviving in this harsh geography fascinated the outsiders. One described the production of nets for catching rabbits:

> The squaws made a long net of oose, a flaglike plant that grows on the foot hills. The mesh of the net was about the size of a jack rabbit's head. The squaws would beat out the fibre of the oose and spin it into two strand twine about the size of a mason's chalk line. The little spinning machine was very simple, being made of two sticks. The handle was about five eights of an inch in diameter and twelve or fourteen inches long, being broader and heavier at one end and tapered to a point. On the extreme end was a button or 'doll's head,' about three-eights of an inch in diameter. This was where the material to be spun was attached, whether it was oose or horsehair. Near the knob, there was a hole through the whirling stick and the handle passed through this hole until the knob on the end prevented it from going clear through. This part was lubricated with deer tallow, and it was no trick at all to swing this spinner eight to one hundred revolutions per minute. The one that whirled the spinner sat still while the one that spun the fibre walked backwards with a bunch under one arm, then two or more strands were twisted together by turning the other way.[11]

The Paiute excelled at basket making and engaged in limited agriculture. They gathered seeds and pulverized them with stone grinders and cooked them into a thick mush.[12] Dried corn, red root seeds, mint, ground cherries, sunflower seeds, sego roots, mustard greens, and wild potatoes provided significant variety and nutrition.

Members of the different bands and groups visited each other's territory to hunt, gather, and trade. Sometimes they intermarried and at other times they carried out raids to acquire women and children to sell as slaves. The Beaver group was among several groups that were more often the aggressors than the victims in the slave raids.[13] The fact that the Spanish Trail passed through Beaver County made it difficult to avoid participation in the slave trade by local Indians because of the high prices that were paid for young girls and boys who were sold as slaves at both ends of the Spanish Trail—southern California and Santa Fe, New Mexico.

The Paiutes first became acquainted with Euro-Americans in 1776 when the Dominguez-Escalante expedition passed through their territory. The Franciscan fathers recorded that near present-day Minersville was the southern extend of the "Bearded Yutas," whom they had first encountered in the Pavant Valley of Millard County. Escalante described these Indians as " . . . people with long beards and pierced noses . . . [who] looked like Capuchin or Bethlemite fathers."[14]

Twenty years after the opening of the Spanish Trail between Santa Fe, New Mexico, and Los Angeles, California, in 1830, Mormon pioneers arrived to settle first at Parowan in January 1851. Brigham Young and other Mormon leaders were successful in ending the slave trade along the Spanish Trail by the 1850s. Within twenty years most of the lands of the Paiutes, including those in Beaver County, had been settled by Mormons. The Paiutes responded by consolidating into larger groups, usually in the vicinity of the Mormon settlements, and with occasional acts of hostility toward the newcomers. For the most part, however, the Indians and Mormons lived peacefully, with the Paiutes trading deerskins and pine nuts to the Mormons for food and clothing.[15] A few of the Paiutes were remembered for their ability with a bow and arrow. On more than one occasion, Pahshaunts impressed the local citizenry. According to Samuel D. Hutchings, " . . . a person could place biscuits on the points of a picket fence and Pahshaunts would get across the street with his bow and arrow and pick a biscuit off every shot."[16]

Itinerant Indians did cause trouble from time to time, including one assumed to be a Navajo who passed through Beaver County in November 1868 and stole a horse from William Allred. Pursuing the Indian across the mountains, Allred overtook him along the Sevier River between Circleville and Marysvale. After circling to get ahead, according to a *Deseret News* report, "When within about 20 or 25 yards from brother Allred, the latter fired one barrel of his shotgun loaded with five revolver bullets, which settled the account with Mr. Indian."[17]

In 1865 several Paiute leaders signed a treaty at Spanish Fork agreeing to relinquish their lands and move to the Ute Reservation in the Uintah Basin. No Paiutes made the move, and in 1873 the United States Commissioner of Indian Affairs sent a special commission headed by John Wesley Powell to Utah and Nevada to look into Indian problems including the removal of the Paiutes from areas of settlement. Given the hostility of Utes toward Paiutes, it was concluded that a better place for relocation than the Uintah Reservation would be the Moapa Reservation in Nevada. The Southern Utah Paiutes agreed to the move on the condition that they be provided sufficient aid to take care of themselves. However, few moved, and most of those who did returned. Little attention was given the Southern Utah Paiutes by the federal government after the 1870s In 1915 the Indian Peaks Reservation was established in western Beaver County—primarily as a home for the Beaver, Cedar, and Panaca Paiute groups. The Kanosh Reservation, established in 1929, drew a few Paiutes from the northern end of Beaver County. Residents of the Indian Peaks Reservation supported themselves with gardens and a few cattle, but the lack of sufficient income made it necessary to seek employment elsewhere, and by 1935 most residents of the Indian Peaks Reservation had moved away.[18] One person who continued to reside on the reservation during the 1940s was named Old Jack. He claimed to be 100 years old and supported himself by making high quality bows and arrows which he sold throughout the state.[19]

The Indian Peaks Reservation and the Kanosh Reservation, along with the Shivwits and Koosharem reservations, were terminated from federal control in 1954 in a controversial action that was challenged by the Paiute tribe. After a long struggle, Congress passed and

President Jimmy Carter signed into law the Paiute Restoration Act on 3 April 1980. The act restored to the approximately 500 members of the Southern Utah Paiute Tribe the rights enjoyed by other American Indians and provided for the return of 15,000 acres of land to the Paiutes.[20]

In 1999 there are no longer any members of the Paiute Tribe living in Beaver County. Nevertheless, the Paiute Indians and their predecessors—the Fremont, Archaic, and Paleo-Indian peoples—have left a rich, if only partially understood, history.

ENDNOTES

1. For a general study of geology in Utah see William Lee Stokes, *Geology of Utah* (Salt Lake City: Utah Museum of Natural History and Utah Geological and Mineral Survey, 1986).

2. Ibid., 176.

3. Ibid., 179.

4. Claudia F. Berry, "Wildhorse Canyon Obsidian Quarry," National Register of Historic Places Inventory—Nomination Form, September 1975; copy on file at the Utah State Historical Society.

5. Dorothy Sammons-Lohse, "Great Basin Style Rock Art Thematic Group," National Register of Historic Places Inventory—Nomination Form, August 1981; copy on file at the Utah State Historical Society.

6. Isabel T. Kelly and Catherine S. Fowler, "Southern Paiute," in Warren L. D'Azevedo, *Handbook of North American Indians Great Basin,* Vol. 11, (Washington,DC: Smithsonian Institution, 1986), 368.

7. William R. Palmer, Map of Paiute Bands, Special Collections, Southern Utah State University.

8. Kelly and Fowler, "Southern Paiute," 380.

9. Ibid., 370.

10. Ibid., 371.

11. Aird G. Merkley, ed., *Monuments to Courage: A History of Beaver County* (Milford: Beaver County Chapter of the Daughters of Utah Pioneers, 1948) 20–21.

12. Thomas J. Farnham, "Indians on the Old Spanish Trail," *Utah Historical Quarterly,* 2(July 1929), 78.

13. Kelly and Fowler, "Southern Paiute," 368–69.

14. Hebert E. Bolton, *Pageant in the Wilderness: The Story of the*

Escalante Expedition to the Interior Basin, 1776 (Salt Lake City: Utah State Historical Society, 1972), 191.

15. Merkley, *Monuments to Courage,* 15–19.

16. Ibid., 26.

17. *Deseret News,* 16 November 1868.

18. Kelly and Fowler, "Southern Paiute," 390

19. Merkley, *Monuments to Courage,* 19.

20. Ronald L. Holt, "Paiute Indians of Utah," in Allan Kent Powell, ed. *Utah History Encyclopedia* (Salt Lake City: University of Utah Press, 1994), 408–10.

CHAPTER 3

EXPLORATION
1776–1856

Until the settlement of Beaver in 1856, the area had been a land to pass through in route to some place else. Franciscan fathers Francisco Atanasio Dominguez and Silvestre Velez de Escalante provided the first written accounts of Beaver County during their epic journey in 1776. Fifty years later American fur trapper Jedediah Smith crossed Beaver County. During the 1830s and 1840s caravans traveled between Santa Fe, New Mexico, and California crossing through Beaver County on their 1,100-mile journey. The first Mormons to enter the county were also California-bound under the leadership of Jefferson Hunt in late 1847. Two years later Parley P. Pratt lead an exploring expedition to southern Utah through the Beaver area. Finally, Mormon Iron Mission settlers leapfrogged over the Pahvant and Beaver valleys to found Parowan in January 1851 and Cedar City in November 1851, approximately thirty and fifty miles south of the future site of Beaver and 250 miles south of Salt Lake City.

Dominguez and Escalante Expedition

The 1776 Dominguez-Escalante Expedition came at the end of

nearly three centuries of Spanish exploration and colonization in the New World that began with the voyage and discoveries of Christopher Columbus in 1492 and drew to a close with the establishment of the California missions beginning with San Diego in 1769 and Monterrey in 1770.

The Spanish presence in the American Southwest began with the 1540 expedition of Francisco Vasquez de Coronado which reached the Zuni and Pueblo villages of Arizona and New Mexico while searching for the Seven Cities of Cibola. Spanish settlement of New Mexico began in 1598 under Juan de Onate. The first Spaniard to reach California was Hernando de Alarcon, when he led a fleet of Spanish ships along the California coast in 1540 as a part of the general Coronado expedition. Alarcon's assignment was to find a water route that might provide access to Coronado, his soldiers, and the Seven Cities of Cibola. No route was found, and it was more than two centuries before the Spanish attempted to settle California. Monterrey was settled in 1770, and within a few years plans were made for an overland trail to connect Santa Fe, the capital of New Mexico, with the new Spanish California capital of Monterrey. The assignment to open the overland route fell to Franciscian fathers Dominguez and Escalante.

Leaving Santa Fe on 29 July 1776, Dominguez and Escalante along with eight companions journeyed through northwestern New Mexico and western Colorado before entering present-day Utah on 11 September 1776 near the crossing of the Green River just north of present-day Jensen, Utah. The long trek to the north was made to avoid hostile Indians and the difficult canyons of a more direct route from Santa Fe to Monterrey. After crossing the Green River, the expedition followed west up the Duchesne River through the heart of the Uinta Basin and across the mountains and through Strawberry Valley before entering Utah Valley through Spanish Fork Canyon. After a brief stay with the Ute Indians at Utah Lake in late September, the party pressed on toward California but first promised to return to Utah Valley to establish a Catholic mission among the Ute Indians. Heading south, the expedition reached the Beaver River bottoms south of Clear Lake in Millard County on 3 October. Escalante recorded:

. . . we came to an arroyo which seemed to have much water, but we found only some waterholes where the horse herd might be able to drink with difficulty. Nevertheless, we stopped here because there was good pasturage. All over the arroyo there was a kind of white scum, dry and thin, which looked from afar like linen spread out, for which reason we named it Arroyo del Tejedor [Arroyo of the Weaver].[1]

Continuing southward, the expedition followed the Beaver River and on 5 October entered a wide valley a few miles north of the Beaver-Millard County line. They named the valley Valle de Nuestra Senora de la Luz—The Valley of Our Lady of the Light. Escalante wrote of the valley, "Through it El Arroyo del Tejedor continues with sufficient waterholes or banked ponds of good water and very spacious meadows abounding in pasturage, of which this valley is very scarce."[2] The night of 5 October a heavy snowfall began that continued all the next day and into the night. Calling on divine intervention to end the storm, " . . . we implored the intercession of Our Mother and Patroness by praying aloud in common the three parts of her rosary and by chanting the Litany, the one of All-Saints. And God was pleased that by nine at night it should cease to snow, hail, and rain."[3] Because of the snow and muddy ground, the expedition had to spend 7 October in camp, " . . . in great distress, without firewood and extremely cold, for with so much snow and water the ground, which was soft here, was unfit for travel."[4]

Resuming their journey on 8 October, the expedition crossed into Beaver County and made camp a mile west of the river at a site eleven miles north of the town of Milford. The arrival in Beaver County was one of the most discouraging days of the entire expedition and brought the first written mention that a return to Santa Fe was under consideration. Escalante recorded:

Today we suffered greatly from the cold because the north wind did not cease blowing all day, and most acutely A bitter cold north wind blew all day and every direction . . . Since winter had already set in most severely, for all the sierras we managed to see in all directions were covered with snow, the weather very unsettled, we therefore feared that long before we got there [Monterey] the passes would be closed to us, so that they would force us to stay

Basalt Rock in western Beaver County. (Don O. Thorpe)

two or three months in some sierra where there might not be any people or the wherewithal for our necessary sustenance. For the provisions we had were very low by now, and so we could expose ourselves to perishing from hunger if not from the cold.[5]

On 9 October the group traveled about 15.5 miles passing the future site of Milford and camping about 6.5 miles to the south. The drier ground in the broad valley along with easy access to water and meadows for pasturage were a welcome relief from the difficulties of the previous days. Continuing southward on 10 October the group reached a short and very low hill with hot springs located south of Thermo Siding on the Union Pacific Railroad line. Taking advantage of what little elevation the hill offered to survey the extent of the valley of La Luz

> . . . we climbed the hill and saw that from here toward the southwest it stretched for more than thirty-five or forty leagues [approximately 100 miles], for where it ends in this direction one could barely discern the sierras, these being very high, as we saw better later on. We also saw three outlets of hot sulphurous water which are on the top and the east flank of said hill. Around it below are

other short patches of nitrous soil. We continued over the plain and, after going two leagues south, we halted, fearing that farther on we would not find water for tonight. Here there was a large good quantity of it from the melted snow, dammed up like a lake; there was also good pasturage. We named the site San Eleuterio.[6]

The San Eleuterio campsite was located approximately twelve miles southwest of Minersville, about seven miles across the Iron County line. The journey through Beaver County was an anxious and difficult one. Although they thought they were on a latitude parallel with Monterrey, the early storm, lack of knowledge by native inhabitants of any Spanish people to the west, the difficulty in finding a passage through the mountains, and the considerable distance they knew they would have to travel raised doubts in the minds of Dominguez and Escalante about ever reaching Monterrey. However, other members of the expedition were reluctant to give up the intended goal. In an attempt to maintain harmony within the ranks, Dominguez and Escalante developed a plan to allow God to determine their course and presented it to the others. Placing the name Monterrey on one stick and the name Cosnina—which they would pass on the return to Santa Fe—on the other, they put the matter in God's hands. But first Father Dominguez admonished the group " . . . to subject themselves entirely to God's will and, by laying aside every sort of passion, beg Him with firm hope and lively faith to make it known to us." This the men did as Escalante recounts, "They all submitted in a Christian spirit, and with fervent piety prayed the third part of the rosary and other petitions while we ourselves were reciting the Penitential Psalms with the Litany and other orations which follow it. This concluded, we cast lots, and the one of Cosnina came out. This we all heartily accepted now, thanks be to God, mollified and pleased."[7]

With the decision made to return to Santa Fe, the expedition hurried southward. After a perilous crossing of the Colorado River near the Utah-Arizona border at the Crossing of the Fathers, now under the waters of Lake Powell, they reached Santa Fe on 2 January 1777, just over five months after their epic journey began. The journal kept by Father Escalante offers the first written description of the land that would become Beaver County.

The decision to return to Santa Fe reached by Dominguez and Escalante while waiting out the snow storm in Beaver County in early October 1776 and substantiated by the casting of the lots a few days later was probably a wise one. California was still hundreds of miles to the west across difficult terrain and, as later travelers would learn at the cost of their lives, early winter storms could seal off any route of escape. It would be more than fifty years before the overland route between Santa Fe and California would be opened and on a route that, of necessity, followed far to the south of the intended route to Monterrey.

Jedediah Smith

It is an anomaly that an area named for an abundance of Beaver in the 1850s saw little activity during the heyday of the Rocky Mountain fur trade of the 1820s and 1830s. Jedediah Smith passed through the county after leaving the fur trapper rendezvous in Cache Valley in 1826. It is unclear what the final destination of Smith's southern journey was to be. Undertaken in search of the mythical Rio Buenaventura River and its hoped-for outlet to the Pacific Ocean, as well as to assess the opportunities for beaver trapping to the south of the beaver- rich areas of northern Utah, western Wyoming, and Idaho, Smith traveled the length of Utah and continued his journey into southern California where he spent the winter and returned crossing the Sierra Nevada Mountains and the Great Salt Lake Desert to reach the annual summer rendezvous at the south end of Bear Lake in July 1827. During his journey southward, he entered Beaver County after crossing through Clear Creek Canyon to the future site of Cove Fort where he turned south to follow the base of the mountains past Beaver Creek on 8 September 1826, which he named Lost Creek, and on to Ash Creek and the Virgin River, before striking across the desert for San Gabriel, California.

A few days after the 1827 rendezvous ended, Smith, with eighteen men, was back on the trail headed southward again passing once more through Beaver County and on to California where he rejoined some of his men left there the previous year.[8]

Spanish Trail

Jedediah Smith proved that no San Buenaventura River existed to connect the Rocky Mountains with the Pacific Ocean, but he did demonstrate that California could be reached by an overland route from Utah. In 1829, two years after Smith's second journey, a Mexican trader named Antonio Armijo carried commercial goods overland from New Mexico to California over portions of what would become the Spanish Trail.

During the winter of 1830–31, two Americans, William Wolfskill and George C. Yount, made their way from Santa Fe to California over the general route of the Spanish Trail. Throughout the 1830s and 1840s, the Spanish Trail was a major route of commerce between the two Mexican provinces. The route was a horse and mule trail, not a wagon road, and travelers usually took about two and a half months to complete the one-way journey of 1,120 miles. Pack mules were used to transport raw wool and woven textiles from New Mexico to California in the fall, and the return trip usually took place in the early spring before snow melt in the mountains swelled the waters of the Green and Colorado rivers. Mules and horses were brought from California to New Mexico in herds of 2,000 or more animals. A secondary item of trade was Paiute Indian slaves taken in Utah, Arizona, and Nevada and sold in both California and New Mexico. Others used the trail, including fur trappers, Indians, California-bound settlers from New Mexico, and government explorers. The trail also formed the western leg of a transcontinental route from Saint Joseph, Missouri, to Santa Fe, New Mexico, across the Santa Fe Trail which was opened in 1821. The trail was most heavily used before Mexico lost California, New Mexico, and what became the Utah Territory to the United States during the Mexican War. After the region became part of the United States, more direct east-west routes were used.[9]

While Los Angeles lay farther south than Santa Fe, the Old Spanish Trail took a northwesterly course through New Mexico and across the southwestern corner of Colorado and into southeastern Utah to avoid the deep canyons of the Colorado River and to make relatively easy crossings of the Colorado River at present-day Moab

Mt. Baldy. (J.D. Osborn)

and the Green River at the town of Green River. Avoiding the barriers of the San Rafael Reef and San Rafael Swell, the Spanish Trail reached its northern apex in Emery County where it turned west passing through Castle Valley and across the Wasatch Plateau where it entered the Great Basin by way of Salina Canyon. Near present-day Salina, the main trail route struck the Sevier River and followed it south to Clear Creek Canyon where one branch turned west to cross the mountains along the general route followed by Interstate 70 to its junction with Interstate 15 near Cove Fort following the route first taken by Jedediah Smith in 1826. Here the trail turned south and passed through present-day Beaver County and rejoined the main branch of the trail which had continued south up the Sevier River at the mouth of Clear Creek Canyon past the future communities of Marysvale, Junction, and Circleville before leaving the Sevier River at Bear Valley Junction to cross the mountains and enter Parowan Valley by way of Little Creek just north of Paragonah. Travelers continued on to Mountain Meadows where animals were rested before the push across southern Nevada and on to California.

Jefferson Hunt

The first Mormon to pass through Beaver County was Captain Jefferson Hunt who made several trips from Salt Lake City to California between 1847 and 1851, including one in 1849 as guide for a group of California-bound gold miners and a company of Pacific-bound Mormon missionaries. One of the members of the Hunt Party, Addison Pratt, reported that they camped on Beaver Creek on 18 October 1849. Pratt described Beaver Creek as " . . . a fine stream. It has wide bottoms on each side and covered with an abundance of good grass. . . . I think this creek would support a settlement of thousands, and the creek has the appearances of affording an abundance of trout in summer. . . . I caught one of about two pounds weight. . . ."[10]

Parley P. Pratt Expedition

In November 1849 Brigham Young and the Legislative Assembly of the Provisional State of Deseret commissioned Parley P. Pratt to lead a group of fifty men to explore the southern area and identify potential sites for future settlements. The expedition " . . . included 12 wagons, 1 carriage, 24 yoke of oxen, 7 beef, 38 horses and mules, and supplies: trade items for the Indians, 150 lbs of flour for each man, crackers, bread, meal, and 60 lbs coffee."[11] Among the fifty men were eight who had been members of the original 1847 pioneer company. Most were experienced frontiersmen, with Samuel Gould, at age seventy-one, the oldest, and Alexander Abraham Lemon the youngest at eighteen.

Preparations for the expedition were completed quickly and the group set out from the Salt Lake Valley on 24 November in the midst of a snowstorm. The winter journey was a difficult one.

> Some days roads were passable and the weather cooperative; some days the company bucked snow, mud, swampy areas and tricky creek crossings. On the way to Sanpete they encountered twenty-three creeks or rivers and forded one, Salt Creek, east of Nephi, six times. Animals and men labored up rocky ascents and descents. North winds stung their faces and penetrated their clothing. At many campsites cattle went hungry; at others, neither man nor beast had fresh water to drink. The mens' energy flagged during frequent backtracking to round up straying cattle and horses. The

Otter Lake in the Winter. (J.D. Osborn)

thermometer seldom stood above freezing. For twenty-one days the temperature dipped into the teens and single digits; six times it registered below zero and on December 10 plunged to 21 degrees below.[12]

The route headed south into Utah Valley past Provo and on to Nephi where it turned to the southeast around the southern end of Mt. Nebo following up Salt Creek to cross the divide into Sanpete Valley. The expedition reached the settlement of Manti just ten days after the pioneer group under Isaac Morley had arrived to found the southern most Mormon settlement to that time. At Manti five men and two wagons joined the expedition. Pushing south to the future site of Salina, the expedition joined the Spanish Trail and continued south along the Sevier River. South of present-day Circleville the expedition left the river and began the ascent into the mountains. After a five-day ordeal of carving a sixteen-mile long road across the mountains using picks, shovels, and axes, the expedition entered the northern end of the valley of the Little Salt Lake through what they called "Summer Gate," because of the valley's welcome contrast to the snow-covered mountains. The route into the valley of the Little Salt Lake followed along Fremont Wash about ten miles south of Beaver.[13]

Continuing southward, the expedition reached the Virgin River and explorered the future sites of St. George, Washington, and Santa Clara, before circling the west side of the Pine Valley Mountains to rejoin their earlier route near Cedar City. The return trip followed the general route of Interstate 15 northward through Beaver County, Millard County, and past Nephi into Utah Valley and back to the Salt Lake Valley. Parley P. Pratt prepared a report of the expedition which was presented to the Utah Territorial Legislature. In his report Pratt outlined the best places for future settlements giving his highest recommendation to the Valley of the Little Salt Lake because of the iron deposits that had been discovered there. Although he had passed through the Beaver area in January, its potential impressed him favorably and he wrote, "This is an excellent place for an extensive Settlement."[14]

The Iron Mission

Two months after Pratt's report to the territorial legislature, Mormon apostles George A. Smith and Ezra T. Benson were appointed during the April 1850 LDS conference as leaders of the Iron Mission which would establish settlements and develop a pioneer iron industry in the Little Salt Lake Valley along with utilizing the agricultural resources of the area. The colony would also help facilitate goods and immigrants which Brigham Young expected to bring to Utah from the west coast. In October 1850 one hundred men were called to the Iron Mission and preparations quickened. Provo was designated as the rendezvous point for the first company which left that community on 16 December 1850.

On 8 January 1851 the main group reached Beaver Valley. John D. Lee, clerk for the mission, recorded a favorable description of the area as he viewed it from a hill at the north end of Beaver Valley.

> . . . here on the summit you have a full view of the surrounding country, of the kanyons that makes into the valley of Beaver, which appear to be well clothed with Pine and Fur timber. The vally is extensive, land good & well adapted for iregation with occasional springs breaking out through the vally immediately on

the bottom is aboundance of grass. Some of which is a rich growth. The hill and S[p]urs of the Mountains are covered with large sage greasewood and rabbit brush; with smawl bunch grass growing among the shrubs. The ceder timber commences about 6 ms from the center of the body of farming land & then continues over the spurs & mountains & in the kanyons & inexhaustible quantity easy of access waggons can be drove among the groves almost in any direction—This is also a splendid situation, for a heavy settlement. . . . [15]

The Iron Mission pioneers camped that night on the north side of Spring Creek near the south end of Beaver. John D. Lee writes that at the encampment they "Tied up the horses and posted strong guards araound the cattle; as the Red men were in our vicinity. This creek is about 1 rod wide and 1 foot deep banks high & steep."[16]

The next day there was much work to be done to locate and build a road south out of the valley and up the ridge to the divide between Beaver Valley and the Little Salt Lake Valley. John D. Lee's entry for 9 January 1851 records:

This morning the pilot Jos Horn and Capt S. Baker were instructed by the Pres. To examine the situation of the land on the south side of Beaver and if possible to look out a rout to avoid crossing the swamp (a wet piece of land made by springs spreading over the land) About 9 bros Horn and Baker returned & reported favorable. Said by driving about 1/2 mile down the stream and making a bridge or rather filling up a smawl ditch with sage brush through which the water runs, the whole camp can go over dry shod. In the mien time Capt. Anson Call by order of the Pres. Engaged as many men with picks and spades on the banks of Spring Creek as could work to an advantage digging down the banks which were very steep. Another portion of the co were collecting the teams about 10 the horse teams commenced crossing and was followed by the 2nd 50. . . . about 3/4 of a mile is the distance between Spring Creek & Pure Creek [South Creek], another tributary of the Beaver. This stream is about 8 feet wide & 1 deep water clear as christale bottom gravely banks hard; but steep bad crossing. Less than a 1/4 mile distance brings you to the main creek. This is about 2 rods wide and 2 feet deep at the ford, banks low and hard bottom gravely. Good crossing—Some willow on the banks near the crossing and about 3 ms up the stream appears to be a considerable body of cottonwood timber.[17]

The night of 9 January was spent at the south end of Beaver Valley and the next morning wagons were double-teamed for the climb to the summit of the ridge. The road up the mountain was " . . . steep rocky & on account of snow, slippery and sideling, hard on waggons & teams."[18] After reaching the summit, George A. Smith " . . . ascended to the top of one of the highest dwarf pine trees . . . & from it had a view of the Little Salt Lake Valley."[19]

After four weeks of travel, the company reached the site of Parowan on 13 January 1851.

The successful establishment of Parowan in January 1851 and the wagon traffic through Beaver Valley back and forth between the Iron Mission communities and Salt Lake City brought greater attention to the potential for settlements in Beaver Valley. For nearly three decades, Parowan was the "Mother" colony for a number of Mormon settlements throughout southern Utah that took hold in some of the most isolated parts of the American West, including the outpost of Bluff settled by Hole-in-the-Rock pioneers on the San Juan River in 1880 after being called to the mission during a conference in the Parowan Rock Church.

Given the favorable reports of the Beaver Valley, it is understandable that one of the first areas for settlement as Parowan residents pushed outward was north into Beaver Valley.

ENDNOTES

1. Fray Angelico Chavez, trans., Ted J. Warner, ed., *The Dominguez-Escalante Journal: Their Expedition Through Colorado, Utah, Arizona, and New Mexico in 1776* (Provo: Brigham Young University Press, 1976), 68.

2. Ibid., 69.

3. Ibid., 70

4. Ibid., 70.

5. Ibid., 70–71.

6. Ibid., 72. Chavez and Warner identify the location as Brown Knoll, about two miles east of the Union Pacific Railroad tracks, noting that "There is a small ravine in the eastern ridge of the knoll which would have been ideal for camping, as it afforded shelter from the desert and mountain

winds. At its base the ground is wet and is used today as a watering place for range cattle."

7. Ibid., 74

8. Dale Morgan, *Jedediah Smith and the Opening of the West* (Lincoln: University of Nebraska Press, 1953), 193–97 and 211–15.

9. C. Gregory Crampton and Steven K. Madsen, *In Search of the Spanish Trail: Santa Fe to Los Angeles, 1829–1848* (Salt Lake City: Gibbs-Smith Publisher), 11.

10. S.George Ellsworth, ed., *The Journals of Addison Pratt* (Salt Lake City: University of Utah Press, 1990) 382.

11. Donna T. Smart, "Over the Rim to Red Rock Country: The Parley P. Pratt Exploring Company of 1849," *Utah Historical Quarterly* 62 (Spring 1994), 172.

12. Ibid., 173–74

13. Ibid., 179

14. Parley P. Pratt, Report of the Southern Exploring Expedition Submitted to the Legislative Council of Deseret, 5 February 1850, quoted in Smart, "Pratt Exploring Company," 188.

15. "Journal of the Iron County Mission, John D. Lee Clerk," ed. Gustive O. Larson, *Utah Historical Quarterly* 20 (July 1952), 263–64.

16. Ibid., 264.

17. Ibid.

18. Ibid., 265

19. Ibid., 266.

CHAPTER 4

THE ESTABLISHMENT OF BEAVER COUNTY AND ITS COMMUNITIES 1856–1870

Travelers to the Valley of the Little Salt Lake easily recognized the rich soil and plentiful water of Beaver Valley. In the early 1850s, residents of Parowan traveled to Beaver Valley to cut the native grass and haul it back for winter livestock feed. Some of the Iron Mission members were so taken with the idea of settling the Beaver Valley that for the first few years church leaders strongly discouraged what they thought would be a premature settlement effort into Beaver Valley.[1] By 1855 it was clear that settlers would be moving into Beaver Valley, and on 5 January 1856 the Utah Territorial Legislature created Beaver County.

Beaver County Created

Unlike most other Utah counties, Beaver County was created before it was settled. Utah's first six counties were created on 31 January 1850. The Beaver area was included in the southern most county first called Little Salt Lake, but changed to Iron County before the end of 1850. The boundaries of Iron County were vague, but were partly defined as the area south of the divide between Beaver Creek and the Sevier River. When Beaver County was created in 1856, its boundaries were set as "All that portion of Utah territory bounded north by Millard County; east by the Territorial line; south by an east and west line crossing the military road on the summit of the ridge dividing Little Salt Lake and upper Beaver Valley; and west by Carson County . . ."[2]

These boundaries were more clearly defined by the Utah Territorial Legislature ten years later when, on 10 January 1866, Beaver City was designated as the county seat and the boundaries were identified as "All that portion of territory bounded south by Iron County, west by Nevada, north by a line running due east and west through a point two miles south from the south side of Fort Wilden on Cove Creek, and east by the range of mountains dividing Beaver and Pauvan Valleys from the valley of the Sevier . . ."[3]

The Settlement of Beaver

A month after Beaver County was created, and five years after the Iron Mission vanguard journeyed south from Salt Lake City to the Little Salt Lake Valley, a group of fifteen families prepared to leave Parowan to establish a new settlement thirty miles to the north in Beaver Valley. Under the leadership of Simeon Howd they left Parowan on 5 February 1856 and arrived the next day, ready to start a permanent settlement in the valley. The original settlers included: Wilson G. Nowers, James P. Anderson, Edward W. Thompson, Ross R. Rogers, Barney Carter, John Knowles, James Low, H. S. Alexander, John M. Davis, Charles Carter, John Henderson, James Duke, Joseph Goff, Benson Lewis, Andrew Patterson, and his sixteen-year-old son Robert.

The first night after leaving Parowan for Beaver Valley, Wilson Nowers recalled:

> the snow covered the ground that was frozen, we built a bon fire of sage brush and thawed the ground then removed the fire and dug a hole in which we cached our potatoes and other provisions, spread our blankets thereon, after covering it with dirt, and slept there for the night. Next morning we opened the cache, loaded our provisions into our wagons and again moved on for Beaver Valley.[4]

The members of the group worked together to clear fields and raise cabins. These first primitive dwellings had cloth windows, rug doors, cobble stone fire places, and dirt roofs.

When the snow finally melted after the first winter, the settlers saw fields carpeted with soft blue sagebrush. Patches of willow, grass, and native plants dotted the valley. Beaver Creek and other tree-lined streams came out of the mountains to the east and ran west through the valley. A number of channels of Beaver Creek returned to one stream in the area eventually known as Greenville. Other streams like South Creek, Devil Creek, and Indian Creek brought enough water down into the valley from the east to be diverted into irrigation canals for agricultural use by the settlers. Beaver Valley had rich range land, soil, and growing conditions for pasture grasses. The temperate climate made it particularly well suited for livestock production.

It was expected that after the initial settlement by veterans of the Iron Mission, additional settlers would come from the Salt Lake Valley and other settlements to the north.

The establishment of Beaver City was typical of the manner of settlement throughout Utah. After choosing a favorable location nearest the most important natural resources, a townsite was surveyed in a gridiron pattern as outlined in Joseph Smith's Plan for the City of Zion. The primary features of the plan included areas for religious, public, and commercial uses in the center of town, surrounded by ten-acre blocks of residential land, each divided into one-acre parcels.[5] Selection of these parcels was made by drawing lots. Settlers built a house, constructed outbuildings and corrals, and planted a garden on their one-acre town lot. Larger tracts of farming and grazing land surrounded the village and were reached on foot, wagon, or horseback. This original layout of a three-tiered, radiating land system is still apparent in Beaver today.

More important to the success of the settlement than the city plan was the colonist group itself. The settling parties were designed to include a compatible group of experienced leaders and craftsmen whose combined talents in milling, carpentry, masonry, blacksmithing, farming, etc., would blend in a cooperative system intent on building and sustaining a flourishing community. Enduring constant difficulties and slow progress at times, the overall effort proved successful, as is evident by the signs of accomplishment visible in the present day city.

Beaver City was first surveyed and platted on 17 April 1856 by James Martineau of Parowan. Martineau's survey laid out oblong blocks with eight lots to the block—four corner lots and four interior lots. When quarrels developed over the choice corner lots, the town was resurveyed by Edward W. Thompson in 1857. He laid out square blocks 396 feet long on each side with streets and side walks 100 feet wide. Thompson's new survey provided for four lots on each block—all corner lots putting the former controversy to rest. Thompson established the survey corner at the northeast corner of the present-day courthouse running east and west. The streets running north and south were given number names, and the streets east and west were designated by the letters of the alphabet. Originally, the township included the east part of Greenville and part of Galeville. The new survey left at least one cabin in the middle of the street, but it was moved to a new location without great difficulty.[6] Nancy K. Nowers, the first white child born in Beaver, was born in the house before it was moved.

All of the city blocks were divided into four lots and included a residence, well, lumber livestock barn, chicken coop, garden plot, and fruit trees. Each of the city blocks had twenty-four hours of city ditch water and six hours of ditch water for each home.

Most of the first residences were log cabins made with roughly hewn cottonwood trees. Red pine, ponderosa pine, black balsa, and white spruce timber were abundant in the local canyons. Before long Beaver homes were built of adobe bricks, native stone including black basalt and pink rock, brick, and sawed lumber.

The town of Beaver was incorporated in January 1867 and John Ashworth became Beaver's first mayor. The city council issued licenses for everything from selling liquor to dancing, and created land taxes, water, poll, and dog taxes. The council also regulated the movement of cattle, horses, and hogs running the city streets; the building of local fences; grazing in town; and traffic.[7]

Beaver County's First Public Officials

The Utah Territorial legislature appointed a full set of county officials and the first official public meeting was held on 4 September 1856. The county court was Beaver County's first administrative body. When originally created, the court consisted of a probate judge and three selectmen. Judge Lorin W. Babitt came to Beaver to install provisional officers until a regular election could be held. These interim officers included Wilson G. Nowers, county clerk; Orson Tyler, sheriff; Lamoni L. Babitt, constable; and James W. Huntsman, selectman. It was intended that Beaver City leaders Simeon F. Howd and Joel W. White would be appointed selectmen, but both were absent at the time of Babitt's visit. In their place, John M. Davis and Ephraim Tompkinson were sworn in to serve temporarily. In addition, Ross R. Rogers was appointed notary public and county recorder; C.P. Liston, county treasurer; James P. Anderson and James Duke, fence viewers; Edward W. Thompson, surveyor; John Ashworth, assessor and collector; John M. Davis, justice of the peace; Charles Carter, supervisor of roads and streets; and James Farrer, pound keeper. The list of offices gives a clear picture of social conditions of the day that reflect the kinds of issues faced by governmental leaders and that established in their minds an orderly community.

The Distribution of Land

The distribution of land in Utah Territory was a complicated matter. Because Utah territory had not been surveyed by the federal government before settlement all land grants were tenuous. Local surveyors had surveyed and platted city lots that were distributed with certificates of survey signed by the surveyor and mayor or probate judge.

Technically, all land transactions were not binding until a federal land office was established in Utah Territory in 1869; all settlers were therefore legally considered squatters. Originally, the land was acquired by the United States government in the Mexican War of 1846 through the Treaty of Guadalupe Hidalgo. One result of the territorial constitutional convention held 2 March 1850 was a petition from the State of Deseret to the Congress of the United States for admittance as a state. The petition was ignored, and Congress passed the Compromise of 1850 on 9 September 1850 which admitted California as a state and divided the rest of the lands obtained from

Mexico into the territories of Utah and New Mexico. However, the territorial legislature was not granted authority over land, water, or timber distribution.

Thus between 1847 and 1 April 1869, twenty-two years later, it was impossible in Utah to secure legal title to land through a federal land office. Because of this unsteady situation, and the absence of governmental supervision of the distribution of natural resources, and because the Mormon church was directing colonization efforts, the LDS church, the State of Deseret, and finally Utah Territory developed their own systems. None of the three claimed more than temporary or emergency jurisdiction over the lands until the federal government stepped in.

The territorial legislature enacted the following provision on 6 March 1852:

> When any conveyance, sale, or transfer shall be made of any legal claim, or right of possession of any city lot, or surveyed lands or land, part or parts thereof within this territory, the seller or vendor of the same shall make and execute to the vendor a full and written claim, and possession to the premises so transferred, and acknowledge the same before the county recorder where the premises are situated.[8]

At the time the provisions of the Pre-emption Act should have remedied this problem. This act had been in force for six years before the Mormon pioneers entered the area and impacted land distribution throughout the West. It provided for a claim of no less than forty acres nor more than 160 acres after fourteen months of occupancy and that payment of $1.25 per acre for heads of families and individuals over twenty-one years of age. However generous this provisions appeared, it was ill-suited to the arid lands of Utah. Even the minimum area was far too large for the typical small subdivision favored by Utah farmers. Because of the precarious situation with the Native Americans, the residency requirement presented a particular problem. The Homestead Act of 1862, which provided a 160-acre piece of land, proved to present the same difficulties for this arid mountainous environment.

When the earliest settlers of Beaver County platted off their lots

and alloted land on the periphery of town, their principal objective
was to establish an agricultural community. The fields that stretched
to the west from the mountain base promised fertile soils for farming and land perfect for stock grazing. The original pioneers brought
with them cattle to begin herds. Soon cattle herds grazed in the Wah
Wah and Pine Valley, and large numbers of cattle grazed in the area
that would eventually be the center of mining activity in the county
around Newhouse and Frisco.

A few years after a federal land office was established in the Utah
Territory in 1869, a branch office was established in Beaver. Some
feared that the land office would give outsiders the opportunity to
claim choice parcels of land which had been farmed by Mormon settlers for over a decade. According to John Franklin Tolton, a small
group of land jumpers did move onto land that others saw as theirs.
The result was violence. One of the land jumpers, John Howard, was
shot dead in his newly constructed cabin. No one was charged with
the murder and, as Tolton recounts the story, "The other jumpers
took the hint and beat a retreat."[9]

Farming and Irrigation

Absolutely essential to the Mormon settlement of the arid west
was irrigation. Born out of necessity, irrigation worked because cooperative work networks were established. Obviously a far too complicated and arduous a task for individuals to complete on their own,
the group effort at irrigation once again united the Mormons in
community building.

In southern Utah Mormons observed that certain Indian groups
irrigated land for crops. It was clear that there would be a constant
need for water, that irrigation provided an efficient and achievable
solution to that problem, and given their group consciousness and
cooperative spirit, a community program of control of water
resources seemed the ideal solution. In a way not unlike the blessing
of the loaves and fishes to thousands, the benefits of the limited water
resources of the Great Basin were multiplied and carefully conserved
to provide for the growing community of settlers in the Mountain
West.

Within a decade after settlement, the inhabitants of Beaver

All members of the family participated in the harvest. (Utah State Historical Society)

County organized in irrigation companies to extract and regulate water from nearby rivers and streams to insure more efficient use. The Kent's Lake Company and the Mammoth Canal Company, among others, serviced local areas and provided water to render the land arable for agriculture.

For irrigation and culinary purposes, each city block had twenty-four hours of city ditch water. Family lots had six hours of ditch water for their gardens, lawns, flowers, and fruit trees. Water rights came along with the purchase of land after 1869.

Farming required long, hard work with primitive tools, and sometimes grasshoppers threatened to destroy entire crops. John Franklin Tolton recalled, "We cut our grain with a cradle, raked and bound it into bundles by hand, and threshed it with a flain. This continued, as well as cutting our hay with a scythe, until as late as 1875. No alfalfa hay was raised in Beaver until a later period, and our principal forage for cattle was wild, or meadow, hay, pea vines, corn-fodder, and straw and chaff."[10] Tolton also described the efforts to combat grasshopper invasions. "So numerous were the grass hoppers during crop growing seasons that the sun would be litterally [sic] obscured at mid-day, so dense would be the swarm. Whole families would be found among the growing crops with willow boughs endeavoring to drive these hords into ditches where straw had been previously placed, and when so driven the straw would be set on fire in hopes of thus getting rid of the pests."[11]

Children made important contributions in doing chores and working on farms.

> Both sons and daughters in the families drove the cows to and from the pastures. Many of these children helped with the milking. At this time the milking was done by hand. The children also fed the calves, chickens, and pigs. They also cut or helped cut the wood for the kitchen cook stove and the heating stove. Oh yes, the wood had to be packed to the wood box near the back door of the house. You can probably guess who did this. Some family children did have one or more riding poinies, but most children walked every where they went. A lot of the boys went bare footed in the summer months, and boy did those gravel and dirt roads get hot.[12]

A woman's life was largely subscribed by the conditions of her home. James Horace Skinner wrote about the varieties of work required of a woman in the production of clothes for her family. "The wool after being carded with hand cards, was spun with the old fashioned spinning wheel, and that was hand work for the women, after being spun, next came the weaving, that too was by hand. Then making up all done by hand, no sewing machines, after a while some parties built a carding machine that took a lot of hand labor off of the women." He continued to describe her other work, saying it is difficult to imagine what all women had to go through on a daily basis. "With baking on a open fire place with bake skillet and frying pan. No carpets, or rugs on the floor, no stoves and few conveniences to cook or work with, and I may say less to wear, with poor and uncomfortable houses to live in, not enough in many cases to keep the wet or cold out, even many lacked enough bedclothes to keep them from suffering from the cold."[13]

The Utah War and Mountain Meadows Massacre

The first real threat to the new settlement in Beaver Valley came from far away in Washington, D.C. The decision by President James

Buchanan to send a federal army to Utah to replace Brigham Young as territorial governor and to put down an alleged Mormon rebellion was made in the spring of 1857, a little more than two years after the first residents arrived in Beaver Valley. The approach of the federal army was met with resistance and plans to abandon outlying settlements, look for other areas into which Mormons could move, and, if necessary, undertake another exodus to relocate the Latter-day Saints to a place where they could practice their religion unhindered by non-Mormons and the federal government. The outside threat also suggested the need to strengthen Mormon alliances with native Indians and to reconsider their treatment of non-Mormon emigrant parties passing through the territory en route to California.

As a result of the force of public opinion, limited actual knowledge of the situation, and his own bias against the Mormon church, President James Buchanan, elected in November 1856, appointed Alfred Cumming of Georgia the new governor of Utah territory. In addition, he appointed William S. Harney leader of a military force that would accompany the new governor to Utah. Secretary of War John B. Floyd, himself bitterly anti-Mormon, believed a show of military force would strengthen the federal presence in Utah and insure that there would be no trouble over the appointment. On 28 May 1857 Floyd order 2,500 troops gathered at Fort Leavenworth "to march then to Utah as soon as assembled." After Harney was reassigned to Kansas, Colonel Albert Sidney Johnston was appointed commander of the force.

Mormons were aware of the impending crisis and quickly prepared for war. They received piecemeal news of the organization of the troops that filtered in informally from travelers through the area. On 24 July 1857, in the midst of a Pioneer Day celebration held in Big Cottonwood Canyon, Porter Rockwell, Abraham Owen Smoot, and Judson Stoddard, returning from a trip to the East, brought the alarming news that an army was moving toward Mormon territory.

Although southern Utah was not in the line of march of Johnston's army, Mormon settlers recognized the severity of the situation and made preparations accordingly. In August 1857 George A. Smith made speeches in Nephi, Fillmore, Parowan, Cedar City, and Pinto, calling upon settlers to take care of their provisions and be prepared to move into the mountains where they would carry out a guerilla war against the federal troops. Smith delivered orders to local militia leaders and found southern Utah settlers ready to defend their homes and resist the federal invasion. Indian chiefs were escorted to Salt Lake City by Jacob Hamblin to meet with Brigham Young to strengthen the Mormon-Indian alliance and to discuss the treatment of emigrants passing through the territory.

One California-bound emigrant party making its way through southern Utah during the chaotic weeks of August 1857 was the Fancher Party. The party of 100 to 150 persons arrived in Salt Lake City on 10 August three weeks after the announcement that federal troops were enroute to Utah. Where earlier parties had taken the Salt Lake Cutoff north to its junction with the California Trail at City of the Rocks, the Fancher Party was probably the first to take the southern route in 1857. Expecting to purchase supplies and trade their trail-worn animals for fresh animals as had previous California-bound groups since the gold rush days of 1849, the Baker-Fancher Party headed south through Utah on the heels of George A. Smith, his admonition to guard their provisions still fresh in mind of the Utah Mormons. Reports and rumors of hostility and misconduct on the part of the emigrant party preceded their trek south.

Late in August the company passed through Beaver about noon and continued south ward for about a mile to a meadow where they set up camp. Local Indians were incensed at the travelers, and Beaver settlers felt threatened by their presence. Indians shot at one of the men as he walked through the sagebrush hunting rabbits. The man was not injured, but in meeting with the Indians, Beaver residents were told that the emigrant party had poisoned a mule and a spring near Nephi which made the Indians sick. The citizens of Beaver tried to placate the Indians, offering them a beef and and urging them not to harm the emigrants because of the numerous women and children in the party. With considerable concern about the Indians, a delegation from the immigrant party returned to Beaver. William B. Ashworth recalled:

> They were told what had been done to dissuade the Indians from making further trouble, but that all their efforts had been to no

avail. The bishop then advised the emigrants to protect themselves as best they could, as the town would not help them on account of all the women and children whose safety depended on the friendliness of the Indians. He urged the men not to come up into the town, as that would jeopardize, not only themselves but the people of Beaver.[14]

The next day most of the party continued on south toward Cedar City where they were also refused provisions and assistance. During the first week of September, they reached Mountain Meadows, thirty-five miles southwest of Cedar City. After resting a few days in preparation for the arduous trek across the desert, the emigrants were attacked by Indians and militia men disguised as Indians on 7 September. After a four-day siege which left them with little water and ammunition, the emigrants surrendered with the understanding they would be taken back to Cedar City. About a mile and a half from their camp, they were massacred by Indians and militia men and only seventeen small children survived.

Fate intervened to prevent a tragedy similar to that at Mountain Meadows from occurring in Beaver County. Philo T. Farnsworth, who was a captain in the militia in 1857, reported:

When the Arkansas Company [Fancher Party] passed through Beaver I was in Salt Lake City and returned as the company that followed them was going through. This company had trouble and divided and its Captain Duke with a portion were left [at] camp just below Beaver and a portion were left back in Indian Creek about six miles. After I got home that evening an Indian . . . came to me and told me the Indians intended to attack the company that was back on Mill Creek. I went to the captain of the company and told him of the intended attack and urged him to go back and bring the rest of the company and protect them. About 9 o'clock that evening he [sent] the Captain to me and said his Company were so demoralized he could do nothing with them. I then got out ten men and finally five of his men joined them and I sent them under command of R.R. Rogers and before [they] had got to their camp the Indians had attempted to drive off their cattle and one of the guards had shot an Indian. My men helped them to hitch up and the company started for town. . . . About 2 o'clock in the morning some Indians came to me and wanted me to join them and get revenge. I told them to send their chief and I tried to pacify him. . . . when I was eating breakfast I heard shots and rushing out I saw that Capt. Duke, Turner, & Collins who had just passed my house and Turner and Collins were both wounded. I spoke to the Indians and ran between them and the men. . . . Later I got the Indians out of town and sent to Parowan for ten men to escort them on their way.[15]

One of the travelers, George Powers, who was part of a small group of only three wagons, reported, "We laid by at Beaver several days, as the Bishop told us it was dangerous for so small a company as ours to go on."[16]

These acts of assistance and aid were overshadowed by the events that occurred at Mountain Meadows, and the tragedy would haunt southern Utah for decades. John D. Lee was the only man arrested in connection with the massacre. Captured in 1875, more than a quarter century after the event, Lee was tried and convicted at Beaver.

On 15 September 1857, Brigham Young declared that a state of military emergency existed and that the militia would resist any invasion of Utah. Under his direction, Porter Rockwell, Lot Smith, Robert Burton, and others led several hundred members of the Nauvoo Legion to hideouts along the route through Echo Canyon, preparing to engage in guerilla warfare to prevent the soldiers to travel through to the Salt Lake Valley.

The principal battles of the "Utah War" were little more than creating havoc for soldiers as they prepared for the advance of the army. Soldiers burned three supply trains, interrupted military communications, and attempted to divert the attention of the military advance parties from accomplishing their mission. Overall there were no deaths from military action. Although reportedly one infantryman "died of fright" after a nocturnal raid on the army's livestock herd. This limited action in Echo canyon did dissuade the troops from traveling through. Instead they wintered at Fort Bridger in perilous conditions.

Thus, according to one historian, "a combination of bungling on the part of the Buchanan administration, vacillating military leadership, hit-and-run raids, and inclement weather stopped the Utah Expedition a hundred miles short of its destination."[17]

Brigham Young's strategy at this point changed and focused instead on removal of his people. Through the intervention of Thomas Kane, longtime friend to the Mormons, Alfred Cumming came peacefully into the valley and assumed his position as governor. Regardless, the Mormons abandoned all settlements to the north and moved south as a body, leaving behind homes and a large amount of property to avoid confrontation with the troops. They stayed for a while in temporary shelters or with friends in Utah County and in counties as far south as Beaver. On 7 June a peace commission arrived from Washington with a proclamation of amnesty dated 6 April. As a result the army moved untroubled through the valley to the southwest, setting up camp in Cedar Valley. The army post was eventually named Camp Floyd after Secretary of War Floyd who had played a prominent role in stirring up the trouble in the first place.

San Bernardino Saints

One of the settlements abandoned during the Utah War was San Bernardino, California, and a number of families moved to Beaver County, including Francis M. Lyman, Marcus L. Shephard, Sidney Tanner, Horace A. Skinner, Alphonzo M. Farnsworth, Jonathan and Alma Crosby, John W. Christian, John P. Carter, Addison Pratt, John Hunt, E .C. Mathews, Thomas Parkinson, James Henry Rollins, Henry Gale, William Moyes, William Flake, Charles Nickerson, Philip Baker, Ephraim Twitchell, William Hawkins, James Henry Rollins, and others. These were part of some fifty-five families that left San Bernardino in November and December 1857, abandoning farms, businesses, and homes.

When John Franklin Tolton's family first came to Beaver, they stayed for a brief time in the Tithing Office Building.[18] Another refugee, James Horace Skinner, described his feelings upon coming to Beaver in a reminiscence written later in his life. When they came, Beaver had only been settled for two years. They had spent much of the previous few years already traveling great distances, building homes, and struggling to survive. Nevertheless, life in this new place provided new and demanding challenges.

I've arrived in time to share in the trials and hardships of making a
home in a desert waste. . . . What with providing something to
keep life in the body—and clothes to cover our persons, to building a shelter to protect us from the cold winter storms, and the
summer heat, building roads, grubbing sage brush, making
ditches, guarding against Indians attacks, herding our stock we
were kept pretty busy.[19]

The experiences related by Horace Skinner also applied to those who
settled Beaver County's other communities, including Greenville,
Minersville, and Adamsville.

Greenville

Greenville, located five miles southwest of Beaver, was explored
and settled by pioneers from Parowan and Cedar City. Well-watered
native pasture was the attraction, and as early as 1857 ranchers were
cutting grass and hauling it home to feed live stock in the winter. In
1860 William and Samuel Edwards, William Richards, and David
Miller decided to stay. They moved in four log houses from Beaver
and made a small encampment beneath a cluster of trees along a
creek. Several other families joined the settlement in 1861–62, including: Robert Easton, Morgan Jenkins, Benjamin Kelly, Robert Hickens,
Lewis Davis, Thomas G. Reese, James Whittaker, Watkin Reese, Orris
Clapp Murdock, Philo Carter, David Williams, Bessir Stredder, David
Reese, Joseph Huntington, James H. Blackner, Benjamin Arthur,
Alfred Heslington, Joseph Morris, David Griffith, Samuel Kershaw,
Charley Booth, Robert Edwards, William Barton, Samuel Maunsey,
and Thomas Butler.

As members of the group claimed plots of ground and built their
homes, the orientation continued to be toward the water. Realizing
the soil was alkaline and unfit for extensive farming, the settlers built
homes, began small farms, and for the most part began stock raising.
Many of them built log homes, but quickly the group joined to make
adobe bricks for construction.

As was true of other small towns feeding off Beaver, business and
industry were slow to come to Greenville. Because nearby mercantile
institutions offered all the goods and services one could need, settlers
here traveled to Beaver rather than start new businesses of their own.

Instead, their economic base depended on farming, dairying, and livestock. Farmers traded the produce from their gardens with the soldiers at Fort Cameron or freighted them to Salt Lake City or to Pioche, Nevada.

William Barton moved to Greenville in 1865 from Beaver. A miller by trade, Barton believed the warm water in Devil's Creek would make it possible for him to operate a mill year round. Farmers came from as far south as St. George to have Barton mill their grist. Jack of all trades, Barton was a particular friend to the Native Americans, conversing easily in their native tongue and also upon occasion was known to pull their teeth. Ruth Reese and Jane Richards were midwives who delivered countless numbers of local babies.

In 1872 the LDS Greenville Ward was organized as a separate ward of Beaver Stake. And like Beaver, Greenville had its own choir, school, and other organizations designed to imitate the cultural life offered by Salt Lake City. Samuel Edwards served as the first bishop between 1860 and 1872, handling the distribution of land, and water rights, as well as his ecclesiastical duties. The Greenville Ward had its own choir with twenty members conducted by James Whittaker, George Eyre, and Robert Brown. Their first log church building was used as a school, as well, until about 1906, when the town replaced it with a rock structure. The Women's Relief Society was organized in 1878, and its meetings were held in a log house on the east bank of Dry Creek. In 1898 the organization purchased a better building and initiated a grain storage project. In 1901 the Relief Society built a pink rock building with donated rock, sand, lime, gravel, and other building supplies, donated labor from the men in the town, and quilts and other products donated by the women for sale to raise much needed cash. A postal road was built by the county from Beaver to Greenville in the late 1870s.

Minersville

Not all exploration efforts were aimed at discovering agricultural sites. Brigham Young had a keen interest in commercial and industrial development and agressively sought to locate the materials and human resources needed to create support technologies. Thus he sent out scouts to find coal, oil, iron ore, lime, and practical precious minerals. Lead was in great demand in 1858 because of the arrival of Johnston's Army that year and the concern that Mormons may still need to defend themselves. The lead could also be used for hunting. In the fall of 1858, Jesse N. Smith, Isaac Grundy, William Barton and Tarelton Lewis discovered a rich lode of ore in what became the Rollens Mine (later the Lincoln Mine). After examining ore speci-mens, President Young "called" Smith, Grundy and others to return to the Mineral Range, open a mine, and build a support settlement nearby. They located two and one half miles northwest of the present Minersville. Eventually it proved most efficient to haul the ore to a small smelting furnace on the Beaver River in what is now Minersville. This location proved superior because water was more plentiful.[20]

In 1859 the first settlers lived in dugouts and covered wagons. From these primitive habitations, they began to farm and raise stock sufficient to sustain Utah's first permanent mining-based commu-nity. In 1859 Minersville was surveyed and laid out, and a mining company was organized with Isaac Grundy president. Although there was brief discussion about calling the settlement Grundyville, it was called Minersville which bespoke its unique position as a church-set-tled town devoted to mining. Besides the mines themselves, the peo-ple built a smelter called the Grundy-Barton Smelter, on the south side of the Beaver River. The smelter's furnace, constructed in 1859, was the first lead furnace west of the Rocky Mountains. Flood water destroyed the smelter in 1861. A stamp mill, blacksmith shop, saloons, and boarding houses spoke to the mining character of the town. Lead for bullets and small amounts of silver and gold were mined locally.

Before the settlement of Minersville, Mormon church leaders, particularly Brigham Young, avoided mining projects, fearing the infiltration of mining interests. Apostle Erastus Snow's attitude typi-fied that of church leaders: "We have all the time prayed that the Lord would shut up the mines. It is better for us to live in peace and good order, and to raise wheat, corn, potatoes and fruit, than to suffer the evils of a mining life, and do no more than make a living at last."[21] Nevertheless, Young also preached that the Lord would provide a way for their material needs to be satisfied. If Mormon Utah was truly to be a self-sufficient empire, it would need some source of mineral wealth. He said in 1849, "When the saints shall have preached the gospel, raised grain, and built up cities enough, the Lord will open up the way for a supply of gold to the perfect satisfaction of his people; until then, let them not be overanxious for the treasures of the earth are in the Lord's storehouse, and he will open the doors thereof when and where he pleases."[22] This opened up the way for an experiment like Minersville, a Mormon town dedicated to the extraction of wealth from the earth.

Isaac Grundy's correspondence with Young provides an interesting glimpse into the town's development. A letter of 24 August 1859 suggests the key issues settlers faced.

> According to your instructions I proceeded to select and organize a company of ten men for the purpose of working the mines in this vicinity. We are located about sixteen miles down the stream from Beaver Settlement the mines are about four miles North of us in the edge of the mountains.
>
> We have prospected several leads and raised between six and eight thousand lbs. of lead ore. I think when the ore is in smelting order it will yield about sixty-eight percent lead.
>
> We intend now to put up a temporary furnace and send up to your city between [6]00 and 1000 lbs. between this time and Conference.[23]

Grundy described their living conditions, and called for more miners to help develop the industry. He clearly expected Brigham Young to respond favorably to his plea for help.

For the first few years after the Lincoln Mine opened, miners hauled the ore to a smelter located on the Beaver River where the lead was melted into bricks to be fashioned into bullets.[24] The temporary nature of the initial shelters reflected the capricious fortunes of mining. Simple dugouts and wooden shacks housed the first wave of miners in the area.

According to local legend, Brigham Young, traveling through the area, stopped his buggy and pointed across the desert to the distance between Minersville and Milford saying that one day they would be joined together by continuous farms. "Produce raised from these farms," he said, "would help feed the world."[25] Irrigating the land for farming was a particular problem here, for Minersville shared one-eleventh of the water rights with Lower Beaver from the Beaver River. Early settler Jesse N. Smith recorded in his journal:

> Sun., March 7, 1859: Brother Grundy and myself mounted at 2 o'clock A.M. and rode down to the "farm." A. Lyman called all parties together and advised that the water claims be settled without dispute, then went to Salt Lake City. It was finally decided that the mining settlement at the cottonwoods should be entitled to one-eleventh of the water of the creek for irrigation purposes, an article to that effect was written out and signed by Bishop Farnsworth on behalf of the farmers and I. Grundy on behalf of the Mining Co. Carried surveyors' claim about seven miles to connect the two surveys.[26]

The Minersville Reservoir and Irrigation Company organized in 1889, and water came into town to be used for farming and culinary purposes. Soon more permanent structures were built along the sides of the valley. Minersville was unique in that it was a Mormon village dedicated to the extraction of ore from the mines with a number of farmers living in the area as well. Because of this, church, school, and merchandising played a different role in the life of the community. More families lived in this mining town than in most, and a sense of community pervaded that was different from the transitory atmosphere of most boom mining towns.

The Minersville Irrigation Company was the first incorporated water company using the water of the Beaver River. Fields of wheat and hay, cattle and sheep grazing on the slopes of nearby hills, expressed that this was a place with a diverse economic base—farmers and miners working for the good of the community.

Isaac Grundy served as Minersville's first LDS bishop until 1860 when James Henry Rollins replaced him. Meetings were held in homes until 1860 when they built their first adobe church building, eighteen by twenty feet. Bishop Rollins doubled as the town ecclesiastical leader and post master, running the post office from his home until 1891.

Many of Minersville's businesses were service industries—blacksmiths, dry goods stores, mills, and boarding houses. Minersville Precinct had 446 inhabitants in 1870, 525 in 1900, and 815 in 1930.

It was undoubtedly the success of this early mining venture that encouraged the exploration of other potential mines, leading to the founding of Milford in 1880 and other mining towns now long abandoned.

Adamsville

In the spring of 1862 David B. Adams and several others settled on the right bank of the Beaver River about nine miles west of Beaver. Among the ranks of the first settlers of Adamsville were: David B. and Lydia Catherine Adams; Thomas and Ann Hougten Gunn; Joseph H. and Mary Ann Richards, Joseph Watkin and Jane Williams Reese; John Walters and Mary Jones Walters; James Simpkins and family; A.G. Wilson; Margaret Griffity; David and Margaret Pearce; John G. Jones; Sarah Griffith Jones; Joseph H. and Mayme Smith Armstrong; David C. and Nellie Adams; Evan J. and Catherine Griffiths Jones; David and Elizabeth Grimshaw Reese; Samuel Johnson; William U. Stewart; John and Mary J. Stewart Limb; John and Kate Evans; John F. Johns and wife.

Their numbers were soon increased by settlers who joined them from Iron, Garfield, and Sevier counties, and included James Simpkins, J. Baker, Joseph H. Joseph, Thomas Gunn, A.J. Wilson, J. Harris, Charles Willden, Joseph Armstrong, D.D. Reese, J. Tattersall, H. Tattersall, Thomas Richards, D.C. Adams, W. Holgate, and W. Hall.

The new populace immediately began to farm, raise stock, and build houses. Some ran sheep and cattle near the Wildcat Ranch, others farmed the land, securing water from the Beaver River through irrigation canals. The terrain nearby was difficult, and there was limited water in Wildcat Creek for irrigation, making settlement difficult, although there was abundant timber for construction. Prospectors equipped by Ebenezar Gillies for their prospecting, roamed through the nearby hills.

Named Adamsville in honor of its leading founder, the town was surveyed in 1867 and a substantial stone meetinghouse was erected in 1868. The next year David B. Adams became the bishop of the Beaver Third Ward, which included Adamsville and Greenville, and school was also held in the meetinghouse. In a creative use of space, desks were built around the periphery of the church's central chamber with seats made of split planks. Usually about forty students attended the school. It remained open until about 1920 when students were transported to school in Beaver.

North Creek, Rock Ford, Manderfield, and Pine Creek

Focusing first on areas near Beaver, the land on North Creek, north of town, was soon sought after due to its abundant water. As early as 1858, the lands and waters of its two creeks were obtained by influential men such as LDS apostles George A. Smith and Amasa Lyman, as well as Dr. John Christian, and Messrs. Holyoke and Baldwin. Among the early settlers of the North Creek area were Alexander ("Scotty") Boyter, known for his fine masonry work on many of the county's impressive stone buildings.

Other venturesome settlers explored similar creeks and streams. A ranch was located on the upper heads of South Creek by John P. Lee, while enterprising Marcus A. Sheperd established what became the Merchant Farm at the head of North Creek. Ephraim Twitchell settled on Indian Creek, and Henry Ceale put down roots on Dry Creek, three miles north of Beaver .

The water from the confluence of two creeks irrigated approximately 3,000 acres of land under the North Creek Irrigation Company and the West Side Irrigation Company. Besides agriculture, two sawmills were located in Harris Canyon and a shingle mill nearby. Population was dispersed throughout the valley, and no physical center existed to the settlement. Nevertheless, in 1893 a school with thirty students opened with Edward Tolton as the first teacher. The North Creek Branch of the LDS Beaver Stake had Henry Green as presiding elder.

In 1863 Sergeant Nathaniel V. Jones, an officer in the Mormon Battalion of Life Guards of the Nauvoo Legion, settled at Rock Ford. Here he built some structures which served as headquarters from which he searched for iron and coal at the request of Brigham Young.

Evenutally, the hamlet of Meanderfield developed in the Indian area. In the late 1860s and early 1870s, several families moved in the Pine Creek range where a small settlement was established.

The Pine Creek settlement was surrounded by thick pine groves along the ridges and valley hills. In the 1860s eight families settled Pine Creek including those of David Levi, George Williams, Jacob Littlebow, and Cunningham Mathews. These families provided milk, butter, and cheese to travelers from the East. Eventually Pine Creek became a mail stop where postal workers would change horses. The Bradshaws, Collis Huntington, Barcloughs, David Levi, and Cunningham Mathews ran cattle. Jacob Littlebow built a one-room house and store, and George Williams built and ran a large corral.

Cove Fort

Charles William Wilden and his wife and seven children settled Cove Valley in 1860. There they built two houses and a dugout. He homesteaded 160 acres and was soon joined by the Charles Wilden family. Brigham Young sent Ira Hinckley to this valley to build a fort which would provide protection from local Native Americans and serve as a supply station for travelers moving south. In 1867 workers from Fillmore and Beaver helped build the 100 foot square fort. Cove Fort was built out of indigenous black rock and lime mortar and was fourteen feet high. The north and south interior walls had six rooms on each side. A courtyard provided a space for community activity.

Strategically located roughly half way between Beaver and Fillmore, the fort provided protection and provisions for locals, travelers, and tourists. The fort complex, carefully restored in the early 1990s by the LDS church, was built next to an even earlier fort, the log Fort Willden established in 1861. The Willden family, fearing harm from the Indians, evacuated their crude log pole and log cabin enclosure not long after completing it.

Early County Government

Beaver County's selectmen first met in their homes or in the schoolhouse until spring 1867 when they began meeting in a room in the LDS Tithing Office Building. They met regularly and enacted regulations to protect the rights and privileges of the citizens of the county. Minutes of their meetings suggest the various issues confronting pioneers of the area. They granted a petition for the right to erect a saw mill and grist mill northeast of the city plot, and the use of the water of North Creek and Beaver Creek to propel the machinery. They gave the right to cattlemen to graze their herds on public land and established a $25 bounty for wolf skins. In 1867 the county court directed a cattle drive and placed the county sheriff in charge. The sheriff was apparently authorized to prohibit anyone from branding or ear marking stock in the public coral during the drive. Brands reflected the owners residency—east Beaver cattle were branded with a B, Minersville with an M, and stray pounds were also established by the sheriff. Licenses for both the manufacture and distribution of liquor came under the jurisdiction of the selectmen.

The early selectmen had proven themselves as effective organizers. Most had helped settle numerous towns, had served in bishoprics, and had proven they could work well with others. Beaver was run, therefore, by two selectmen and one designated as judge. Together they acted as a county court and selected other county officers.

Obviously, a selectman designated as "judge" wasn't a court judge as traditionally understood, although the group attempted to proceed in an orderly manner and, according to some assumptions about what was appropriate and, therefore, legal. At the first of each meeting, the minutes of the previous meeting were read and approved; if both selectmen (a quorum) could not be present, they rescheduled the meeting. Judges rotated frequently, more often than selectmen. Each county officer chosen by the judge and selectmen had to furnish a bond supported by approved security, sometimes several hundred dollars.

These three men were in charge of virtually all official county business, which included water, forests, roads, animal grazing, grist mills, lumber mills, and regulating the production and selling of liquor. The county assumed the responsibility for the poor, handicapped, and disabled. Selectmen passed taxes and directed the treasurer to receive wheat, oats, barley, and corn for payment of taxes. Regulations establishing election procedures and qualifications for candidates were established, as were rates of compensation for all elected officials. In 1860 they appointed Philo Farnsworth superintendent of schools. Two years later they divided Beaver County roads into four districts and appointed a road supervisor for each district.

Selectmen passed an appropriation for a bridge across the Beaver River in 1861, this was typical of their sense of responsibility for roads, bridges, and regulating the use of water—clearly the key issues dealt with routinely by the selectmen. In 1862 Orin Twitchell and Company petitioned the court for the rights to build a toll road through North Creek Canyon. The selectmen decided instead that they would hold a special election to raise $525 in tax funds to build the road. They recommended that it be paid in wheat at $1.50 per bushel. The road was located in Road District No. 1. In 1875 James R. Lindsay, D.P. Whedon, and others petitioned the court to build a highway from Minersville through Shauntie to Florida, a small mining town located in the San Francisco Mining District west of Milford.

In 1869 precincts were established and presiding officers appointed for Adamsville, with James Simpkins as magistrate; Pine Creek, William Dotson, justice of the peace; and Indian Creek (Manderfield), Willis Coplan, justice of the peace. The selectmen designated brands to distinguish stock belonging to individuals in various precincts. The court created Greenville Precinct in 1865 and designated it as School District No. 2, Beaver as District No. 1, and Minersville as District No. 3. Milford Precinct was established in 1876, with William H. Lighthall as justice of the peace.

During the first decade after settlement, Beaver City and Beaver County jockeyed for control over local resources. From the first, Beaver City controlled water that came from the Beaver River and the head water from the upper parts of the Tushar Mountains. Also the city collected taxes on water from the east part of the valley. All land grants were arranged by the city council and deeds issued by the mayor who met in a room in the county court house. Town lots sold from between $10 and $70. Further, the city council arranged for irrigation ditches to bring water to lots in the city out of the Beaver City Canal. After the land was surveyed into sixteen ten-acre lots, the city council awarded plots by casting lots. The settlers immediately planted a few acres of land, drawing water from nearby streams. This original area was soon known as the "Old Field." Early in May 1856 the settlers built a dam east of town to divert water for irrigation. Those who planned on using water for irrigation helped build the canals that brought it out of the canyons. James Horace Skinner worked on the first canals coming down out of Beaver Canyon. He remembered, "All this work was done free. We furnished our own tools, and food, and bedding, the food we cooked on the camp fire, our bed was two or three quilts laid on the hard ground, and 2 or 3 to cover us. No tents to protect us from the rain or cold. If it rained or snowed we had to take it as it came, many nights I have lain in wet bedding, shivering with cold."[27] The mill race was also constructed by community cooperative effort and was completed in 1857. By 1857 more than a hundred settlers lived in Beaver. In the center of Plat A, they built a log meetinghouse in the block set aside as the public square.

The lumber for the structure was processed at Edward Thompson's sawmill and hauled to the lot by the town's men. Thompson, himself a carpenter, directed the construction. James Horace Skinner worked on the building, as did all workers, without any pay. "I labored on the building," he later wrote, "from hauling the lumber out of the canion [sic] untill the completion of the building, even making benches and desks, all of this without one dollar of recompence in any shape or form. I helped build the central school house, the Rock house, the Park building meeting house, all on the same terms."[28]

Indian Relations

When Mormons began settlement of the Great Basin, they believed they were acting in fullfillment of scripture. Building the kingdom of God imbued their efforts with a sense of justification, like the American ideology of Manifest Destiny. Because Mormons believed the American Indians were the descendants of Book of Mormon peoples, they sympathized with the Native Americans. But, as was true throughout the frontier, it was perhaps inevitable that the Indians would resist the encroachment of Mormon settlement onto their lands. Their opposition endangered the continued existence of Mormons in this new environment "a thousand miles from nowhere." Here, in Utah territory, Mormon pioneers acted like many of their predecessors in other locations. On the frontier they occupied the land, they confronted the resistance of the Indians to their occupation, and asked for the federal government's assistance in the removal of the Indians to reservations.[29] This culture clash was part of the American settlement of the West, which meant the acquisition of traditional Native American lands. Mormon policy was often occupation without compensation to the owners. Acting in Young's absence, Heber C. Kimball advised the Mormons against paying the Indians for their land: "If the Shoshone should be thus considered, the Utes and other tribes would claim pay also. The land belongs to our Father in Heaven and we calculate to plow it and plant it and no man shall have the power to sell his inheritance for he cannot remove it. It belongs to the Lord."[30] This was justified because of their intention to convert the Indians to their religion and their way of life.

Most of these Indians were nomadic, seed-gathering peoples. Many groups, especially the Goshutes, Piutes, and Shoshone, constantly traveled from place to place foraging for food. Relations between Mormons and Native Americans remained fairly calm through the winter of 1852–53. But military action began against Chief Walker in Central Utah and against Jim Bridger and the mountain men in the Green River country who were allying with the Indians there. Brigham Young had taken a personal interest in Walker and the other Ute chiefs and had in fact baptized a number of them. In June 1851 Indian chiefs Walker, Sowette, Arrapine, and Unhwitch were ordained elders in the LDS church. Nevertheless, Young was acutely aware that the priesthood had not turned the Indians into allies. Walker and the others were disturbed by the continued advancement of Mormons into tribal lands. That Young was conscious of this growing tension is evident the following in dictation to his scribe on 18 May 1853: "I shall live a long while before I can believe that an Indian is my friend when it would be to his advantage to be my enemy."[31] Two months later the pressure broke and the Walker War began. Over the next nine months Walker led his band on the warpath eventually killing twelve white men and causing an estimated $2 million in property losses. An equivalent number of Indians lost their lives. Fear over war with the Indians spread through Mormon territory like a prairie fire.

Although the United States Congress appropriated $53,512 for territorial losses, none of the personal losses were compensated. The war was entirely over by the end of October, and a formal peace treaty signed in May 1854 at Chicken Creek (south of present day Nephi) by Young and Walker. Walker died a year later and was buried at Meadow Creek.

Since the 1850s the Mormon church had run four Indian farms in conjunction with the Bureau of Indian Affairs and the territorial government. These were closed in 1865 with the official removal of the Indians to the Uintah Reservation despite the objections of Chief Black Hawk and others.[32] The resulting confrontation between the Native Americans and white settlers resulted in at least seventy deaths and considerable property loss. In fact, Utah territorial officials estimated the cost of the war at $1,121,037 for military action alone. During the height of conflict, settlers abandoned their homes and towns in Wasatch, Sanpete, Sevier, Piute, Iron, Kane, and Washington counties.[33]

When the Indians raided James Horace Skinner's and other's stock and stole a number of horses belonging to the Tanner family, "they also took some 10 or 15 head of horn stock, mostly work oxen and cows. A company of some 21 or 23 men was soon collected and took the trail in persuit [sic], we followed them as far as what is now known as Fish Lake." They knew they were close behind them because they found meat cooking on an open fire. Regardless, they were forced to turn back because of their lack of provisions, despite the fact that they "had men in our party that would fight that had been tired, and were some of the best shoots in this part of the country, as for me, I guess I would have run if I could if I hadn't been too scared to run."[34]

The settlers' homes in Beaver County were attacked sporadically during the 1860s. On 23 September 1866, Paiute Indians attacked John P. Lee's ranch on South Creek. They burned the house and wounded a ranch worker named Joseph Lillywhite. The Lee children left the house during the fire and walked eight miles to Beaver for help. When they arrived in Beaver, the "Beaver Minutemen" were shingling the church tabernacle. This attack may be the cause of the temporary removal of Adamsville settlers to Greenville in 1866.[35]

The next September the same Paiutes raided Beaver itself and drove off 200 head of horses and cattle. Regardless of the number of attacks and skirmishes, eventually some measure of compromise was reached between the Beaver settlers and the local Native Americans.

An important consequence of the Black Hawk War was the abandonment of Circleville in June 1866. When Circleville settlers requested help, Beaver men and teams crossed the mountains and assisted a number of families to flee to the safety of Beaver. Edward Tolton, William J. Allred, Hyrum and Roan Fowler, Elijah Hoopes, John and Henry Bryant, and Fred Clark were among those Circleville settlers who took up residence in Beaver. Other Circleville settlers returned to Ephraim in Sanpete County from which most had come.

Beaver residents did their best to accommodate the Circleville settlers but the first years were difficult. John Franklin Tolton, who was four and a half years old when his family left Circleville, recalled:

> On our arrival, there being no hay or pasturage available, we were obliged to turn our oxen and cows upon the public domain which resulted in our losing them, all through Indian depredation. Picture if you can, a family of eleven souls, living in such quarters with all their earthly possessions, consisting of an old wagon, and wagon box, no food nor shelter, no clothing except what covered our bodies, and with scarcely sufficient bedding to protect us from the coming of winter.

During the two years following, we moved from one home to another, where charity invited us, by which time father had secured a lot and dug a cellar for our protection.[36]

Territorial Militia

Throughout the nineteenth century, rural Utah local militias offered the principal means of defense. Under Lieutenant-General Daniel H. Wells, Utah Territory's militia included all able-bodied men over the age of fourteen and under the age of seventy-five. The Beaver Militia was part of the Iron County Military District under the command of Colonel William H. Dame. Originally, Joseph Betensen was the captain of the Beaver County Militia.

Troops were mustered at least once a year for three or four days. Beyond that they were told to keep guard night and day so that "houses, stables, corrals, pastures, and ranges may not be robbed; nor men, women, nor children carried off in the night time, nor the day

time, and none but the sufferers know of it until it is too late to help
it."[37] Militia men were supposed to be ready to come to arms at a
moment's notice upon demand. To insure that this was possible, each
unit was to have sufficient horses, equipment, and weapons.
According to Daniel H. Wells, "Let every arrangement be quietly but
perfectly made and not wait till wanted and then have to hunt up
bullet molds, saddles, wagon-hammers, linch pins, harnesses, or anything else, but be 'minute men,' in fact, and let all these arrangements
be made immediately upon the recipt of this letter—make due report
to me of the condition of things in your district, the number of men
you can rely on and their equipment, ammunition, etc."[38] Wells
advised Beaver's militia to maintain watches at points along the trail
between Iron and Beaver counties and to maintain Fort Sanford
(near Circleville). During the Indian conflicts in the 1860s, Beaver
men helped guard Fort Sanford, along with men from Panguitch,
Circleville, Cedar City, and Parowan, usually for periods of two
weeks.

James Skinner recalled, "For several years we kept this up, we—
the cavalry—quartered from Pine Creek on the north to Fremont on
the south, day after day, sunshine or storm we were out, two to 4 or
often as many as 10, at a time, watching for Indians to keep them as
much as possible from raiding and steeling [sic] our stock and perhaps killing some of our people."[39]

The militia came together for exercises twice a year and for special three to four day training periods. Each man had to furnish his
own horse, saddle, gun, pistol and ammunition and to be ready to
muster at a moment's notice. William Booth Ashworth remembered
organizing into a militia to prepare for defense of the county. He considered them lucky that a former soldier, Dan Martin, had settled
nearby. "He was capable and a very agreeable officer. We got together
every Saturday afternoon, dressed in our uniforms—blue trousers,
with a red stripe down the outside of each leg (and by the way, [he
says] my mother carded the wool, spun the yarn, dyed it, and had it
woven on a hand loom, and made my trousers.) We had our saddles,
bridle spurs, fire arms, colts, pistol and springfield rifle and sabres."[40]

James H. Skinner recalled, "Our company even went so far as to
get uniforms and armed ourselves with sabers. . . . We needed a drill

master, there was one Dan Martin, but he had no horse, saddle or bridle, we took the matter and bought him a complete outfit and mad[e] him a present of it. In return he put us through our paces." The long hours of drill were, on occasion, spiced with levity. Skinner recalled one incident while the militia was drilling. " . . . the order came to draw sabers and charge. One man by the name of Nelson had a horse that was kind of slow or lazy, to hurry him up a little he hit him a whack across the rump, the blow broke his saber having about a foot in his hand, if that wasn't a funny scene, him charging a foe with about a foot of broke saber . . . how we did laugh when we came to rest."[41]

Ecclesiastical Affairs

The Church of Jesus Christ of Latter-day Saints organized the Beaver Branch on 8 February 1856 with Simeon Howd as president. Howd homesteaded 280 acres of land along the Beaver River. His land included seven forty-acres pieces. Three sections ran north-south from just above the South Fork of the Beaver River, south to Birch Creek Lake, then west four sections (or one mile) almost to the Left Hand Fork of Cane Canyon. Howd ran cattle on this land.

Howd proved ineffective in dealing with a lack of unity among the original settlers, and Philo T. Farnsworth was called by Brigham Young to move to Beaver to become bishop of the Beaver Ward in December 1856. Bishop Farnsworth directed the construction of a church building to accommodate a hundred members which was completed in 1858. Located in the center of Plat A, the church was the literal center of town. Farnsworth was not sucessful in dealing with the factions and, in the view of Brigham Young, to properly handle church affairs in Beaver. As a consequence, President Young appointed John R. Murdock of Lehi to become the new bishop of Beaver in 1864. "It gave me a severe shock," Murdock wrote, "when, upon invitation, I entered the office of President Young and was informed that he wanted me to be the Bishop of Beaver."[42] Murdock quickly organized community building efforts, and within years Beaver felt the results of his competent leadership. "I bought a farm and some town lots and built houses for my families to live in." Murdock wrote in his biography. "I also immediately set about building school houses, a meeting house and other public buildings. I was very zealous in this labor and carried much responsibility myself."[43] It was common practice of the church to plant powerful, influential businessmen and community leaders in other regions to facilitate growth bringing needed expertise and capital with them. Other men called from Lehi to lead communities included Abram Hatch in Heber City and Canute Peterson in Ephraim. Murdock oversaw the construction of the stake tabernacle, the original co-op store, the central school house, and the brick tithing office. In March 1866 Murdock became the stake president of the newly organized Beaver Stake.

The Beaver Stake was first created in 1866 but reorganzied in 1877. Again church leaders paralleled local community and governmental leaders. Murdock became stake president two years after he arrived in Beaver. With population growth, new wards were created in the stake. Murdock also encouraged several other Lehi residents to join him in Beaver including William Fotheringham, who had served two missions, one to India and another to South Africa. Fotheringham served as first counselor in the Beaver Stake. Thomas Frazer, a convert from Scotland who immigrated to Utah in 1861 and settled in Lehi, moved to Beaver in 1868 at the request of Murdock. A trained stone mason, Frazer's rock buildings and homes are now landmarks in Beaver.[44]

The women's organization—the Relief Society—was first organized in Nauvoo, Illinois, in the early 1840s but reestablished in Utah in 1867 and presided over by Eliza R. Snow. Local Relief Societies cared for the poor and the sick, owned property, operated cooperative stores and granaries, and supported home industry. After 1869 they helped organize comparable groups for adolescent women— Retrenchment societies. Throughout the nineteenth century, these groups promoted home industry, frugal practical economic and cultural activities, and advocated women's suffrage and equal rights throughout the settlements.

James Horace Skinner empathized with the difficulties women had in providing the necessities for their families, challenged by primitive conditions in this pioneer place. Clothes were produced primarily by hand through the industry of women and their daughters. Wool shorn from local herds was carded and spun on spinning wheels, then woven into cloth.

Buildings and Architecture

Encouraged by Brigham Young to build permanent structures to last till the Millennium, the pioneers' preference was for masonry over wood construction. During an 1862 tour of the towns of southern Utah, Young was critical of the quality of the built environment in Beaver. Recorder J.V. Long wrote,

> He showed the lack of local improvements of every kind, and stated that instead of visible improvements calculated to attract his attention . . . everything had remained in the statu(s) quo since his last visit. . . . We left the folds at Beaver feeling well, most of them showing signs of contrition and evincing a determination to improve the habitation of both man and beast by the time of the President's next annual visit.[45]

No progress had been noted by the next year, as one of Brigham Young's associates complained,

> we were unable to discover all those marks of enterprise and improvement so eagerly looked for by the Presidency on their entrance into the various settlements. The houses are chiefly of logs, with a few adobies, and I saw two shingle roofs and one frame stable. The meeting house is built of logs also. There has been great neglect on the part of the people of Beaver.[46]

Given the existence of many fine masonry structures dating from the late 1860s on, it is apparent that major changes occurred in Beaver at that time. The marked improvement in construction quality seems to be the result of several new influences: a new leader, a suddenly prosperous economy, an influx of new settlers, including some gifted masons, and the use of local rock and kiln-fired brick. Unsatisfied by the progress made under the town's early leaders, church authorities called John Riggs Murdock, then of Lehi, to lead the colony. Founded in 1851, Lehi had become an impressive community of adobe, brick, and stone structures, among them Murdock's own large residence. Murdock's experiences in Lehi and Salt Lake City allowed him to

One of Beaver's Pink Rock Houses. (Utah State Historical Society)

understand what was possible for Beaver, and within a short time, the town took on a new, more advanced appearance.

Adobe bricks were produced at an adobe yard west of Beaver near a spring in an area called the Adobe Yard Slough. Almost every Mormon community had eventually identified a lot in town that had the soil best suited for adobe making, and designated it the adobe yard. There they produced bricks for use in construction of their homes, their business buildings, and sometimes their churches and schools. They did this in the absence of available timber or professionally produced bricks.

The process was simple and just about anyone could help produce adobes. The night before the work was due to begin, the men would dig loose dirt at the bottom of a large circular pit. After drenching it with water, they would let it soak all night. The next day the dirt and water were mixed and then stamped or tromped on until it was just the right consistency. Men, children, and even a town's women would join together to produce adobe, the women pulling their skirts precariously high above their feet in the effort to prevent them from becoming soiled.

After the adobe mixture was just right, it was placed in molds formed with strips of wood to simulate the approximate size and dimensions of traditional kiln-fired bricks—familiar to these Saints from their homes in the eastern states or in other parts of the world. The molds were then placed in the sun for about two weeks until they were properly dried, then laid in even courses with a simple mortar— just mud and water. Pioneers from every social class and economic status used adobe bricks for building, sometimes covering them with a veneer of tar paper or stucco, but it was a cheap, quick, socially acceptable method of building up until the second decade of the twentieth century.

Among the first and still extant adobe houses in Beaver was the hall-parlor residence erected for Robert Kershaw in about 1864. Because adobe has relatively low compressive strength, and because it returns to mud when it gets wet, it is much less durable than brick or stone. Thus few adobe structures remain in Beaver.

From the 1860s, the period from which Beaver's oldest extant buildings survive, the burgeoning town had begun to develop a fairly sophisticated construction industry. Due to an abundance of building materials and the presence of a talented work force, construction technology allowed local craftsmen to employ their knowledge of eastern states and British/Scottish designs in building substantial, architecturally impressive dwellings, meetinghouses, public buildings, and commercial structures. Among Beaver's settlers were masons and builders with construction experience gained in their homeland counties of Fife and Clackmanan in Scotland. Others hailed from England, and several had constructed northern European-influenced American building types while living in Parowan, Salt Lake City, and Nauvoo, Illinois. In the beginning, Beaver's builders were not short of knowledge and experience, but of the materials and technology necessary to put their abilities to good use. The early years were spent developing the needed technology.

As soon as the technology could be developed, citizens of Beaver began to make fired brick. They were among the first people in Utah to build with this much superior masonry product. The earliest known commercially manufactured brick in Utah was produced in 1865 in the Atwood kiln in Murray. The first brick made in Beaver is believed to date from the same time, or perhaps a year later. There

One of Beaver's Black Rock Houses. (Allan Kent Powell)

were at least two early brick-making plants, one operated by the
Patterson family near a clay deposit near South Creek about four
miles south of town, the other run by Anciel Twitchell and sons at
Indian Creek (now Manderfield). The red brick from both plants was
soft when compared to later pressed brick, but was superior in
strength and durability to adobe. Its greater expense meant that some
settlers would continue to build with adobe.

It appears that after the arrival of stone mason Thomas Frazer in
1868, black rock structures could be built somewhat less expensively
than brick but at greater cost than adobe. Thus residents could chose
between three masonry products based on cost and architectural
preferences.

Among the important early brick buildings was the Beaver Stake
Tabernacle, started after the first log meetinghouse burned down in
1865. The construction of the tabernacle epitomized the cooperative
effort for which pioneer society is known. Robert Wiley and Samuel
Edwards laid the stone foundation. The brick was supplied by
Twitchel and sons, while the lime was burned by Joseph Tattersall,
David Powell, and David Davey. Edward Thompson's sawmill pro-

vided the lumber, and Jonathon Crosby's finishing shop produced the planed-and-turned trim. The carpentry work, including the framing, windows, doors, pulpit area and later gallery, was done by the city's leading mechanics, Jonathon Crosby, Charles Bird, John Ashworth, and Roberts Keys. Wood shingles for the roof were made at Edward Nelson's mill. To ensure a high quality interior finish, church leaders sent to Beaver painter and grainer John Wicker and his assistant, a Mr. Schepelli, who had come from Europe with Wicker.[47]

Completed after several weeks of effort, the east-facing tabernacle was a monument to pioneer craftsmanship and devotion. The tall, spacious assembly room had ample windows and a balcony or gallery at the east end. In the full basement were two big rooms used for Sunday school classes, priesthood quorum meetings and parties. Later Richard Maeser used the building for a church school. A bell tower with a "large, clear-toned bell" called students to class. Used for church, school, social, and civic meetings for sixty years, the beloved edifice was razed in 1931, its materials salvaged for continued use in building the West Ward Meetinghouse.

It was also in 1868 that stone mason Thomas Frazer arrived in Beaver as an LDS convert and immigrant from Scotland, following seven years in Murdock's former town, Lehi. During his first two years, Frazer was kept busy doing masonry work on the Beaver Woolen Mills, Beaver Co-op Store, and other business buildings. About 1870 he found himself free to build houses, for which he used the black basalt rock found in the foothills and bench areas east of the city. The equivalent of what we now call a general contractor, he built scores of stone houses during the 1870s and 1880s, apparently employing his own designs which he modified and perfected over the years. Many of Frazer's well-built structures remain, mostly on the west side of town.

Frazer's own home, a modest one-story stone building, is still extant. It typifies his style—well-cut, squared stones and carefully beaded mortar joints of uniform width, extraordinary craftsmanship, dormer windows, white-stained mortar, and Greek Revival and Federalist style influences. Eventually, between 1872–73 Frazer served as the major contractor for Fort Cameron, an enterprise that employed craftsman from all over the area. Sixteen of his stone houses still stood in 1999; perhaps the most beautiful of these is the Duckworth Grimshaw house. Built in 1877, the Grimshaw house exhibits masterful stonework, dormer windows, a steeply pitched roof, and gable in the center of the facade, over the entrance.[48]

Just east of Beaver's main street is a house built for Marcus L. Shepherd, most likely by Thomas Frazer, in 1876. This two-story house included a full attic and a half-basement. Frazer's attention to detail is shown in the stone bay windows, decorative cornice, dormers, and careful stone work. A central hall plan house, it has two gable ends with chimney stacks and windows immediately below.[49]

The earliest method of lighting homes was with candles produced at home by housewives. Part of the traditional round of domestic work was creating candles from mutton tallow with molds made out of tin pipes one inch in diameter and joined together in sets of six. Coal oil lamps and lanterns, eventually hanging gas ceiling lights after 1884, made it possible for interiors to be lighted in the evening.

Timber, Saw Mills, and Early Construction

Timber was plentiful in the Tushar Mountains east of town, and capitalizing on the available water power, a number of saw mills soon operated in North Creek. Judge Babbit and his associate Wilson G. Nowers received a franchise from the first county court on 4 September 1856 for a saw mill and grist mill to be built a half mile north of the town plat. Three years later, in December 1859, W.W. Willis and P.K. Smith were authorized to build a saw mill on North Creek along with control of all water on the mill site, control of the timber along the creek in the canyon, and the right to build a toll road.[50] A Mr. Harris owned a saw mill in Pole Canyon; Tom and Frank Holbrook ran a saw mill along the South Fork of North Creek. Thomas Whornham had a shingle mill in the North Creek Mountains, and James Valentine, William Twitchell, and Titus Greenwood of North Creek had a lime kiln at the west mountains, now called the Mineral Range. Mills also were located near Indian Creek. The prospects for a substantial timber industry are suggested in the authorization given by county officials to Edward W. Thompson and William Barton to clear out the channel of the Beaver

River so that timber could float down the river during high water. They were also given permission to charge a toll of one-fourth of all timber sent down the river by other individuals or companies.[51] However, the plan did not appear successful, and saw mills continued to operate in the canyons and lumber was hauled out by teams and wagons.

John R. Murdock and Edward W. Thompson installed a steam saw mill in 1868. Edwin Swindlehurst, saw mill operator for forty years, remembered a number of local saw mills:

> As nearly as I can remember there was the Joseph Huntington Mill of Beaver; later the Samuel Hooten and Fred Harris Factory Mill at Indian Creek, later moved to Beaver. Charles Oakden and Joseph Tanner bought the Huntington Mill. The Mining Revenue Mill at Pine Valley (where Mr. Swindlehurst helped to cut 120,000 feet of lumber); the Henry Blackner and Sons Mill at Ranch Canyon; the William Hutchings Sawmill; the Arthur Lightner and Frank Pryor Steam Mill; the James Robinson Mill at Indian Creek; the Thornton Mill bought from Arthur Lightner and John Ayers).[52]

Much of this lumber was used in Beaver, Greenville, and Adamsville to build houses and businesses. But an important market was provided also by Frisco, Newhouse, and Pioche. Lumber freighted to the mining region ranged in price from $70 to $100 per thousand feet.

By 1870 four mills were producing sawn logs and dimensional lumber for wall studs, floor joists, roof rafters, siding, and flooring. Early shingle, sash, and planning mills soon provided machine-sawn cedar shingles and molded trim for baseboards, casings, mantels, and, eventually, doors, windows, and wooden ornament. These early mills were the Beaver Machine Shop, First Shingle Mill, North Creek and Indian Creek mills, run by Jonathon Crosby, A.M. Farnsworth, U.V. Stewart, and Willis Coplan, respectively. Two of the saw millers also ran lumber companies, and one of them, Jonathon Crosby, was also a building contractor. An early business directory (1871–73) lists three other men as contractors or "carpenter and builder," namely C. Bird, H. Walters, and Charles Harris. By 1880 others had entered the construction work force. W. Holt was a major builder, while Willis

Coplan and C.C. Harris had become lumbermen, and Coombs and Wand, and George Owen specialized in painting.

Economic Life

Brigham Young clearly stated the goal of pioneer activity in general conference addresses, exhorting his Saints to concentrate on the work of what he called the building of the literal Kingdom of God on Earth. Believing that their work called in the advent of Christ's millennial reign on earth, Young and the other church leaders organized a wide variety of programs to establish an acceptable nucleus of the kingdom. These included missions to the United States, Canada, and Great Britain, colonization of the area, and community building.

Communities were built by volunteer labor and donations of the members, wealth acquired and developed in colonization, and economic windfalls from travelers through the region. The wealth of the church was collected by the tithing system of the church and administered by leaders in public works projects, agricultural and irrigation programs, merchandising, banking and industrial developments, transportation and communication systems. All of these projects were designed to build the kingdom and render it self-sufficient.

This entire effort was driven by the belief in the imminent millennial reign of Christ. People who believed the world's end was approaching were empowered by a sense of dedication to the work. Equally as important was the Mormon belief that the line between the spiritual and the temporal was insignificant, that for God all things are spiritual. The temporal practical work required to build a place—digging and laying out canal systems and building reservoirs, driving herds of cattle and sheep, plowing under miles and miles of land for planting, building structures for businesses, families, and public gatherings were for the Mormons religious acts—embued with a sense of significance that gave meaning to their labor. The peculiarly Mormon understanding of the earth as the "Lord's" enabled them to justify seizure of Indian lands without compensation and the creation of land distribution policies, control over natural resources like water, timber, and mineral wealth, and the accumulation of considerable material wealth to help the people become self-sufficient and united, and created a general feeling of equanimity.

First instituted in July 1838 to replace the ideal, though seemingly impractical law of consecration and stewardship, church members officially accepted the Law of Tithing in 1841. This law called for the donation to the church by members of one-tenth of their possessions at the time of conversion and one-tenth of their annual increase thereafter. During the exodus and early years of settlement, many settlers actually experienced a decrease rather than an increase which rendered the system less efficient than it would later be. Collecting tithes also proved to be difficult because more than 70 percent of all donations were paid in agricultural produce or livestock. According to Leonard Arrington, in his *Great Basin Kingdom,* five different kinds of payments were used: property, labor, produce, stock, cash, and institutional tithing. After 1850 the system became much more efficient, based in the General Tithing Office and Bishops' Storehouse in Salt Lake City. An elaborate network of local tithing houses helped distribute goods and services throughout the territory. Church farms, granaries, and storehouses were located at strategic points to facilitate the care of colonizing groups and settlers throughout the area. The bishops' storehouses dealt with goods over and above the tithing totals. These surplus goods were frequently exchanged for needed items, for credit, or to benefit the community. To facilitate these exchanges, "tithing script" was issued by the church, thereby creating an internal monetary system of exchange.

In 1867 Richard Curfew, an English weaver and convert to Mormonism, built a carding plant near Beaver. John and William Ashworth assisted Curfew in the plant located a few hundred feet north of the Messinger and Sons Flour Mill. Until the Beaver Woolen Mills took over their business, the carding plant provided a needed service to wool producers.

In 1869 South African Samuel N. Slaughter opened a tannery. Slaughter immigrated from Cape Town, South Africa, to Salt Lake City. There, John R. Murdock and William Fotheringham invited Slaughter to come to Beaver where, they suggested, he could be successful in the manufacture of leather into shoes, harnesses, and other products. The tannery was located in a small adobe building located on the edge of town towards the south. When business increased, Slaughter built a second, this time two-story rock building on the site. The tannery employed several men from Beaver in the manufacture of shoes until the late 1880s.

Dairies and creameries were located in several Beaver County communities. Abundant native grasses made Beaver's open fields ideal land for grazing cattle and farm animals. Many local women were employed by the dairy industry, churning butter at home, forming it into rounds, pressing a fancy pattern on the top and wrapping it in parchment and bartering it for other household products. Women like Sarah Nowers, Mary Low, Amelia Smith, Ann Levi, and Sophia Dean, among others, marketed their products locally and supplied the officers at Fort Cameron with butter while stationed nearby. The first creamery was established in 1889 in an old tannery building south of town.

Specialty businesses followed in the wake of farm settlement. Handcart pioneer Joseph Ash opened a gunsmith and locksmith shop in Beaver. Ash, a particular friend to local Indians, fashioned and repaired guns for both anglo settlers and Native Americans. John Eardley, formerly of St. George, came to Beaver in 1887 and established a pottery in town. Known for his high quality earthenware, Eardley was also a local musician and band leader. East of the Messinger Grist Mill, James Boyter established the Beaver Marble Works. There he made tombstones with a gangsaw out of native marble extracted from a marble quarry near Newhouse in the west end of Beaver County. This white marble had a slight streak of blue running through it and did not take on a high polish. Granite for tombstones was found in a quarry six miles south of Beaver City. Before he came to Utah, he had worked as a stone cutter in Scotland. After Boyter retired from business in 1912, his son Henry K. Boyter made tombstones until 1926.

Mail Service and the Telegraph

As was true of most of rural Utah, Beaver's mail was delivered first by freight wagon and distributed by the bishop. In 1864 an office was established in a single-room adobe building in town owned by Judge Thomas. For a period of time, Ephraim Thompkinson received mail at his home.

The Deseret Telegraph Company extended its lines as far south as Beaver by 1867, and from there to the mining camp of Pioche, Nevada, to the west and St. George to the south. This connected Beaver to both Salt Lake City and points east. William Fotheringham was the first telegraph operator; Robert Fotheringham the second; and Daniel Tyler the next. Beaver also became the junction of two stage coach routes, with one line going to St. George and the other to Pioche. The road to Pioche was also used by local freighters hauling timber for the mines and burgeoning community.

Schools and Education

As soon as families built log or adobe shelters to house their families, they joined together to build buildings to house worship activities and the education of their children. In Beaver the first public building was a multipurpose log meetinghouse that doubled as a school house for several years before a separate building was built. Teachers of younger students held schools in private residences. In December 1856 the town built a twenty-by-twenty-five-foot school building on the northwest corner of the Public Square. It was constructed of cottonwood logs, with two windows on each side, a fireplace on the south end and door on the north, and a roof formed with board planks. For several years the school year included only the three or four coldest months of the winter. Children were kept busy helping their parents prepare fields, build fences and barns, and improve their shelters. In school the children were not above some mischievousness. Jacob Henry White, an early teacher from England who everyone called "Daddy" White, taught school in Beaver for many years. "He began each day with prayer, but always prayed with his eyes open to be sure that the pupils were in good order. Often he would stop in the course of his supplication to chastise some unruly child. when order was restored he took up his prayer where he left off."[53]

Books and supplies were very scarce. Among the first school books to reach Beaver were a few blue-backed spelling books and McGuffey's *Readers* brought to Beaver by the San Bernardino, California, exiles in 1858. A student in 1864 recalled that " . . . she had only a piece of pine board 12 inches wide, planed smooth on both sides, which she wrote on with a piece of charcoal from the fireplace. When the board was covered with writing she took it to the ditch and scoured it clean with sand, then it was ready for use again."⁵⁴ Almost all reading and spelling were done in concert because of the large classes and lack of adequate books and supplies. Louisa Barnes Pratt described her classes in her journal. "In January 1860, I again engaged to teach school. The education of the children, owing to so much moving about, had been sadly neglected. I labored with great diligence, using every possible means to make them learn, but want of suitable books was a constant annoyance."⁵⁵

In 1855 the territorial legislature passed a law placing all public schools under the direction of county courts. The Beaver Ward bishop, Philo T. Farnsworth, was appointed the county superintendent of schools in 1860.⁵⁶ The county was divided into new districts in 1865. Beaver City⁵⁷ became District No. 1, Greenville No. 2, and Minersville No. 3. Four years later Beaver City itself was divided into four districts, with a schoolhouse for each division. The schools became known by their particular building material—the Lumber School, the Rock School, and the Brick schools were each single chamber buildings with simple wooden benches for students.

Teachers were paid in kind, with room or board, or with baskets of eggs, jugs of butter or jelly, bags of potatoes, wood, or grain. On 21 March 1860 Louisia Barnes Pratt wrote: "I closed my school. The pupils had made creditable improvement. The house of worship where I taught was a dread to me, so neglected and out of repair. It was, however, improved a little by the vigilance of the women of the community."⁵⁸ Barnes taught a few months out of every year for twenty years in her home, a small adobe-and-log three-room house in Beaver. Because of growth, in 1869 Beaver was divided into four school districts and each area had its own school building.

Richard S. Horne taught for several years at a one-room red brick school built in 1870, called the Institute. His students ranged in age from fifteen to twenty-five years. He used the traditional teaching materials—McGuffy's *Readers,* Ray's *Third Part Arithmetic,* and *Blue-Backed Spelling Book.* "Almost all reading was done in concert, owing to the large classes, and spelling was conducted orally. It was regarded a signal honor to spell others down until one reached the head of the class. Medals or other prizes were given at the end of the year to those having the highest averages in spelling and other subjects."[59] Horne also included physical education in his curriculum, outfitting the school grounds with horizontal bars, trapezes, and jungle gym. Ball games, wrestling contests and other sporting events became common occurrences.

In addition to semi-public schools run by the Mormon settlers, in 1873 the Reverend Clark Smith came to Beaver to establish the Methodist Episcopal Church to conduct school for members and patrons. School was held in a small lumber building located across the street to the east of the county courthouse.

One of the county's first native sons to gain national and even international attention was George LeRoy Parker, alias Butch Cassidy. Born 13 April 1866 in Beaver to Maximillian and Ann Campbell Parker, George was the first of thirteen children born to the couple. Maximillian carried mail from Beaver to Panguitch through Circle Valley and became enthused about the area's agricultural potential. In 1879 he persuaded Ann to leave Beaver and they acquired a ranch three miles south of Circleville. After the move to Circleville, Maximillian returned to the county to work at Frisco, cutting ties for the railroad and studding for the mines. As a mail carrier while living in Beaver and as a laborer after the move to Circleville, Maximillian spent considerable time away from home. Consequently, George LeRoy, thirteen years old when the family moved from Beaver, did most of the chores and was considered by the family to be his father's "right hand man."[60]

Later, after the young man chose to follow the Outlaw Trail, he changed his named to Butch Cassidy and became one of the West's most famous outlaws. Cassidy developed a reputation as a western Robin Hood—stealing from the rich and giving to the poor and never shedding innocent blood. He became the subject of one of Hollywood's most famous westerns, *Butch Cassidy and the Sundance Kid*, in which actor Paul Newman played Cassidy and Robert Redford his friend the Sundance Kid. Even his alleged death in South America has met with controversy as many believe he returned to the United States and lived many years under an alias. Books continue to be written about him and suggest that during the first thirteen years of his life in Beaver, he developed the skills as a horseman and cowboy that became part of his outlaw legend.[61]

Culture and Recreation

Beaver's first dramatic companies were organized in the 1860s by Robert Stoney and Henry Blackner; Professor Reinhard Maeser gathered another group of actors and musicians at the school for theatrical presentations. One favorite drama was uniquely expressive of this group of settlers' story. *Nick of the Woods* was a hands down favorite of local audiences. This western depicted the terror the pioneers suffered at the hands of invading parties of Native Americans. Maeser himself played the role of "Jibbernansey," the great spirit of revenge, who alone had enough strength to frighten the attackers. One Daughters of Utah Pioneers' account of the play captures the light-heartedness of this very serious presentation. Scenery plays a significant role in the play. "One night in this very serious scene, the Indians had the white people encircled with no help anywhere. At this point the Spirit came over the falls with a lighted torch in his hand, striking terror to the Indians who are supposed to flee, but as the Spirit came down, the falls came with him, filling the "whites" as well as the Indians with dismay, not to speak of the dust and canvas that covered them all, but Oh, think of the joy and the laughter of the audience."[62]

Many of these performances were given in "Field's Hall," a long narrow hall with a gallery, a stage that stretched the length of the building, and wooden benches that were reputedly in constant disrepair. Frequently, "the backs [were] always falling off just at the wrong time, leaving a dozen or more of the audience on the floor and the rest of the people convulsed with laughter, and of course one of the most dramatic scenes ruined by the actors joining in the mirth."[63]

Dramatic companies were organized in Minersville and Milford and produced such plays as *Ten Nights in the Bar Room*. Except for dances, the plays were the most popular entertainment activities in most Utah communities, and local actors and locally secured props often generated humorous stories that became part of the local lore. In Minersville one actor was supposed to be shot during the play. When the gun failed to go off, he fell to the stage floor, exclaiming,

"Go on, I'm dead anyway." The laughter of the audience was remembered after the plot of the play was forgotten.[64]

Beaver County had several talented musicians who joined martial bands for parades, orchestras for dances and musical presentations, and for summer concerts under the stars. Beaver's Brass Band members wore uniforms of blue cloth, locally produced at the Beaver Woolen Mills, and felt hats with narrow rims and creased tops. The number "General Hancock's Grand March" was a local favorite frequently requested. Their first conductor, arranger, and occasional musical teacher was Lorenzo Schofield. When the San Bernardino Saints first came to Beaver in 1858, they included several talented musicians. That same year Beaver's choir was organized with John Weston as director.

William Booth Ashworth was a member of the martial band that would serenade the town on Christmas Eve and New Year's Eve. The band would stop at individual homes and frequently be invited in for refreshments while they warmed their hands at the hearth.[65]

Dancing was the most popular social activity. During the first years, a fiddler was the only source of music. In time the accordion and even the organ were used as instruments for dance music. Two of the most popular dances were the Christmas Dance and the Wood Dance, the latter held in the fall after crops were harvested. Men and boys drove teams and wagons into the mountains to gather wood for the widows and needy in the town and were rewarded for their efforts with free tickets to the banquet followed by a dance.

During the summer most Beaver residents paused from the full schedule of farm work to celebrate Pioneer Day on the 24th of July—a commemoration of the arrival of the first pioneers in the Salt Lake Valley—with a parade, speeches, toasts, band music, picnic, games, races, a dance, and cannon salute.[66]

It is possible to examine Beaver County's early history and be struck by the relative homogeneity and tranquility of the picture and the significant accomplishments in community building during the first two decades of the county. But according to cultural geographer Ben Bennion, Beaver is also an example of the significant variety and diversity that existed just beneath the surface. John R. Murdock early noted the diversity of his people. According to one Murdock biographer, he "found the people considerably divided into factions. . . . His position was a delicate one, as Beaver was then, as it has since been, made up of a great diversity of elements . . . He not only had the opposing [Mormon vs. gentile] elements . . . , but he also had more or less of the contentious element with the Church to reckon with."[67] This, according to Bennion, was due to a number of factors about the origins of the original settlers. The majority of Beaver's settlers came from "points south and west, *not* north and east."[68] Members of the original party came north from Parowan and the aborted Iron Mission at Cedar City. A large group of Mormons vacating the San Bernardino colony joined the group in 1857–58. This diversity would become even more pronounced in the 1870s with the location of the Second Territorial District Court in Beaver in 1870 and the establishment of Fort Cameron in 1873.

ENDNOTES

1. Dale L. Morgan, "Historical Sketch of Beaver County," 5. A copy of this history prepared as part of the WPA writers project is in the Utah State Historical Society Library.

2. Laws of Utah, 1856, section 9, 7, quoted in Morgan, "Historical Sketch of Beaver County," 2.

3. Laws of Utah, 1866, chapter 146, sect. 4. quoted in Morgan, "Historical Sketch of Beaver County," 2.

4. Reinhard Maeser, *Sketches from the Life and Labors of Wilson Gates Nowers* (Beaver: Weekly Press, 1914), 41

5. Early in its history, the Mormon church surveyed new towns beginning in Missouri according to a design Smith presented to his people in 1833. The "Plat of the City of Zion" was introduced in the form of a revelation from God and was first planned for use near Independence, Missouri. This city plan would become the standard for Mormon colonization and settlement over the next fifty years. It was natural that in its regional effort at settlement that Brigham Young would follow this precedent.

The Plat of the City of Zion called for a mile-square grid of streets, each 132 feet wide, with three large squares at the center of the grid. Each block would contain ten acres, cut into half-acre lots providing for twenty houses to the block. Houses would be set back twenty-five feet from the street. Streets would be eight rods wide and intersect each other at right angles and run north/south and east/west. This middle tier of squares was to be fifty percent larger than the others and the site of the bishop's storehouse, temples, and meetinghouses. The plan further stipulated that all community members were to live in town with farm fields located beyond the town's boundaries. Ideally, stables and barns would be located outside of town on farm land, although many families built small barns and other out buildings on town lots.

As a physical plan for settlement, the Plat of the City of Zion incorporated much that is familiar to students of New England towns. Its gridiron plan typified the settlement of the American West as proscribed by the Land Ordinance of 1784. There is obviously much in it that was already part of the cultural milieu of the times. However, even still it is, according to rural sociologist Lowry Nelson, an invention of the Mormons because of its unique reflection of the ideologies of millenialism, communalism, and nationalism which they derived from the social environment of the early nineteenth century and their reliance on the Old and the New Testaments. See Richard H. Jackson, "The Mormon Village: Genesis and Antecedents of the City of Zion Plan," *BYU Studies* 17 (Winter 1977); Lowry Nelson, *The Mormon Village—Pattern and Technique of Land Settlement* (Salt Lake City: University of Utah Press, 1952); and Robert Alan Goldberg, "Building Zions: A Conceptual Framework," *Utah Historical Quarterly* 57 (Spring 1989).

6. Aird G. Merkley, editor, *Monuments to Courage: A History of Beaver County* (Milford: Beaver County Chapters of the Daughters of Utah Pioneers, 1948), 10–11.

7. Beaver City is situated in Sections 15, 16, 20, and 22 Township 29 South, Range 7 West, Salt Lake Base, and Meridian. The townsite patent was issued to John Ashworth, mayor of Beaver City, 20 June 1878, and embraced 1,280 acres of land. In 1882 George Buckner homesteaded the N E quarter of section 22 of the same townsite and range. Beaver city officials obtained by purchase this 160 acres from Buckner, 30 March 1882, for a total of 1,440 acres.

8. George Thomas, *The Development of Institutions under Irrigation,* (New York: Macmillan Co., 1920), 37.

9. John Franklin Tolton, *History of Beaver,* 18–19.

10. John Franklin Tolton, "From the Halls of Memory," typescript, n.p. chapter nine.

11. Tolton, *History of Beaver,* chapter four.

12. Patterson, "Legacy of a Great People," 143.

13. James Horace Skinner, "Reminiscences," 2, Utah State Historical Society

14. William B. Ashworth, "Autobiography," quoted in Juanita Brooks,

The Mountain Meadows Massacre (Norman: University of Oklahoma Press, 1970), 50–51.

15. Philo T. Farnsworth, From Utah Notes, a collection in the Bancroft Library, collected in 1884 under the supervison of Franklin D. Richards and quoted in Brooks, *The Mountain Meadows Massacre,* 115.

16. Brooks, *Mountain Meadows Massacre,* 114.

17. Poll, *Utah's History,* 168.

18. "Memories of the Life of John Francis Tolton." Utah State Historical Society

19. James Horace Skinner, "Reminiscences," Utah State Historical Society.

20. Keith Belly and J. Kenneth Davies give a very interesting overview of the story of the settlement of Minersville in "Minersville: The Beginnings of Lead-Silver Mining in Utah," *Utah Historical Quarterly* 51(Summer 1983): 229–45.

21. Erastus Snow quoted in Leonard Arrington, *Great Basin Kingdom: An Economic History of the Latter-day Saints, 1830–1900* (Cambridge: Harvard University Press, 1958), 242.

22. Brigham H. Roberts, *Comprehensive History of the Church of Jesus Christ of Latter-day Saints,* 6 vols. (reprint ed.; Provo, UT: Brigham Young University Press, 1965), 3:347.

23. Isaac Grundy to Brigham Young. 24 August 1859, LDS Church Library Archives. Quoted in Kelly and Davies, "Minersville: The Beginnings of Lead-Silver Mining in Utah," 238.

24. Reportedly the ore was soft with gold assays running as high as one-half ounce to the ton, silver from 19 to 30 ounces, and 38 per cent lead.

25. Alvaretta Robinson and Daisy Gillins, *They Answered the Call: A History of Minersville, Utah* (Minersville: Minersville Centennial Committee, 1962), 5.

26. Ibid., 7.

27. Skinner, "Reminisciences,"

28. Ibid.

29. "The largest Indian group was the Utes. They had divided into eastern and western bands sometime before 1848. The western Utes occupied the eastern two-thirds of what is now the state of Utah, situating themselves south of the Shoshoni, north of the San Juan River, and east of the southern Piutes. They were divided into smaller bands known as the Uintahs (in northeastern Utah), the Timpanogas (around Utah Lake), the Pavantes (around Fillmore and the Silver Lake area), the San Pitch (in the same general north-south area but ranging further east), and the Weeminuche (in

southeastern Utah and across the border into Colorado). The Navajo had moved from northwestern New Mexico and northeastern Arizona into the region of Utah south of the San Juan River and traded regularly across the river with some of the Utes. Further south into the Arizona region were the Hopis and the Havasupis." Eugene Campbell, *Establishing Zion* (Salt Lake City: Signature Books, 1988), 95.

30. Ibid.

31. Ibid.

32. See Edward Everett Dale, *The Indians of the Southwest: A Century of Development under the United States* (Norman: University of Oklahoma Press, 1949), 132. See also United States, Congress, House, 43rd Cong., 1st Sess. 1873–74, House Exec. Doc. 157, Serial 1610, 19–21. One the negotiations see, "Journal History," LDS Archives; Gustive O. Larson, "Land Contest in Early Utah," *Utah Historical Quarterly*, 34 (October 1961), 318.

33. United States, Congress, House, *Memorial of the Legislative Assembly of Utah Territory*, 41st Congress, 1st Session, 1869, House Misc. Doc. 19, 1. *Salt Lake Tribune*, 20 April 1947.

34. Skinner, "Reminiscenses."

35. Andrew Jenson, *History of Beaver Stake*, cited in Dale Morgan, "Historical Sketch of Beaver County," 14. See also the account of this incident by Gideon A. Murdock in Merkley, *Monuments to Courage*, 15–17.

36. Tolton, "From the Halls of Memory," chapter 9.

37. Merkley, *Monuments to Courage*, 186.

38. Ibid.

39. Skinner, "Reminiscences."

40. Autobiography of William Booth Ashworth, Vol. I, 32, copy in Utah State Historical Society Library.

41. Skinner, "Reminiscences."

42. Merkley, *Monuments to Courage*, 115.

43. Ibid.

44. Linda L. Bonar, "Thomas Frazer: Vernacular Architect in Pioneer Beaver, Utah," (M. A. thesis, University of Utah, 1980). In her thesis, Ms. Bonar examines the entire building career of Thomas Frazer, but gives special emphasis to eight houses: the Thomas Frazer House; the Edward Tolton House; the David Powell House; the William Robinson House; the Joseph Tattersall House; the Duckworth Grimshaw House; the Charles D. White House; and the Robert Stoney House.

45. Gordon Irving, "Encouraging the Saints: Brigham Young's Annual Tours of the Mormon Settlements," *Utah Historical Quarterly* 45(Summer 1977): 235.

46. Lyman O. Littlefield quoted in the *Deseret News,* 12 May 1863.

47. Among significant studies of Beaver's architectural tradition are: Duckworth Grimshaw House Nomination Form, National Register of Historic Places files, Utah Division of State History; Richard C. Poulsen, "Stone Buildings in Beaver City," *Utah Historical Quarterly* 43(Summer 1975); Linda Bonar, "Historical Houses in Beaver: An Introduction to Materials, Styles, Craftsmen," *Utah Historical Quarterly* 51(Summer 1983).

48. See Bonar, "Historical Houses in Beaver."

49. This was accomplished by splitting the flue and running them around the sides of the windows and rejoining them at the ground floor fireplaces.

50. Morgan, "Historical Sketch of Beaver County," 11.

51. Ibid.

52. Merkley, *Monuments to Courage,* 103.

53. Ibid., 70.

54. Ibid., 69.

55. Ibid.

56. The board of examiners included Robert Wiley, John Woodhouse, and Jessie N. Smith. Alphonzo M. Farnsworth became superintendent in 1862.

57. William J. Cox, Wilson G. Nowers, and Horace A. Skinner were elected school trustees for Beaver City.

58. Merkley, *Monuments to Courage,* 70.

59. Ibid., 74.

60. Lula Parker Betenson as told to Dora Flack, *Butch Cassidy, My Brother* (Provo, UT: Brigham Young University Press, 1975), 31–33.

61. See Larry Pointer, *In Search of Butch Cassidy* (Norman: University of Oklahoma Press, 1977); and Richard Patterson, *Butch Cassidy: A Biography* (Lincoln: University of Nebraska Press, 1998).

62. Ibid., 46.,

63. Ibid.

64. Robinson and Gillins, *They Answered the Call,*180.

65. Autobiography of William Booth Ashworth, Vol. I, 22,

66. Merkley, *Monuments to Courage,* 47–49.

67. Joseph M. Tanner, *A Biographical Sketch of John Riggs Murdock* (Salt Lake City: The Deseret News, 1909), 136, 172.

68. Lowell "Ben" Bennion, "The Gospel Net Gathers [Fish] of all Kinds:" A Diverse and Divided Beaver, Utah, 1856–91," unpublished paper, copy in my possession.

CHAPTER 5

THE WORLD OUTSIDE COMES TO BEAVER 1870–1900

The last three decades of the nineteenth century brought great change to Utah and especially Beaver County. Many of these changes developed in part because of the completion of the transcontinental railroad on 10 May 1869, more than 300 miles north of Beaver at Promontory Summit. The railroad greatly stimulated Utah's infant mining industry, which expanded into Beaver County during the 1870s. Just over a decade after the Union Pacific and Central Pacific linked the Pacific and Atlantic coasts by rail, the railroad reached Beaver County.

In preparation for the economic challenges to the Mormon Kingdom that Brigham Young anticipated would come with the railroad, a cooperative movement was launched that grew into the United Order Movement, both of which took root in Beaver County. With the establishment of the Beaver Co-operative Commercial and Manufacturing Institution and the Beaver Woolen Mills, Beaver became an important commercial center in southern Utah. In the western part of the county, Milford became the principal shipping and freighting point for southern Utah from 1880 until well into the twentieth century.

During the 1870s two federal institutions greatly impacted the county. Beaver was the location for the Second Judicial District for the Territory of Utah from 1870 until 1896. The establishment of Fort Cameron near the mouth of Beaver Canyon in 1873 marked a decade of the United States Army presence in southern Utah—the only time during the nineteenth and twentieth centuries that federal troops were stationed on permanent assignment south of Fort Douglas in Salt Lake City.

In retrospect, Beaver County prospered during these three decades. Substantial homes, schools, and public buildings were erected; new reservoirs and irrigation canals were built; more farm land was developed; cattle and sheep herds multiplied; and mines at Frisco, Newhouse, and other locations constituted a mining boom equaled only by a few other locations in Utah. Statehood for Utah in 1896 brought changes to county government and an outpouring of patriotism and optimism that carried Beaver County well into the twentieth century.

Second Judicial Court

The Second Judicial Court for Utah Territory was established in Beaver by proclamation of territorial governor J. Wilson Shaffer on 15 July 1870. Before this time, the Mormon settlers had dealt with many of their legal conflicts in the bishop's court and high council tribunals. The Second Judicial Court had been established on 8 November 1869 by a proclamation from Shaffer's predecessor, Charles Durkee. The first court session was held in St. George on 21 December 1869 and the next in Parowan on 2 September 1870. Judge C. M. Hawley was assigned to the bench, N.P. Wood. The first court session held in Beaver was in December 1870 and sessions were held in Beaver until Utah was granted statehood in 1896. The court's venue included Beaver, Iron, Washington, Kane, Garfield and Piute Counties. Local supporters of the court argued that Millard, and Sevier counties should be added to the second district as a way to save both time and expense for those who otherwise had to travel to the first district court which held forth in Provo and Ogden. The proposed expansion of the Second Judicial District was calculated to lengthen the court term and keep the judges in Beaver. Otherwise, "under existing circumstances the court is dismissed for the term and the judge off for Salt Lake all in a hurry. It seems to some people as though, the eagerness of our judges in the past to get to Salt Lake has caused some cases to be rushed through hurriedly not giving them that consideration and time that they demanded in justice to the defendant or the government."[1]

Those who served as Second District judges were: C. M. Hawley, 1869–1874; Jacob S. Boreman, 1874–1880; Stephen P. Twiss, 1881–1885; Jacob S. Boreman, 1886–1889; Thomas J. Anderson, 1889-September 1892; James A. Minor, September 1892-February 1893; and George W. Bartch, 1893–1896. Without identifying those who were sympathetic or antagonistic towards Beaver citizens, John Franklin Tolton found that "Some of the Judges were an honor to their profession, others should have worn sack cloth rather than the ermine of judicial authority with which they were clothed."[2]

Fort Cameron

On 7 March 1873 the United States Army established a military camp at Beaver City. After the Mountains Meadows Massacre, it was generally believed that a federal presence in the area was needed. The fort was located at the mouth of Beaver Canyon just two miles east of Beaver City.

Federal intervention in Beaver County during the territorial time period was marked by an imperialistic fervor. Clearly, territorial autonomy seemed to threaten the security of the United States for many, and seemed to justify extraordinary efforts to put down the efforts of the Mormon church. Because of that, one important theme of the story of Beaver County's relationship with the federal government is persecution and intervention.

As a result of confrontations with the Indians, the House Committee on Territories conducted an investigation of whether additional military forces were needed in the area in 1867. Nonetheless, it was not until 1872 that Secretary of War William W. Belknap received letters from the Associate Justice of the Utah Supreme Court, Cyrus M. Hawley and territorial governor George L.

Fort Cameron near the mouth of Beaver Canyon. (Utah State Historical Society)

Wood stating that "annual Indian raids upon the settlements," a few miles south of Beaver, made Beaver a suitable location for a military installation. The idea had significant local support; in fact, Utah's inhabitants believed that yet another Indian war was imminent. Already attacks had commenced in central and southern Utah. In 1872, Secretary of the Interior Columbus Delano solicited Brigham Young's assistance in quelling the tide of conflict.

A second consideration that in Hawley's mind justified the installation was the fact that the perpetrators of the Mountain Meadows Massacre had not yet been brought to justice. In fact, according to Hawley, it was unlikely that they ever would, considering the current political condition where anyone who testified against their fellow Saints might be punished. A "military force established in that [the second] district, say at the city of Beaver, of at least five companies," would facilitate those efforts.[3] As a result of this testimony, Secretary of War Belknap suggested that the government appropriate $120,000 for the construction of a military base near Beaver.[4] After the appropriation had been given, during mid-1872, Lieutenant General Philip H. Sheridan, a civil war veteran, appointed Colonel John D. Wilkins to lead a command of four companies (181 men) to open the post.

When they arrived at Beaver after having traveled 200 miles from Salt Lake City, they camped just a mile north of town. From that vantage point, Wilkins conducted reconnaissance of the area, searching for the most advantageous site for a military base. Wilkins found a site on the north side of the Beaver River near both Beaver Canyon and town. Initially, the base was called the "Post of Beaver," but later Fort Cameron in honor of Colonel James Cameron, a hero of the Civil War who was killed in the Battle of Bull Run. Twenty-one and one-half acres of timber land was added to the post as a reserve in 1879.[5]

On 7 September 1873, 250 troops arrived in Utah under the command of Major John D. Wilkins. The setting was a lovely ten-acre plot of ground in the foothills a mile from the mouth of Beaver Canyon. Large cottonwood trees bordered the fort on every side. Fourteen buildings facing toward the central parade ground were constructed of black igneous rock, quarried in nearby canyons. To the north was the hospital, a two-story structure with a veranda running around both the lower and upper floors. To the west of the hospital were two smaller buildings—the adjutant's office and the Commander's Storehouse. Other buildings included a bakery and two long rectangular one-story barracks. Five large two-story buildings served as the officers' residences, four for two families each, one for a single family and the residence of the commanding officer. Laundry, storage, and an armory structures were also located near the square.[6]

The fort was unique in appearance because of the black, basaltic lava stone used to build it. Quarried in a nearby canyon, the rock was hauled by local settlers who also furnished the bulk of the labor. All types of workers, stonemasons, carpenters, and artisans found work on the project that provided them with badly needed cash. The interior was rough plastered except for the two-story, twelve-bed hospital, which was more carefully finished with plaster of paris.

As was typical of western forts, the walls stretched 700 feet in one direction and 620 feet in the other. A parade ground located in the center of a series of rooms that ran the length of both sides was the

The officers quarters section of Fort Cameron after it became Murdock Academy. (Utah State Historical Society)

scene of public activity. Both the east and west walls were built into barracks for the troops, the officers rooms were located on the south, and the hospital to the north, as were the commissary and the base offices.[7] A network of aqueducts brought water into the fort. The parade grounds were landscaped with trees and grass. All in all, the cost of the construction and furnishing of the fort was $120,000.

The fort brought revenue to Beaver City in other ways. Fifteen women were employed as laundresses, a blacksmith and carpenter were hired for $160 month income. Local boardinghouses and hotels benefitted from the officials who came to town on fort business. Soon auxiliary businesses began operation like a brewery established in an old carding mill nearby.[8]

Because Beaver County was relatively self-sufficient, the post was able to purchase needed supplies locally. Gardens grown by the soldiers themselves located outside the fort provided a number of vegetables, including potatoes, turnips, cabbage, lettuce, beans, and peas. But beyond that they purchased what they needed from local merchants. According to one report, the army rented milk cows from farmers in Beaver City.[9] What supplies they could not purchase

The parade ground at Fort Cameron used for recreational activities by
Murdock Academy. (Utah State Historical Society)

locally they shipped to the nearest railroad terminus in Juab County.
Again, locals benefitted from this as well. Joshua C. Hall was paid
$1.50 per 100 pounds for supplies he freighted from the station to the
fort.[10]

Typically, in western territories, being chosen for the site of a military installation was seen as good news. Threatened by attack from
Native Americans, it was a distinct advantage to have the presence of
the federal government in western land. Nevertheless, as was true for
Mormons throughout the territory, the residents of Beaver County
looked at the establishment of a United States military installation
nearby with suspicion. With the exception of Camp Floyd, which was
the result of the 1857 episode, each of the Utah installations was
related to the threat posed by the Native Americans. Conflicts during
the Walker War of the 1850s and the Black Hawk War of the 1860s
seemed to justify military forts in the territory.

After the fort was built, there was little for the soldiers to do. The
contrast between the religiously homogeneous locals and the men
housed in the fort led to occasional conflicts. "Some of the officers

were honorable men," wrote Louisa Barnes Pratt, but "the soldiers with few exceptions were intolerable drinkers of ardent spirits. It was terrifying [to the women] to hear them on the streets at night."[11] Some of the soldiers had wives and families, and the group developed a lively cultural and social life to help pass the time. Occasionally, they organized musical shows and plays, for a period the Fort Cameron Band, and supported a parochial school. Population at the fort ranged from a high point of 203 enlisted men and twelve officers in 1873 to eighty-seven enlisted men and seven officers in 1882. After the Utah Southern railroad reached Milford in 1880, Beaver County's isolation ended. Two years later the army decided to shut Fort Cameron down. On 1 May 1883, Secretary of War Robert Todd Lincoln ordered it abandoned and the troops removed to Fort Douglas.[12]

The Fort Cameron buildings and property were sold on 30 May 1883 to Philo T. Farnsworth and John R. Murdock who subsequently donated half of the property for the Beaver Branch of Brigham Young Academy which later became Murdock Academy. The military hospital became office and classroom space, the enlisted men's barracks became dormitories, and the commissary a bookstore.

Mining

Although most of the Mormons settlers who came to Beaver County were farmers, discoveries of rich veins of minerals in mountains surrounding the valley made Beaver one of the most important mining centers in the West. Gold, silver, lead, copper, zinc, bismuth, sulphur, as well as marble, granite, sandstone, potash, and other rocks used as building materials attracted those willing to extract the riches of the earth. Towns sprang up around the locations of these resources across the base of mountain ranges bordering Beaver Valley. Many of these boom towns were vacated as the mines became exhausted and fortunes turned, but others survived the mining era and became rural villages with redefined identities. Local mining activity, recent finds and profits were carefully noted in the *Beaver County Blade* and other local newspapers as well as the *Union Vedette*. Beaver's mining activity put the county on the map, so to speak, and drew the attention of entrepreneurs from Salt Lake City and throughout the nation.

Miners in Beaver County. (Utah State Historical Society)

Several mining districts were created during the 1870s in Beaver County. These included the South Star District (1870); Beaver Lake District (1871); North Star District (1871); Lincoln District (1871); and the San Francisco (1871); Pruess District (1872); Rocky Mining District (1872); and Bradshaw District (1875). The San Francisco District is situated in the center of the county about 225 miles south-southwest of Salt Lake City and 98 miles northeast of Pioche,

Nevada.[13] Although the district was organized on 12 August 1871, the most significant discovery was not made until 1876, a year after the discovery of the Horn Silver Mine and the settlement of Frisco.

When the Star District organized on 8 July 1870, Shauntie became the main settlement. Rapidly growing in the 1870s, it was the hub of freighting and smelting activites until the railroad came to Milford in 1880. Mines like the Mammouth, Red Warrior, Moscow, and St. Mary's brought sudden wealth and a population of transient workers into the area. Shenandoah, another South Star town, reportedly had 300 inhabitants in 1875.

Both towns housed mine workers, served as supply stations, and provided needed services. Shauntie had a telegraph office, and Shenandoah was the main distributing post office in Beaver County. Both towns were real communities with families and various social activities. Every Saturday night everyone in town went to the school house for a dance and a dinner. "They had square dances and then they had Virginia reels, and all of that stuff," one Shauntie old timer, Florence Barnes, remembered.[14] Children would go to school, on picnics, and enjoy the freedom afforded by life in an isolated environment. Although Shauntie had surface water, water shortages plagued the two towns, and water often had to be shipped in from other locations. Because so many of the buildings were frame construction, fire was another perpetual problem. In June 1875 much of Shauntie burned, causing $40,000 in damage. When the smelters were out of operation, many of the mine workers were unemployed. Reduction of ores produced in Beaver's mines was always a problem. Isaac Grundy's primitive lead furnace was succeeded by a series of smelters with charcoal kilns that worked well enough until the railroads made shipment of ores outside of the county more profitable.

Shauntie had two smelters in 1873. The Riverside Smelter fed power off the Beaver River, about seven miles north of Milford. Up and running for only a few months, this smelter processed copper ores from the Beaver Lake and Rocky Mining districts. Arvin Stoddard leased property in Milford to be used by the Harrington and Hickory Consolidated Mining Company to build a $45,000 mill. This mill processed ore from the Hickory Mine in 1873 and 1874. By 1878 it was completely shut down. Two years later a larger smelter

This headframe stands over a mine shaft at Newhouse. (Utah State Historical Society)

was built in Shauntie. The Troy Furnace was built six miles southwest of Milford to handle ore from the Mammouth Mine until 1880, when it burned down. Elephant Canyon was the dividing line between the South and North Star districts after November 1871. By 1875 mining in the Milford area had dwindled.

The Horn Silver Mine was first prospected by Samuel Hawkes and James Ryan, two men working the Grampian Mine, a source of galena ore. Finding a good source of anglesite ore, they developed the mine to the 500 foot level. Fearing the failure of the mine to produce, they sold the claim to A.G. Campbell, Mathew Cullen, Dennis Ryan, and A. Byram on 17 February 1876 for $25,000. The new mine revitalized Milford and created a new town, Frisco, almost overnight.

Besides selling the ore, these three erected a smelting works and developed the ore in the mine. Eventually they sold the mine to investors in the New York and Salt Lake Company for $5 million. This new company sank the mine to the 800 foot level, resulting in a good profit from production until 1884, when the mine caved in.

William A. Hooper described the property in 1879 as follows:

The quantity of ore extracted up to February 1, 1879, is given as 22,712 tons. During February about 90 tons daily were raised, making a total of 25,00 tons of ore. The extraction of this 90 tons was barely enough to keep the mine in good shape and prevent the breasts of ore from crowding too much upon the timbers. The present expense of mining is low. We have as the cost of taking out 90 tons daily:

Labor $144.00
Timbering 90 tons . . . .$ 73.00
Superintendence . . . .$ 6.00
Supplies and expenses . . . .$ 50.00
Total $273.80
Cost per ton . . . .$ 3.05

The Grampian Mine was located on the hill beyond the Horn Silver Mine in the dolonite. Originally a vein of ocherous ore assaying about $50 silver and some gold was located near the surface and trailed down eighty feet varying from one to eight feet of ore. Although the total cuttings have amounted to 515 feet, less than 200 tons have actually been shipped.

Several large ledges of pyrite and copyrite ore were located in the northern part of the San Francisco District, resulting in a very high grade silver ore in claims called the "Comet," "Cactus," and the "Copper Chief."

The mill at Newhouse. (Utah State Historical Society)

The Cactus Mine, for one, was owned by the South Utah Mines and Smelter Company. Located in Copper Gulch about 2.5 miles northeast of Newhouse, the main body of ore is sited about 6,450 feet above sea level or 200 feet above Newhouse itself. First identified in 1870, the mine is one of the earliest in the district. Regardless, successive companies have failed to make the mine a success. A small smelting plant built in 1892 was also unsuccessful and produced little ore.

The Williams Smelter, built after the discovery of the Horn Silver Mine, utilized a special construction to improve safety, be more environmentally responsible, and catch the fumes and particles before they escaped into the air up the chimney. Also at Frisco a variety of smelting techniques was experimented with, but scarcity of water, the difficulty of getting sufficient charcoal, and other complications limited their success.

The Moscow Mine was one of several mines in the South Star District. Owned by Matt Cumming, this mine was first started on the west side of the mountain just west of Milford. Mine operators hauled ore from the Moscow Mine to Milford on the Frisco switch with teams and horses. The ore ran high in silver and lead. Water was brought to the mine with a pipe line laid by Harry and Gil Martin. A small gasoline engine pumped water up the hill some thousand feet.

Most of the miners who worked at the Moscow Mine lived in Shauntie five miles away. As was true of most mines, miners with families chose to keep a house in town where their family would live and their children could go to school. Joe Smith remembered that the Harrington Hickory Mine had a number of places for miners to live—boarding houses and a few timber houses. After the mines were closed down, the houses were relocated closer to Milford.

Milford

In some ways the settlement of Milford was a spill over from Beaver. However, like Minersville, Milford was a town that originated because of the rich mineral resources of surrounding mountains and was truly a mining town with a difference. The townsite was located on the route used by miners to reach the San Francisco Mountains and at a crossing of the Beaver River where a stamp mill was located. Therefore the name Milford emerged by combining the two words "mill" and "ford." Milford was first settled by Arvin Stoddard and his family in 1880. Later that year Stoddard, who was himself a surveyor, surveyed the townsite.[15] From the first Milford was not an agricultural community but a supply station, serving freighters and feeding off the mines, although crops were planted as early as 1859. Therefore trade boomed here, and by 1890 Milford had an impressive Main Street lined with saloons, mercantiles, hotels, and a variety of service businesses like blacksmith shops and livery stables. Alton Smith counted five saloons in Milford at the turn of the century—the Atkins Bar, Milford Saloon, Crescent Bar, Oxford Saloon, Long Tom Martin Saloon, and the East Side Saloon. Besides serving the miners liquor and a meal, gambling, dancing, and eventually vaudeville were added entertainments offered by the saloons.[16]

When Milford became the railroad terminus for the Southern Utah, it became a major loading place for Southern Utah cattle.

During the 1880s and 1890s, the area around Milford had excellent grazing conditions.

Most settlements south of Utah County were anxious to be connected to outside markets by the railroad. Being chosen as a railroad terminus was a sure-fire promise of success. Beaver County's flourishing mining industry proved to be a sufficient draw to the Utah Southern. In January 1879 it announced that an extension line would be built to Frisco, the home of the Horn Silver Mine. Mine owners would pay a quarter of the construction costs.

Frisco's citizens petitioned the county court for a local jail in the late 1870s. Selectman James Low met with several men from Frisco to determine what they could contribute to the construction. At the same time, the Union Pacific with its interests in the Utah Central railroad was constructing a line through Milford. By the fall of 1879, rail lines had been laid as far south as Deseret in Millard County. By the beginning of 1880, the road bed was graded within ten miles of Milford before the Utah Southern extension had been built through Frisco. Electric power went from Beaver to Milford to Frisco in 1908, a year when Frisco was the largest town in Beaver County.[17] Rather than locate the railroad station in the original plat, swamp land to the east of the original survey was drained and a second series of streets was laid out on a diagonal to the original grid.

Saturday, 15 May 1880, was an important day for Milford. When the first engine roared into town, it signaled future prosperity and business. Governor Eli Murray and other dignitaries traveled to Milford to mark the event, staying the night in the Stoddard Hotel. Soon new businesses, hotels, stores, feed yards, and other facilities were built. Consolidated Implement Company was one of the first new businesses to supply freighters and miners throughout southern Utah. As was true of other new enterprises, it was located along the west side of the tracks on the road to Beaver to the south.

Visitors to Milford reacted in different ways to either the town's promise or stark reality. One predicted Milford would become a "second Cheyenne,"[18] another characterized it as the "perfection of desolation."[19] Yet another described it as little more than "a frog pond surrounded by five saloons."[20] Regardless, this town near the geographical center of Beaver County fed off all the major economic industries of the region—the freighting of agricultural products, the railroad center for the transportation of cattle and sheep to markets, and the site of a mining mill and smelter.

The valley had already been identified by stock raisers from Beaver as fine grass land for grazing. Some estimates suggest that as many as 20,000 cattle ranged in the area between the 1870s and 1880s.[21] Frequently settlers built their homesteads on land with readily available water rather than in town.[22]

In 1873 a Scotch-Canadian Company called the Harrington-Hickory Consolidated Mining Company erected the Milford Stamp Mill (also known as the A.G. Campbell Mill) for $45,000. The mill processed the ore of the Hickory Mine between 1873–74, producing between $9,000 to $12,000 in bar bullion. The company was in business for only five months.

Besides mining, cattlemen worked out of Milford. During the early 1870s, three stock raisers from Pioche, Nevada, known as the "Dodd Brothers," settled at Pine Grove in southeast Pine Valley west of Milford. There they established a cattle ranch with 2,500 head of cattle. Over the years various owners ran cattle and sheep on the ranch, eventually shipping stock to market from the rail station located in Milford.

When Milford became the county's main railroad terminal, it became critical to the stock raising industry. The owner of one of the largest cattle herds, B.F. Saunders of Salt Lake City, grazed his sheep and cattle on the Pike Springs Ranch located in southern Utah and northern Arizona. He shipped his stock out of Milford.

The land around Milford was perfect for grazing cattle—native grasses, white sage, and other native plants grew abundantly. Both the Beaver and the Milford valley floors were covered with a blanket of meadow grass from Hay Springs to Black Rock. It was estimated that it could sustain at least 20,000 head of cattle and 5,000 horses.

Because of the number of timber structures in town, fire was a perpetual problem. The number of stables, barns, and blacksmith shops spoke to Milford's importance as a freighting center as well. A number of hotels and boarding houses, saloons, and restaurants serviced the transient population feeding off the railroad. A few Chinese workers were employed by the Atkins Hotel, including a cook called

Two travelers pose for this picture with a railroad trestle in the background. (Utah State Historical Society)

only "Monday."[23] The Williams Hotel was built in 1881 by John D. Williams. A barber shop was located on Main Street in the McKeon Building on the corner of Fourth Avenue and Main Street. The barber, Phil Arwin, had a big bath tub in a back room. On Saturdays miners lined up outside to get a shave for 25 cents, a "shingle" hair cut for 35 cents, and a bath with plenty of water and soap for another quarter.[24]

After the railroad came to Milford, interest in continuing the line farther south faded away. Milford, therefore, became even more significant as a freighting and trade center. Bullion from Nevada smelters, healthy mining in the Star and San Francisco districts, and new supply businesses that stocked implements, wagons, buggies, and other products serviced the freighting industry.

Cattle and sheep shipped through Milford required stock yards and feed stores. Saloons, boarding houses, and restaurants provided respite for cowboys traveling through. By 1882 there were as many as seven stables with feed yards, four saloons, five blacksmith shops, two groceries, a drug store, Chinese restaurant, meat market, and a grainery. Because of the lack of water, farming was less important to Milford's growth, but many farmed some acreage and, coupled with other businesses, were able to make a living.

South of the Forgie Hotel a brothel operated during the peak years of the mining boom. A woman known as "Nigger Mag" ran a similar business down the wash from the mineral springs to the northeast of Milford. The area, later known as "Nigger Mag Wash," provided hot baths, massages, and a swimming pool at the springs.

Frisco

After the accidental discovery of silver and lead ores in Beaver County in 1875, Frisco was settled at the southern tip of the San Fransisco Mountains. Two prospectors, James Ryan and Samuel Hawkes, working a small claim nearby, passed by a limestone ledge on the way to their site from their camp. One day they chipped some of the limestone away and found silver-bearing galena. They sank a twenty-five foot shaft through what appeared to be solid ore. They sold the find the next year for $25,000, thinking they had made a good investment.

The Horn Silver Mine, as the new owners called it, proved to be enormously rich and soon yielded silver valued at $100 per ton. In 1879 banker Jay Cooke and other Salt Lake money interests bought out the Horn Silver mine for $5 million. They induced the Utah Southern Railroad to build a line to Milford and then to Frisco to transport ore to distant markets. In 1879, the *United States Annual Mining Review and Stock Ledger* called the Horn Mine "unquestionably the richest silver mine in the world now being worked."[25]

Frisco quickly sprang up around this mine and miners, merchants, and interested bystanders came by the hundreds. Soon other mines were discovered—the Carbonate, Rattler, Golden Reef, and Grampion. Each mine had its own smelter, and five beehive shaped charcoal ovens were built to serve the smelters using local woods like cedar, dwarf pine, mountain mahogony and sagebrush.

According to one historical account, the "story of the Horn Silver Mine, one of the great producers in Utah and American mining history, reads like pulp fiction: Two prospectors casually discover a rich ore body, a bankrupt financier promotes the venture, the boomtown of Frisco becomes one of the wildest mining camps in the West with a murder or two every evening, a tough lawman who shoots on sight begins to clean up the town, after producing millions the huge mine collapses, and Frisco becomes another ghost town."[26]

The Carbonate Mine, located 1.75 miles northwest of Frisco, is found at an elevation of 6,750 feet and consists of a group of eleven claims and fractions. The site was first discovered in 1878 and sold the next year for $10,000. The mine produced concentrates with an average assay of 43.63 percent of lead and 94.09 ounces of silver to the ton. As well, the tailings contained a significant amount of minerals.

Within years Frisco had twenty-three saloons, false fronts stores, boarding houses and restaurants, enough to service a population that reached as high as 6,500 between 1880–85. According to one historian, "Frisco became as wild and tumultous a town as any in the Great Basin, . . . and the wildest camp in Utah. Twenty one saloons had so many killings the undertakers wagon made daily rounds."[27] It was so wild that Marshal Pearson from Pioche, Nevada came to town to clean up the criminal element—promising to shoot on sight anyone breaking the law.[28]

Water, supplies, and food were shipped in from Wah Wah Springs to the west, from Black Rock and Salt Lake City. Houses, shops, schools, and churches attested to the presence of a substantial population. Articles in the local paper, *The Frisco Times*, speak to the growing diversification of the local population and the colorful nature of local politics.

Fred Hewitt, a mining engineer traveled from California to Frisco, first by railroad and then by stage where he worked first for the Champian Silver Mining Company and later for the Horn Silver Mining Company. He wrote to his wife several letters which described the journey to Frisco, work inside a Frisco mine, life in the 19th century mining camps, and a strike staged by miners at the Horn Silver Mine when their wages were reduced. The first letter, dated 1 February 1880, describes the railroad trip to the end of construction in Juab County and the stage coach ride on to Frisco.

The stage left at 1 P.M. I wrapped my feet up as well as I could and put the shall around my shoulders and after riding about half an hour found my feet so comfortably warm that I congratulated myself on the nice arrangements. Jerkey stopped, driver looks in and sees my fellow passenger on front seat. I was on the back. "You will have to take the back seat sir. I must put a bag of corn on the front." So my companion with some grumbly takes the back seat. Of course this somewhat disarranges our things. Then the driver gets in to handle the bag of corn and walks on our legs in so doing. The corn laid on the seat and the driver back in his place we start again, somewhat colder than before. We are evidently going to have a cold night. The breath freezes to our whiskers. Pretty soon the bag of corn comes off the seat on to our legs and it takes considerable exertion to get it back again. It keeps coming off until some time in the night the driver takes it away. Not very long after the advent of the corn, another stoppage, "gentlemen you will have to get out and help me over the railroad crossing. So the pins come out of my blanket the wraps are laid aside and out we get. The drivers tries to cross the track which is here in an unfinished. . . .

Nothing particular happened only the usual stage bumping. First it bucks you up a foot or so, then a quick jerk sideways another from the other direction, then a twisting jerk that seems to go all around you, then a few minutes of ordinary jolting and then we are bucked up again and the side jerks and twists are repeated. We became colder and colder until it seemed as if I could not bear it much longer. The stage stops we think we will get out at station and warm, but no, no stoppage here only taking on another passenger. This at half past two in the morning. On we go again until about 4 o'clock we hear the drivers hallo to the next station. We are to have breakfast here but the people are not up, and so we stamp about in the snow for some time until the door is opened. The table is set, there is a bed in the room from which the man and his wife have just risen she is buttoning or hooking something as we enter, a child is in the bed. A good wood fire is soon going in the stove but it takes us a long time to thaw out. After about an hour breakfast is ready such as it is. I could hardly eat any, but the warmth and the coffee was worth the 50 cents it cost. After that we did not get so cold and did not stop again until we arrived at Frisco about 9:30.

February 7, 1880

After reaching the [Belcher] mine somewhat behind time, as the mining time is half an hour ahead of town time, I found that I was expected. I was taken into a back room of the office. A flannel shirt was handed to me and a pair of flannel pants fastened with a string round the waist. The whole outfit like a Coney Island bathing suit. I was requested to strip, when I inquired how much I was told everything. After dressing as requested, they made a parcel of my money and took care of it, they gave me socks and opened a long box filled with shoes from which I fitted myself. Then I went out to the shaft house the costume being very airy for winter, and was put in charge of the pump man. Visitors to mines do not generally go down the pump shaft but go in the large cage down the regular hoisting compartment. My object being more to examine the engineering arrangements I went down the pump shaft. There was a little cage if it may be so called, a little shelf or bracket guided only on the back on which we stood. It was about 16" wide one way, just large enough for the two of us to stand on with feet close together and standing up straight. . . . The word was given and we went 900 ft on that, slowly and stopping at different stations to examine pumps, balance bobs etc. At the 900 ft station we got off and walked down an incline of 31 degrees to the 1600 ft station. Walking down stairs, it was all steps for 700 ft is pretty fatiguing work. It was very warm down this incline, the perspiration pouring off of me. A regular Turkish bath arrangement. At this point we drank ice water and rested going to a point where cold air came through for this purpose. Then we took a large car and were lowered down to the 2400 ft station that being the lowest part of the pumps. The mine is 3000 ft deep but we did not go to the bottom. . . . The water that came up from the pumps was too hot to be able to bear the hand in, and in some of the drifts it felt like being in an oven. . . .

February 11, 1880

About the mine is a collection of shanties mostly belonging to the Co. I think. One or two you could almost call houses. The Co's boarding house and the shanty over the mine shaft. . . . I have had a 9 x 12 shanty allotted to me. It is furnished with a bedstead of pine wood made by the carpenter, a very rough table and sundry boxes, one of which I use for a seat. Like all such shanties this one

is full of cracks. There is a fire place at one end made of rocks and
mud and so far I have been supplied with fire wood. I had to buy
blankets at the store—also bed tick which I filled with hay at Co's
stables, also wash basin and tin cup. I moved over here Monday
morning, and started a fire in the afternoon, and kept it up all
evening . . . Last night I had to move my bed to get out of the snow.
Mud and gravel also blows in.

July 20, 1880

The new superintendent of H.S. Mg. Co. A Mr. Hill made an
attempt to cut down the miners wages, resulting in a strike yester-
day. The men last evening went in force and compelled them to
stop the smelters and declared that no other work should go on
and Mr. Hill backed down and sent word for them to go to work at
the old wages. The miners are getting slightly higher wages than in
some other places $3.50 per day, but it ruins the health of every
man that works in this mine, and I think that a man that once gets
"leaded" will never be the same again.[29]

Also important to the mining economy in the area, thirty-six
beehive charcoal kilns supplied the furnaces of the San Francisco district with fuel. Eight groups, each under separate management, were
found within six to eighteen miles of Frisco. The kilns were constructed of granite float extracted nearby and lime mortar. Varying
in size from sixteen to twenty-six feet in diameter, they generally were
as high as they were wide and had walls from twelve to fourteen
inches thick at the top. Two openings, each closed by sheet iron
doors, provided access to the kilns. One at ground level was four by
six feet, and the side door located two-thirds of the way to the apex
was three by four feet. A series of vent holes in rows eighteen inches
apart, three by four inches in diameter, was found near the ground.
Wood burned in the kilns was usually pinon pine cut for $1.25 the
cord, transported to the site on wagons or sledges for between $1.50
to $2.50 per cord.

Operators fired the kilns from the center at the bottom and drew
the fire to the top through a small space above the door. Further regulation of the fire was accomplished through the vent holes. The fire
was maintained for three to seven days, then cooled for three to six

days. The charcoal produced through this method was shipped to the smelters in racks at a cost of from 3 cents to 5.5 cents per bushel.[30]

W.S. Godbe managed the Frisco Smelting Company and its five distinctive beehive charcoal kilns, with Benjamin Y. Hampton as superintendent and M. Atkins as agent.[31] In 1879 the company reorganized as the Frisco Mining and Smelting Company with a capital stock of $2,000,000 in 80,000 shares, property including the smelting plant at Frisco, the Carbonate mines, the Cave Mine in the Bradshaw District, and an iron flux mine in the Rocky District.[32] The United States Tenth Census described the smelter in 1880 as a "complete one" which consisted of a Blake rock-breaker, a Number 5 Baker blower, two horizontal boilers, one 40-horsepower horizontal engine, numerous pumps, a shaft furnace and flue-dust chamber, a reverbertaory flue-dust slagging furnace, and five charcoal kilns on the site.[33]

Originally, the fuel for the smelting process was produced in pits. But in Frisco cone shaped ovens produced a higher grade of charcoal. Each kiln cost between $500 to $1,000 to build, according to one author.[34] First designed by Michigan engineer, J.C. Cameron in 1868, an article in the *Utah Mining Gazette* described his plan as conforming to the shape of a "parabolic dome, with a base of twenty to twenty-four feet in diameter and altitude of nineteen to twenty-two feet," for a cost of about $700.[35]

The 1880 United States Census Mining Compendium detailed the kilns of the Frisco Mining and Smelting Company:

> The kilns are made of granite float found in the neighborhood and a lime mortar. They are of various sizes, from 16 to 26 feet in diameter. It is the rule in this section to make the height of the kiln equal to the diameter. The thickness varies from 18 to 30 inches at the base and from 12 to 18 inches at the summit. There are two openings, closed by sheet iron doors, one at the ground level, 4 by 6 feet, and the other in the side two-thirds of the distance to the apex, 3 by 4 feet. There are also three rows of vent holes, 3 by 4 inches, near the ground. The lower row is at the surface of the ground. The rows above are 18 inches apart, having vent holes 3 feet apart in each row. The kilns cost from $500 to $1,000 each, and last a very long time if used regularly. The 16-foot kiln holds about 15 cords of wood and the 26-foot kiln 45 cords. Sometimes

the wood is piled radially, but generally very closely in cord-wood fashion. The wood is all pinon pine, and is cut at all seasons by Mormons at $1.25 per cord. It is brought from 1 to 4 miles by sledges or wagons to kilns for from $1.50 to $2.50 per cord. The kilns are fired in the center at the bottom (though sometimes at the top), and the fire is drawn to the top by leaving a small unsealed space around the upper door. This is then closed entirely, and the fire is regulated by the vent holes. The duration of burning is from three to seven days, and of cooling from three to six days. Charring, which includes packing the wood in the kiln and drawing the coal, is usually done by contract, and costs from 2 3/4 to 3 1/2 cents per bushel. About 50 bushels are produced per cord charred. The coal is bought by weight, 17 pounds making a bushel. It is shipped to the smelters in racks, at a cost of from 3 to 5 1/2 cents per bushel for hauling, depending on the distance. The price received is 18 cents per bushel. Kiln hands were paid from $2 to $2.75. The labor required averages one man per kiln per twenty-four hours.[36]

Census data give some indication of how many men were employed in charcoal production. Again the Tenth Census suggests that there were twenty-one coal burners, seven stonemasons, one brickmason, two wood contractors, and five wood choppers. Fourteen of them were single men who lived in boarding houses.

Production was most active during the period between 1879 and 1884. After the railroad came through the county, coke replaced charcoal as a cheaper and more efficient fuel. The Frisco Mining and Smelting Company no longer appeared in the *Utah Gazetteer* and in 1900 the Horn Silver Mine was the only producer in the area.

In 1885 the Horn Silver Mine caved in. Frisco and Milford both suffered dramatically because of it—many miners left town altogether, the mills and charcoal kilns laid dormant. After only ten years, the mines had produced $54 million, and although a new shaft was drilled farther down to 900 feet, only a few of their families stayed on. Ten years later vacant buildings stood as a silent reminder of what had been lost.

The Horn Silver Mine was important to the economy of Beaver County. When a fire destroyed most of the mine works on 5 April

Mine buildings at Newhouse. (Utah State Historical Society)

1894, John Franklin Tolton wrote in his diary, "This is a hard blow to Southern Utah and Beaver County in particular, and will be keenly felt as it was a means of circulating a great deal of money in this and other communities."[37]

Newhouse

A second silver mining town settled in the 1870s centered on the interests of the Cactus mine. For the next thirty years, attempts were made by a series of investors to operate the mine, but lack of capital always plagued these efforts. In 1900 Samuel Newhouse, already successful in mining in Bingham Canyon, purchased the property. Originally called "Tent Town," because everyone lived in either tents or in covered wagons, Newhouse soon had permanent buildings and took on the look of a company town. Stone, brick, stucco structures, a restaurant, library, livery stable, hospital, several stores, and even a company owned and operated hotel rounded out the town. An opera house, dance hall, and the "Cactus Club" provided locals with entertainment opportunities. The Utah Southern Extension Railroad depot welcomed newcomers and processed imports and exports.

In an article published in *The Salt Lake Mining Review,* Leroy A. Palmer gave a brief description of Newhouse. "It contains forty-two attractive three and four-room cottages with cement finish, thirty two-room houses, two boarding houses, opera house, store and club house." Palmer went on to describe the Cactus Club which any employee could join for an initiation fee of 50 cents and monthly dues of 25 cents. "The club house has a reading room, card room, billiard room and bar. The reading room is supplied with the leading general and technical magazines and dailies from the principal cities of the country. Out of its profits the club has built the opera house and one of the boarding houses. It gives a free dance every week, a Christmas entertainment for the children, and in many other ways makes life more attractive in this out-of-the-way spot."[38]

Newhouse's boom period lasted only five years before the Cactus Mine gave out after producing $3.5 million. As miners left town and businesses relocated, a number of buildings were simply moved to Milford. The Newhouse Mine, located in the Preuss District, yielded between 1905 and 1912, 25,341,183 pounds of copper, 9,959 ounces of gold, and 224,911 ounces of silver.[39]

Star District

Yet another mining district, the Star District, was twelve miles square and positioned a few miles southwest of Milford. Here mines are at an altitude between 5,000 and 6,000 feet above sea level in rises above the Beaver River Bottoms. Shauntie, Shenandoah City, Elephant City, and South Camp were temporary mining camps located in the area. Rather than organized efforts by large mining companies, most of the prospecting here was done by individual miners who met with minor success.

Nevertheless, at one time Shauntie had forty houses, and in 1873 a two-stack smelter was built. Most of the structures burned down at different times.

In the Beaver Lake Mountains, the Beaver Lake District's most productive mine was owned by the Majestic Mining Company located in the southern part of the mountains at an elevation of 6,150 feet. First organized as early as August 1871, the mine was little noticed at a time when silver, gold, and lead were bigger draws. Copper was the most important mineral located in these mountains.

Sulphurdale

Yet another type of mining town was Sulphurdale, concentrating on the extraction of a single mineral—sulphur. U.S. Deputy Surveyor Charles Dickart first located a large ore body in 1870. Nevertheless, it was not until 1883 when a thermal processing plant was built to extract sulphur that a company town arose at the site. Continuous production of 1,000 tons of sulphur per year began in 1890 and continued for the next fifteen years by open pit stripping. With the help of a team of horses and scrapers, the miners pared away the overburden and ore which was less than 15 percent sulphur. Only the highest grades were worked. The town included between twenty-five and thirty homes, a schoolhouse, company store, and offices and a large stone processing plant. All miners, teamsters, and company workers lived in town with their families. Twice a week freighters hauled between twenty and twenty-four tons of sulphur the thirty miles in five-wagon trains to the Union Pacific loading docks at Black Rock to the northwest. For a period after 1918, the town was known locally as Morrissey for the mine organizer.[40]

Plans to extend the Utah Southern Railroad farther south began again in the spring of 1890. Because of that, Milford filled up again with transient workers, this time men prepared to work on grading the road bed and laying railroad ties. Large tents served as temporary quarters for those unable to find lodging at local hotels or boarding houses. This time organized under the name the "Utah and Pacific Railroad Company," the railroad stimulated yet another economic boom. Milford's population rose from 150 people in 1890 to 279 in 1900.

Protestant Churches

As was true throughout the state, religious denominations other than Mormonism established churches in Beaver County. In addition to religious services, they often held school classes to provide an alternate to the LDS dominated school systems. In 1873, for instance, Reverend Clark Smith helped establish the Methodist Episcopal church and school in Beaver City. The school was an act of faith, and, as Reverend Smith recalled, he waited anxiously for any students to arrive. "On the first day of September 1873 I opened day school Towards noon of the first day Mrs. E.W. Tompson brought three of her children and wished them entered as pupils. These three constituted the school for several days when Mr. C.C. Woodhouse brought a few more. At the end of the first month there were eight names on the roll."[41]

Reverend Smith was followed by Reverends George Janes in 1875 and Reverend Erastus Smith in 1879. Services were originally held in a small lumber building across the street to the east of the county court house. Originally, the building had been used for worship services by the Josephite church. The next year, the group purchased property north of the current location of the Public Library. The school continued until 1891. The Methodist Episcopal church ran a school in the front part of their church and organized a church choir with Alice Woodhouse-Lindsay as their first organist. Classes were taught in the school until 1891 with a series of principals: Reverends Brock, Coplin, J.B. Gehr, D.J. Frew, J.D. Gililan, E.C. Graff and M.O. Billings. When public school began at the turn of the century, the school was only open part of the time. Although the church property was sold, Reverend Karl L. Anderson served in Beaver between 1908 and 1912 and preached in the Richard Smith home which had been bought by the church. This two-story black stone house was located across the street from the Mormon East Ward Building.

Politics

The decade after the Utah War was one of increased tension in which the Mormon church continued to dominate politics, especially at the local level, through the People's Party. Church leaders in Beaver County dominated all local elections and controlled the nominating and electoral procedures during these years. Indeed, most candidates were part of the ecclesiastical hierarchy as well as community leaders. When selecting nominees for public office, the Mormon settlers of Beaver County voted for those they knew as church leaders. This changed somewhat with the increased number of non-Mormons who came to the county with the mining industry and with the

building of the railroad. When in 1880 the Liberal Party was organized by non-Mormons to challenge the People's Party, meetings
were held in Frisco and Minersville.

The Liberal Party experienced surges in popularity before statehood. In 1880 the party decided to adopt a new political strategy—
rather than insulting their opponents they would address issues. The
Deseret News could not resist commenting.

> One of the most striking characteristics of the so-called "Liberals"
> of this Territory, apart from their extreme illiberality, is their
> remarkable inconsistency. In illustration of this we quote two or
> three paragraphs from the resolutions of the Beaver County
> "Liberal" Convention. They occur apart, but we place them
> together to show how much harmony there is between them:
> "Whereas the party which has held power in this Territory since its
> first settlement have denied all exercise of political rights to
> American citizens who do not worship God according to their
> peculiar forms and mode of religious faith, . . . Be it resolved, that
> this convention of the Liberals of Beaver County believe that the
> cause of progress and enlightenment will be best subserved, and
> the moral and material interests of the community best promoted,
> by our candidates for county and precinct office being exclusively
> chosen from that class of the community who have no connection
> with the dominant Church, . . . Resolved, that we wage war upon
> no class of the community, and disavow that we have any wrongs
> to avenge; but insist upon the right of the majority to choose and
> elect men to office whom they regard most fit for public position.[42]

The *Southern Utonian* was unabashedly supportive of the
People's Party and in fact, published a warning in February 1890 that
there were "Liberal hosts" about, trying to gain support, supposedly
finding temporary work so they could vote in local elections.[43]

In the 1870s the county divided into election precincts which
included: Beaver (with 301 votes); Minersville (99), Grampion (91),
Milford (50), Adamsville (46), Greenville (41), and Star (35).
Remembering that women could not vote gives a picture of the relative number of registered voting members of the county.[44] The
scarcity of non-Mormon candidates caused many of the non-
Mormon population to cry for change:

The non-Mormon population of Beaver County pays no small or mean portion of the taxes, yet no Gentile has ever been elected to a county office. We ought to have had the one Selectman, who is to be elected next Monday, but no effort has been made to elect him. As individuals, the *Times* has nothing to say against the present officers of Beaver County. We believe them to be honorable, upright gentlemen, who administered the affairs of the county, honestly, fairly, and impartially, yet we do most emphatically object to their being elected by an ecclesiastical instead of a political party. We most decidedly object to any church exerting such control over politics, believing as we do, that it is contrary to the spirit and institutions of our Republic.[45]

Both parties organized local members with countywide conventions advertised and reported on in the newspapers. Stake president John R. Murdock discussed People's Party politics in stake conference in July 1889, reminding the Mormon congregation to attend their conventions to insure that American principles would prevail.[46] People's Party meetings were held at the LDS meetinghouse in Beaver to elect delegates to attend district and county conventions.[47]

Frequently political races became quite heated in Beaver County. Because of the large non-Mormon populations in the mining towns, the Liberty Party (composed primarily of non-members of the Mormon church) made a significant effort to put good strong candidates in local races. The 1880 election typified the disputes over numbers of registered voters, fair election procedures, and political issues. Throughout the county, over 1,100 votes were cast. But of that, apparently, 145 votes were cast by non-registered voters in Frisco. After a subsequent review, the entire vote from Frisco, Milford, Minersville, and Adamsville was cast out. The key political issues were the location of the telegraph office, land use policy, and which party should be in power.[48] That same year the Liberal Party nominated Allen G. Campbell to run for delegate to Congress against incumbent George Q. Cannon. Campbell had made millions in Beaver County through investments in the Horn Silver Mine. Although he lived part of the year in Salt Lake City, he spent the majority of his time in Beaver County. Periodically, Campbell had run for selectmen of Milford.[49] Cannon was running for his fifth term and was a LDS apostle.[50]

The election was covered by papers as far away as New York City. Claims of improprieties were thrown at both sides. "The clamors of indignation and murmurs of revenge began when they arrived at the brand new town of Milford. Here ambition had o'er leaped itself and the 'Liberals,' probably in the majority even in a fair election, resorted to 'stuffin', by means of the swearing in process."[51] The *Deseret News* (the Mormon newspaper) maintained that the People's Party had one election judge for every two of the Liberal Party, hinting again at problems with election procedures.

While there was generally unity within the People's Party in Beaver, it was not always the case outside the county. When the Beaver and Iron County central committees could not agree on a candidate for the territorial legislature, representatives of the People's Party from outside the area used both committees to compromise in selecting Silas S. Smith of Paragonah as the representative from Beaver and Iron counties.[52]

Effective party management and campaigning did not have nearly the impact of the Edmunds Act on causing change in local politics. The Edmunds Act of 1882 disenfranchised anyone who was practicing plural marriage. The *Frisco Times* jubilantly saluted this change in affairs. "Gentiles are rejoicing with *The Tribune* over the fact that God and the Governor will run Zion for awhile. They can beat the old Mormon revelators out of their boots."[53] The federal government sent out non-resident officials to preside over the territory during this period. Eventually, on 10 June 1891 the People's Party met to officially disband. Members were encouraged to join either of the two main national political parties.

John Franklin Tolton described the end of the People's Party and the creation of the Democratic Party in several 1891 diary entries.

> May 20th/91 Much agitation is being waged by politicians to disband the old Liberal and People's parties and adopt one or the other of the two national parties. This move seems to be growing here and in other counties north. This together with the diphtherial scare has created a great agitation.

June 5th Attended a rousing meeting at Fields Hall. The object of said meeting being to organize a Democratic Club. Resolutions were adopted last Tuesday evening by the County Central Committee of the People's Party, recommending the disbanding of said party which was the initiative for the present step.

June 18th In the first Democratic primary held under the new order of things, that is, division on the National Party lines, I was tonight nominated for the position of School Trustee for Beaver School District. From present indications it would seem that the people who are afflicted with political itch in any manner are almost unanimously Democrats. No move has yet been made by the Republicans to organize, and encouraging and flattering reports come from the lower settlements that the masses of people are there Democratic as well as in Beaver.[54]

At the Beaver Stake Conference attended by Apostle Amasa M. Lyman on 20 June 1891, he was surprised at the " . . . political craze as had apparently struck us," and inquired why so many Beaver County residents had become Democrats. Lyman went on to explain that LDS church " . . . authorities desired us to divide about equally on National Party lines in order that we could receive favors from which ever party was in power. Said that those who had not already declared themselves Democrats and could conscientiously do so, should ally themselves with the Republicans." Apostle George Q. Cannon, who was also in attendance at the conference, was somewhat disturbed by Lyman's remarks and sought to restrain his companion with the admonition, "Bro. Lyman, don't go too far."[55]

The excitement continued right up until the election on 2 August 1891. Tolton recorded:

Aug. 2nd The election tomorrow promises to be quite lively as there are several tickets in the field. The Republicans are not well organized, and the name of P.T. Farnsworth having been placed upon their ticket without the proper authority, will weaken their cause.

Aug. 4th Reports from various precincts show an overwhelming Democratic majority. The entire county ticket is conceded by large majorities. Returns also show that the Liberals have carried Salt Lake City which has caused considerable excitement here.[56]

In 1898 John R. Murdock was elected to the Utah House of Representatives as a Republican, even though, according to his biographer, "the county had always been Democratic."[57] Within only a couple of decades, however, the county became overwhelmingly Republican.[58] Beaver County participated in statewide party conventions, sending seven delegates to the Republican conventions and eleven to the Democratic statewide convention.[59]

During the last half of the nineteenth century, the most persistent political issue was that of statehood. During these decades Utah territory went through six aborted efforts at statehood. Non-Mormons resisted the effort, believing that once the territory became a state, government would fall back into the hands of the church. Numerous petitions circulated in Beaver County during these decades against statehood, signed primarily by the inhabitants of the mining towns.[60] One message sent from the San Francisco Mining District, 28 June 1876, revealed the lines that had been drawn on the issue. "Whether James G. Blaine is the nominee or not, he has many warm friends in this district who wish him success. I can safely say that about two thirds of the miners of Beaver County are Blaine men, for they consider him a staunch friend to the Gentile cause and true to the Union."[61] It is interesting that the political battles that waged in Beaver County were best reported in Salt Lake City newspapers. The *Deseret News* bias was toward the People's Party, or the Mormon church viewpoint, and the *Salt Lake Daily Tribune* leaned toward the Liberal Party, or the non-Mormon political interests. Interestingly, Beaver County was one of the strongest centers of the Liberal Party, particularly Milford and the mining towns.

The John D. Lee Trial

In November 1874 federal marshals under the direction of William Stokes left Beaver and crossed the mountains to Panguitch to arrest John D. Lee for his involvement in the 1857 Mountain Meadows Massacre. In her biography of John D. Lee, historian Juanita Brooks describes the actions of Stokes and his men:

They camped for the night out of town, and early in the morning of November 7, 1874, dashed into the village, galloping at full speed up through the main street. At once people hurried out to discover the cause of the excitement, and when the posse turned and stopped in the center of town, they were immediately surrounded by curious questioners. . . .

The crowd became so large that the officer began to fear for the safety of his men, so he resorted to the strategy of asking each citizen his name, writing it down, and ordering the man to assist in finding and arresting John D. Lee. Each man was ordered to go home, get his gun, and return in five minutes. This had the desired effect, for the men dispersed and not one came back to carry out the order.[62]

Stokes found out where Caroline, one of John D. Lee's wives, lived, and with a stroke of luck was able to locate Lee who was in hiding behind a pig pen. Threatened with being shot if he did not surrender, Lee gave himself up. Brooks continued her description of the dramatic event:

Together they walked to the house. There some of the women and children were crying with fear, others talking at once with excitement. Lee quieted them, telling them it was time that he was brought to a fair trial. It would be much better to face up to it and be a free man again.

By this time the neighbors had gathered around until half the village was in the yard. Lee's sons took him aside and told him that if he didn't want to go to Beaver to say so and they would arrange it so that he wouldn't have to. But there were six well-armed men in the posse, and any attempt to break would mean death to too many people. When Stokes asked where they could get breakfast in the village, Lee apologized for his lack of hospitality and ordered his wives to feed the men. He also furnished the team and wagon to take them back to Beaver, with his son-in-law, Henry Darrow, to drive it.[63]

The trip to Beaver took two days and when the party arrived about noon of the second day, "The whole town was thunderstruck that they had been able to take Lee alive."[64] Lee was incarcerated at Fort Cameron from 10 November 1874 until 23 July 1875. He was a model prisoner, giving his guards no trouble and making friends with soldiers and officers and being permitted to spend some time out of doors each day. If Lee caused no trouble, the same could not be said of his wife Emma. According to one account, after she visited him at Fort Cameron, one of the soldiers asked, "Who is that handsome woman?" A companion answered "Oh, that is one of John D. Lee's whores." Emma did not hesitate to defend her honor. "In a flash he was struck across the face with the buggy whip, as Emma turned fiercely upon him. Surprised, he ducked to miss the next blow, and then turned and ran outside before the third."[65]

Lee's first arraignment was on 6 April 1875. Because of difficulties securing evidence, the trial did not begin until 12 July 1875. The first trial was held in a saloon located at 98 North Main—the current location of Lee's Clothing Store. The second trial was held in the upper room of the Beaver Co-op, the scene of community-wide dances, celebrations, and school graduations. Judge Boreman presided. On 21 July Lee pled not guilty and a jury was empaneled to hear evidence presented by both sides. The jury was made up of eight Mormons—who voted for acquittal—and four non-Mormons— who voted for a conviction.

At a second trial an all-Mormon jury found Lee guilty on 20 September 1876. He was sentenced to be executed on 26 January 1877 by firing squad. Lee had been writing his autobiography while in prison. Waiting for an appeal to the Supreme Court, which was denied, he wrote what was in his heart, still believing God and his church could save him. He wrote:

Camp Cameron
13 March 1877
Morning clear, still and pleasant. The guard, George Tracy, informs me that Col. Nelson and Judge Howard have gone. Since my confinement here, I have reflected much over my sentence, and as the time of my execution is drawing near, I feel composed and as calm as the summer morning. I hope to meet my fate with manly courage. I declare my innocence. I have done nothing designedly wrong in that unfortunate and lamentable affair with which I have been implicated. I used my utmost endeavors to save them from their sad fate. I freely would have given worlds, were

they at my command, to have averted the evil. I wept and mourned over them before and after, but words will not help them, now it is done. Death to me has no terror. It is but a struggle, and all is over. I much regret to part with my loved ones here, especially under that odium of disgrace that will follow my name. That I cannot help . . . I have been treacherously betrayed and sacrificed in the most cowardly manner by those who should have been my friends, and whose will I have diligently striven to make my pleasure for the last thirty years at least. In return for my faithfulness and fidelity to him and his cause, he has sacrificed me in a most shameful and cruel way. I leave them in the hands of the Lord to deal with them according to the merits of their crimes, in the final restitution of all things.[66]

Before he was shot, he sat on the edge of his coffin, posing for pictures for each of his wives. He stood and spoke in a clear, strong voice of his lack of fear of death and faith that those who had wronged him would eventually pay for their dishonesty. He said, "Center my heart, boys. Don't mangle my body!" When the shots were fired, he fell back quietly and was brought to his family in Panguitch, Utah, for burial. His grave was marked with a simple marker which said, "Know the Truth, and the Truth shall make you free."[67]

Anti-Polygamy Crusade

The federal government was particularly forceful in its efforts in the anti-polygamy crusade of the 1870s-80s. Partly because of Beaver County's non-Mormon population, and its location on the transportation route, Beaver City was chosen as the site for the Second Judicial Court for Utah Territory. Beaver, Iron, Washington, Kane, Garfield, and Piute counties were all included in the Second District between 1870 and 1896. In some ways local businesses benefitted from the number of people who came into town to attend court cases, but the prosecution of violators of anti-polygamy laws in the Second Judicial Court brought additional responsibilities to local Mormon leaders. J. M. Tanner, in his biography of John Riggs Murdock, reveals:

Men and their wives were brought to Beaver, where many of them were strangers. These had no opportunities to provide themselves with assistance and they must either give bonds or go to jail. The requirement of the court in the matter of bonds was strict. Only those of well-known ability to meet financial obligations were accepted. John R. Murdock's financial standing in Beaver was first-class and he was ever ready to render every possible assistance to his unfortunate brethren, and went on the bonds of not fewer than fifty different men.[68]

In addition to posting bonds for accused polygamists, Murdock and other Beaver residents opened their homes to the families of men sent to Beaver for trial.

Beaver polygamists were also subject to arrest. On one occasion two federal marshalls, known only as McGarry and Armstrong, searched for Marcus Shepherd, a polygamist with two wives and several children. Marcus was a sheep man who was frequently away with his sheep or in the mountains. Neighbors kept him appraised of the movement of the marshalls through town and warned his wife when they were coming too near the Shepherds' home. While searching for Shepherd, the federal marshalls questioned people all over town about the whereabouts of Shepherd's second wife. Because she hadn't had warning ahead of time, she had to dash out the back door and run across the back of her lot to hide at a neighbor's house down the street.

Mae Crosby White's mother worked for the Shepherds and tended the children when both were gone. She also helped Mr. Shepherd load up big bags of flour, rice, or sugar to haul up to his flocks to feed the other herders. Mrs. Shepherd came to hide in her home, staying for most of the day and night. The next morning the men in the family rose early to begin their morning chores, milking the cows and tending to the other farm animals. A marshall came up to the front gate and quizzed the children about who was inside the house. They lingered there for hours eventually leaving to get a search warrant from the county court clerk.

While they were gone, the Crosbys' oldest daughter came to the house with her husband, dressed in their church clothes. The woman changed clothes with Mrs. Shepherd who then left the house, passing the marshalls on her way down the street where she climbed into a buggy waiting for her by the church. The marshalls searched the entire house, looking behind furniture, rummaging through boxes and chests, and searching every room.

Everywhere in Utah territory, Mormon polygamists suffered because of increased prosecution and the intense pursuit of men and women on the underground. Federal marshals came to be figures to be feared and avoided at all costs. Tales of the underground abound in narrative histories of the era, focusing on the ways the Mormons avoided being caught. One particularly scandalous pursuit in the area aroused the fear and ire of Mormons in Beaver County and intensified the tension on both sides.

In 1886 Mormon polygamist Edward M. Dalton was shot by Deputy United States Marshal William Thompson. Dalton had been indicted for unlawful cohabitation in the spring of 1885 but had escaped while under arrest. He fled to Arizona where he stayed for a number of months before traveling to his home in Parowan. Deputy marshals Thompson and Orton, in Beaver at the time, heard of Dalton's return. They left during the night of 15 December, planning to re-capture Dalton in his bed. They solicited the help of Mormon apostate Daniel Page. The next afternoon Dalton was herding cattle down a street near his home. Thompson and Orton, hiding in the Page home, waited till he passed by. They shouted out the order, "Halt, you are under an arrest." But when Dalton failed to stop, Thompson shot him in the back with a Winchester rifle. Dalton fell off his horse and died on the street.[69] Panic spread from Parowan to towns near by with the news. Parowan sheriff Adams arrested Thompson and Orton and took them to the county courthouse in Beaver to appear before a judge at the Second District Court.

Federal marshall Frank H. Dyer was notified about the shooting. Dyer immediately dismissed Thompson and sent another marshall, Arthur Pratt, to Beaver to take charge of the case. Thompson's matter was heard on 6 January 1887. All members of the jury were non-Mormons, primarily from nearby mining camps. They found Thompson "not-guilty" after two days of deliberation.[70]

At least eleven Beaver citizens were convicted of unlawful cohabitation and sentenced to prison terms: William Fotheringham, three months, 23 May 23 1885 to 11 August 1885; John Lang, four months, 17 May 1885 to 29 September 1885; James E. Twitchell, seven months,

9 May 1885 to 22 December 1885; Henry Gale, seven months, 12 May 1885 to 15 December 1885; William G. Bickley, twelve months, 9 May 1885 to 27 May 1886; M.L. Shepherd, six months, 28 May 1886 to 29 November 1886; William J. Cox, six months, 28 May 1886 to 29 November 1886; William Robinson, four months, 7 May 1885 to 16 September 1886; George Hales, four months, 11 May 1886 to 16 September 1886; Thomas Scofield, six months, 26 September 1886 to 26 March 1887; and James Farrer, six months, 26 September 1886 to 26 March 1887. In addition to these men, " . . . John R. Murdock, John Ashworth, C.D. White, William Ashworth, William W. Hutchings, Duckworth Grimshaw, Philo T. Farnsworth and David Levi . . . were regarded as violators of the Edmund-Tucker Law."[71]

Beaver Female Suffrage Association

While Mormon polygamists faced prosecution for plural marriage, the Beaver Female Suffrage Association promoted universal suffrage by reminding men that women were their moral equals. Beaver County presents an interesting case study in nineteenth-century female suffrage, because of the large population of non-Mormon women in the county and because of the mining industries or the presence of the military there was a more diversified population during the late nineteenth century than was typical of the rest of the territory. As the county seat, Beaver City was the center of political, social, and religious action in the area, the likely location for a county suffrage association. The initial association was organized through the direction of general LDS Relief Society leaders—Eliza R. Snow and Zina D. H. Young who had been traveling throughout the territory organizing local units of the suffrage association. Therefore Mormon women felt the ecclesiastical support of their association in the women's rights movement.

Scorning criticism that said that women would be exposed to "drinking, fighting and profanity that goes on" at the voting booths, women seeking the voted argued they were well suited to withstand such forces. As the secretary of the Beaver Women's Suffrage Association recorded:

> Let no man or woman be mistaken as to what this movement for
> suffrage really means. None of us want to turn the world upside

down, or to convert women into men. We want women, on the contrary, above all things to continue womanly—womanly in the highest and best sense—and to bring their true, honest, just, pure, lovely and of good report to bear upon conduct of public affairs.[72]

Beaver's women published a monthly, hand-written newsletter, the *Equal Rights Banner,* to promote their ideology, stating regularly that women had a "purifying influence" on government in the territory and encouraged the territorial legislature to support the idea of female suffrage.[73] Politically the group was neutral but adamant in its support of the single issue of suffrage. A typical meeting would include discussion of relevant contemporary issues—the free coinage of silver, readings, singing, and other activities. For instance, on 16 January 1894 the Beaver WSA secretary recorded the following:

> Programme next in order. Musick Instrumental by W. G. Bickley. Civil Government Class omitted, Prest. Farmsworth not prepared. Song by Mrs. Fernley, "The pardon come too late" next Reading from Womans Suffrage History by Louissa Jones lady not present. Speech by w.G. Bickley. . . . The Gentlemen, not being prepared with a lecture, he read a selection from W. Tribune.

Typically, the members were from the elite of Beaver society—their husbands were ecclesiastical and governmental leaders, and businessmen or farmers. They were connected by familial, religious, as well as social ties. Sarah Caroline Maeser, for one, in 1892, was the daughter of the prominent educator—Reinhard Maeser, the first school principal in town and the son of Karl Maeser of Brigham Young Academy. The Beaver Female Suffrage Association provided women a social outlet as well as place for them to put their creative energies in the effort to create a better environment for women in Utah territory.[74]

Architecture

Despite its relatively small size and isolation from major urban centers, Beaver County contains a veritable treasury of architecturally significant buildings. Its oldest town and county seat, Beaver City, is especially rich in its variety of materials, styles, and early Mormon house types, so much so that it has been the subject of field studies and

The Beaver County Courthouse. (Allan Kent Powell)

has been featured in architectural and historical publications. Beaver's unique collection of fine black rock (basalt) and pink rock (tufa) houses are well known and admired, as are its brick houses and its variety of historical building types. Less well documented but of importance is the historical architecture of the county's later, smaller Mormon towns, as well as the mining town architecture of Milford. Significant for helping to understand life in a more secular community with a non-agricultural-reliant economy, building construction and the town layout in Milford are distinctly different from that of the pioneer towns.

Beaver's most spectacular historic brick building is its Territorial Court House—the eventual county courthouse. In 1876 a group of selectmen petitioned the territorial governor and legislature for $15,000 to build a courthouse in Beaver City. The courthouse would house the Second Judicial District Court. Started in the mid-1870s and completed in 1882, the three-story, Victorian creation is one of the finest buildings of its type in Utah. Its architect is unknown, but William Stokes, a U.S. Army soldier and one-time U.S. marshal of Beaver, was superintendent of construction. The full basement was built of black basalt, while the main superstructure and four-sided clock tower is of red brick. The original court house size of 42 by 52 feet was expanded by a later addition measuring 29 by 32 feet. The building included a clock funded with $250 from the county and $625 from the city. Facing north, the main building contained county offices on the first level, a large court room on the second level, and rooms for officials and juries on the third floor. In the addition were vaults for records storage. Partially destroyed by a fire in 1889, the damaged sections were immediately rebuilt and improved, with the addition of a tower to house the town clock as well as a bell. Today the architectural gem finds service as a museum.

Other early brick buildings of importance include the Beaver Institute, an 1870 school which, when enlarged with a two-story addition, became the Central School. Both the Low Hotel, built in about 1865, and the Mathews or Beaver Centennial Hotel, erected in 1876, were two-story brick structures. Many fine, nineteenth-century brick homes are still extant. Many commercial buildings, along with the high school and library, feature impressive brick architecture.

Newspapers

Beaver County has had an active and varied history of locally produced and published newspapers which were of particular importance in connecting settlers separated by considerable distance in land. The *Beaver Enterprise* was first edited in August 1873 by George W. Crouch and the Carrigan brothers. For a period of time, the paper's mascot was the image of a donkey. The new editor, Scipio A. Kenner, who purchased the paper in 1875, got the idea from a group of mules Bishop John R. Murdock kept for a period of time in the tithing office yard. The mules created quite a disturbance during the night, braying incessantly, banging into the fences, and keeping the neighbors up all night. Kenner entitled the image, "The Beaver Nightingale." An alternate paper, *The Beaver County Sentinel* was published during the same years and managed by G. W. McLaughlin. *The Square Dealer* first appeared on 29 January 1877, during the months before the execution of John D. Lee for the Mountain Meadows Massacre. The editor commented on 23 March 1877 about Lee's confession: "One particular statement he had adhered to from the first. He had at all times declared that Brigham Young and the Church leaders had nothing to do with the Mountain Meadow Massacre."[75] A daily newspaper, *The Beaver Daily Chronicle* began publication on 16 October 1876. This four-column, four-page paper was 11 by 16 inches and published every day but Sunday. The paper's fifty or sixty subscribers paid their subscription fees with wood, vegetables, and wheat, or even occasionally with liquor. *The Beaver Chronicle* had a less than advantageous beginning. The first issue, dated 20 January 1879, was only one sheet and included this apology: "The public must bear with our shortcoming for a few days. We had paper ordered which started from Salt Lake on the 2nd, and it was not shipped from Juab until the 11th. We expect it every day. Hence a short coming may be caused by a long coming."[76] By October the *Chronicle* had changed hands and changed names to the *Beaver Watchman* under the management of Joseph Field. Briefly after February 1881, the *Southern Utonian* surveyed public auctions of government barracks, stores, officers' quarters, and other buildings at Fort Cameron and other local business news. Reinhard Maeser and George Hales were editors. On 5 October 1883, the paper's name was changed to the *Beaver Utonian,* and finally in 1904 the paper again changed hands and became the *Beaver Press.*

Post Offices and Mail Service

Utah's first post office was established in Salt Lake City in August 1850 as the official center of communication in the territory. Beaver County's first post offices were established in Beaver, 24 July 1857; Minersville, 7 December 1864; Greenville, 8 December 1865; and Adamsville, 10 April 1868. With the coming of the railroad, trade and communication with the world outside and increased mining activity prompted the establishment of post offices in Shauntie, 3 November 1874; Star City, 25 January 1875; Frisco, 30 August 1877; and Milford, 8 June 1880.

Before 1870 mail came through Beaver County with freight wagon trains. In 1870 a mail route from Beaver to Fillmore was established. Riders traveled from Beaver to Cove Fort where fresh horses were obtained. John A. Skinner and Alonzo Hinckley were among the first riders, keeping their horses at the stables at Cove Fort and Corn Creek between the two towns. At that time the mail was delivered to the James Low Hotel. The first official federal post office was built in 1874 on the southeast corner of the Milton Anderson lot—with Horace A. Skinner as the first postmaster between 1874–1877. The post office shifted locations several times before a federal building was built. Because of its location on the railroad, Milford was an important distribution point for mail addressed to the eastern Nevada communities of Pioche, Panaca, Bristol, and DeLaMar, as well as communities in Iron and Washington counties in Utah.

Water

Beaver County's settlers were cognizant of their church leaders' commission to make the "Desert blossom like a rose." But before local farmers could make their land a success, they had to secure a predictable and constant source of water. Most of them had experience with farming in the humid climate of New England or the Northeast. They were unfamiliar with the demands of a desert environment with different soil conditions, available water, and seasons. In the East, riparian rights had created the legal base for the distribution of water. Riparian rights represented a radically different attitude toward water use and regulation than was necessary in Utah.

The riparian water right concept centered on the rights of land owners whose land bordered lakes or streams. They were entitled to have water flow naturally, undiminished in quantity and unpolluted in quality. In one case decided in the State of California in 1884, for instance, riparian rights were defined as follows:

> The right of the riparian proprietor to the flow of the stream is
> inseparably annexed to the soil, and passes with it, not as an ease-

ment or appurtenance, but as a part and parcel of it. Use does not create it nor disuse destroy or suspend it. The right in each extends to the natural and usual flow of all the waters, unless where the quantity has been diminished as a consequence of the reasonable application of it by other riparian owners for purposes hereafter mentioned. The right of enjoying this flow without disturbance or interruption by any other proprietary is one of pure nature and is an incident of the property in land, not an appurtenance to it, like the right he has to enjoy the soil itself, in its natural state unaffected by the tortuous acts of a neighboring land owner. It is an inseparable incident to the ownership of the land, made by an inflexible rule of law an absolute and fixed right and can only be lost by grant or twenty years of adverse possession.[77]

Utah's social and physical environment created a unique situation. The policies and procedures of water distribution and use reflect on that particular set of problems. In Utah the system of water law and custom that developed applied the doctrine that water belongs to the public and is subject to appropriation by individuals or to grants by the legislature or other bodies (like canal companies) for this purpose. The diversion of water for use by the people was the accepted policy of the territory.

During the territorial legislature's first session, the body gave the power over water to the county courts. Section 39, written 4 February 1852, defines the powers of the court: "The County Court has the control of all timber, water privileges, or any water course, or creek to grant mill sites, and exercise such power as in their judgment shall best preserve the timber and subserve the interest of the settlements in their distribution of water for irrigation or other purposes. All grants or rights held under legislative authority shall not be interfered with."[78] Therefore the county courts held extensive power and the principle of public ownership of water was established.[79] Possibly the most important power delegated to the county in this desert environment was the granting and adjudicating of water rights.

Water legislation gave the power over regulation of natural resources to the courts, the probate judges and three selectmen in the county oversaw administration of the water network which included the appointment of a water master to oversee the regulation and main-

The John and Nellie Griffith house in Minersville. (Utah State Historical Society)

tenance of irrigation systems and to insure that orders of the court were properly executed. Beaver County was divided into water districts according to the source of water—streams, rivers, or springs coming into the valley from nearby mountains. Districts exercised their authority under and according to charters received from the territory.

Furthermore, the court directed the location of dams and canals; in fact, the location of reservoirs and canals could not be changed without approval of the court. The court controlled as well regulation of wells, springs and streams. Although local wards, irrigation companies, and groups of individuals provided the bulk of the labor required in building canals, reservoirs, and water systems, county and local government provided support and direction as well, and frequently the best work represented a combination of public and private. Occasionally the court directed the preservation or conservation of natural resources.[80] On 11 April 1866, for instance, the court discussed a measure to prevent anyone from cutting down cottonwood trees that belonged to the county.

In 1877 John R. Murdock, I.P. Carter, and William Barton petitioned the county court to build dams and reservoirs on North Creek for irrigation. C.P. Bord, Edward Tolton, John A. Smith, Muir, Skinner, Frazer and forty others objected to this petition and made it known to the court. After studying the situation, the court decided that all water in North Creek and its tributaries should be declared an irrigation district and should be regulated as such. Within days the court called for an election so that citizens could vote on whether the North Creek Irrigation District could charge $2.00 an acre on all irrigated lands for water from the creek.[81]

The Utah Territorial Legislature passed a subsequent act in 1880 establishing the idea that territorial water, when appropriated, became private property.[82] This essentially repealed the 1852 law giving the county court control over territorial water. From that point forward, the control over water passed into the hands of the selectmen who became water commissioners of the county. Under this new law, it was no longer the responsibility of the territory to enforce a beneficial and economic use of the public water, but to create a forum for the adjudication of conflicts that arose over the separate parties. It defined their duties as follows:

> to make or to cause to be made and recorded such observations from time to time as they may deem necessary of the quantity and flow of water in the natural sources of supply, and to determine as near as may be the average flow thereof at any season of the year, and to receive, hear, and determine all claims to any right to the use of water, and on receipt of satisfactory proof of any right to the use of water having vested, to issue to the person owning such right a certificate thereof, and to generally oversee in person or by agents appointed by them, the distribution of water within their respective counties from natural sources of supply, and to fairly distribute according to the nature and extent of recorded rights and according to law, to each said corporations as to the nature or extent of their rights to the use of water, or right of way, or damages therefore, of any one or more of such persons, or corporations, to hear and decide upon all such disputed rights and file a

copy of their findings and decisions as to such rights with the County Recorder, and to distribute the water according to such findings or decision, unless ordered by a court of competent jurisdiction.[83]

Beaver County had numerous irrigation and canal companies that organized the distribution of water on the local level. The companies initiated the construction of canal systems, reservoirs, and regulated the maintenance and distribution of water.

Nevertheless, water rights and the need for greater regulation were often debated in local papers. Some believed water legitimately belonged to the city, whose obligations it was to distribute it equally; others, the promoters of individual rights, supported the notion that individual private ownership of property brought with it control over water as well. Again water was the key to agricultural prosperity in the area.

Minersville built a reservoir across the lower Beaver River as early as 1860 about two and one half miles below Minersville itself. Their dam was a makeshift affair constructed with dirt, rocks, and branches, and soon fell apart. Nevertheless, water was so scarce the settlers became discouraged and planned to move elsewhere. Brigham Young visited their community and encouraged them to stay, promising them eventually the valley would be filled with farms.

Nelson Hollingshead supervised the construction of an irrigation dam at the mouth of the canyon near Minersville so that he could provide power for his grist mill. This dam was constructed with logs and lumber and was used eventually as a diversion point as irrigation was organized for the area. It also eventually washed away.[84] Other farmers built two dams at Rocky Ford, one of brush and gravel and the other of diamond-shaped pens filled with rock. Despite their efforts, both dams flooded out and were washed out down river.

The first incorporated company on the Beaver River was the Minersville Irrigation Company. The original bill of incorporation was drawn up by lawyer Frank R. Clayton and was signed on 7 February 1889 by Edwin Eyre, George Marshall, Soloman Walker, James W. McKnight, William Wood, William Hamblin, and Joseph H. Dupaix, and other residents of Minersville precinct. The purpose

This building was used as a hotel in Minersville. (Utah State Historical Society)

of the dam built at Minersville was to store and control water from the Beaver River for irrigation purposes at the point near Minersville Canyon known as Rocky Ford. It was intended that the river would proceed naturally through the canyon to canals, ditches, and other waterways constructed and maintained by the company and diverted to land of the stockholders. Originally, the company had $30,000 capital stock and 2,000 shares valued $15 each.

Agriculture and Livestock

Cattle raising also required a certain type of individual, well seasoned by the environment and the challenges of settling in this difficult terrain. Pioneer families like the Murdocks and the Farnsworths had the largest cattle herds and large tracts of land north of Milford on the Beaver Bottoms. Here they pastured several thousand cattle yearly. In the western part of the county, operations like the Pine Valley Ranch ran as many as 5,000 head of cattle. Owners of large herds hired cowboys to handle their animals. Quintessentially western, the cowboy's life played out in the natural environment, with only minimal interruption and marked by the shifts in prices for cattle.

Sheep also grazed in the Tushar Mountains as early as the 1870s. The discussion over land use was always strained; hence, relations between cattlemen and sheepherders and between livestock raisers and forestry proponents were tense.

Some felt local herds taxed resources and made life unpleasant. One angry citizen wrote in an editorial to the *Southern Utonian,* 18 April 1889, "Our County road has been filled up with muck making it very perplexing and annoying to the traveling public. Our canals and ditches that have cost considerable means and hard labor are filled with rock pushed by their herds of sheep crowding the roads."

Farming life in Beaver County was dictated in part by the distribution of resources—water, land, and man power. Beaver County is overwhelmingly rural in nature, but here we see a greater diversification of land uses than is typical in other counties. The farmer's life was driven by the changing seasons and the effort to work the land with limited water. David A. Tanner recounted his father's efforts at raising enough food for his family and to sell at market:

> I remember that when I was a small boy my father raised potatoes and a small garden without irrigation. Alfalfa was raised, but the water was so close to the surface that it deteriorated in about two years time. . . . in my teens I was old enough to plow for corn. We used a Red Bird Sulky plow. I would make about a four inch deep furrow and make sort of a circle and then go along and drop the next row. Sometimes father would ride through the corn on a horse and you could just see the top of his head. This was over across the fields on the other side of the river. We raised red top, timothy, blue grass, and other grasses down the fields along the tracks to the north.[85]

Lucy E.W. Burns remembered her father's farm three miles west of Beaver. Their home in town consisted of one-quarter of the city block, with a house barn, out buildings, and a yard full of chickens, pigs, cows, and horses. A vegetable garden, a small patch of alfalfa, and some fruit trees were the responsibility of the mother. The father farmed land located on the periphery of town and usually owned twenty-five acres.[86]

Besides the endemic problems with rabbits feeding off crops during the night, wolves roamed freely through fields in Adamsville and Greensville.[87] Fire plagued farmers who heated their homes with coal or wood stoves and worked over fires in the fields for a variety of purposes. The *Southern Utonian* reported a fire caused by Mrs. John Smith making soap in the yard beside her house when a high wind came up and carried the sparks into a nearby peastack.

> A cry was raised and the neighbors came running to the scene. The fire spread to the fence, and burned about two rods of it before its ravages were stopped. The sparks were carried by the wind to Heber Dean's correl across the street and several times the manure and straw got to a blaze but were extinguished before any serious results were experienced there. It was a close call and should be a warning to all to be careful with outside fires, especially while the wind is blowing.[88]

Beaver Woolen Mills

Perhaps the single most important manufacturing institution was the Beaver Woolen Mills first incorporated in 1870 with a subscribed capital of $30,500, largely through the efforts of John Ashworth. The mill building was three stories tall, 60 by 120 feet, equipped with machinery shipped to Utah from New England. When installed, the production floor included nine looms for flannels and finer fabrics, one loom for men's wear, and one loom for the production of blankets. Three cards, one spinning jenny of 360 spindles, finishing and fulling machines, warpers, and other miscellaneous machines made possible the production of virtually all types of cloth.

Both converts from England, John and William Ashworth managed the mill initially. Department heads included William Robinson, John Dean, Henry Tattersall, Enoch Cowdell, Richard Curfew, Heber C. Dean, William Holgate, William Dean, and Thomas Schofield. English immigrant and experienced weaver Eliza Slater Moyes wove the first set of blankets.

Key to the economic development of Beaver because of employment opportunities it provided and revenues it brought into the area,

The Beaver Woolen Mill. (Utah State Historical Society)

the Beaver Woolen Mill was the first of its kind in southern Utah. Wagons loaded down with goods to be exchanged for mill products brought more varied products into local markets. Mining towns to the west provided steady markets for mill products as well.

In both 1889 and 1890, additions were built on the original building which extended the building by thirty feet to the west. In addition, capital stock increased by $15,500 resulting in $46,000. Upgrades on machinery, the addition of new card sets and spinning jennys improved the quality of the product. A new manufacturing department producing shirts, socks, underwear, and other articles of ready-to-wear clothing broadened the range of products the mill provided. The organizational structure of the company also became increasingly specialized. William Ashworth replaced his father as superintendent, John F. Tolton and Charles Woolfenden both worked as bookkeepers and salesmen for the company. Other superintendents: included William Farnsworth, Franklin D. Farnsworth, and O.A. Murdock. By the 1890s it became increasingly difficult for the mill to market its manufactured goods for sale and the mill closed down by the end of the century.

Beaver Co-operative Commercial and Manufacturing Institution

Besides cooperating for building projects and town settlement, Mormon pioneers organized in cooperative merchandising institutions under the centralized control of church owned Zions Cooperative Mercantile Institution (ZCMI). Each local ZCMI branch functioned as part of a regional merchandising network designed to minimize non-Mormon competition and facilitate the distribution and production of home manufactured goods and the importation of states goods. Aimed toward territorial self-sufficiency, ZCMI allowed church members to purchase stock certificates and share in company profits.

The Beaver Co-op Store was a two-story building constructed in 1872 of black igneous rock quarried from mountains east of Beaver. For its time, the store was the largest mercantile south of Salt Lake City. The Beaver Co-operative Commercial and Manufacturing Institution became an important part of the cooperative network of which the Salt Lake City ZCMI was the parent institution. The largest original shareholders of the Beaver Co-operative and Commercial and Manufacturing Institution were James R. Murdock with 865 shares at a value of $4,325; P.T. Farnsworth, Jr., 320 shares worth $1,600; and M.L. Shepherd with 165 shares worth $825. Most shareholders purchased only a few shares. The original board of trustees reads like a Who's Who in Beaver County and includes many of the original pioneers to the area: John R. Murdock, M.L. Shepherd, P.T. Farnsworth, Jr., A.M. Farnsworth, William Ashworth, John White, David Levi, James Lowe, John Ashworth, Edward Tolton, Robert Easton, W.G. Nowers, William Greenwood, Thomas Frazer, Isaac Riddle, and James Farrer.

In the effort to become self-sustaining, a variety of industries soon provided residents with a variety of products and services— woolen, flour and saw mills, dry goods stores, shoe and tailor shops, and bee keepers helped to provide a more substantial and diversified base for settlement efforts. A number of businesses that fed off stock and sheep raising also were located in the county. Some farmers broadened their resources with small flocks of sheep, usually between ten and twenty. Wool production provided a variety of different jobs. It needed to be shorn, carded, spun and eventually woven into cloth. One Scandinavian immigrant, Charsta Lunblad, wife of Hans Lunblad former president of the Scandinavian Mission, wove the wool that her husband, himself a tailor, fashioned into men's suits.

United Order

The community attempt at cooperative living was no where better expressed than in Beaver's effort at living the United Order, first organized 12 April 1874. The objectives of the united order were " . . . to carry on a general business of farming, manufacturing, merchandising, fruit-growing, stock-raising, dairying, and as many other pursuits as will tend to the material prosperity of the order."[89] The minutes of the organization read as follows:

> Realizing by the Spirit and Signs of the Times, and from the results of our past experience, the necessity of a closer union and combination of our labors for the promotion of our common welfare, and whereas we have learned of the struggle between Capital and Labor, resulting in Strikes of the Workman with their consequent distress, and also the oppression of monied monopolies and, whereas, there is growing distrust and faithfulness among men in the Political and Business relations of life as well as a spirit for extravagant speculation and over-reaching the legitimate bounds of the Credit System, resulting in Financial Panics and Bankruptcy, Paralyzing industry, thereby making many of the necessities and conveniences of life precarious and uncertain and whereas our past experiences has proven, that to be the Friends of God, we must become the friends and helpers of each other in a common bond of brotherhood, . . . we must be self-sustaining, encouraging home manufacturing, producing . . . and not only supply our own wants, but also have some to spare for exportation.[90]

This very interesting document helps illustrate nineteenth-century values and social conditions in Utah. It outlines as well the basic materialistic assumptions of the day, what was considered essential to existence, what was thought to be of value. It further says that "we believe the beauty of our garments should be the workmanship of our own hands and that we should practice more diligently

Inside the Beaver Woolen Mill. (Utah State Historical Society)

Economy, Temperance, Frugality, and the simple grandeur of manners which belongs to the Pure in Heart."[91] The order's objective was to create a self- sustaining people, capable of meeting the difficulties presented by socially, morally, politically and commercially perilous times. Foolish fashions and and the use of imported luxuries was to be shunned. Trade and business relations with individuals who were not members of the order were to by avoided " . . . unless absolutely compelled by our necessities."[92] Meetings of the United Order opened with prayer, with group singing, and felt much like a church gathering. Work was divided among members of the order by the same ecclesiastical figure who would call them to repentance on Sunday. Clearly, Beaver's United Order was an expression of a religious ideal.

The Beaver United Order operated under a cadre of nineteen officers, with the most prominent positions going to John R. Murdock, president; William Fotheringham, secretary; and William J. Cox, treasurer. Initially, resources were divided among three superintendencies—one for horses, one for cattle, and another for the tannery. The tannery remained in private ownership but an agreement was made for the united order to operate the tannery for which it received one-fourth of the tanned skins. This arrangement led to the establishment in June 1874 of a shoe shop as another united order operated undertaking. The united order also acquired W. Coplan's steam saw mill and signed a contract to provide beef for nearby Fort Cameron at the rate of 6.5 cents a pound for live cattle and 8 cents a pound for dressed beef.

In spite of these promising beginnings, the Beaver United Order lasted only a few months. It was apparently a trial for some members of the Mormon faith. One non-Mormon in Beaver wrote to the *Salt Lake Tribune*, " A number of the faithful are distressed over this matter. They dislike to give up their fellowship in the church, and they dislike to give up their property."[93] Historian Dale Morgan explained that "Only about a third of the settlers had joined, and whether the difficulties of the organization were occasioned by communal conflicts, lack of adequate capital, internal dissension, or other reasons, the order was abandoned and the property redistributed among the members.[94]

Economic Life

The United States Census helps paint a demographic image of the county's social makeup and reveals patterns of population dips and plateaus. At the time of the county's first enumeration in 1860, 785 persons were recorded as residents. That number had increased by 155 percent by 1870 (2,007), and another 95.2 percent by 1880 (3,918). The county's population dropped by 14.8 percent (3,340) by 1890.

A Beaver County Tax Roll for 1873 provides an interesting look at local occupations. This roll of the territory was used to select persons qualified to serve as jurors for the Second District Court. Of fifty-six men permanent male residents of the county, thirty-eight were farmers. Five were miners; two were freighters; and the rest were businessmen—a blacksmith, merchant, two shoe makers, liquor dealer, and stock raiser. Thirty-eight were from Beaver, the clear political center of the county.[95]

During the nineteenth century, locals made their livelihood through farming, freighting, stock raising, mining, or through business.

Prosperity in one economic sector spread to the others. As long as the mines were doing healthy business, freighters, miners, and service businesses prospered as well. For instance, in the 1880s Milford's business district included five stables and feedyards, five saloons, five blacksmith shops, two grocery stores, a drug store, Chinese restaurant, meat market, granary, and numerous boarding houses. The *Deseret Evening News* gave a view into Milford's business district in April 1896:

> some two dozen buildings . . . among which are four very creditable hotels, two or three general merchandising establishments, two saloons, and a commodious and well appointed railway depot. There are no streets, and when a person with a conveyance sets out to go anywhere, he is pretty sure to strike some sort of structure amidship before going very far; when this happens either of several courses can be taken—he can tunnel under, climb over, go through, go around, turn back or remain where he is. In nine cases out of ten he goes around.[96]

Success in business seemed to depend on success in mining, stock raising, and freighting, each of which brought needed revenue into the county.

Freighting

Freighting was also another important industry that brought customers and goods through the county. Particularly before the railroad traversed the county, freighting companies played a particular role in connecting Beaver County with the world outside. Original roads followed Indian trails, but all were difficult regardless of the weather. Traversing rocky trails, muddy in inclement weather, freighters welcomed the services provided by these rural communities. They hauled ore mined in the area, timber from Beaver Canyon to Frisco to build mining structures, hay from Adamsville to feed their animals, farm products to feed miners or to be shipped to more distant markets. It took three days to make the round trip from Beaver to Frisco. Customers themselves, freighters bought butter produced by local housewives,

Freighting was such a profitable enterprise that many local farmers took it up for part of the year to earn money to supplement their other income. Besides shipping goods between county towns, many

would bring their wagons up to Sanpete or Sevier counties fill them
with farm produce and bring them back to supply local mercantiles.

Bill Wood's father joined his father or his older brother in
freighting when he was only ten years old on trips between
Minersville and Salt Lake City. They would drive the teams hard, resting periodically for a day or two to let the horses recuperate and feed.
Soon he drove his own smaller wagon behind his father's, still loaded
down with supplies. To climb hills, they would double up their teams,
from time to time stopping the wagon, blocking the wheels and letting the horses rest.[97]

Freighting was particularly demanding work that proceeded
regardless of the season. When the weather was warm, drivers rode
on wagons with clouds of dust billowing in the wake of a team of
horses or oxen. Even worse when wet, the roads bogged down with
mud that rendered some places unpassable. Businesses lining
Milford's and Frisco's main streets reflected the importance of the
freighting industry—stables, blacksmith shops, feedyards, and boarding houses provided vital services. On the average a single load would
range in size from 6,000 to 8,000 pounds. Ingenious freighters would
travel loaded each way—hauling machinery and merchandise out
and ore from the mines back to the county's towns. Wagons were
usually covered with sheets of canvass to protect the goods, and a
standard wagon would be three or four feet deep. The driver sat on a
seat high over the "jockey box," a tool box carrying tools, grease, and
food, and supplies. Wooden water barrels tied to both sides of the
wagon insured that driver and team would not perish in the desert
environment and feed bags hung off to the sides as well. After the
railroad was built to Milford, freighting occurred in three directions:
east to Beaver, south through Minersville to Parowan, Cedar City, St.
George, and other southern Utah towns; and west to the mines at
Panaca, Pioche, and Delamar in Nevada. The round trip from
Milford to Delamar often required nearly two weeks. While ore was
the usual commodity hauled back from the mines, west-bound wagons hauled everything from produce and hardware to heavy mining
equipment. On one trip Joe E. Eyre of Minersville and two other men
drove an eight-horse team across Panaca Summit where the snow

was up to their hips. When a piece of the mining machinery rolled off the wagon, it took them four days to get it back on the wagon.[98]

Railroad

Beaver County's settlers benefitted by the coming of the railroad in a number of ways. Because the need for railroad ties was great a number of men cut timber in local canyons for the rails. The ax men cut the trees, then rolled them down the steep mountains. At the bottom they were cut into rail ties seven or eight inches thick. Most of the ties were finished with axes.

The coming of the railroad to Beaver County facilitated the rapid transportation of ores extracted from the mines to distant markets. Before the railroad, teams of freighters hauled ores and agricultural products across the desert land separating Beaver County from eastern Nevada and markets in towns like Panaca. The railroad came first to Milford in 1880 and soon after to Frisco and Newhouse. The line coming into Beaver County was potentially an extension of the Utah Southern Railway.

Settlements south of Salt Lake were conscious of the economic impact a railroad depot had on community growth and competed for selection. Despite vigorous boosterism promoting Beaver as the perfect location for a railroad line, Milford was chosen as the destination on the route south. For a while it seemed Minersville would be the Beaver County city to be chosen. The *Deseret News* published excerpts which illustrated the heated contest being waged over the issue.

> Minersville is steadily coming to the front, the surveyors having marked out the Southern Extension through the burg.
> Uncle George Adair, who resided at Minersville, some 18 years ago, used to relate a dream which he had about that town. He said that in his dream he saw a railroad built into said town and the place transformed from an insignificant little farming settlement into a live, bustling mining and railroad town. It is beginning to look as if Uncle George's prophecy might be fulfilled.[99]

When the railroad came to Milford, it also left its stamp on the community. The depot, storage warehouses for goods being shipped in and out of the area, and perhaps four dozen other buildings lined the streets contiguous to the railroad station.

Milford's railroad station was constructed in 1880 when the railroad came to Beaver County. The railroad that came through Milford was an extension of the Utah Central Railway which started in Ogden (in 1870) and extended into the south. Original investors included Joseph A. Young, William Jennings, Bishop John Sharp, LeGrand Young, and other businessmen from Salt Lake City. Upon its completion, the Utah Central, Utah Southern, and Utah Southern Extension were all consolidated under the name the Utah Central Railway.

In 1872 Brigham Young purchased stock in the Union Pacific Railroad Company, which joined with the Utah Central Railway in extended tracks even farther south into Utah territory.

Perhaps the most important objective of the Utah Southern Extension was providing transportation for the rich silver and lead mining products coming out of the Frisco area, particularly the Horn Silver Mine. Sometimes as much as 150 tons of the rich galena ore coming out of the Horn Silver Mine were shipped per day.

It would be difficult to underestimate the importance of the railroad to the development of Milford City. Diversity in businesses, people, and challenges marked this town as a place apart. Although Beaver was the county seat and center of agriculture and the stock raising industry, Milford became the principal location for the shipment of goods in and out of the county.

When the Utah Central was engaged in construction of its southern line in 1889, Beaver County newspapers attempted to draw attention to what Beaver had to offer, arousing its citizens to action. "The Railroad. Surveyors at Work. Fremont Canyon Being Surveyed. Shall We Let Them Pass. Never! Never! Never!" one article was titled. It continued:

> Every citizen arouse! Every man to his post! A company of railroad surveyors is now located near the mouth of Fremont Canyon just over the ridge south of Beaver. Their apparent object is to survey through Fremont pass via Dog Valley on to the Sevier river, thence travel northward passing by Marysvale through Sevier and Sanpete counties. The route selected is very impractical, difficult, and hazardous, besides being a long way around.

Via Beaver the route would be materially shortened, and notwithstanding the fabulous amount estimated by some that it would cost nearly $600,000 more to cross our way, it would be of incalculable more benefit to any road.[100]

In a series of editorials, articles, and other promotional material, the benefits of the railroad coming through Beaver were paraded before a willing audience. "Beaver is not dead but only sleeping," one wrote. "Sleeping to the great benefits that could be derived by a wide awake, rustling people; asleep to the many gigantic resources that lie dormant from lack of a little push; dosing over the untold resources of wealth that everywhere surround us. It is high time that there should be a shaking among the dry bones, and that further opportunities be not permitted to slip by us."[101] "It is an established fact that railroad men in this part of the country mean push," another maintained. "Our money would be returned to us in more ways than one."[102]

Beaver's mayor believed Beaver ideally suited for a depot: "We have the facilities here to make a beautiful city, if we can get a railroad through here. We have the land and plenty of water if it is utilized. If a road will pass through Beaver it will greatly enhance the value of property. A railroad is the only thing that will advance Beaver in the proper scale." William Ashworth, superintendent of the Beaver Woolen Mills, was pessimistic about Beaver's future without the line. "If the road passes along and misses us entirely we have nothing to remain in Beaver for. If Beaver should have a railroad it will rank among the leading cities of the Territory. We have the facilities. We have the best water in the Territory."[103]

Settlement in Beaver County was spread out over miles and miles of land. Therefore transportation between the separate towns and communication were critical in creating a sense of community in the county. Early transportation was not with out danger. On 4 January 1894, John Franklin Tolton left his home in Beaver for Milford and the train which would take him to Salt Lake City for a session of the territorial legislature.

While enroute to Milford I met with a mishap while crossing the Beaver River at a point near Minersville. The ice broke and caused

my team and bugy to drop into the current, the water being so
deep as to flow into the buggy and came nearly upsetting the contents into the river. Reached Milford o.k. and took train the following morning for Salt Lake City.[104]

Hotels and Boarding Houses

Beaver's first hotels were the Thompson Hotel, run by Mrs.
Edward W. Thompson and the Low Hotel, operated by Mr. and Mrs.
James Low. While these establishments offered lodging for travelers,
they functioned more as boarding houses for miners and other work-
ers. The Lee Boarding House was located above Charley's Saloon. The
boarding house was operated by an African-American couple named
Lee who came to Beaver because of Fort Cameron. Other early
Beaver hotels include the Betensen Hotel, the Mathews Hotel, the
Farnsworth Hotel, the Baker House, and the Beaver Hotel.

Milford had several quality hotels. The Williams Hotel, built in
1881 by John D. Williams, housed smelter workers, mining magnates,
and visiting religious leaders including Laurence Scanlan, Catholic
bishop for Utah. The Smithson Hotel was the largest of Milford's
early hotels, with as many as forty regular boarders plus other travelers in need of accommodations. The Tanner House, originally built
as a private residence for Ebenezer Tanner and his family, was
adopted as a hotel by the Tanners and became a popular stopping
place for "drummers," as traveling salesmen were usually called.[105]

Schools

Beaver schools operated in several different locations and under
separate districts during the 1860s and 1870s. In 1873 the Methodist
Episcopal church opened a school which operated continuously until
1891. A second Methodist school was operated by Reverend Karl L.
Anderson from 1908 to 1912. These two schools were part of a
Protestant missionary initiative in Utah to provide a good education
for Mormon children with the conviction that with such an education the children would turn away from Mormonism.

In 1881 Beaver's local schools underwent consolidation. All the
separate districts became one unified district to facilitate tighter
administration of funds and programs. The problem of housing
Beaver County students was periodically met with special school

taxes for the purpose of enlarging existing facilities or build new ones.[106] Reinhard Maeser was Beaver's first school principal. Maeser recorded in his diary,

> My father and James E. Talmage were about to make a trip through Southern Utah as far as St. George, in the interest of education, and I was invited to go along. While visiting at Beaver the trustees consulted my father respecting a teacher for their school. The three or four districts having been consolidated, would make this a large and important one. I was asked if I would accept the position, which I did. After returning from St. George in the latter part of July, 1881, I remained in Beaver to arrange for the opening of school in the latter part of August.[107]

In part because of Maeser's influence, the Mormon church established their first school south of Provo, the Beaver Stake Academy in 1886. First held in rooms over the Beaver Co-op store, the academy held daytime classes for school aged children and nighttime sessions for adults. In 1890 the academy built its own building, a two-story pink sandstone structure located at the center of town.

In 1888 the Utah Territorial Legislature passed a bill establishing a Free School System in Utah. The *Southern Utonian* published a census of school aged children in 1890 that described the expenditures of the system in the county. Beaver had a total 988 children, 153 determined as non-Mormon, 835 as Mormon. Beaver had the largest population with 545, Minersville with 148, Greenville with 105, and Adamsville with 86. The state would spend $2.50 per year on these children, between the ages of six and eighteen, for teachers salaries, supplies, and school buildings.[108]

Because of the impracticability of running the academy in this changed situation, with free schools, the Beaver Stake Academy closed in 1890 and the building rented to the county for use by a new school called the Park School.[109] In 1909 a new two-story red-brick eight-room school building was built on the same lot to the north. Besides organizational changes, Beaver County schools saw an evolution in the concept of gradation. Before 1894, school age children were separated into five divisions, which ranged from the First Reader to the Fifth Reader. In 1894 that changed and students were placed in eight

The Murdock Academy Band. (Utah State Historical Society)

grades. Policies varied some according to the principal in charge, but discipline was particularly strict under J.S. Hanks (1907–1915). He was particularly exacting in the way children entered and exited the building. To walk as a group, they lined up at the door, two abreast, from the lowest grade to the highest, with each teacher stationed nearby. Disobedient or unruly students were placed in the "Awkward Squad." And those who created the most challenging discipline problems were given a special drill by Mr. Hanks.

The Beaver Branch of the Brigham Young Academy, later known as Murdock Academy, began its tenure in September 1898. After Fort Cameron was abandoned, the Mormon church became owner of half of the property, with John R. Murdock and Philo T. Farnsworth owning the other. The two men donated their share to the church, which represented a value of $15,000. The property was used during the interim for summer schools and recreational uses. Responsibility for renovating the space was given to the Beaver Stake with the stake presidency responsible for raising funds necessary for the construction and remodeling. The campus included 240 additional acres around the fort buildings. When it opened, a procession marked the

day attended by two Mormon general authorities and a public concert and ball. Thirty-eight students enrolled the first day, and within
two weeks the enrollment reached 100. The school was directed by E.
D. Partridge who was sent to Beaver from the parent institution in
Provo. He remained until 1900 when he returned to Provo and
Andrew B. Anderson was assigned as principal. Students from all
across the region came to complete the two-year high school course
offered. Classes were offered in chemistry, physics, mathematics,
English literature, and music. Physical education, elocution, and the-
ology rounded out the offering.

The Beaver Branch of Brigham Young Academy became an independent school in 1908 and was renamed Murdock Academy. With
the construction of a beautiful two-story pink stone building
between 1908 and 1913, and a full four-year high school program
offered, Murdock Academy stayed open until 1922, when declining
enrollment because of the development of public high schools in the
area led to its closure on 12 May 1922. Much of the school equipment
was given to the Beaver High School.[110]

Health Issues

Settlers of Beaver County were dependent on a group of dedicated midwives who delivered babies and cared for other medical
needs as best they could until medical doctors arrived in the county.
Traditions and customs affected health care in Beaver County as in
other parts of the country. Women and usually their husbands were
adverse to using the services of a male doctor during child delivery.
Consequently, until well into the twentieth century a cadre of dedicated midwives took charge of this important responsibility.
Midwives not only assisted in the delivery process but stayed on to
help both mother and child with whatever needed to be done including the necessary house work. Some, including Elizabeth Grundy,
received training in Salt Lake City in child birth and other medical
techniques. One midwife, Ruth Reese of Greenville, took pride in
greeting the young men she had delivered with, "I was the first one
to see you, my boy."[111]

The first doctors, John Ward Christian and George Fennemore,
came to Beaver with the San Bernardino exiles in 1858. Both men

remained in the county for the rest of their lives. Fennemore turned one of the rooms in his house into a drug store. In 1872 Dr. Wayne Smith came to Beaver with the soldiers at Fort Cameron, and following the closure of the fort he remained in Beaver to practice. Other doctors arrived later including Seymour B. Young in 1890.[112] Still, the practice of medicine remained an imprecise science. When John Franklin Tolton was afflicted with a rash, sores, and swelling on his hands in the summer of 1892, he went to two local doctors but found little or no relief from their treatment. He then " . . . consulted Dr. Yellowstone who was visting Beaver, with a wonderful show and advertising his celebrated medicines, and was unable to make any satisfactory terms with him on promise of a permanent cure, as the doctor would not back up his guarantee."[113] After suffering another two months, Tolton finally paid a specialist—Dr. Elison—$50 for treatment. The guaranteed cure proved successful.

Until the first trained dentists arrived around 1880, blacksmiths often handled the necessary extraction of aching teeth without any anaesthetics but with the assistance of several men who held the patient. For children, a string tied to the loose or aching tooth was attached to a door knob and the door slammed shut to accomplish the extraction.[114] In a time when good dental hygiene was not commonly practiced, many people lost their teeth and were outfitted with bridges and dentures.

One local dentist, Elijah Smith, learned the practice from a dentist whom he assisted and went into business for himself. In 1906 when the Utah State Dental Board learned that he was practicing without proper training or a license, he went to Salt Lake City and took a course in dentistry. Among the techniques he learned was how to freeze teeth before extracting them. However, "Many times he would put the freezing agent on the teeth and then pull them before it had a chance to deaden the pain. By the time the gum was numbed, the tooth was out and if a patient remarked that it hurt he would say, 'Oh, I knew you could stand it.'"[115]

In 1889 the managers of the Beaver Woolen Mills planned to install public bathing rooms. "It is intended," the *Southern Utonian* reported, to "have one large plunge bath, 12 X 20 ft. long, and a number of private baths."[116] A diphtheria epidemic broke out in 1891 causing many to move out of town for a period of time.[117] During the epidemic William and Hattie Fotheringham lost three children. Meetings and all public gatherings were canceled and the town was placed under quarantine.[118]

Recreation

Beaver County, as a community, is first of all a geographic setting. Marked by mountains to the west and east, the broad and sweeping valley floor, the arid climate and environment, and relatively homogenous population present a particular set of resources with which the community is built. Beaver County's cultural life reflects an effort to go beyond the geographic setting to find ways of interacting to build a shared bond of social meaning and satisfaction with life.

Dances were favored entertainments, joining all ages in the quadrille, the waltz, the polka, and scotch reel. Dances were scheduled in conjunction with July 4th celebrations, Pioneer Days, or other holidays; in observance of weddings, changing seasons, or the harvest. Dance music might be as simple as a combination of fiddles and accordions, organs and whatever variety of instruments was available. Settlers joined for dances in school houses, churches, and sometimes at home. Summer dances were staged in barns, under boweries, or in fields lighted by hand-made candles. Beaver County residents joined for philanthropic purposes in the "wood dance," an event scheduled after the fall harvest for the area's widows and poor. Men and boys hauled wagon loads of wood in exchange for tickets to the dance, wood that was then donated to those in need. The women of the Mormon Relief Society prepared a delicious meal spread out on long tables—steaming hot vegetables, meats, pies and cakes, homemade bread and jellies. Often a group of young men would generate the idea of staging a dance and covering the costs themselves. Expenses included $1.50 for the fiddler, $1.00 for the caller, and candles to light the room.[119] Refreshments might be simply squash and potatoes roasted in the coals of the fire. Candy pulling was also a popular activity that accompanied evening dances. Dances were also held each time a company of pioneers pushed through town on their way south.

One long remembered dance in Minersville was an April Fools Dance in 1889 when a prize was offered for the best "April Fools Surprise." The prize went to two sisters, Melissa Ellen Wood and Emma Wood, for the cupcakes they baked with cotton on the inside, but delicious looking frosting on the outside.[120]

Basket dances were also popular, and women and girls decorated baskets which they filled with fried chicken, biscuits, fruit, and cake to entice the highest bid. Sometimes the bids reached $10 and more for a basket, which entitled the winner to share the food with the lady who had provided it. "If a boy found out which basket belonged to his beloved he would really bid, while the other men added to his worries by also bidding to keep him from getting it. . . . It was common to see an older man eating lunch with a young girl, or a young man eating with an older woman, but people were good sports, eating and dancing with the girl whose basket was drawn."[121]

Pioneer children were encouraged to learn to dance by watching their parents and other adult members of the community and at special dances held in the afternoons for children. "The music was the same as they had in the evenings and there were always older people in attendance to supervise the teaching and enjoyment of thse dances for the children." Dances included the Virginia reel, quadrille, cake walk, Chicago glide, highland fligh, 7-Up, Berlin polka, Danish slide off, lanses, shottish, square dances, and waltzes. [122]

Beaver staged numerous parades through the year, but none so impressive as the Pioneer Day parade. Leading the parade was Beaver's martial band complete with piccolo, four fifes, four snare drums, and one large drum. The parade marshal wearing a plumed wide brimmed black hat and red sash, sword to his side, riding his finest horse followed close behind. Perhaps the most interesting entry in the parade were the figures representing President Brigham Young, the handcart companies, Indian war parties, and pioneer farmers. The local 24th of July queen, Miss Utah, and Miss Beaver rode in a special wagon, later a float, down Main Street. The parade ended near the town park, where a picnic lunch met all participants, accompanied by band music under the shade provided by an ample bowery.

The 4th of July gave Beaver County another occasion to celebrate. The variety of sponsors for one day's festivities paints a picture of

An early Beaver horse race. (Utah State Historical Society)

the stratification of the local society. Supporters included the Beaver Co-op, a merchant and photographer, a brewmaster, a liquor sales-man, several saloon, hotel, and drug store owners, an ice cream par-lor owner, an editor, and butcher. A parade led off the day's activities. After the grand marshall began the parade, a "Goddess of Liberty" on an elaborate float drawn by four well matched horses proceeded down the street. Individuals representing the thirteen original colonies, the other states and territories followed. The band members rode in a wagon also pulled by four horses to the park where they embarked and played through the afternoon under the bowery. During the afternoon, children's games and foot races and sports activities entertained all who joined for the celebration. A patriotic program including readings of the Declaration of Independence, orations by local teachers and political officers, and songs sung by school-aged children continued through the after-noon.

John Franklin Tolton described the 1893 4th of July in Beaver in his diary and concluded that Beaver's patriotism and ability to cele-brate matched that of any other place in the United States.

A bowery was constructed in front of meetinghouse and a nice program rendered. Miss Laura Ashworth represented the Goddess of Liberty; R. Maeser, orator of the day, did credit to himself and the occasion. The town was well represented with traveling men and strangers generally, who pronounced the celebration equal to anything they had seen in cities of similar size in any part of the Union. In the evening a grand display of fireworks was witnessed by a vast gathering of people.[123]

As early as 1876, Beaver saw baseball games in a ball diamond located on the west side of town. One team, composed of boys between the ages of fifteen and sixteen, was called the "Rough and Ready." The older team, comprised of twenty-year-old men, was called the "Resolutes." Rules for games were decided upon by the town.

> First, in the delivery of the ball by the pitcher, overhand pitching not being permitted. The hand in making delivery must pass below the hip line. Second, the catcher was required to stand some ten feet behind the batter and take the ball on the rebound. No player was permitted to use a glove or mask. Bare handed he must handle the ball, and be assured it required some pluck.[124]

Frequently the most popular group activities were informal sporting contests. The *Salt Lake Tribune* mentioned one such match:

> A party of Friscoites and Milfordites who are now making the Clift House their headquarters, modest gentlemen, but egotistical enough to believe that they have among their numbers gentlemen of superior athletic ability, and whose proficiency in that line is only overcome by their personal attractions, are soon to have an opportunity to display their prowess at Black Rock or any other place they may select along the Lake Shore, in jumping, running, putting the stone (Caledonia style) or at single handed talking. And while we entertain towards them the highest feelings of friendship, we believe that they will meet their match on the Lake Shore.[125]

Statehood

Beaver celebrated the arrival of statehood for Utah in 1896 by staging a grand parade which began at 10 o'clock and proceeded down Beaver City's Main Street. Clubs and individual citizens drove floats, wagons, and other vehicles along the route. Both city and county officials waved cheerfully to appreciative crowds that lined the streets. "Utah, the Queen of the West" was represented "tastefully" by Sadie Huntington. The bicycle club members fell back three blocks before reaching the meetinghouse which had been artistically decorated. Mayor W. H. Bakes conducted the general meeting, which began with Beaver's band's presentation of military music. Beaver's choir sang, "Utah, the Queen of the West," and Lizzie Nielsen read the proclamation of statehood. Precisely at noon, a salute of forty-five guns echoed through the air.[126]

For John Franklin Tolton, statehood marked the dawning of a new era for Utah and for Beaver County. "For twenty-five years . . . the people had been under the dominance of carpet-bag rule in its most vicious form. Those who came as our rulers were actuated with a spirit of prejudice and often times hatred toward the Mormon people, and under such stress there was little hope for a spirit of amity and 'good Will Toward All Men.'"[127]

County Government Changed with Statehood

Statehood brought a change to county government when the county court was replaced by a three-member commission. The commission met in the commission chamber of the county courthouse. Beaver's County government reflected patterns established by the Utah legislature and supplemented those services provided by the state itself. In some important ways, county government functions as an administrative arm of the state, and in others as an extension of state programs. Article XI of the Utah Constitution described counties as "legal subdivisions of this state."[128] The county acts in a way as an agent, administrating state programs within the county, always bound by state regulations and restrictions. In this same hierarchy of government services, the county enlarges upon city government. The county uses federal grants-in-aid, shared state revenues, county property taxes, the local option sales tax and other fees and license fees gathered locally. These monies are used for internal improvements construction, and control of county roads, sidewalks, ferries, bridges, public buildings, airports, cemeteries, as well as flood control, fire

The courtroom inside the Beaver County Courthouse. (Utah State Historical Society)

protection, mental health, substance abuse services, medical care and welfare services, resource development, and other services. "Among the many things that might be done in and around our city, to assist in beautifying it, is the cleaning and fixing up of our cemetery. The home, or resting place, of our loved ones who have gone before us, we cannot say is much of a credit to the city," one Beaver correspondent to the *Southern Utonia* reminded her fellow citizens.

The Beaver County Courthouse was the scene of much of this activity and activities of the Beaver City Council often overlapped with county projects. In 1889 the county built a reform school to house juvenile delinquents outside the adult jail.[129]

Beaver City passed an ordinance in 1889 restricting the sale of liquor, gambling, and other dubious activities.[130] Animals could no longer run freely down city streets—from then on, cattle, horses, mules, sheep, goats, and hogs could be driven through town toward pastures if carefully monitored. If they were running loose, the town marshall could confiscate them and put them in the pound.[131]

At the end of the century, Beaver County boosters were confident that their future was secure:

> There are prospects ahead of us which, shall they be realized, will cause Beaver to take a front position. With the advent of the railroad and other modern conveniences we can see a future of great prosperity and growth for our city. And those who seize time by the forelock and are preparing for these near events, will be among those who will reap the greater benefits.
>
> Property in this city is being inquired about, the climate, the general surroundings, the business status and all questions that tend to show that Beaver has a name abroad and that cannot be downed but is continually rising into greater prominence.[132]

These optimistic sentiments were shared by many but would be tried by changed economic conditions and a new century.

ENDNOTES

1. *Southern Utonian,* 24 December 1889, 5.

2. J. F. Tolton, *History of Beaver,* (np, nd) 50.

3. United States, Congress, House, 42nd Congress, 2nd Session, 1871–72, House Exec. Doc. 285, Serial 1520, 2.

4. Ibid., 1.

5. United States, War Department, Surgeon General's Office, *A Report on the Hygiene of the United States Army, with Descriptions of Military Posts* (Washington, D.C., 1875), 328; Aird G. Merkley, ed., *Monuments to Courage: A History of Beaver County* (Milford, UT: Daughters of Utah Pioneers, 1948), 30; "Military Forts of the West," *Heart Throbs of the West,* 3 (1941): 174; Orson F. Whitney, *History of Utah* (4 vols., Salt Lake City, 1892–1904), II, 718; United States Congress, Senate, 47th Congress, 2nd Session, 1882–83, Senate Exec. Doc. 45, Serial 2076, 2–3; Thomas G. Alexander and Leonard J. Arrington, "The Utah Military Frontier 1872–1912: Forts Cameron, Thornburgh, and Duchesne," *Utah Historical Quarterly* 32 (Fall 1964): 330–38.

6. Mae Crosby White, "A Brief History of Fort Cameron," manuscript at the Utah State Historical Society.

7. Surgeon General's Office, *Report,* 329–31.

8. "Military Forts," *Heart Throbs,* 3 (Salt Lake City: Daughters of Utah Pioneers), 174–75. War Department, *Report,* (1878), 1, 316.

9. Surgeon General's Office, *Report,* 331.

10. War Department, *Report* (1877), 1: 302, and (1881), 1: 368 ff.

11. Louisa Barnes Pratt, "The Journal of Louisa Barnes Pratt," *Heart Throbs,* 8 (1947): 381- 82.

12. R.C. Drum to R.T. Lincoln, Adjutant General, Washington, D.C., 12 January1883; Robert Todd Lincoln to Chester A. Arthur, Washington, D.C., 18 January 1883; in United States, Congress, Senate, 47th Congress, 2nd Sess, 1882–83, Senate Exec. Doc. 45, Serial 2076, 1–3.

13. The district is about seven miles square and lies upon both flanks of a small range called the San Francisco Mountains.

14. Florence Barnes, interviewed by Rosemary Davies, 25 February 1975, Milford, Utah.

15. *Deseret News,* 30 June 1880.

16. Alton Smith interviewed by Rosemary Davies, 30 September 1978, Milford, Utah.

17. Evan Patterson, "Summary of Beaver County Minutes, 1856–1883," 6, copy in my possession.

18. Essay Caigh, "One of the Places that went up like a Rocket," *Deseret Evening News,* 23 April 1896.

19. Ibid.

20. Merkley , *Monuments to Courage* , 243.

21. George A. Horton, Jr., "An Early History of Milford Up to Its Incorporation as a Town," M.A. thesis, Brigham Young University, 1957.

22. Abstracts in the County Clerk's Office, Beaver, Utah.

23. Florence Barnes Interview, 17.

24. Joe Smith, interviewed by Rosemary Davies, 7 October 1974, Milford, Utah.

25. Ibid.

26. "When the Fabulous Horn Silver Mine Caved In," *The History Blazer,* Utah State Historical Society, n.d., n.p., 1.

27. Frank Robertson (author of *Boom Towns of the Great Basin*) quoted in the *Deseret News,* 8 September 1969.

28. "When the Fabulous Horn Silver Mine Caved In," 2.

29. Fred Hewitt Letters, Utah State Historical Society.

30. Merkley, *Monuments to Courage,* 259.

31. *Salt Lake Tribune,* 1 July 1877.

32. Philip F. Notarianni, "The Frisco Charcoal Kilns," *Utah Historical Quarterly* 50 (Winter 1982): 40–46.

33. Ibid.

34. Nell Murbager, "Forgotten Industry of the West," *Frontier Times,* May 1965, 26.

35. *Utah Mining Gazette,* 25 July 1874, 381.

36. *Tenth Census,* 13, 471. The *Engineering and Mining Journal,* 18 November 1882; 273, described the kilns as well: "Each kiln burns at one time 32 cords of wood, making from 1200 to 1500 bushels of charcoal-pinon pine, at a cost of $6 per cord, being used. It takes from six to ten days to burn a kiln. The company uses about 30,000 bushels of charcoal a month, besides about ten cords of cedar wood per day, at a cost of $3 per cord."

37. John Franklin Tolton, "Memories of the Life of John Franklin Tolton," typescript at the Utah State Historical Society.

38. *The Salt Lake Mining Review,* 30 August 1911, 17.

39. *Rich County Reaper,* 30 August 1937.

40. The Utah Sulphur Industries operated until about 1949. In 1961–62 the Sulphurdale Chemical Company built a new mill for $250,000 and began once again commercial production about 1965.

41. quoted in "History of the Methodist Episcopal Educational Work in Beaver, Utah," *Southern Utonian,* 24 December 1889.

42. *Deseret News,* 4 August 1880.

43. *Southern Utonian,* 14 February 1890.

44. "Record of the County Court, 1856–1883," 403.

45. *Salt Lake Daily Tribune,* 2 August 1881.

46. *Southern Utonian,* 11 July 1889.

47. Ibid., 27 June 1889.

48. *Deseret News,* 21 July 1880.

49. Ibid., 29 September 1880.

50. Cannon received 515 votes, Campbell, 223. Statewide, Campbell received 1,357 votes to Cannon's 18,568.

51. *Deseret News,* 4 August 1880.

52. John Franklin Tolton, *History of Beaver County,* chapter eight.

53. *The Frisco Times,* 15 August 1882.

54. "Memories of the Life of John Franklin Tolton."

55. Ibid., diary entry for 20 June 1891.

56. Ibid.

57. J. M. Tanner, *A Biographical Sketch of John Riggs Murdock* (Salt Lake City: The Deseret News, 1909), 190.

58. See Stewart L. Grow, "The Development of Political Parties in Utah," *Western Political Quarterly* 16 (September 1963): 39–40; G. Homer Durham, "The Development of Political Parties in Utah: The First Phase," *Utah Humanities Review,* 1 (April 1947):, 122–23; Charles C. Richards, *The Organization and Growth of the Democratic Party in Utah, 1847–1896* (Salt Lake City: Sagebrush Democratic Club, 1942).

59. Frank H. Jonas, ed., *Politics in the American West* (Salt Lake City: University of Utah Press, 1969), 359.

60. *Deseret News,* 12 June 1872.

61. *Salt Lake Daily Tribune,* 28 June 1876.

62. Juanita Brooks, *John D. Lee: Zealot, Pioneer Builder, Scapegoat* (Glendale, CA: Arthur H. Clarke, 1961), 335.

63. Ibid., 337

64. Ibid.

65. Ibid., 337–38

66. John D. Lee quoted in Juanita Brooks, *Mountain Meadows Massacre* (Norman: University of Oklahoma Press, 1962), 207.

67. Brooks, *Mountain Meadows Massacre,* 210.

68. Tanner, *John Riggs Murdock,* 171.

69. *Deseret Evening News,* 16 December 1886.

70. Orson F. Whitney, *History of Utah,* 3, 536–37.

71. Tolton, *History of Beaver,* 51–52.

72. Quoted in Lisa Bryner Bohman, "A Fresh Perspective: The Woman Suffrage Assocations of Beaver and Farmington, Utah," *Utah Historical Quarterly* 59 (Winter 1991): 10.

73. *Equal Rights Banner,* undated, 8, in Beaver Suffrage Association Minutes, Special Collections, Harold B. Lee Library, Brigham Young University, Provo, Utah.

74. See Bohman, "The Woman Suffrage Associations of Beaver and Farmington, Utah," 4–21.

75. *The Square Dealer,* 23 March 1877.

76. *The Beaver Chronicle,* 20 January 1879.

77. George Thomas, *The Development of Institutions under Irrigation* (New York: Macmillan Co., 1920), 43.

78. Ibid., 45.

79. See Ibid., 46. This proposition included five basic ideas: "the right to grant preference of use for irrigation; the right to grant a restricted use for power purposes, as in the case of flour and saw mills; the right to limit the amount of water a person or corporation can appropriate; the right to pre-

scribe the territory where the water shall be used; the right to fix the place of usage or the point of diversion which shall not be changed save by permission of the same power that made the grant at the pleasure of the granting power where the flow was not great or not sufficient or not needed."

80. On 9 December 1859 (Beaver County Records), the court ordered the preservation of timber in Beaver's canyons.

81. Evan Patterson, "Summary of Beaver County Minutes," 7.

82. Thomas, *Development of Institutions under Irrigation,* 54.

83. Ibid., 140.

84. Alvaretta Robinson, ed., *They Answered the Call: A History of Minersville, Utah,* (Minersville, UT: Daughters of Utah Pioneers, 1962).

85. David A. Tanner quoted in Horton, "History of Milford," 71.

86. Lucy E.W. Burns, Oral History, interviewed by Jay Haymond, 27 February 1974, Beaver, Utah.

87. *Southern Utonian* 31 October 1889.

88. Ibid., 9 May 1889.

89. Article II, included in "Record of the United Order of Beaver Stake of Zion," typescript on file at the Utah State Historical Society.

90. Record of the United Order of Beaver County of Zion, Beaver City, 12 April 1874, 1, Utah State Historical Society.

91. Ibid.

92. Article XV, in "Record of the United Order of Beaver Stake of Zion."

93. Quoted in Leonard J. Arrington, Feramorz Y. Fox, and Dean L. May, *Building The City of God: Community and Cooperation Among the Mormons* (Salt Lake City: Deseret Book, 1976) 145.

94. Morgan, "Historical Sketch of Beaver County," 22.

95. "Beaver County 1873 Tax Rolls," Beaver County Courthouse.

96. *Deseret Evening News,* 23 April 1896.

97. Bill Wood, Charles K. Jamison, and Randall M. Banks, interviewed by Jay Haymond, 24 February 1977, Minersville, Utah.

98. Robinson and Gillins, *They Answered the Call,* 131.

99. *Deseret News,* 11 February 1880.

100. *Southern Utonian,* 14 November 1889.

101. Ibid., 13 June 1889.

102. Ibid., 27 June 1889.

103. Ibid., 25 April 1889.

104. Tolton, "Memories of the Life of John Franklin Tolton."

105. Merkley, *Monuments to Courage,* 151–54, 243–45.

106. *Southern Utonian,* 30 December 1890.

107. Reinhard Maeser, quoted in Merkley, *Monuments of Courage,* 76.

108. *Southern Utonian,* 20 August 1890.

109. The school district bought the Park School in 1932 and razed it to make room for a play ground.

110. Merkley, *Monuments to Courage,* 82–87.

111. Ibid., 158–159.

112. Ibid., 91–92

113. Tolton, "Memories of the Life of John Franklin Tolton," 6.

114. Merkley, *Monuments to Courage,* 94–95

115. Robinson and Gillins, *They Answered the Call,* 177.

116. *Southern Utonian,* 23 May 1889.

117. Ibid., 19 May 1891.

118. Tolton, "Memories of the Life of John Franklin Tolton," 2.

119. Autobiography of William Booth Ashworth, Vol. I, 22, copy at the Utah State Historical Society Library.

120. Robinson and Gillins, *They Answered the Call,* 184.

121. Ibid., 185–86.

122. Ibid., 182–83

123. Tolton, "Memories of the Life of John Franklin Tolton."

124. Tolton, *The History of Beaver,* 27–28.

125. *Salt Lake Tribune,* 19 July 1881.

126. *Southern Utonian,* 10 January 1896.

127. Tolton, *History of Beaver,* 49–50.

128. *Utah Constitution,* Article XI.

129. *Southern Utonian,* 11 April 1889.

130. Ibid., 27 June 1889.

131. Ibid., 23 May 1889.

132. Ibid., 26 August 1890.

CHAPTER 6

ENTRANCE INTO THE TWENTIETH CENTURY 1900–1920

If you are a stranger within the gates of Zion and wish to make the best use of your opportunities, you will finish up your business during the day, visit some one of the various amusement resorts during the evening, partake of a light repast afterward, then repair to the Salt Lake Route Depot, where you will purchase a ticket via the San Pedro, Los Angeles and Salt Lake Route to Milford.[1]

This flowery travel account of a journey through Beaver County written by A.B. Blainey in 1911 gives a sense that the county held a certain attraction to outsiders. He continues:

In a few minutes, after anointing the porter's palm with a generous piece of silver, you step off the train in the bustling town of Milford near the geographic center of Beaver county. Substantial business houses are in evidence and attractive homes surrounded by growing shade trees, delightfully green, greet the eye. As you stretch your legs and incidently your neck to get a better view of the landscape, a young man with a weather-beaten, but withal a genial countenance, approaches. The young man takes the visitor on a drive through the county introducing him to the various vis-

The west side of the Beaver County Courthouse. (Utah State Historical Society)

tas, and sites, through towns and across the valley floor. When twelve miles out, at the top of a slight raise, a delightful strip of green comes in view, straight ahead. This is Minersville, . . . As the eye shifts from the dusty sage green of the desert, to the vivid coloring of the cultivated land, with its lofty Lombardy poplars latticed with silver streams, it must be concluded that water is the soul of the West.[2]

It wasn't only the land that inspired Blainey with feelings of awe, but efforts at civilizing the area moved him to comment as well. Speaking of Beaver, he said, "Wide streets, magnificent distances, electric lights and cement sidewalks lend a metropolitan air. An afternoon spent in getting acquainted with the people and investigating conditions, impresses you with the possibilities of this valley, instead of 3,000 people Beaver should have 30,000.[3]

As part of the new state of Utah, Beaver County miners and farmers entered the twentieth century optimistic about the future, depending on the area's resources to continue to support their efforts to make livings, run businesses, and improve their communities. In this they were fully in line with the agenda of the Progressive Era—a time when Americans could pay new attention to the quality of life, not just survival. Enthusiastic boosterism benefitted Beaver County towns as they attempted to provide new services for local residents— gas, lights, telephone, and a more consistent water supply.

Beaver's 50th anniversary celebration in the Beaver Stake House in 1906 acclaimed the efforts of the settlement generation. Over the next few years, city government directed a number of city improvement projects—paving sidewalks in District No. 1, building in the southeast part of the city, and installing fire hydrants and drinking fountains in the business section of the city. The city council announced on 5 February 1909 that 2,888 feet of the business district would be paved as a sign of the local commitment to "progress and improvement."[4] The city applied to the Andrew Carnegie Foundation for a $10,000 grant to build a public library. They passed an ordinance prohibiting gambling in town.

Civic leaders in Beaver were painfully conscious of the difficulties created by the distance they had to travel to transport products for trade to Milford and the railroad. Efforts to attract rail lines continued throughout the first two decades of the twentieth century. Locals organized in the Milford and Beaver Railroad Company to build a branch of the railroad to Beaver. W.M. White conducted a survey during the winter of 1901–1902 with the intention of identifying the best route for rail lines through Minersville, Adamsville, and Greenville. The line would have crossed the Beaver River five times and covered 30.62 miles, but was never started.

Two Beaver businesses in the early twentieth century—The Mansfield
Murdock and Company Building, and the J. F. Tolton General Merchandise
Building. (Utah State Historical Society)

While White was carrying out the survey of the long-hoped for
railroad line, an earthquake rumbled throughout southwestern Utah
during the night of 13 November 1901. In Beaver the tremors dam-
aged the church, courthouse, the academy building, and most of the
houses in town. The earthquake also temporarily increased the flow
of water in City, Bullion, Cottonwood, and Beaver creeks as much as
50 percent.[5]

Public Services

As Beaver City entered the twentieth century, civil government
helped provide amenities that raised the standard of living. William
R. Hurst and W.M. White were hired by Mayor Frank D. Farnsworth
and his city council N.P. Ipson, James H. Yardley, S.F. Howd, James
Farrer, and J.E. Bennett to create an updated map of Beaver City for a
fee of $125. This six-by-nine-foot map designated new expanded city
boundaries, school and water fire districts, and monitored growth.
This map is on exhibit at the Beaver Daughters of Utah Pioneers
Museum.

In 1898 the city granted Rocky Mountain Bell Telephone

The southeast corner of Main and Center Streets in Beaver with the Equitable Co-op Building on the corner and the tower of the Beaver County Courthouse in the background. (Utah State Historical Society)

Company a franchise to install a telephone system. Under Mayor Lewis W. Harris in 1904, the first municipal electric light system was installed and a central electrical plant built on the edge of town. Main Street businesses and several homes were supplied with electricity at a time when there were still no paved highways and transportation was still limited to horse drawn buggies and wagons. Minersville obtained electric power a decade after Beaver in 1913–14; however, some locations, like Greenville, did not receive electric power until 1941 and continued to use coal oil lamps for lights long after most homes in the county had electric lights.[6]

Floods were a perpetual problem for each Beaver County town. Every spring Beaver City streets were flooded with irrigation water used by farmers, but because of the nature of the soil the water did not filter down but spread through the streets, creating havoc for the citizenry.[7]

In 1907 businessmen joined forces in a Commercial Club to boost Beaver's image abroad. "Why?" an article in *The Weekly Press* asked. "Because a community needs to advertise its advantages just as much as any merchant, manufacturing institution or other individual enterprise."[8] A community must not hide its "light under a bushel."

> Because Beaver is one of the best towns in Utah naturally and yet hardly any one knows it. Very few people in this state, let alone, those out of the state, know of the excellent lucern, beef, butter, cheese, potatoes, wheat, oats, eggs, poultry, etc., produced here. The same is true of our meadows and pastures which are the most wonderful in many respects in the state, and which can be doubled and trebled as well as not. Beaver is naturally the best dairy town in Utah, admitting the superiority of no other town in the state. But where have you ever read any statement of the fact in the newspapers or any kind of advertising literature?
>
> Because Beaver has not one single manufacturing industry worthy of the name. The woolen mills are sitting up here against the hillside almost begging for some one with a little nerve, energy and capital to make them over into a profitable enterprise employing a large number of people who would live here, spend their money here, and by their taxes and moral support help maintain and increase the efficiency of our schools, town government and every other public utility. The working people of this community wear enough of the coarser grade of shoes to keep a shoe factory of fair size running a good part of the year, and this portion of the state offers a good market for its surplus product. A tannery is one of the crying needs of the community. Our Creamery today cannot come anywhere near producing enough butter and cheese to supply its demand. The list might be enlarged indefinately. Everyone here almost knows of the building rock in our hills, and yet not one soul is trying to find a market for it.[9]

This, then, was seen as the important role to be played by a Commercial Club—advertising Beaver's strengths.

After 1896 fire protection and law enforcement also was regulated by county offices. Beaver, Milford, and Minersville each had a few trucks, and each had a volunteer fire crew. Limited assistance was provided by the forestry and federal fire control programs in times of crisis. The county sheriff's office and the police departments joined forces for law enforcement. Some full-time officers and several part-time officers insured that the county was well regulated.

Murdock Academy. (Utah State Historical Society)

Schools

Both Beaver City and Milford have high schools. Beaver, Milford, and Minersville each have elementary schools. It is interesting that school enrollment declined along with population during each decade of the twentieth century, but at a faster rate.

Despite the reorganization of the districts and construction of new buildings, education in Beaver followed traditional curriculums and required strict discipline in the classroom. John Samuel Hanks was a teacher in Beaver between 1905 and 1915, where he taught at the Belknap School, served as principal, and eventually as County Superintendent of Schools. Former students remembered that under his instruction classrooms were absolutely quiet, no roaming about the room or leaving or speaking was permitted. Ilene Hanks Kingsbury was late for school one day in 1912 when she was in the third grade. She was ushered outside to the entrance of the building with other latecomers. "We became the Awkward Squad!" she later recounted. "We formed a double line and at rigid attention awaited the pleasure of Principal Hanks. When the entire school was quietly settled, then Mr. Hanks stood on the front steps. He was half through

Beaver High School opened in 1920. (Utah State Historical Society)

his lecture before he focused in on me, his oldest, frail girl of eight, afraid to breathe, and on the verge of tears."[10] His daughter, but also a student, the one important lesson she remembered learning in the third grade was to be on time.

In 1908 the school district erected a new $30,000 school in Beaver City. The building included eleven class rooms, offices for the principal and faculty, an auditorium, lavatories, and physical plant. Reflecting the natural environment, the structure's foundation was built with blue lava rock and the building itself with Beaver's locally produced brick and distinctive pink tufa rock trim.[11] The 1914 bill calling for the consolidation of the state's school districts pulled all Beaver County schools into one district. The new board of education superceded the authority of local boards of trustees and received jurisdiction over all school matters. The first board of education included C.F. Harris, E.R. Smyth, W.J. Burns, J.H. Rollins, and R.B. White, with Edgar White serving as superintendent and Gertrude W. Gillies as clerk to the board. When White resigned in 1918, he was replaced by Karl Gilbert Maeser.

On 25 September 1917, Beaver held a special bond election to raise $130,000 for a high school building. Ideally, the bonds would run for twenty years, with an interest rate of 5 percent. The county

A train of ore cars crossing a trestle at Newhouse. (Utah State Historical Society)

voted in favor of the bond, purchased Block 36, and began construction on a building designed by architects Nelson & Ashworth. Members of the board of education who supervised the construction project included William Hurst, John P. Barton, A. L. Dotson, D.K. Barton, and W.J. Barns. The new high school opened September 1920, with C.B. McMullin as principal of the junior high. High school classes did not begin until 1922, when the Murdock Academy closed. At that time H.S. Alvord became the first high school principal.

Railroads

Rumors of the railroad finally coming to Beaver County frequently appeared in local newspapers. If negotiations were successful with Kentucky capitalists, one article maintained, "a steam railway will be built from Milford to Beaver this summer."[12] "It should not take much of an effort to raise the bonus asked for, and the right-of-way is already secured, with good terminal facilities. There is no question but what the road will pay from the start, as a heavy ore tonnage is now in sight."[13] On 14 October 1910, "Railroad for Southern Utah Practically Sure" confidently stated: "The prospects for a railroad into

Beaver are getting brighter all the time. At a meeting which was called by the promoters of the enterprise in Salt Lake last Saturday the sentiments expressed by those present were very encouraging. Men who are recognized authorities in the financial world—Senator Reed Smoot, A. Hanaur, M.H. Walker and a number of others—have signified their intention to become identified with the proposition, and will put considerable money into it. It's up to us to take the initiative and get in on the ground floor."[14] In spite of the high hopes, the railroad was not built.

The one railroad line in Beaver County with its depot at Milford came under the control of the Union Pacific Railroad in 1921. Five hundred miles of railroad owned or being developed by the Oregon Short Line south of Salt Lake City under the San Pedro, Los Angeles, and Salt Lake Railroad was consolidated with the line constructed by Senator William A. Clark of Montana in 1903. Owned by Clark and E.H. Harriman of the Union Pacific and the Oregon Short Line, the company name was changed to the Los Angeles and Salt Lake Railroad Company. In 1921 Senator Clark sold his one-half interest in the stocks and bonds of the Los Angeles and Salt Lake company to the Oregon Short Line, owned by the Union Pacific, which assumed full ownership.

Mining

As Beaver County entered the twentieth century, mining continued to be an important part of the local economy. Samuel Newhouse purchased the Cactus Mine in 1900 under the auspices of the Newhouse Mines and Smelting Corporation operating until 1910 when they reorganized as the South Utah Mines and Smelter Company. Production in the mine began in 1905 and continued until 1909, resulting in the production of 19,419,319 pounds of copper, 7,510 ounces of gold, and 176,365 ounces of silver. Originally powered by a steam plant, eventually electrical equipment and power were furnished by the Beaver River Power Company.

By the 1920s the Horn Silver Mine consisted of the original claim, 1,440 by 600 feet; two five-acre smelter sites located in Frisco; a complete three-stack smelting plant; a refining works located at Chicago, Illinois; iron-flux mines near Frisco; charcoal kilns, a forty

Newhouse, Utah. (Utah State Historical Society)

mile telegraph line to Beaver, two large stores in Frisco, and other less important property.

After putting a new mining shaft in the mine in 1884, the mine continued to produce well. In 1911, however, the Salt Lake Company sold its interest in the enterprise to the New York Mining Company, which sent W. H. Hendrickson from New York to manage the mine and serve as superintendent. He managed the mine until 1943, when the Metal Producers Company of Los Angeles, California, assumed control of the mine under three men: George W. Clemson, general manager; James H. Wren, superintendent; and W.H. Hendrickson, mining engineer.

An article in *The Weekly Press* described the Hub properties finds in the Star District, which had also been surprisingly rich. The article concluded, "Another year will see Beaver County one of the most active mining Sections of Utah, and a goodly tonnage of copper, silver, lead and gold is promised. With men like Samuel Newhouse and the Knights, 'blazing the trail' the results have been assured for sometime past."[15]

Finds on Wild Cat Creek in 1914 sparked more interest in min-

Children in front of the Newhouse School. (Utah State Historical Society)

ing Beaver County's mountains, as well as discoveries in the Sheep Rock Mine at the edge of the valley and at the foot of the same range seven miles south of the Wild Cat and about nine miles northeast of Beaver City. A "stampede" to Fortuna in the Bald Hills, where, according to *The Beaver Press*, "a remarkable series of outcropping ledges in Rocky Hollow were found to pan gold freely," and then discoveries on Mt. Baldy, ten miles east of Sheep Rock and on South Creek, fifteen miles southeast of Beaver City. The Sheep Rock Mine was considered the "star property" of the group in that it had the greatest amount of development work and high grade ore running as high as $1,000 a ton. "This mine is situated about mid way of a series of veins that strike north and south along the foothills of the Tushar mountains and can be traced by their outcroppings for a distance of ten miles." In short, "splendid outcropping veins can be traced along this zone over hill and valley, where never a hole has been sunk, but where the free gold can be panned at a surprising number of places."[16] This mining revival brought new energy into the effort to find further mineral sources and brought Beaver's mines once again to the attention of the international markets.

In April 1915 Potash was discovered near the town of Marysvale.

Residents of Newhouse enjoy some leisure hours. (Utah State Historical Society)

Before the world war, Potash was shipped from Germany. This new source was being tested to determine the quality of the product.[17]

The O.K. Mine was developed by owner Theodore Kronholm and operated by Jesse P. Villars and associates. Lying in an entirely igneous, quartz-monzonite or laccolith ore body, the mine is bordered on the north and west by talisman quartzite of the Pennsylvania Age, and was first opened along a fissure vein striking about N 80 degrees west and dipping to the north at about 60 degrees. The ore from the O.K. Mine was processed at the Milford Smelter; in 1903 thirteen cars of O.K. ore were shipped across the country, flying banners on the box cars labeling the contents as "Beaver County Ore," exhibiting the ore abroad as well before it returned to Milford and sent through the smelter. According to old-timers, this was "the most beautiful ore ever mined."[18]

The Weekly Press predicted that Beaver County was in 1908 about to enter a new period of mining prosperity:

A number of changes are taking place in the mining properties of Beaver county, which are to mean much from a productive
standpoint. Additional equipment is being installed, and operators
are placing large forces of men at work. The Red Warrior property
has recently developed fine ore bodies, and made several consign-
ments of ore to the local market, which tells of the richness of that
product, now being mined.

Superintendent Merritt of the Red Warrior has just purchased
the gasoline hoist plant that was formerly used by the Copper Kinz.
It has been removed to the Red Warrior shaft and is doing its work
nicely. This equipment will give the company ample facilities and
the management intends to have ample tonnage mined and for-
warded to the valley smelters beginning with the latter part of this
week.[19]

Electricity

Electricity first came to Beaver in 1902 when the Pelton Water
Wheel was purchased by Beaver City under Mayor Lewis W. Harris.
The Beaver River Electric Company organized in 1900. After searching for a number of years for a suitable site for a hydroelectric plant,
a site was located where the Beaver River exited Merchant Valley.
From this narrow ledge area, the Beaver River plunged rapidly
through the gorges below. Initially, the survey called for a thirty-four-
inch steel pipe line that reduced in size farther down the mountain.
In January 1904 the Beaver City council and mayor called a public
mass meeting to discuss the hydroelectric plant proposal. They held a
bond election the next week to raise the needed funds to built it. The
mayor and council appointed various committees of local men to
oversee the different jobs for the project. The ditch and bridges committee worked on the power canal. Another constructed the building
to house the electric generator. A third committee dug holes for the
poles, four feet deep for 60 cents a hole; others cut red pine poles
thirty feet long from the east mountains, hauled them into town, and
delivered them to the site where they were to be used. The city paid
them $2.00 a pole. The pole line came down the center of many city
streets. The work commenced in April, and by October Beaver had
electricity. Eventually the Beaver Electric Company used water out of
the LaBaron Reservoir and piped water out of Dry Hollow Canyon.

Inside the Newhouse Power Plant. (Utah State Historical Society)

The electric company built a new dam, pipeline, and station building in 1906. The pipeline from Dry Hollow down to the station again was larger at the top of the line and declined in size by the bottom. There were two generating units in the new power station which produced 90 kilowats of power. Powered with water from the Beaver River diverted by a canal to the site, this plant and distributing system supplied Beaver City until 1927.[20]

The Upper Beaver Power Plant, also known as the Telluride Power Plant, constructed in 1907 by L.L. Nunn, pioneering hydroelectric entrepreneur, was located in Beaver River Canyon about twelve miles east of Beaver. The plant provided a cheap and predicatable source of power for the silver mines and towns nearby. Stimulated in part by Nunn's recognition that the Newhouse mining operation had a deficient steam-generated electrical supply, he surveyed the Beaver River area and located a perfect spot for a hydroelectrical plant.

When Lucien L. Nunn first came to Beaver County in the early 1900s, he had already established his reputation by building the Ames power plant in Telluride, Colorado, and the Olmstead hydroelectric plant in Provo Canyon, Utah. His speciality was high-head hydroelectric technology for small mountain streams. Despite Beaver County's growth during the mining years, its significance as a wool manufacturing center, and its easily accessible markets by rail lines through Milford, it lacked hydroelectric power. For instance, the Newhouse Mines and Smelters Company depended on an unreliable source of power—a steam system fired by coal and wood for electrical power.

Nunn was drawn by the area's potential and sent survey crews into the Tushar Mountains to locate a potential power plant site. Twelve miles to the east of Beaver City in Beaver Canyon, they located a steep incline where several different streams flowed into the Beaver River at a sufficient grade and supply to provide power for several good-sized generators. As a result, Nunn organized the Beaver River Power Company, designated himself as president, and hired a core of engineers who began measuring how water flow varied in different seasons and began drawing up plans for a power plant. A. B. Blainey superintended construction of the dam which began in 1905. Besides the dam, they laid 2.25 miles of wooden pipeline from the reservoir to a riveted steel pentsock or a sluice that guided water to the wheels. The powerhouse itself was built in 1907. Eventually a complex of offices, houses, a boarding house for workers, and shops for the company post made it a self-sufficient company community site, designed by W. H. Lepper, Salt Lake City architect. Using the pink tufa stone so familiar to Beaver residential building, his designs were in the craftsman style with shingled upper walls and roofs. The two turbine-generators sat in a sunken floor area designed to house the transformers, switches, and other equipment. The generators had a total capacity of two megawatts.

The penstock was built in 1908 and was 4,500 long, descending 1,000 feet. At the top the pipe measured twenty-eight inches and twenty at the bottom. The plant began production that same year, transmitting electricity to the Newhouse Mines' Cactus Mill, fifty-three miles away along a 40,000-volt line. Power was distributed from there by substation transformers to the Consolidated Mining Company's Indian Queen operations. Yet another substation transported power to Milford City. Other customers eventually purchased power from the company, including Minersville and Marysvale.

In 1910 the company built smaller diversion dams on three streams that fed into the Beaver River and built feeder lines to the

An early airplane lands at Beaver. (Utah State Historical Society)

main conduit. Although costly, these improvements proved to pay off in terms of increased capacity. That same year the company engineers installed a surge tank at the top of the penstock.

Also important, the Telluride Power Plant became a training institute for electrical engineers learning Nunn's generating and transmission technology. Every summer apprentice engineers and student engineers boarded at the site and received on-site instruction. The Beaver River Power Company and the Southern Utah Power Company combined shortly after World War I to form the Telluride Power Company.[21] Eventually the plant was purchased by Utah Power and Light.

Water

The innovative idea of pumping water was first discussed in Beaver in 1918. The government sank a test well in land near Milford under the supervision of G.C. Haskell. After its success, several wells were drilled throughout the farming area. Milford farmer Charles Baxter was the first farmer to successfully harvest a crop by pumping water.

Beginning in about 1910, the Delta Land and Water Company

began buying land and surveying in anticipation of building yet another dam at Rocky Ford. In 1913–14, the company constructed the Rocky Ford Dam in 1913 at the head of Minersville Canyon, and much of the land between Minersville and Milford was purchased by the company. During that first summer they sold 14,000 acres of land and water but were unable to establish water rights for farmers farther down the river. During the 1920s, the Delta Land and Water Company assumed water rights from Minersville. And the next year the Rocky Ford Irrigation Company purchased existing rights from individuals in the Lower Valley. When the Telluride Power Company built a line through the area in 1920, pumping wells offered a consistent water supply. In addition to alfalfa seed, grain, corn, and potatoes were also grown. Between 1920 and 1929, another sixty wells were drilled.

In 1919 the state legislature appropriated funds to support research of alternate sources of water for irrigation from wells. Tests were conducted in various areas to determine if underground water was sufficient to create a flow for irrigation purposes, and to investigate what types of wells and well casings would best facilitate the maximum flow of water. They found that formations at about sixty to seventy feet could produce 400 gallons per minute, which was more than enough for a very good irrigation stream. In 1920 fifteen wells were drilled in the district and the Telluride Power Company constructed a power line seven miles through the district's center.[22]

Animal and Predator Control

Rabbit control was frequently mentioned in both county and city council minutes as a principal concern of local farmers. The ingenious methods for trapping, slaughtering and diverting rabbits ranged from the practical to the ridiculous. Bill Woods and Charles Jamison remembered a time when the problem was so serious in Minersville that the town held a mass meeting where they decided to fence the fields of the entire community with special rabbit guards.

> Their stockade fence around there to keep the other stock out was a rip gut fence, . . . made out of cedar posts and limbs, and well, some of that old fence is intact today down on my farm. And then on the outside of this rip gut fence, they cut small cedars and cedar

limbs or anything that could be stood on end and made a solid fence right around the whole Minersville. It took women, kids and everything.[23]

According to Jamison, the rabbits got so bad, they were trying to break into the barns and feed storage sheds. So "the people cut some holes through and dug a pit, and then the rabbits would try to go through that hole, and they'd fall down in the pit, and then they'd have to make a trip around that fence and kill the rabbits and get rid of them."[24] Sometimes they would kill as many as 500 rabbits in a single night.

At other times coyotes would plague Minersville farmers, roaming their fields and sometimes coming into town. Animal life, like the agriculture itself, was affected by drought cycles. Oldtimers remembered times when wild horses ran thick in the mountain valleys and then cycles when cougars or coyotes were thick and would eat the colts, a condition which Bill Woods described as making "a balance in nature."[25] Antelope and deer seemed to run in cycles as well.

Agriculture

Farming changed during the 1900s, largely driven by continuing problems with water. The Beaver Arid Farm Company organized in February 1907 with a group of solid businessmen at its core—J.M. Murdock, C.E. Murdock, C.D. White, D.A. McGregor, N.P. Ipson, G.B. Greenwood, J.T. Tanner, J.F. Jones, and H.A. White. The group secured 4,000 acres of land on Indian Creek and in Wild Cat from the state—arid land that they intended to make "blossom like a rose." To do so, the company purchased a thirty-two h.p. traction engine, a Reeves double-cylinder type capable of drawing eighteen plows and turning forty-five acres per day. The engine would also be used to transport fuel from Milford.

Local farmers would build and maintain canals, first clearing them with plows pulled by horses and then lining them with stones or hard-packed earth. Eventually, they paved them with cement. Regardless of the precautions they took in the preparation of canals, in Minersville sometimes floods would carry gravel and debris into town.

The Farmer's Institute sponsored a series of speakers—professors

Mechanized farm equipment brought major changes to agriculture in Beaver County during the first decades of the twentieth century. (Utah State Historical Society)

from the state's universities to introduce the latest techniques in dry farming, reclamation, and irrigation techniques.[26] They conducted a dry land experimental farm to discover the best methods of raising grain in local conditions.

David A. Tanner remembered that his father would transport water from the Beaver River to irrigate their family farmland. Before the reservoir was built, the water would often flood the land, "so thick and heavy down here in the north part of Hall's field that sometimes cattle would dig right in there and almost hide up away from me."[27] This flood cycle would influence the crops his father would plant. "Well, father tried alfalfa, but the first year it would come all right, and then it would drown out, but he raised corn, potatoes, oats and different things of that kind and grass hay, such as red top and timithy [sic] and clover and so on, and fields to haul it in and hundreds of loads every year."[28]

A group of Beaver County residents gather around an early tractor. (Utah State Historical Society)

An informative editorial appeared in the *Beaver County News* during 1913 which identified the important link between mining and agriculture. Recognizing that mining was the dominant and perhaps flashier producer of wealth for the county, the author described the mining companies and their workers as "patrons" of husbandry. Mining pumped needed revenues into local markets for supplies and agricultural produce. Therefore, he writes, it is important to focus attention on developing new sources of water—determining underground water flow. "There is no mistaking the facts, however, that a great acreage now barren can be made productive by the application of water that has been going to waste." At that time government engineers were conducting a study of 15,000 acres.[29]

In 1910 Beaver County had a total 319 farms with a total acreage of 45,986.[30] The average value of the typical farm was $7,123. Ninety-five percent of them were irrigated by a system of canals with water furnished by streams. A proposed reclamation project would make productive land that in 1913 was covered with sagebrush in part by the construction of a reservoir that would impound 27,000 acre feet of water. In addition, its potential for grazing could be augmented. Another similar project was organized by George A. Snow and W.I. Moody of Salt Lake City who proposed investing a million dollars in a dam, reservoir, and ditches to reclaim 48,000 acres near Adamsville.[31]

John R. Murdock and John C. Murdock were among the first promoters of the Beaver Bottoms project. Both homesteaded property in the area. Other individuals who farmed there were Jim Curfew, George Hardy, John Andrew Smyth, William Armstrong, Joe Hickman, John C. White, John Ashworth, Jim Robinson, W.S. Bond, and Nels Schow.

What made this effort different was that the water for irrigation was pumped out of wells dug deep beneath their fields. After dismal failures with dry farming, subirrigation yielded good crops of hay, wild hay and alfalfa seed. By 1920 farmers were typically making between $6,000 and $7,000 yearly on their alfalfa crop.

Creameries

Thomas Cartwright lived at and ran the creamery located in the old Slaughter Tannery building in 1902. He ran the business for nine years, producing various cheeses and butter. Daily production from the herds at Beaver, Greenville, and North Creek was estimated at 1,200 to 1,400 pounds except during peak seasons of June, July, and August when production reached 4,000 pounds daily. Butter fat was sold during that time for fifteen and sixteen cents a pound.

Gunner Gunderson operated the creamery after Cartwright until it became more popular for farmers to use separators and ship the cream to Salt Lake City and other markets. Some dairymen continued in the traditional industry to churn and package butter locally and ship it to Milford, Frisco, and other mining centers in the area. In 1913 Thomas Cartwright joined with Warren Shepherd and Lester E. Harris to organize the Beaver Valley Creamery on the Shepherd Farm west of town.[32] The plant processed milk from Beaver and other town herds nearby.

The Forest Service and Natural Resources

In 1902 chief grazing officer Albert F. Potter of the Department of the Interior's Division of Forestry came to Utah to conduct a sur-

vey of natural resources and begin an era of public management of
natural resources. His exploration took five months and led eventually to the establishment of a series of forest reserves in the state.
Potter's interests included ecological balance, conservation, and the
relation of forest resources to the social needs of Utah's population,
and was pragmatic in its orientation.[33] He studied among other
things the relationship of grazing and livestock to the mountain forest areas. In fact, a compelling interest of Potter's was the potential
for stock raising on mountain range land. The mountains were an
important resource for both irrigation and stockraising. Opinions
varied according to geography about Potter's findings. Stockmen in
Beaver County, perhaps because they had not experienced a shortage
of timber or had problems with watershed, were generally opposed
to the idea of conservation. Economic investment in the sheep industry seemed to determine public opinion more than any single factor.
A commitment to private ownership also was a significant factor.
Repeatedly Potter was told that selling public lands was the best solution to overgrazing and management problems. His report helped
form the base for land use decisions and policies during the next several decades.

One of the decisions influenced by Potter's report was the creation of the Fillmore Forest Reserve in May 1906. The reserve later
became the Fillmore National Forest, then the Fishlake National
Forest. Most of the western slope of the Tushar Mountains in Beaver
County was included in the reserve. Initially headquarters for the
Fillmore Forest Reserve were in Beaver with William Hurst the first
forest supervisor. Later, because of consolidation measures, the headquarters moved to Richfield. While there was some resistance to the
establishment of the national forests, many local people signed petitions calling for federal action as the last resort in dealing with the
serious problems of over-grazing, erosion, loss of valuable timber
resources, and destruction of watersheds.

Every county in Utah contains government-owned land—in
some places the land surrounding schools and public buildings,
alongside roads or parks. But in Beaver County large proportions of
county land are owned by the federal government and managed by
the Bureau of Land Management (BLM) and the Forest Service.

The Public Lands Grazing Issue and the Taylor Grazing Act provided guidelines for the organization of public lands for stock raising. The Taylor Grazing Act sought "to stop injury to the public grazing lands by preventing overgrazing and soil deterioration; to provide for their orderly use, improvement, and development; [and] to stabilize the livestock industry dependent upon the public range" by leasing the public domain to stockraisers. Although much of the county's land was arid, broken, mountainous, it was perfect for grazing. Overgrazing the public domain had always been a concern to local stockraisers.

The Reclamation Act of 1902 was based on the experience of the Mormons with irrigation. This law provided for the construction of federal irrigation projects in western states and territories with monies from the sale of public lands. According to irrigation historian George Thomas, "The federal government supplies the capital for construction, and the costs are paid back, without interest, over an extended period of time."[34] Construction and management of such projects came under the jurisdiction of the Reclamation Service, later called the Bureau of Reclamation. The Bureau of Reclamation was responsible for the investigation of irrigation resources, preparation of plans, construction, operation, and maintenance of irrigation projects, including power development, and the administration of funds for such projects. J.R. Alexander of Salt Lake City was the district counsel for projects in Beaver County. In 1920 the Mineral Leasing Act changed the disposal of oil and gas, coal, and other minerals to leasing. The Bureau of Mines was given responsibility for these programs.

Politics

Beaver County remained predominantly Democratic during the first four decades of the twentieth century, and in 1912 one of the local party stalwarts, John Franklin Tolton, was selected as the Democratic party nominee for governor of Utah. Tolton recounted his nomination and the election battle.

When the 1912 State convention was called, my name became prominently mentioned for the Governorship. Realizing that such a nomination and expense of statewide campaign meant that

Beaver's Carnegie Library built in about 1915. (Utah State Historical Society)

expenditure of considerable money, I was in no sense enthusiastic, but allowed the movement to proceed of its own volition. After a hard contest wherein several prominent Democrats were arrayed against me, the nomination was accorded me amidst much acclaim. In the campaign which followed, the newspapers, being all Republican, waged a war against me personally, being so biased politically that my speeches were allowed to pass unnoticed. Governor William Spry, who was my chief opponent, was well fortified, having all of the State political machinery back of him through the influence of his appointments, and won out in the race, defeating me by a small margin, only about 5,000 votes. Residing as I did, more than two hundred miles from the more thickly populated sections of the state, many regarded my race as quite marvelous.[35]

Tolton's opponent, William Spry, won the election with 42,552 votes to 36,076 for Tolton. Among the reasons for Tolton's defeat was his campaign against an incumbent—Spry had defeated the popular Mormon mining magnate Jesse W. Knight in the 1908 election and, as Tolton observed, had the advantage of political appointments in place to assist with the campaign. Nevertheless, Tolton did

Murdock Academy Musicians in 1912. (Utah State Historical Society)

better in the 1912 election than had Jesse Knight who lost the 1908 election by a vote of 52,913 to 43,266. William Spry, a resident of Tooele County, was a close associate of Reed Smoot—the LDS church apostle, Republican, and United States Senator from Utah. During his first term as governor, Spry created a state road commission, obtained authorization to begin construction of the State Capitol building, and campaigned for tax reforms. During the 1912 election, Spry campaigned effectively for William Howard Taft, the Republican nominee for president. Taft won in Utah by 42,013 votes over Democrat Woodrow Wilson 36,579 votes and Progressive candidate Theodore Roosevelt's 24,171. In the three-way presidential battle, Taft carried only Utah and Vermont, while the split vote between Republicans and Progressives sent the presidency to Woodrow Wilson. In addition to Spry and Tolton, there were two other candidates in the 1912 election: Nephi Morris, who ran on the Progressive ticket and received 23,590 votes, and Homer P. Burt, who, as the Socialist candidate, received 8,797 votes. The votes for the Progressive and Socialist candidates likely hurt Tolton and helped Spry win a second term, as did the lack of newspaper support as recognized by Tolton.[36]

Life in Beaver County

The largest decade of growth in population was between 1900 and 1910, when the population increased by 30.6 percent. Beaver County's population peaked in 1920, with a total of 5,136 residents. This represented an increase of 9 percent increase from the preceding year, and was 1.1 percent of the state's total population. By 1940 the population had again dropped, this time to 5,014.

Lucy E.W. Burns described a typical farm at the turn of the century, that of her father, Hyrum Alonzo Walker.

> His farm was about three miles from west of town, besides our home in Minersville, which consisted of 1/4 block where we had a large barn and other out buildings. We kept a few chickens, pigs, cows, and horses, so there was always plenty of work for every one. We also had a vegetable garden, a small patch of alfalfa and some fruit trees. I remember a man who was admiring his beautiful garden one day who asked where his weeds were? My father replied that weeds didn't grow in his garden.[37]

Burl Ashworth was Beaver's ice supplier. Families would bring their wagons to Ashworth's ice house where he would dig a large block of ice out of the sawdust, and with a large cross cut saw he would cut off what he needed. Ashworth's house was near a pond near the city park. During February he would cut the ice at the pond, haul it to his ice house, and lay it with sawdust until his ice house was full.

Most homes were heated by coal or wood burning stoves and were extremely cold during the winter months. One woman remembered the back of her nightgown being scorched from backing up against the fire to get warm and that the bread would be frozen in the morning and the water frozen.[38]

Fire heating created perpetual problems with fire control. On 9 July 1915, *The Weekly Press* reported a fire on Main Street in Beaver City at the New York Store that totally destroyed the structure. Shortly after the fire erupted, owner E. Papkin left the building after having tried to douse the blaze. As neighbors were confused about how to open and use the fire hydrants, the fire went on without interruption until the building was completely lost. By the time the fire-

The Beaver Hospital. (Utah State Historical Society)

man arrived, their primary attention was spent preventing neighboring buildings from also burning.[39]

Diseases spread through whole communities quickly and created danger not unlike uncontrolled fires. In Greenville, in 1900, a case of smallpox caused neighbors to take precautions against contact with those outside their families. "That dread disease," an article in *The Weekly Press* announced, "has been traveling throughout the state and finally made its way to Beaver County." The same article quoted the state constitution, empowering the State Health Inspector to call quarantines and take extraordinary measures in the containment of communicable diseases.[40]

Smallpox was a feared disease, and when it struck, precautions were taken to quarantine the victims. In 1903 a small pox epidemic broke out in Minersville, Milford, and other isolated places in Beaver County. William J. Burns, the husband of Lucy Elizabeth Burns, was stricken with smallpox at Milford in April 1904. He came home from teaching school one day feverish and sick to his stomach. He tried to fight it by taking a long walk and eating lemons which he had an odd craving for. Within a few days he was extremely ill and covered with pox marks. After diagnosis by a doctor, it was clear that Burns could not remain in the house with his family nor complete his teaching assignment for the rest of the school year. His wife recalls:

> He took his fathers bedding which was stored in a large piano box out in the yard, which included some bed springs and feather bed. A tent was put up in the back yard and this is where he stayed until he got better. His food was taken out and set on a bench near the tent and he would have to get it there. He was very ill for several days so it was quite an effort for him to get up, but he did, so I wouldn't know that he was so bad. It was very painful, especially when the pox was trying to come through the callouses on the bottoms of his feet and the palms of his hands. . . . We were quarantined and everyone was very frightened. People would walk by on the opposite side of the street. Even the country doctor, Fennemore, wouldn't go in to see my husband, but brought some ointment or something to rub on his face and body, handing it over the fence to him. He made the remark that he looked like a real plum pudding. It was true that he looked just awful. His hair standing up, his face blue and swollen with pox marks, which looked like oatmeal splattered all over it. I don't think that anyone would have recognized him, had they not known he was there.[41]

The quarantine lasted for one month.

In 1905 an outbreak of scarlet fever was announced in the paper as "alarming." State health inspector Woodard arrived in Beaver in August 1905 to visit 250 homes, enumerating cases of scarlet fever. He encouraged families to cooperate with quarantines, and to exercise common sense.[42] Most public gatherings were canceled during the outbreak.[43]

Baseball and dancing continued to be the hands-down favorite social activities in this rural county. David A. Tanner remembered dances held in the school hall. "The school halls was partitioned. They laid the partion and two big doors, and they'd open them up, and there's where they'd dance. And they'd dance in the Williams' home up here. Up at the Williams home they could get down there and put on four or five different sets at a time in the big dining room. Johnson from Rush Lake and a man from Parowan used to come over here and Marge Stoddard used to play the organ. One of them would play the piccolo and one would play the violin . . . They'd go

Young ladies exercising in front of the Murdock Academy. (Utah State Historical Society)

over there and sometimes they'd forget when daylight come. They was still dancing."[44] After its construction in 1908, the Beaver Opera House became a popular location for dances, especially on Friday nights. Masquerade and costume dances were also popular, especially in Milford where they were held in the school house, Williams Hotel, and other locations.

According to one observer of local culture, in a letter written to editor D.I. Frazer of *The Weekly Press,* changing dance and dress styles, including bathing suits, reflected an evolution that is "only natural." Reacting to some expression of public outrage, she stated her belief that public condemnation is also natural because, on the inside, people secretly wished that they had the "courage to attempt such actions!"[45]

The first county fair was held 1905, the last week of June. Agricultural and mining exhibits, games, food booths and dances offered a variety of entertainments. Prizes were given for the best draft horses, dairy cows, hogs, home made butter, and "best sacked garden peas" among other agricultural produce.[46]

A crowd gathers in front of the Beaver Opera House. (Utah State Historical Society)

The year 1914 marked the arrival of the "agitated film." The Beaver Opera House offered films including, *When Rome Ruled, The Reign of Terror,* and *The Perils of Pauline.*[47] One of the largest and most popular celebrations held in the county was the Labor Day festival featuring food, athletic events, music and dancing, and animal races.[48] Chautauquas were held annually at the Opera House. These week-long festivals centered on theatrical performances, music, and orations.[49]

The Opera House, completed in 1908, was a material statement of Beaver County's assumption that it would be the center of Utah's cultural life for the lower half of the state. Supported by town leaders R.R. Tanner, G.N. Greenwood, D.I.Frazer, J.P. Barton, J.R. Murdock, A.J. Hardy, and W. J. Robinson, the architectural design was created by Liljenberg and Maeser. This three-story building was constructed for $20,000, with a dance pavilion on the first floor, an auditorium and stage on the second, and a third-floor balcony. Built of local pink tufa quarried stone, its style was Classical Revival with huge Roman arches, massive round columns, and rectangular piers flanking the dramatic entry steps leading to the front doors. At the

The Isis Theater and Progress Meat Market in Beaver. (Utah State Historical Society)

top of each column is a monumental entabulature with a decorative frieze and ornate cornice.

Important for years as a community center, the Beaver Opera House was the scene for vaudeville performers shows like Ralph Cloniger, Luke Cosgrave, Shelby Roach, and Walter Christensen. Eventually it was renovated into a motion picture theater and was sold to the National Guard in 1929 which used it until 1955.

Roosevelt Hot Springs, located about twelve miles northeast of Milford was developed as a resort by P.B. McKeon family in 1910. The McKeons built a large swimming pool, bath houses, and raised several hundred chickens, some of which were cooked for special occasions and Sunday dinners for which the resort was well-known. Because there were no telephones at the springs, reservations would be taken at various businesses in Milford and relayed to the McKeons and their workers when they came to town for supplies. Some visitors suffering with rheumatism stayed for a week or ten days, taking baths daily in the hot natural spring waters. The resort operated from 1910 to 1912, however P.B. McKeon continued to live at the springs until his death in 1927.[50]

On 29 December 1902, the Beaver Masonic Lodge organized with Grand Master Ephraim Homer, Grand Secretary W.J. Moore, and A.B. Cline, W.S. Keesee, and W.S. Thompson. Fifteen men were inducted the first night. Originally meeting in the Thompson Building, the lodge eventually moved to the Low Building.[51] Young men participated in the scouting program. Each week, *The Weekly Press* featured a column devoted to the scouting program, making appeals for support, leadership, reporting on projects and accomplishments of the boys.

While attending a ball at the Odd Fellows Hall, the family of Jas. A. Hutchings was robbed. The first to arrive home was Albert, who had returned home because of a bloody nose. As he stumbled through the house in the dark, he noticed the outline of a figure standing in the shadows of the room. Albert wrestled the man to the ground and ended up with a deep gash on his scalp from a knife wound.[52]

The juvenile court began meeting in Beaver City in 1908 with Judge Greenwood presiding over juvenile proceedings. Probation officer John Barton appeared with three young men who had reportedly stolen eggs from a barn and had thrown them at people walking down the street. The judge told the probation officer to visit their homes, watch their conduct, and return and report in a month.

Liquor licenses were both a means of controlling alcohol consumption and a good source of revenue for local governments. Where John Ashworth had been granted an unconditional liquor license in 1860 for $10 a year, by 1909 the license cost $800 a year, paid in quarterly installments of $200. In order to retain the license, saloon proprietors had to make sure that there was " . . . no gambling at place of business, no liquor sold to habitual drunkards nor to minors, nor enough sold to any customer to make him drunk; no blinds, benches, or chairs to be allowed in the saloon, and the doors to be closed from 10 P.M. to 7 A.M. and all day Sunday."[53]

News of local and national events was printed throughout these years in *The Beaver Press* published first by Robert Shelton as manager and O.A. Whitaker as editor until 25 November 1904, and David I. Frazer and Sons, as publishers until 1916. Between 1916 and 1920, the paper was run by Karl S. Carlton.

The Bank of Milford. (Utah State Historical Society)

Physically Milford changed little during the first decades of the twentieth century. Telephone service came to Milford in 1902, with Lottie Barton Bardsley as the town's first operator. A petition for incorporation circulated during 1903. One hundred and forty-one of Milford's 172 inhabitants signed the document received by the county commission in November. E.S. Sawyer became the first town president, with Arvin M. Stoddard, then seventy-eight years old, Angus Buchanan, J.L. Tanner, and James Forgie as trustees. One of the first orders of business was selecting a town marshal and establishing ordinances for disturbing the peace. The first Sunday School union of the Methodist church was organized 7 July 1905 by Reverend D.E. Carter.

Spanish American War

A few men from Beaver County volunteered for the brief Spanish American War in 1898. John Frank Tolton recruited volunteers to serve under Theodore Roosevelt's command in the Rough Riders. In the spring of 1898, Orson P. Allred, Lorenzo Bohn, Wilford

Beaver veterans of World War I in front of the newly dedicated Dough boy statue on Memorial Day 1927. (Merle Lessing)

Cartwright, Robert B. Findlay, Stephen H. Fotheringham, Harry Harris, John Mathews, George Roosevelt, Joseph Robinson, Joseph Skinner, and Arthur Smith volunteered. Regardless of their willingness to serve, this group of locales arrived in Jacksonville, Florida, after the war ended. Nonetheless, they were honorably discharged and returned home in July 1898.[54]

World War I and the Flu Epidemic

World War I was another matter. The United States entered World War I in April 1917, a conflict that had erupted in Europe with the assassination of Archduke Francis Ferdinand, heir to the Austria-Hungarian throne, and in his wife, Sophie, in Sarajevo in June 1914. Beaver residents shared the majority opinion that the United States should remain neutral and avoid involvement in the conflict if at all possible. However, when the United States declared war on Germany in April 1917, young men from the county served in the armed forces and families adjusted to the loss of manpower on their farms and local businesses. Beaver residents supported the United States commitment to "fight the war to end all wars" and "make the world safe for democracy." Representative of this patriotism are the statements of John Franklin Tolton, a Beaver County Democrat who was elected to his fourth term in the state house of representatives in November 1916. During the 1917 he was selected as Speaker of the House of Representatives, and on the eve of war with Germany he reported:

> Before the close of the Legislature in March, while Germany was heaping indignities upon us, and we were hesitating about entering the war, I made some timely remarks, upon the floor of the House, about our duties in the premises, which quite electrified members and visitors, and led to a speedy conclusion of the debate.
>
> When we had fully entered into the arena of the World War, and organization of our forces as a State began, the responsibility of Chairman of the County Council of Defense fell upon me. I continued so to act until the termination of the War in November 1918. Every drive for money and man power was fully met, and that speedily, by my department, for which prompt service we were fittingly complimented.[55]

A Beaver County Council of Defense was set up soon after entrance into the war. This group organized local efforts in preparation. They included the following: J.F. Tolton, chair and finance; D. Frazer, secretary-treasurer, publicity; Russell E. Parsons, legal; Dr. Jos. T. McGregor, sanitation and medicine; Henry Frazer, food supply and conservation, industrial survey; William Hurst, labor; R.H. Strickland, vice-chair, military affairs; J.H. Barton, state protection; George Jefferson, transportation; H.T. Hanks, survey of man power; W. J. Burns, George Marshall, Mrs. Margaret Murdock, women's work.

The Council of Defense set up a committee on child welfare to insure that children would not be neglected during the war. The national slogan of such groups was: "Save a hundred thousand babies and give the children a square deal." The group had four basic goals: (1) to protect women during periods of maternity, children during infancy; (2) to encourage mothers to care for elder children usually left to fend for themselves; (3) to enforce child labor laws, compulsive education laws; and (4) to provide recreation for all children.

A welcome to members of the 145th Artillery Regiment of the Utah National Guard. (Utah State Historical Society)

Members of this committee included representatives of the P.T.A., the school board, and local women's clubs.

R.H. Strickland headed the county food administration committee. He traveled throughout the county, held meetings, and supervised the observance of food regulations. He distributed rationed food products, like sugar. Chesley Barton was the county fuel administrator. His principal duty was monitoring coal traffic.

Some people of Beaver County contributed to the war fund. The county also contributed foodstuffs to be distributed in supply stations in Europe. Red Cross units engaged local women in preparations for relief work. Classes in elementary nursing were held locally. There women made bandages of old cloth to be sent to European medical units. Beaver County women and children conducted clothing drives to gather clothing, blankets and other supplies to be sent abroad

Beaver County's young men started to leave for service in Europe during April 1917, and by the end of the war at least 256 Beaver County residents saw military service including 130 from Beaver, 82 from Milford, 28 from Minersville, 9 from Adamsville and 7 from Greenville. Five men lost their lives in military service, including

Downtown Beaver. (Utah State Historical Society)

Joseph M. Martinez of Beaver who was killed in Germany in November 1918; James Gilbert Yardley, who died in a hospital in France after combat service in the Argonne Forest; William Wallace Ipson, a sniper with the Marines who became a casualty on the high seas off Brest, France; Rural King Dorrity, who died of influenza on 23 October 1918 and Leroy Q. Eyre of Minersville who died of unidentified causes. Two Beaver residents, Roland G. Nowers and Bert Swindlehurst, were wounded in combat and spent several months in government hospitals.[56]

All Utah men inducted into service left Utah to be trained at Camp Lewis on American Lake in Washington State. Most of them were in the 362nd Infantry. The division landed in France on 22 July 1918. There they stayed first at Chaumont and other locations in rugged battle camps, hiking over hills and through marshes nearby.

After their division disbanded, their commander, Major General Johnston, wrote Utah governor Simon Bamberger a letter praising their performance.

> The people of Utah have reason to be proud of the record made by their representatives in the Ninety first division. It has been a plea-

sure to command men of this kind. They have demonstrated that no better soldiers exist than can be made of young American citizens. They will return to their civil pursuits, not only with the experience gained as soldiers, but will return better citizens because of their service during the war. They have learned how to command and how to obey; how to bear with fortitude the unavoidable inconveniences and even sufferings of the campaign. I congratulate you upon the return of such men to the citizenship of your state, and with equal sincerity I part with them with genuine regret.[57]

When the "doughboys" returned from Europe after the war, Beaver City had a pageant in the Beaver Opera House commemorating their brave efforts. Organizers included the Boy Scouts, R.H. Strickland, Margaret Murdock, Laura Shepard, and Dr. Gibson. The program was based on a series of tableaus representing the "great" moments in American armed forces history.[58]

During and just after the war, many both in Europe and at home suffered with the Spanish Flu epidemic which was felt in every Beaver County town. Thirteen-year-old Florence Barnes remembered how in 1918 it seemed that virtually everyone was sick with high temperatures and congested lungs. Treatments included mustard plasters and bed rest. Many died from the flu, including Florence's father. Another woman, Rosemary Davis's mother, remembered that when she was a little girl, "a wagon that would come by everyday and pick up the dead. They would just put them out the door. Everybody was afraid to go anywhere. They were afraid to buy groceries. . . . they would call the flu wagon and pick up the bodies that were left on the front steps."[59] A volunteer crew drove through Beaver County towns to pick up the dead, according to Alton Smith. "I think that they got so scared that if they got that flue [sic], they thought they were going to die. I think that's what killed a lot of them, fear."[60] Smith remembered, "They used to quarantine all the time when I was a kid. If you had measles or anything, they usually locked you in the house for three weeks. I don't care whether you'd had it or not." The family would post a sign on their front door warning of the quarantine. Groceries would be dropped off on the porch.

With a world war concluded, and the threat of a catastrophic influenza epidemic diminishing, Beaver County residents, as did their fellow citizens throughout the country, looked forward to a return to what newly elected President Warren G. Harding called "normalcy." Little did they realize that the next decades would bring the worst economic crisis in America's history and involvement in another world war that would take Beaver County's sons and daughters back across the Atlantic to North Africa, the British Isles, and Europe, as well as to the islands of the Pacific.

ENDNOTES

1. 1 A.B. Blainey, "A Trip into Beaver County," *The Arrowhead* (August 1911): 61.

2. Ibid.

3. Ibid.

4. *The Weekly Press* (Beaver, Utah), 5 February 1909.

5. Dale Morgan, "Historical Sketch of Beaver County," 28–29.

6. Arid G. Merkley, ed., *Monuments to Courage: A History of Beaver County* (Milford, UT: Beaver County Chapter of the Daughters of Utah Pioneers, 1948), 161, 220.

7. *The Weekly Press,* 5 February 1909.

8. Ibid., 24 May 1907.

9. Ibid.

10. Ilene H. Kingsbury, "The Life and Times and Teaching Career of John Samuel Hanks," typescript, Utah State Historical Society, 9–10.

11. *The Weekly Press,* 8 July 1908.

12. Ibid., 3 April 1908.

13. Ibid.

14. Ibid., 14 October 1910.

15. Ibid.

16. *The Beaver Press,* 10 July 1931.

17. *The Weekly Press,* 2 April 1915.

18. *The Beaver Press,* 22 February 1946.

19. *The Weekly Press,* 21 August 1908.

20. *The Beaver Press,* 12 December 1948.

21. In 1958 Utah Power and Light bought Telluride Power.

22. Merkley, *Monuments to Courage,* 358.

23. Bill Woods, Charles Jamison, and Randall Banks, oral interview.

24. Ibid.

25. Ibid.

26. *The Weekly Press,* 22 December 1905.

27. David A. Tanner, interviewed by Gladys Whittiker, 12 October 1974, Beaver, Utah.

28. Ibid.

29. "Beaver County Resources," *Beaver County News,* 1913, Clipping File, USHS.

30. Ibid.

31. Ibid.

32. Later this became the site of the Brooklawn Creamery owned after 1936 by investers from Salt Lake City.

33. See Charles S. Peterson, "Albert F. Potter's Wasatch Survey, 1902: A Beginning for Public Management of Natural Resources in Utah," *Utah Historical Quarterly* 39 (Summer 1971): 238–50. Thomas Alexander, "The Powell Irrigation Survey and the People of the West," *Journal of the West* 7 (January 1968): 48–53; and Thomas Alexander, "John Wesley Powell, the Irrigation Survey, and the Inauguration of the Second Phase of Irrigation Development in Utah," *Utah Historical Quarterly* 37 (Spring 1969): 190–206.

34. George Thomas, *The Development of Institutions under Irrigation* (New York: Macmillan Co., 1920), 33.

35. John Franklin Tolton, "From the Halls of Memory," chapter thirty-one, typescript at the Utah State Historical Society Library.

36. Allan Kent Powell, "Elections in the State of Utah," *Utah History Encyclopedia* (Salt Lake City: University of Utah Press, 1994), 189 and William L. Roper and Leonard J. Arrington, *William Spry: Man of Firmness, Governor of Utah* (Salt Lake City: Utah State Historical Society, 1971), 110.

37. Lucy E.W. Burns, interviewed by Jay Haymond, 27 February 1974, Beaver, Utah.

38. Florence Barnes, interviewed by Rosemary Davis, 25 February 1975, Milford, Utah, 10.

39. *The Weekly Press,* 9 July 1915.

40. Ibid., 7 April 1900.

41. Lucy Elizabeth Walker Burns, interviewed by Marian Sund, 22 February 1974 Utah State Historical Society.

42. *The Weekly Press,* 18 August 1905.

43. Ibid., 28 July 1905.

44. David A. Tanner interview.

45. *The Weekly Press,* 16 July 1915.

46. Ibid., 30 June 1905.

47. Ibid., 20 November 1914.

48. Ibid., September 1909.

49. Ibid., 24 October 1919.

50. Minnie McKeon, Roosevelt Hot Springs, Milford, Utah. Typescript provided to the author by Gladys Whittaker of Milford.

51. *Beaver Press,* 7 November 1940.

52. *The Weekly Press,* 1 January 1909.

53. County Court Record, vol C., p. 96, cited in Dale L. Morgan" Historical Sketch of Beaver County," 28.

54. Merkley, *Monuments to Courage,* 190.

55. John Franklin Tolton, "From the Halls of Memory," chapter 32.

56. Merkley, *Monuments to Courage,* 161, 190–94, 201, 222, 333.

57. Noble Warrum, *Utah in the World War* (Salt Lake City: Arrow Press, 1924), 50.

58. *The Weekly Press,* 4 April 1919.

59. Florence Barnes, interviewed by Rosemary Davis, 25 February 1975, Milford, Utah.

60. Alton Smith, interviewed by Rosemary Davis, 30 September 1978, Milford, Utah, 10.

CHAPTER 7

PROSPERITY AND DEPRESSION
1920–1950

Two men from Beaver County became national personalities during the period between 1920–1950—Philo T. Farnsworth and Abe Murdock. Both Farnsworth and Murdock had roots that ran deep in the county—their ancestors had been men and women of the founding generation. But each lived lives that were anything but ordinary, and made contributions that drew them to the attention of the world outside the county.

After receiving his education at the University of Utah, Murdock returned to his home town to set up his law practice in 1922. During the next several decades he served in a number of public roles on the Beaver City Council; as county attorney; and as attorney for the Beaver County School Board. He and his wife, Mary V. Yardley, also of Beaver, raised six children—William Orrice, Abram Riggs, Daniel Beck, Jane Elizabeth, Mary Violet, and Cinda.[1]

Abe Murdock served as a representative from Utah to the United States House of Representatives between 1933–1945 and a United States Senator between 1941–1947. While in Washington D.C., he served on various committees, including the Committee on Banking

221

Horse riders parade down Beaver's Main Street in the 1920s. (Utah State Historical Society)

and Commerce; judiciary; public lands and surveys; territories and insular affairs; post offices and post toads; and privileges and elections. During his time in office, he participated in numerous special senate investigations into silver production and the effects of centralization on heavy industry.

Murdock had earned his reputation locally as a lawyer specializing in irrigation law, helping to negotiate Utah's share of the division of water from the Colorado River. Described in the *Congressional Record* as "a strong defender of working people and organized labor," he was appointed by President Truman to the National Labor Relations Board in 1949, where he served until 1957. He became a member of the Atomic Energy Labor-Management Relations Board in 1960.[2] He died in Bethesda, Maryland, on 15 September 1979, and is buried in the Beaver cemetery.

Also born and raised in Beaver, Philo T. Farnsworth won his first national contest by age thirteen after the family moved to Frankliln, Idaho, a year earlier. The contest, sponsored by *Science and Invention*

magazine, highlighted his invention—a thief-proof lock. At age sixteen he drew a design for his high school chemistry teacher, Justin
Tolman, that explained his belief that one could transform electricity into pictures by controlling the speed and direction of fast-flying
electrons. Philo called his invention an "image dissector"; his teacher
kept this drawing.

Farnsworth attended Brigham Young University for two years,
but learned most of what he knew about physics from correspondence classes he took from the University of Utah. Eventually,
Farnsworth moved to Salt Lake City and began efforts to raise funds
to develop his idea for the "image dissector." He married his longtime
sweetheart—Pem Farnsworth—and moved to California. Although
he had no training or previous experience in high-vacuum physics,
Farnsworth was a quick learner—finding a new way to seal a flat lens
end on a dissector camera tube to create a very high vacuum. This
new application of this technology led to his demonstration of the
first television system in September 1927. Although others were
working on the transmission of visual images, his high school design
allowed him to establish the claim—that he was the first to conceive
of the basic technology of television.

In 1936 he attracted the attention of *Collier's Weekly* which
described his work in glowing terms. "One of those amazing facts of
modern life that just don't seem possible—namely, electrically
scanned television that seems destined to reach your home next year,
was largely given to the world by a nineteen year old boy from Utah
. . . Today, barely thirty years old he is setting the specialized world of
science on its ears."[3]

Over the next decades, Farnsworth secured two patents to his
designs, and his corporation eventually secured over 150. He died in
1971 at the age of sixty-four. Farnsworth never became financially
wealthy because of invention, nor did he ever during his lifetime
receive the recognition he rightly deserved as the "father of television." In 1987, however, the Utah legislature passed House Joint
Resolution No. 1 sponsored by Donal R. LeBaron and Richard B.
Tempest to commission an artist to sculpt a bronze statue of Philo T.
Farnsworth, the father of television, for the Utah State Capitol.[4]

A 1920s float with dancers and musicians in Beaver. (Utah State Historical Society)

Beaver County in the 1920s

Because of the advantageous markets created by World War I, Utah's economy experienced a boom during the war years, but dipped into a depression soon after. In the early 1920s, several years before the of the nation entered into the Great Depression, Beaver County's mining and agricultural towns began to experience economic decline. Nevertheless, it is stunning how little things changed on a local basis with the end of World War I. Business continued as usual. Town government was concerned primarily with providing services that made life easier—improvements on property, fences repaired, water systems improved and maintained, streets and irrigation ditches cleared and resurfaced. The county commission included, in the early 1920s, Oren Burke, C.C. Sloan, C.A. Arrington, Homer D. Thompson, C. Frank Harris, and Ross B. Cutler.

Beaver City held a bond election in 1940 to raise $130,000 for a new hydro-electrical plant to be located in Beaver Canyon. The plant and new system was built under Mayor Homer D. Thompson.

Since the late 1920s, Beaver has had a motion picture theater, large dance halls, and various clubs, like the Ladies Home Economic Club of Beaver, lodges, and other social organizations. Mormon church activities staged by wards and auxiliary organizations continued to provide an important forum for community social interaction. Evan Patterson remembered these times:

> I was a teenager during this period. Remember, there was no TV, radios were very few here in Beaver. The dance halls and sports were the entertainment of the day. There were many dance halls in our area. . . . Hanging Rock in Minersville canyon, Brown Derby at Parowan, Utah, Purple Haze and Shadydell over along the Sevier River, Anderson Ranch dance hall located just east of the road where one turns off Interstate I-15 going to Zions Canyon. Yes, I'll not forget Kenyon Grove, just south of the present-day race tract in Beaver.[5]

Young people loved to dance, he concluded. High school dances were also mentioned in numerous articles in local papers. The Radium Warm Springs swimming pool opened a half mile east of Minersville in July 1931. These hot springs were undeveloped until Albert and Roy Smith built a swimming pool, a dance pavilion, and a resort nearby and capitalized on this natural resource.[6] Besides formal activities, neighbors visited each other often, offering help in times of hardship, but for the most part just socializing.

Rabbit hunting was very popular in the 1920s and went a long way in dealing with the problem of rabbit control in the county. Team competitions resulted in the destruction of literally hundreds of rabbits, as reported in a 16 February 1923 article in *The Weekly Press.* Teams usually consisted of fifteen men, armed with their own ammunition and assigned to a predetermined area.

In 1927 a Hollywood film company came to the county and persuaded some local residents to invest in a silent film entitled, *The Urge Within.* Several local people acted in the film, including William A. Firmage and his son Bill, Cy Davis, Howard Fotheringham, Orville Harris, and Faye Jensen Williams. The film was about a town drunk and the efforts to get rid of him and his two children—played by Faye Jensen and Bill Firmage.

A Scene from the movie *The Urge Within,* filmed in Beaver in 1927. (Courtesy William Firmage)

Orville Harris and Bill Firmage went to Hollywood following the completion of the film to pursue acting careers. Harris found he did not like Hollywood and returned home. Firmage found the depressed economy offered practically no hope for the talented young man.

The Urge Within was shown around the county for at least two decades including during World War II during county-wide war bond drives. However, when the highly volatile film caught fire in the Milford theater, the only known copy was lost.[7]

The 1927 Minersville Basketball Team

In 1927 the Minersville High School basketball team defeated B.Y. High for the Utah State Championship and departed by train from Milford for Chicago and the national high school basketball tournament. The town and the entire county were excited. Heber Gillins was so excited that, although he had just come from the fields to say farewell and was dressed in his farm overalls and old hat, he jumped on board the train and went with them—money and a change of clothes to be worried about later.

The train slowly pulled away from the platform to the cheers and

The 1927 Minersville Basketball Team traveled to Chicago for the national high school basketball tournament. (Courtesy Dell Hollingshead)

shouts of the crowd of well wishers. The team members included DeLose Baker, DeWayne Carter, Marcine Davis, Haratley Eyre, Ty Gillns, Henry Hall, Arshel Hollingshead, Newell Marshall, Wallace Osborn, Thel Smith, and coaches Stan McKnight and Melvin Whittwer.

There were only ten boys in the eleventh and twelfth grades of Minersville High and all were on the team. When they reached Chicago, they were amazed by the sights, sounds, and smells of the big city. Their country roots were soon apparent. The story is told that when mashed potatoes were scooped onto their plates with a ice cream scoop, they thought that the potatoes were ice cream and saved them until last to eat as dessert.

The team was eliminated from the tournament after losing their first two games. They found that their style of basketball did not meet with favor from the officials.

Minersville went on to win the state championship again in 1931, and the winning tradition has continued with town and church teams, although high school students now attend school in Beaver and the old Minersville school no longer stands.[8]

The Four Wheel Drive Auto Company operated by T. E. Parkinson takes on a load of freight and passengers at Milford. (Beaver County Travel Council)

Communications

The Beaver Press continued to be the best local source of news connecting the various sections of the county together—noting the deaths of oldtimers and local celebrities, discussing the most current issues of concern, and detailing new business start-ups and changes in the infrastructure. Between 1920 and 1950, The Beaver Press had a series of editor/publishers. Starting with Timothy Brownhill (1920–1922), Karl S. Carlton (1922–1927), A.C. Saunders (1927–1933), Karl S. Carlton and his son, Walter Carlton (1933–1942), Charles S. Wilkinson (1942–1945), and Aird G. Merkley (1945–1947).

Two U.S. highways ran through the county from the north/south and east/west. Highway No. 91 passed through Beaver City's Main Street and connected the town with most other important cities and towns of central Utah to the north and south. Highway No. 21 traversed the county east and west, providing a route to Nevada on the west and to Piute County to the east. Highway 21 runs through Milford, Frisco, and near the Indian Peak Indian Reservation and into

Nevada near the Lehman's Cave area near Baker, Nevada. The Los Angeles and Salt Lake railroads traveled through Milford and provided daily passenger service. Also in Milford was a large freight depot, located on the main line of the Union Pacific.

An airport was constructed in Milford during the early 1920s—a simple landing strip scraped out of the sagebrush fields. Used primarily as a stopover when the army flew the mail through the area, lights were installed in 1934 making it a twenty-four-hour landing field. Used as a CAA reporting station until 1958, the city of Milford maintained the field which served as a landing field for planes in distress, including many military jets and transports.

Like the rest of the United States, Beaver County felt the impact of the 18th Amendment adopted in 1919 which prohibited the consumption of alcoholic beverages. Known as Prohibition, the era from 1919 to 1933 gave rise to hidden stills to produce illegal liquor and bootleggers to transport the alcohol to willing customers. Oldtimers remembered a number of stills producing liquor during the days of prohibition, a time they called the "days of Sara Walker."[9] At least six distilleries were reportedly operating. Charles Jamison worked with the sheriff's office during these years and made periodic runs through the county to shut the stills down, arrest offending operators and discourage the production and sale of alcohol. Often he met with heated resistance. On one occasion he arrested three men and took them to Beaver to be housed in the city jail. He remembered,

> A few days after that, the U.S. Marshall come down with a couple of deputies and a machine gunner, fresh out of the army, and they got up, they found and located the still, and got upon the hillside, and made a brush front to hide them, and waited until they got down there and lit up the distillery, and got it to working, and they kicked these brush out, and there was this man with this machine gun pointed right at them, and the U.S. Marshall says, put your hands above your heads and come this way, and they hancuffed him and put him in the car and took the distillery.[10]

The Weekly Press editor, Timothy Brownhill, described the rising problem with bootlegging in a 14 July 1922 editorial. Brownhill, who reminded his readers that he was a non-Mormon suggested that his

readers remember that Mormon church president Heber J. Grant had
spoken out about obedience to the Mormon doctrine the Word of
Wisdom, which prohibited the consumption of alcohol, and had
specifically addressed the issue in a recent general conference address.
He also spoke about of the problems of enforcing the law without the
support of the county's people. He said that it had created a serious
problem with juveniles who were having to appear before the juvenile court. Expressing disappointment that the citizens of Beaver
were not more attentive in desiring the enforcement of the law, he
stated, no self-respecting citizen should want less.[11] There is a certain
irony in the destruction of 300 gallons of mash produced with government wheat by Beaver County sheriffs in June 1932. High above
the Wah Wah Valley, about thirty-five miles west of Milford in an
abandoned cattlemen's cabin, some boot-leggers were producing illegal mash ready for distilling. Spotting the sheriffs long before they
arrived, the guilty parties made an easy escape, but nevertheless the
officers destroyed the mash and the possibility of their making an
illegal profit.[12] Prohibition ended in 1933 with the passage of the 21st
Amendment which repealed the 18th Amendment.

The American Legion and National Guard

Veterans of World War I first met on 2 December 1924 for the
purpose of organizing a Beaver post of the American Legion. Twenty
men originally subscribed for membership, paid their dues, and
became charter members. During the next several months, they
drafted a constitution and applied for a charter. On 8 January 1925,
Beaver Post No. 32 of the American Legion was granted its charter.
Three weeks later, on 30 January, a grand ball and banquet initiated
the group's activities. From its inception the American Legion has
made a substantial contribution to the county's well being as a social
and civic organization. Frequent and substantive involvement in 4th
of July celebrations and other patriotic activities was traditionally
supported by legionaires. Over time the Beaver post sponsored
county fairs, and round-ups. The legion veterans also had rodeo
grounds near the city park and each year went out into the western
ranges and caught wild horses and staged authentic western rodeos.
Dances, city beautification projects, patriotic oration contests, and

Dedication of the Doughboy Statue in Beaver on Memorial Day 1927. (Utah State Historical Society)

numerous other types of activities were supported yearly by the Beaver post. In the mid-1920s, the American Legion built a Legion Dance Hall. Today used as a sewing factory run by John Powell, the dance hall was the scene of all kinds of social functions during the Depression years. The American Legion maintained a weekly column in *The Weekly Press*.[13]

On Memorial Day 1927, ten years after the United States entered World War I, the Beaver Post of the American Legion dedicated a monument in commemoration of those who served during the Great War. The monument was located in the center of Beaver's Main Street for several years before it was moved to its present location on the lawn of the post office. The American Legion raised $2,000 to purchase the monument.

In addition, the wives of members of the American Legion joined together since 20 April 1925 to support post activities. Like their husbands, the auxiliary raised money for the Doughboy monument, supplies and medical aid for war veteran's children, contributions for school and civic clubs, and help for the needy. These women planned and executed Memorial Day, Independence Day, Washington's

Downtown Beaver during the dedication of the Doughboy Statue May 1927.
(Utah State Historical Society)

Birthday, and Armistice Day programs for local schools. Not only a
philanthropic organization, but one which placed an emphasis on
education and American patriotic values, the American Legion
Auxiliary made an important contribution to the life of this community.

The Milford American Legion Post was organized on 6 March
1928 with twenty-six charter members. That same year the Milford
American Legion Auxiliary was organized with twelve women as
charter members. The Milford members were also involved in many
patriotic, civic, and humanitarian programs and projects.[14]

During the spring of 1929, Beaver City organized a National
Guard unit. When first established in April 1929 as Headquarters
Battery, Second Battalion, 222nd Field Artillery was led by First
Lieutenant S. Taylor Farnsworth as Battery Commander; Second
Lieutenant Grant H. Tolton as junior officer; Joseph A. Manzione as
first sergeant; E.S. Tattersall as supply sergeant and caretaker. When

it was first organized, there were thirty enlisted guardsmen. Each year the group mustered for a two-week training camp at the Jordan Narrows in June. Occasionally they traveled to California for brigade camps and to other locations in the northwest. Before the United States entered World War II, National Guard units began to mobilize.

Mining

After World War I, the development of new mines continued at a slower rate than during the boom times of the late nineteenth century. For instance, in the 1920s finds in the vicinity of the Horn Silver Mine indicated that rich veins stretched in several directions. The owners of the King David and Frisco Silver-Lead mines pumped fresh revenue in sinking and drifting the mines.

> At the King David, six mineralized veins, striking toward the Horn Silver, have been penetrated by a long crosscut to the north on the 750-foot level of the main working shaft. The most promising leads are being developed through a raise. Further west on the same zone, within less than 300 feet of the surface, the Frisco Silver-Lead has opened shoots of high-grade silver-lead ore from which many shipments have been made to the smelters.[15]

The shear zone, which was 4,200 feet in length and 500 feet wide, led directly into the Horn Silver Mine and contained many veins and deposits of pay ore in its fractures. North and south of the Horn Silver Mine finds located on a fault, originally identified in 1878 as the Beaver Carbonate, were called the Quadmetals by 1930.

Mining companies continued to prospect for new sites of mineral deposits. Joe and Bernett Swindlehurst opened the Gold Basin property three miles above the old Rob Roy Mine in the Indian Creek area where they struck a large body of gold-bearing quartz at a depth of twelve feet.[16] That same week R. J. Finley of Los Angeles began assessment of a large body of galena- lead ore which also had the potential for yielding good silver and copper values in the West Mountain Range. Finley, who was raised in Beaver, located this site thirteen years earlier about four miles west of the Fortuna Mine. Reportedly, this was one of the largest bodies of ore ever discovered in this section—the outcropping ledge was nearly a thousand feet in length and ran several hundred feet in depth. Average assays along the vein averaged $40 per ton in lead, in addition to having value in silver and copper.[17] By 1931 the Fortuna Mine, first developed in 1914, was yielding significant amounts of lead and renewed interest in mining in the Indian Creek area. "The success at Fortuna this year is giving an impetus to mining on Indian Creek, the west mountains and other mineralized zones, with the result that new discoveries and rock assays are being reported daily," according to the *Beaver Press*.[18] Mine manager John Bestelmeyer stated the Fortuna district "shows undeniable promise. Both in the igneous rocks or in the sedimentaries remarkable mineralization can be found. Surface indications are splendid, but not enough work has been done at depth."[19] The gold values ran from 60 cents to $108 a ton in gold. One boulder yielded $854 a ton in gold. The company stored ore in a hundred ton bin at their property.[20] Thomas and Fay Harris, who were working a claim just west of the Utah Gold Mining Company's property at Fortuna, were so excited about their claim that they built a log cabin at the site and worked continuously through the winter.[21]

Besides the work at the Fortuna site, work was underway during the same decade at the Oak Leaf property. A tunnel reaching 308 feet produced good quartz that assayed for $20 in gold, and which broke into Buckskin lime with an eight-foot vein of $35 to $40 in gold ore. The manager of the site boasted that nearby they had also opened a three-foot vein of manganese ore six feet under the ground that ran more than $25 in gold to the ton and promised even better results as the vein widened.[22]

A group of men in Milford including R.E. Ellingsworth, Jim Hemby, Don Workman and Bert Nichols installed a gasoline hoist at the Big Project site in the Bradshaw district, seven miles southeast of Milford. Earlier in 1931 they had found a two-and-one half foot ledge of lead-silver-zinc ore which they determined was at least 2,500 feet long and several feet deep.[23] Also in 1931 a new prospect was developed by the Horn Silver Company in an area called the Buckhorn Shaft.[24] Plans were under way in 1931 to reopen sulphur mines twenty-two miles north of Beaver.[25] Sulphurdale's mines opened in June 1932 and fifteen families moved back into homes nearby.[26] The principal product manufactured by the company was

The Park at Newhouse. (Utah State Historical Society)

sulphur dust, used extensively in California for dusting melons, lettuce, and other vegetable fields to prevent mold.

Generally, there was enthusiasm in the early 1930s about the potential still lying in the county's rich mineral mountains. According to the *Press*, "There is an apparent optimistic trend in the mining situation over the country that is being noticed in Beaver County as well as in other sections. That the price of silver is due to come back to a point where mining of that commodity will again be profitable is not a far distant future is confidently felt by the mining fraternity."[27] An editorial in the *Press* on 21 July 1933 expressed the common sentiment, that mining was helping to turn the tide of bad times and promised future profits.

> With metal prices again at a profitable level and moving higher, the west is preparing for a genuine old-fashioned mining revival. Talk of reopening old properties is rife and the prospector and promoter is beginning to venture forth again after several years of inactivity in silver, lead, zinc and copper mining. . . . In this transi-

tion a mine has been turned from a liability into a profitable venture once more. As yet, however, the margin of profit is small and producers feel that it will be better to await the consumption of some of the surplus stocks before reopening their mines and placing production again ahead of consumption. By late summer and early fall this condition should be classified and a number of producers will undoubtedly see their way clear to reopen properties and thousands of men will be returned to their normal occupations. Reopening of the mines will be followed by the reopening of the smelters. The railroads will again be moving long trains of ore cars, supplies, etc., and the farmer will begin to find a market for more of his products. The start toward all this has been made, now the conclusion is up to the industries themselves. Men must be put to work now to perpetuate the improvement. This is no time for timidity. If consumption is to improve, it must be made to improving placing men back to work.[28]

Businesses feeding off the revived mining activities also were organized in the county. A rod mill for handling ore was installed in Beaver in September 1932 by D.W. Jeffs, John M. Bestelmeyer, and John M. Broomcamp, among others. The company was formed to handle the ore of the Utah Gold Mining Company out of Fortuna, but milled ore for other mines as well.[29] The Forrester Balanced Rod Mill would grind, elevate, and classify ore for immediate amalgamation, flotation, or concentration, and did so with four to seven horsepower per fifty ton unit.[30]

The first shipment of ore from the Utah Gold Mining Company at Fortuna was made to the mill company in November 1932. It consisted of forty-two tons of ore which yielded $38 per ton.[31]

Besides benefitting from new mining activity, several mines were sold outright—Edward Schoo sold eighteen mining claims, known as the "Prosper" group, in 1935 for $250,000 to Harry Murtha, a mining engineer from South Africa.[32] The owners of the Sheep Rock Mining and Milling Company leased their property to E.Bissell of Beaver and Charles A. Sihler of Glendale, California—who anticipated commencing work before the next month.[33] By the next fall, they were shipping high grade gold and silver ore to smelters in northern Utah for processing.[34]

Mining activities stepped up at the Horn Silver Mine as well as at the King David property in April 1935.[35] In May 1935 news of a rich new strike in the Horn Silver mine west of Milford was announced. The vein was allegedly eight feet wide and contained gold, silver, and lead.[36] By 1935 one newspaper headline described the area as "teeming with mining activity."[37] The heaviest producing mines were the Lincoln, Moscow, Carbonate, Rob Roy, Shamrock, Beaver Copper, Old Hickory, Montreal, and the Horn Silver, which had produced by 1935 more than $50,000,000. The rising price of silver in part explained the renewed activity—but success in terms of new sites, high yields, and generally optimism about future efforts proved contagious and spread through the district.

After having been closed for forty years, the Quadmetals Mine in the San Francisco district was leased in 1935 to a group of Chicago investors who planned to bring in new equipment, unwater the mine, and commence work as soon as possible.[38]

The San Francisco district was described in 1937 as "alive with mining activity." That same year discovery of an extension of the $50 million vein system of the Horn Silver Mine drew the attention of national mining engineers, mine operators, and others who visited the district to examine the find.[39] One visitor, lead smelter owner E.R. Phelps, described the claim as being convincingly rich in potential yields. "Conditions south of the Horn Silver are so nearly identical with those in the Horn Silver that I look for conditions to ore deposits for considerable distances."[40] The Bonanza Mining Company was driving a tunnel to tap the vein at 110 feet. In what was called the "Lulu" was a 900-foot shaft that had been driven by the American Smelting and Refining Company in 1929. Work on the site had stopped with the stock market crash of 1929 and had not been the scene of further activity until 1937.[41] The San Francisco Mines, Inc, company was chartered in 1938 to carry on mining activities near the Horn Silver Mine as well.[42] In the 1930s Beaver County mining districts produced $489,155 worth of ore. Despite the devastation to the mining industry caused by the Depression, higher prices and revived production stimulated new activity. By the mid-1930s, and since the inception of mining activity in 1860, Beaver County had produced 453,422,708 pounds of lead and 23,354,296 ounces of silver. Copper,

Two automobiles loaded with passengers in front of the Cactus Club in Newhouse. (Utah State Historical Society)

next in line with 53,946,296, and zinc, with 42,123,360 pounds, were both important sources of revenue. The Horn Silver Mine had its best year in a decade in 1939—producing 10,590 tons at a gross value of $128,000. This total included 1,470 ounces of gold, 77,330 of silver, 1,444,000 pounds of lead, and 139,299 of zinc.[43] By the 1940s the Horn Silver Mine had produced approximately 190,192 tons of lead, 17,104,544 ounces of silver, 33,000 ounces of gold, 9,177,853 pounds of copper, and 19,192 of zinc.

Rich deposits of scheelite or tungsten were found at the Old Hickory Mine in 1940, having an estimated value of $10,000,000.[44] Clarence H. Hall, engineer of the U.S. Vanadium, headed the work which included core drilling on the tungsten vein, drifting in the McGarry shaft to cross-cut the vein, and working the surface to try and determine the width, extent, strike and value of the vein on the leased property.[45] A second tungsten claim in the west mountains was operated by M.M. Ward and Edith Ward, who owned one-half interest in twenty-four claims known as the Scheelite group. Working for them on the project, miner E.A. McCarry was sinking a double compartment shaft to the 200-foot level. They also hired a number of engineers to study the site.[46] Tungsten was of particular benefit to the war effort, which increased interest in the thriving mining efforts.[47] Used for filiments in electric light globes, and for hardening and toughening steel, tungsten was a vital element in modern industry.

In 1943 Lew Lessing discovered a rich tungsten deposit in a tunnel first dug more than fifty years earlier, in an event described by the *Beaver Press* as seemingly like an "Arabian Knights Fable; Affects all Beaver County's Future." It describes it with glowing language: "It remained for Lewis Lessing, a comparatively young prospector in his late 30's while prospecting the surface ground for indications of tungsten to enter the old abandoned workings with his 'Aladis' (fluorescent) lamp and discover a veritable enchanted chamber, shimmering and scintillating with a billion tungsten crystals."[48] Beaver County tungsten mines were remarkably productive during the 1940s. On 3 March 1944, Strategic Metals Incorporated shipped three car loads of tungsten ores from the Granite Mining District to U.S. Vanadium Corporation in Salt Lake City.[49] Reportedly, this mining district which was under intensive prospecting showed "a tremendous granite-lime contact, geologically conducive to the existence of tungsten ores." It was believed at the time that future development would reveal even larger deposits of shipping and milling grades of this particular strategic metal.[50]

Also important to the county were the number of outside investors attracted by the increased mining success in the west mountain district. In 1942 a group out of Chicago leased the Garnett property owned by A.E. McGarry and James E. Robinson's property—the "Rattler Claims"—was leased as well to outside investors.[51] A group of investors from Pennsylvania joined with investors from Utah in the Penn-Utah Mining Company to purchase mining properties and leases, and to begin mining operations in the Frisco district. At the time of their incorporation, they had twenty promising claims to further investigate.[52] Out of California, the Metal-Producers Company acquired a lease on part of the Horn Silver property and cleaned out the King David shaft, repaired it to depth of 800 feet, and extended a lateral from the 800-foot level of the shaft 2,000 feet to the Horn

Silver ore channel. There they discovered new ore and expected a 200-ton output daily.[53]

During World War II, seven major mines were under various levels of development—the Horn Silver Mine, the Moscow Mine, the Wah Wah Mine, the O.K. Mine, the Harrington Hickory Mine, the Gold Reef Mine, and the Old Hickory Mine. Five other mines were preparing to produce and ninety local men were employed in mining activities, for an average monthly payroll of $30,000. The average daily production was between 175 and 200 tons.[54] Milford became increasingly central to southern Utah's mining activities during these years.[55]

A new 400-ton processing plant was charted to begin operation in the fall of 1947 to process low-grade ores from the Horn Silver Mine. Huge quantities of low grade copper, lead, and zinc ores adaptable for milling were to be charted and blocked out for processing at the new mill. Built by the Metal Producers Company out of California, which had run the old Horn Silver mine in western Beaver County since 1941, the facility would represent an accommodation to the amount of ore that was produced locally.[56] But in 1947 a presidential veto of the metals subsidy bill broke the mining trend and the Horn Silver Mine closed down altogether.[57]

Under the management of Jack Lowe, the mine reopened in September and began plans again for the construction of a mill to handle the low-grade ores.[58] The mill neared completion in February 1948, and it was generally believed that this $300,000 facility would benefit the entire district. Powered by two large diesel-electric motors, a several thousand gallon reservoir and a sixteen-inch well would supply the mill, which would employ twenty-five local men.[59] By July the mill was grinding out ore at the rate of 500 tons per day and producing concentrates which were then shipped to Salt Lake smelters.[60]

Regardless of increased local mining activity, some rail lines were taken up in 1937 and 1943. After the 1940s there were only thirty-four miles of main track and twenty-one miles of side tracks in the county. Originally laid in 1899, the Utah and Pacific Railroad Company extended the main line southwesterly from Milford to Uvada at the Utah-Nevada state line and the sixteen and one-half miles of the old main line between Milford and Frisco became the Frisco Branch.

Agriculture

Stock raising continued to be important to the county's economic well-being throughout the period, the shearing season starting in April each year and ending a month later. In April 1932, for instance, sheepmen began the process of shearing their sheep at the Newhouse shearing corrals. The Newhouse facility had thirty machines with a capacity of between 2,000 and 3,000 heads per day.[61] The Newhouse shearing corral was built in 1913 and was one of the largest in the state. Most of the sheep sheared at the corral were owned by people from outside the county who brought their herds into the area from Sanpete Valley, the Salt Lake Valley, and other locations. Most of the Beaver County sheep were sheared at the Minersville corrals where local men began shearing with hand-operated blades about 1900 with the sheep held in brush corrals. Later corrals were built, machinery installed, and almost every local man worked as a sheep shearer at one time or another. One shearer, Obra Myers, won a shearing contest held in Craig, Colorado, in 1946. The prize was awarded for both speed and the quality of the shearing. Myers sheared five sheep in twelve minutes and thirty-one seconds and was featured in a photograph that appeared in *Life Magazine.*[62]

According to county agent Lew Mar Price, 20,000 pounds of turkeys were shipped from Beaver County in November 1932. Killing and processing the birds were done in Beaver before shipping by truck to Los Angeles for the Thanksgiving market. Farmer Fay Hall of Minersville had the largest flock with between 700 and 800 birds, but most farmers in the Milford Valley and in Greenville had between 400 and 500 turkeys. Before they were butchered, the turkeys assisted the farmers in combating a grasshopper invasion. Farmers let their turkeys loose in their fields and they allegedly greatly reduced the pests. The local turkey association made it easier for many local farmers to go into the turkey raising business on a large scale.[63]

Also important to the county's economy was the dairy industry. In 1932 the Brooklawn Creamery began business on the site of the old Beaver Valley Creamery and employed several men and women

A Fourth of July parade in Beaver. (Utah State Historical Society)

from the county. Despite the Depression economy, the company undertook extensive remodeling of the plant, laying new concrete floors, repairing and plastering walls, and bringing the building up to a much improved condition.[64] Before the Depression years, the Shepard Creamery was the sole dairy industry in the valley, but by 1933 Beaver had two modern, well equipped creameries, and produced approximately one-sixth of the state's total cheese, surviving the low prices for butter and cheese during the first years of the Depression.[65] The Beaver Dairy Association stressed the importance of the dairy industry to the county, stating in January 1938 that the Brooklawn Creamery alone paid over $175,000 for dairy products. "Beaver is the ideal dairy center of the state," they boasted. "We have the market and pasture. We raise the finest alfalfa hay and corn for silage in the state." The association's objectives were to increase production by increasing herds and improving feeding and housing of dairy cows and eliminating low producers. "We are going to make a drive for a better quality of milk, giving out in formation as to the best method of caring for same. We plan on dairy excursions thru the state to see how others are doing in their locality." All high-minded objectives, through the association's local dairy, farmers found ways to weather bad times and come out on top. To help recruit new members and popularize their work, the dairy association invited the public to join them in a celebration. "Don't forget to watch for the Big Dairy Association Supper and Dance soon," they announced in *The Beaver Press,* "Don't say Beaver is a pretty good place. Or Beaver could be a better place. Say Beaver is the Best place in all the world. Thanks to the cow."[66]

In 1940 the names of eight local dairymen were added to the national honor roll by the National Dairy Association, recognizing their accomplishment of developing a herd of cows with an average butter fat production in excess of 300 pounds per cow.[67] The association attributed this to attention to "good breeding, good feeding, wise selection of individual cows, and general good management."[68] In 1947 the plant processed milk from Beaver and other nearby towns at the rate of 58,000 pounds of milk daily. By 1947 the price of butter fat had increased to $1.00 per pound.[69]

In 1935 there were 447 farms in Beaver County with a total of 50,127 acres of land of which 9,998 were irrigated. The farms were generally small in size, most between 20 and 99 acres, and the average farm size 112.1 acres. Seven farms totaled more than 1,000 acres.[70]

In 1941 it was estimated that the county had 6,000 head of beef cattle and 3,000 head of dairy cattle, representing the principal source of agricultural income. Primary crops grown by local farmers were alfalfa, corn, barley, oats, and wheat—some planted potatoes. The county planning board suggested that the county included 6,500 acres of pasture land, ranging from highly productive to water-bogged lands which couldn't be used for grazing. The work of the state agricultural experiment station was particularly critical in planning for the future and attempting to find more efficient ways of using available resources.[71] The Potato Marketing Company came to Milford in 1943, and after suffering significant losses in their first year ($32,000), they began making a profit within a few years.[72] The Boston Land Company began large scale farming in the Milford Valley in 1944, focusing initially on the conservation and careful management of water resources, and planting 3,000 acres with

California Mariot Barley, White Rose Potatoes, alfalfa, wheat, and vegetables.[73]

By the end of World War II, Milford Valley was producing potatoes, and in 1945 shipped 500 car loads of potatoes from the Milford Union Pacific station to markets in Chicago, Amarillo, Texas, and Detroit, Michigan.[74]

By 1946, 1,000 acres were planted in potatoes in surrounding fields in anticipation of a harvest that would exceed 1,200 cars of potatoes ready to be shipped out of the county to markets across the U.S. Two storage cellars had been used by the town for several years, but two more were constructed in 1946. Each had a storage capacity of between 25,000 and 35,000 potatoes.[75]

Managing Water Resources

Dams had been built and maintained by Beaver farmers during the nineteenth century who received $2.50 a day for hand labor on the dams and canals. Drivers of wagons and teams received $5.00 for their difficult trek up the canyon. Stockholders joined together to form the Kents Lake Company for joint ventures like the Kents Lake Reservoir. The company organized and began building dams in 1903. Shareholders worked on the site every fall, bringing their plows, rock boats, scrapers and wagons for the work. In 1910 the original dam was enlarged to provide enough space for fish planting. After 1925 the Utah State Engineer took control over the distribution of water. In 1948 the Utah State Engineer questioned if there was enough water to fill this reservoir and required that the Kents Lake Company drill more core drill holes where the dam would sit. Resistance to the project came from those who thought there were already enough dams on Beaver Mountain and didn't want it further altered.[76]

The district court in Beaver was the scene for numerous battles over water—the key to agricultural development and survival in the area. Ownership of virtually every part of the Beaver River was in constant dispute between 1915 and 1931, with law suits between farmers, county government, and private citizens, and between municipalities. In some ways it seemed like an irreconcilable conflict in which everyone would always be fighting for their own self interests. In 1929 the state engineer's office attempted to adjudicate water

allotments, but a continuing debate over amounts led to further controversy. "The fight by no means was settled, it was only begun. The
east end of the county contended that the duty on the water was too
high, the west end that it was too low. The filing of 150 protests
resulted and were heard by the district court for an entire month in
1931."[77] For many, building new reservoirs to store water in peak
times and regulate more fairly in dry months for irrigation purposes
was the only fair solution to the enduring problem.[78] When Utah's
Soil Conservation Service was organized, the state offered local farmers help in these discouraging efforts. Under their direction, they
built dikes, reservoirs, and underground canal systems, controlling
better the flow of water from rivers to irrigated farm fields.
Organizations like the Minersville Reservoir and Irrigation Company
continued these efforts on a local level.

A perpetual problem plaguing Beaver County farmers was an
inconsistent and unpredictable water supply. On 3 September 1936,
Minersville was seriously flooded. Cedar trees flowed down town
streets, pigs swam in the water, haystacks scattered through town.
Farmers would clear out the irrigation ditches two or three times a
year, but eventually they would become blocked. Water was irregular
and would flood out fields or dry them up. When washes ran down
through the canal, they would "come in and move the shocks of grain
out of the field, and just cover rocks and silt over everything. The
early settlers back then, they hauled rock and they brought cedar
limbs in and piled within the rock, and making a bank to turn the
flood. It might be good for one or two years, and then they'd do it all
over again, and it was just taking the fields, and it was a failure."[79]
Using WPA funds, Minersville attempted to resolve its water dilemma
by updating its water system and running new six-inch pipes
throughout town.[80] When D. Low visited the county representing the
Utah State Agricultural College in December 1937, he assessed the
county's single greatest obstacle to further agricultural development
as being limited water resources. "Greater intensification of agriculture on the small scale Beaver County is dependent on the development of added irrigation water and these factors are vitally important
to determining the wealth and success of any community."[81]

Finally in August 1941, Judge Will L. Hoyt of the district court decided in the case of Rocky Ford Irrigation Company and Telluride Power Company vs. Kents Lake Reservoir Irrigation Company and T. H. Humphreys, state engineer, in favor of the defendants. The Kents Lake Reservoir Company had applied to transfer their storage rights from the Kents Lake site to Three Creeks. This decision was of significance to the county because it made possible construction of a reservoir at Three Creeks in Beaver Canyon, providing significant water for Beaver County irrigation on the bench land and would result in an increased production of alfalfa on this land from 3,000 to 5,000 tons.[82]

Preparation for the Three Creeks dam involved building a road around the northwest side of the proposed site, rerouting a phone line through Three Creeks valley to Puffer Lake, and clearing a significant amount of land. After the 1920s, reservoir projects in the Tushar Mountains were collaborative efforts. The Utah State Engineer, the local forest service personnel, the electric power company, and the Utah State Road Commission, among other governmental entities, all played a role. The Three Creeks Reservoir construction project was bid out at $142,000, begun in the summer of 1948, and completed the next year.

The Three Creek Reservoir received little of the spring water run-off, so the tunnel headgate was shut down by the company. The dam started to leak just a few days later, causing them to install ten-inch galvanized pipes to pick up the water spilling over. The company was also involved in legal action with Minersville Reservoir over Beaver River water. The result was that water from the river was stored in both reservoirs.

Forestry and Wildlife Management

In part the management of water was a matter of regulating spring run-offs in nearby canyons that related to the erosion in the valley caused by long dry periods. In 1931 forest officials anticipated serious flooding because of the erosion that had occurred on ranges throughout the district. H. M. Christensen, forest ranger, suggested that the situation was particularly precarious because of the cumulative effect of a series of bad years. Because the county had so many of the conditions that led to flooding, the Fish Lake Forest Service

The Beaver Game Club Entry in a Beaver Parade. (Courtesy Dell Hollingshead)

requested aid from the state authorities. A group of eleven representatives of local organizations—the Lions Club, forest service, Pine Creek Forest Users Association, the Fish and Game Commission, county commissioners, among other men, visited various areas of the watershed to access current conditions. They observed that much of the range grass was cropped short and had an overabundance of weeds, a condition common to overgrazed land. Few young trees were growing in any of the areas. Depletion of the range was the principal concern of the group, caused in part by the large number of deer grazing in mountainlands which had forced cattle and sheep down into lower areas and overgrazing resulted.[83]

Success came gradually, but by the mid-1940s it was clear that planning efforts had had positive results. The Fish and Game Commission announced in March 1945 that it was transplanting part of Utah's antelope herd in the western desert section of Beaver County. "This range is rapidly coming back under the intelligent administration of the grazing service which has built water holes and restricted grazing," according to Ross Leonard of the Utah Fish and Game Commission, "as such, it is an ideal habitat for prong horns."[84]

The government established the Intermountain Forest and Range Experiment Station, a division of the research arm of the United States Forest Service, in 1929–30. The focus of the station was the study of the range areas of the Intermountain West. A general survey of the ranges was made between 1930–31 to determine a permanent experimental site to study grazing management. Approximately 51,000 acres of winter range fifty miles west of Milford were selected after the preliminary survey.

In 1933 the Desert Range Branch Experiment Station was established about fifty miles west of Milford. Operated by the Intermountain Forest and Range Experiment Station of the United States Forest Service out of Ogden, the station was established to study the management of sheep and cattle. Of particular interest were grazing capacities and the most effective methods of utilization of the arid semi-desert areas of the west. The area around the station typified much of the 50 million acres of range land in Utah, central Nevada, southwestern Wyoming, southern Idaho, and eastern Oregon.

The government revealed plans to establish a reforestation camp employing 200 men in April 1933 at Big Flat, just above Puffer Lake. The plan included building a road on the east side of the mountain to Puffer Lake; the construction of a road to Kents Lake on the west side of the mountain; poisonous weed control in various areas of the Beaver mountains, and erosion control. The 200 workers would be recruited by the labor department but managed by the army. The camp would be run like an army camp in terms of feeding, clothing, and housing. The forest service would regulate their work activities during the daytime.

It was rumored that men would be recruited from the ranks of the unemployed in southern Utah, recommended by local relief agencies. Workers had to be at least eighteen years old and, if married with dependents, would be given first consideration.

In May 1933 the government announced plans to build a Government Forest Conservation camp at the Tushar Ranger Station in Beaver Canyon as well as a timber camp in Beaver Canyon. This meant that several roads would be constructed into the area, that 200 local men would be employed at the camp, and another 200 at the camp near Ibex, in the western part of the county.[85]

County officials met periodically with government officials to discuss the conditions of grazing lands, nearby forests and other natural resource development and use. In July 1933 regional, district, and national representatives from forestry agencies met with representatives of the grazing district, Fish Lake Forest, and the inspector of fish and game in region four. Forester C.E. Fave conducted a discussion about the way land was currently being managed in the area and suggested that "the already greatly depleted areas of the watershed that serve this beautiful valley may be harmed to such an extend that restoration of undergrowth may be impossible."[86] Emphasizing that planning was critical to the preservation and appropriate use of local resources, they described their aim as striking a "happy medium, not sacrificing game, stock or watershed but to maintain a balance that will tend to benefit every one."[87]

Limited vegetation on these range lands consists of low shrubs and grasses from the salt-desert shrub group. Throughout the region, lands similar to these provide forage for as many as 4.5 million sheep and 250,000 cattle during the winter months. In Beaver County about 1.1 million acres of winter range land, or 65 percent of the total acreage of the county, were used this way. Water was limited. In fact, precipitation was about half that in Beaver itself or about six inches per year. Light snowfall also facilitated winter grazing.

The sole sawmill operating in 1947 was run by Walter Mackerell and Robert Draper. Located west of the Beaver Race Track grounds, it was built on the Fort Cameron site. Timber milled there was cut in the high region of "Big John's Flat" and hauled to the mill in an old army truck.

Until the 1950s, the district forest ranger had no permanent staff and, except for some fire fighting equipment, had very little equipment. Hanmer (Ham) Christensen, who became district ranger in 1930, was the only full-time forest service employee, and at the outset of his service in Beaver he used his own auto. In time he was furnished a pickup truck; a horse trailer was added later. Christensen personally tagged all the cattle that were legally permitted on the forest service land, counted the sheep twice each season, and marked with a "U.S." each tree that was permitted to be cut for lumber. His horses were kept in pastures at the ranger stations during the summer and at his home in Beaver during the winter. During the summer he lived with his family at the Big Flat Ranger Station until about 1936 when they started using the Delano Ranger Station which had been recently constructed by the Civilian Conservation Corps.

The Great Depression

The people of Beaver County may have felt like the stock market crash of October 1929 was a rich people's game in New York City and wouldn't have much of an impact locally. If they did, they were wrong. The cycle of credit, inflated securities investments, and real estate booms fell flat, and created a depression that swept across the country like a devastating tidal wave. Businesses, banks, farms, and mines were all effected and many closed down completely; others struggled to stay in business but could barely pay their bills. Millions of Americans were unemployed, penniless and disoriented, unsure about where to turn for help.

Continuing in the laissez-faire tradition of republican government, President Herbert Hoover believed the market would heal itself and proceeded to confront short-term issues of immediate welfare and relief rather than address the struggling economy in general. The most sweeping of his Depression proposals, the Reconstruction Finance Corporation, was presented too late in the game and offered only indirect relief to those individuals and families stricken by the Depression. By the early 1930s, the American people wanted a new leader, someone they believed could save them from the Depression and turn the economy around. Franklin D. Roosevelt and his promise of a New Deal for the American people swept the 1932 election.

Because Beaver County was largely agricultural in character, its people did not starve during the Depression. Nevertheless, the county did experience sweeping and devastating economic change. Farmers were able to continue to feed their families but rarely had money in hand with which to purchase new clothes or tools. Professionals and businessmen, on the other hand, frequently had to barter their goods and services for food. Many remembered long years of sacrifice and tighting of belts as local residents struggled financially.

The Wood family had a "bunch of fine hogs and they was bringing such money, we said we'd let them get a little bigger and when they did get a little bigger, the bottom went out so fast, we never got anything, and the cattle the same. We never had no money to buy any. That's why as a kid, I came over here [Beaver] and tried to keep the cattle a long."[88]

Evan Patterson remembered that the local bank went broke early on and many farmers had to sell their adult animals to the government for $20 a head, calves for $2.00. Complicating their difficulties even further, Beaver Valley experienced a drastic drought.

Direct relief came in a variety of forms. The Red Cross shipped nine cars of feed wheat to Beaver County in May 1932. The wheat was used to feed families as well as cattle. The wheat was apportioned to farmers according to the number of head of cattle they owned. The wheat arrived by rail at Milford but was hauled to local farms by the farmers themselves or for a fee of 15 cents per 100 pounds.[89] The *Press* acknowledged the benefit this would have on local farm conditions: "This wheat will be of great help to the hard-pressed farmer and stockmen who have been compelled to run their stock on short rations, and will assist materially in getting the stock back in shape."[90]

The county commission between 1929 and 1935 included Fred R. Levi, Herbert C. Eyre, Frank D. Williams, James Patterson, Grant H. Tolton, R.E. Ellingsworth, and H.A. Christiansen. Required to address the same concerns as their predecessors: road maintenance and construction, water regulation, local ordinances, as well as the new challenges presented by the Depression, they were responsible for forming committees and agencies to administer the separate programs of the New Deal, manage local projects, and distribute resources and appropriations. County commission minutes indicate that the commissioners believed it was the county's responsibility to provide for the poor and the indigent. In their commission meetings during 1930, they discussed poor relief, provision of care for dependent mothers, old age pensions, county and state roads, and distribution of general funds. The county was supporting at the time two young girls at the Children's Service Society of Utah at considerable expense.

The New Deal

When Democrat Franklin D. Roosevelt became president in 1932 within 100 days he had initiated several programs that directly addressed the problems suffered by Beaver County residents. Together these programs, called the New Deal, provided relief for the needy, created jobs, encouraged business, and set up government agencies to address special interest groups—farmers, home owners, banking, and business. New Deal programs brought federal money into the county, helping to build the infrastructure, provide jobs for the unemployed, and help the needy to survive in their time of greatest need. T. L. Holman, chair of the governor's central committee for relief, met with the Beaver County commission during the second week of December 1932 to access local needs. After examining the reports of the way the county was distributing relief, he advised that no more money be given to the needy but rather groceries, supplies, clothing, and other resources be provided directly. He gave the commission a check for $2,500 to purchase these types of materials for distribution.[91] Holman also played a role in the establishment of Civilian Conservation Camps in the county during 1933.[92]

The Beaver City canning center prepared food for individuals and families on relief rolls. In August 1935, for instance, they canned 919 cans of beans; 263 cans of peas; 839 cans of corn; 147 cans of beets; and 219 cans of tomatoes; or 158 cans a day. This work was originally done in the high school kitchen but moved because of better facilities to the LDS East Ward Relief Society Hall. Canned corn was apparently in the greatest demand. All the produce used in canning was donated by area farmers.[93]

National Reemployment Office

The government established an office of the National Reemployment Service in the county in November 1933, located in the old Post Office building on Beaver's Main Street. As manager, Joseph A. Manzione worked with the Beaver County Relief Committee which consisted of E.A. Griffith, W.W. Farrer, Warren Neilsen, Lew Murr Price, O.F. Hubbell, George Marshall, and W.H. Varley. All workers employed on public works projects—highways, municipal and county school district projects—had to be hired

Neilsen's Garage in Beaver. (Utah State Historical Society)

through the service office. While this was one way to begin to deal with the problem of unemployment, the committee emphasized that most of the work needed to be done in the private sector, and that the county should not rely too heavily on federal projects for reemployment of its citizens.[94] By December, fifty of Beaver's unemployed men were put to work on improvements on the water system and cleaning, improving, and repairing streets, sidewalks, and in the Beaver city park.[95] By April, unemployment figures had dropped by 26 percent, largely due to the work of farmers in spring planting.[96] The Beaver County Relief Committee attempted to track those individuals who claimed the need for aid but refused employment when offered. "No individual is entitled to relief until they have exhausted all of their resources and are unable to support their families longer."[97] The re-employment office was closed in January 1937 because of the limited number of federal projects in the county.[98]

Banking

As was true of banks across the United States, the State Bank of Beaver County suffered with money shortages and closed its doors— declaring a holiday for a two-day period, putting its business in the hands of a state bank examiner.[99] The bank then responded with a variety of incentives to those who would redeposit their savings. In February 1934 the bank offered a 10 percent dividend to depositors to the bank, an offer that had been cleared by Royal Kimball, examiner in charge of the bank's affairs by the Fifth Judicial District judge. The total amount of the bank's obligations at the time was $157,932.60; according to the newspaper, this 10 percent dividend would "put $15,793.26 in circulation, quite a nice amount these hard times."[100] At various times over the next two years, the bank issued additional dividends on the liquidation of the State Bank to depositors. In August 1935, for instance, it issued a 7 percent dividend or a total of $9,915.59.[101] By October 1936 the bank had issued 64 percent in dividends to depositors.[102]

A new bank opened in Milford in October 1937—the Milford State Bank. "The opening of this new bank is a big step in the forward progress that is being made by the community," the *Press* asserted, "and will be a big inducement for outside capital to build a bigger and better Beaver City." By the end of the war, deposits increased dramatically in both Milford and Beaver County banks, representing a return to economic good health and more predictable sources of income.[103]

Agriculture

The purchase of cattle by the federal government had a significant impact on the livestock industry in Beaver County. Of an estimated 10,000 cattle in the county, 8,500 were made available by their owners for purchase under the government program. Of these, the federal government purchased 4,752 by the end of August 1934. About 25 percent, or 1,134, were slaughtered for local use, while the remainder were shipped out of the county to be canned for relief supplies.[104]

Beaver County residents benefitted from a number of programs of the New Deal. After years of unchecked use of agricultural lands in the county, the Agricultural Adjustment Administration set up programs locally to monitor soil fertility, and promote the economic use of and conservation of land. In Beaver the chair of the AAA committee was Arnold J. Low. He oversaw the organization of soil erosion and flood control programs among other projects to benefit farmers in the area. Also in the interests of agriculturalists, the Farm Security Administration organized rural rehabilitation projects to benefit needy farm families. Utah came under the jurisdiction of Region No. 9 located in Logan, Utah.[105] The FSA supervisors in Beaver County were D.D. Bushnell and Arthur B. Smith. The Home Management Supervisor was Hannah H. Wells. Farm produce was regulated by the Federal Surplus Commodities Corporation which purchased goods, managed the exchange and processing of farm products, and worked with farmers in the distribution and transportation of their goods. The purpose of the corporation was to remove surplus agricultural commodities from the normal channels of trade and divert those products to the needy and underfed. Farmer Aubra Cartwright of Beaver City managed such efforts in Beaver County. A.R. Hovey of Cedar City was the field supervisor for the Emergency Crop and Feed Loan Office that provided loans for farmers for fallowing, production of crops, planting, cultivating, and harvesting crops, and the purchase of supplies for agricultural purposes. The Farm Credit Administration also benefitted local farmers through the creation of funding sources more readily available for farmers. The Federal Land Bank of Berkeley made long-term mortgage loans more easily attainable for agricultural purposes, for the purchase of equipment, fertilizer, livestock, or farm buildings. R.H. Billings of Delta processed loans for Beaver County. Furthermore, an extension service of the Utah State Agricultural College was established in Beaver County. Expressing the close relationship between this service and the county, their offices were located in the county courthouse. The purpose of the extension service was to stimulate and maintain the interest of farm families in progressive agriculture. In 1938 the County Agricultural Agent was Hyrum Steffen of Beaver City. Under the state department of public instruction, a Vocational Agriculture Education program managed research projects about field agriculture in the area. S. Melvin Wittwer of Beaver City was the local superintendent of the county schools. And finally H.A. Christensen of Beaver City headed the Beaver County Planning Board which provided procedures for the development of sound land use plans, programs, and policies on the county level.

The Farm Debt Adjustment Committee assisted the governor's

committee in assisting farmers who had fallen into debt. The
Conciliation Commissioners handled cases in which farm debts had
reached the conciliation court. Ray L. Lillywhite, assistant supervisor
of the Farm-Debt Adjustment Association, suggested that farm
debtors who were confronted with foreclosure or who had difficulty
paying off their debt, "FIRST, meet your principal creditors, and try
to arrange a settlement with them. SECOND, go to a member of the
local Farm-Debt adjustment committee and ask his help and advice,
which is recognized by creditors the country over, THIRD AND
LAST. If these methods fall, apply for Debtors Relief with the
Conciliation Commissioner, who has legal authority and who can
enforce decisions."[106] In 1937 the Resettlement Administration had
received applications for loans from 124 farm families, for a total of
$130,761.[107]

Some attributed Beaver County's farm problems to the low rural
income, which was, in 1933, $800 or less. One-fifth of local farmers
earned between $800 and $1,000 gross per year, and another one-fifth
between $1,000 and $1,500 per year. Also the small average size of
farms and the large farm indebtedness contributed to the problems
faced by farmers. The large acreage of noxious weeds throughout the
county was also a perpetual problem and reduced productivity of
farm land.[108] Between 1934–1936, drought compounded financial
problems already faced by farmers and stockmen.[109]

Civilian Conservation Corps

The Civilian Conservation Corps provided employment for several local young men as well as embarked on projects in local recreational areas that benefitted the county as a whole. The CCC's
principal mission was to conserve and develop natural resources,
relieve unemployment, and create a well-ordered program of extensive public works.[110] Enrollment was limited at first to single unemployed men between eighteen and twenty-five years of age whose
families were on relief roles.[111] Workers from CCC camps in Cedar
City (managed by the Division of Grazing), Bryce Canyon (managed
by the National Park Service), and at Duck Creek (managed by the
forest service) worked on projects in the county.

In June 1933, twenty-eight CCC recruits from Salt Lake City and

Garfield between the ages of nineteen and twenty-five arrived at Milford to be sent to one of the two Beaver CCC camps. The news editor of the *Milford News* met with the men along with Mayor O.F. Hubbell and J.C. Smith. All three men had played a role in the selection of the camp sites and the organization of the work. Together they visited the "Wah Wah camp Friday of last week and had chow with the camp officers and those of the workers who were not out on work detail at the time."[112] The Beaver camp was located originally at Little Reservoir, near the upper Telluride Power Plant, but relocated to the area near the Tushar ranger station, and was called Camp Delano (for Delano Peak). The camp commandant, Captain N.C. Snidow, was quoted in the *Beaver Press* as speaking "in glowing terms of Milford and the hospitality and friendly help he has had on every hand from Milford townspeople—something which incidentally," according to the newspaper, "has brought our town country-wide notice innumerable times in the past." It further reported that the camps had been relatively sickness free, particularly the desert camp, although the extreme altitude had bothered CCC workers from Virginia living at the camp. Each camp housed about 110 workers.

For several summers a CCC camp was located at Britts Meadows between Three Creeks and Puffer Lake in Beaver Canyon. In winter the men were moved to the Milford area. William Oakden of Beaver was the civilian supervisor. Most of the CCC workers were from Kentucky and were under the command of a U.S. Army captain.

Each Thursday evening men at the Britts Meadows camp on the Beaver River were entertained with a special program; at one, Congressman Abe Murdock delivered a speech titled, "Your Part in Our National Recovery." He reminded the young men that, when President Theodore Roosevelt helped create the reforestation program, it had two purposes: conservation and improvement of the nation's forests and "building of better American citizens." Each Thursday at the close of the program, the men sang and danced long into the night.[113]

In July 1933 Lieutenant W.E. Kraus from Fort Sam Houston, Texas, joined Snidow in leading work on a connecting road between Beaver Canyon and the junction road by way of Puffers Lake. It was also announced that the camps would soon each have 200 workers.

At the same time, the government announced that the national forest camps in Utah would get an additional 1,379 men and that Zion National Park would get forty-nine additional workers. These new recruits were described in the newspaper as being "selected from among those who have had some experience in mountain and forest work and who are fitted to exercise a wholesome leadership among the younger enrolled men; they may be married or single and the eighteen to twenty-five year age limit does not apply, but the men selected must come from among the unemployed."[114] After the specific projects were completed, the men left the camps and returned to their homes.

In July 1934, CCC workers came to the Delano Camp again, this time to execute what was called "Drouth Forest and Drouth Relief." A total of 235 men would be lodged at the camp including at least sixteen local men.[115] Beaver County welcomed the CCC men with a "homecoming" held at the camp, including a dance, and made plans for a number of exchange programs between the camp and local organizations, including baseball and football games.

In 1935 seven of the forty-one new men who came to Camp Delano were from Beaver County—Bill Bacon, Vernon Black, Ray Hodges, Ray Hutchings, Ray Orton, Tom Pedigo, and Fred Potter. The camp published its own newspaper—*The Mirage,* later called the *Delano News,* which published news about progress on the various projects and personal anecdotal information about the men in the camp.[116]

The CCC men began immediately to clear sixteen miles of road, clearing the sides of underbrush and debris to minimize fire hazards, and building a number of experimental grazing systems. Crews of men were located at camps at Kents Lake and other locations along the construction route. In addition to road construction, the CCC men worked on the Little Beaver resort campsite, building tables, restrooms, cook stoves, and other recreational amenities. They built more permanent structures at the Beaver Dam Ponderosa Campgrounds, earlier known as the Boy Scout camp.

Other projects included construction of fences around forty acres of land in Bakers Canyon for grazing reconnaissance projects and construction of an experimental grazing station. Timber stand improvement would also proceed in the area surrounding the camp itself. The *Press* reported, "The boys are taking hold nicely and seem to show interest in what they are doing. Many of them are interested enough that they plan to go into Forestry as a career."[117] By September 1934, ranger stations had been constructed at Big Flat and Delano, six grazing reconnaissance enclosures were completed at Grindstone, and four at Merchant Valley Watershed.

The county recognized the tremendous impact CCC projects had on the area and tracked their completion in the local paper. The *Press* quoted Lt. E.M. Squire, Welfare Officer of Camp Delano, who said: "When one considers that all of these accomplishments are done through the manual labor of the CCC boys and adds to this good food, regular hours, healthy out-of-door life and supervised recreation it is small wonder that the CCC is rapidly developing over 650,000 clean, strong, healthy, quick-thinking, and fearless young men of whom the citizens of this country may justifiably be proud."[118] Although many of the projects were conducted during the summer months, a winter camp was established fifty miles west of Milford in Pine Valley. Projects at this camp included a nine-hole golf course, a tennis court, hand-ball court, and indoor basketball court. In November 1935, 190 CCC enrollees arrived in Milford from Kentucky to work on projects under the Taylor Grazing Act. These projects included work on the Parowan Wash Reservoir, the Greenville Hollow Reservoir and other water projects designed to prevent flooding and lead to greater water mangement.[119] That same month, the Desert Range Camp and the Beaver River Camp began a variety of projects described in the *Beaver Press* in its 22 November 1935 issue.

> Pipe lines, 13,200 feet; Tree Seed collection (conifrers) 1 bu.; Planting grass 4 acres; 7 vehicle bridges; 2 carrals; 4 latrines; 1 Shelter; 1 drinking fountain; Water supply systems 280 Mandays; 26 camp stoves; 2 portals; 18 rods stone walls; 36 table and bench combinations; 34 articles under miscellaneous structure, 15 miles of horse trails; 10 acres of seeding grass; 5 acres soil preparation; 210 feet of rock walks; 1 mile of stream development; 180 cubic yards earth filled dams; 375 cubic yards rock filled dams; 97 miles of fence; 50 miles of telephone lines; 7 reservoirs; 6 cattle guards;

4 markers and gates; 1 amphitheatre; truck trails (roads) 107 miles;
64 check dams; 3,000 square feet of riprap, rock; nurseries including 645 man-days; 113 acres of landscaping; 3,084 trees and
shrubs, moved and planted; 58 experimental plots; 62,059 acres
surveyed for type and soil; roadside clearing for fire hazard reduc-
tion 15 miles; fire fighting 97 man-days; 67 acres of public camp
ground development; 3 public camp ground buildings; other cam
ground facilities, 27 in number; bank protection and erosion control 2,314 square yds; 40 acres of rodent control; 50 acres larkspur
eradication; barns 2; 1 dwelling; 1 garage; 1 woodshed; 1 cellar; 1
office and store room.[120]

In the county CCC men worked on a program of reseeding
rangeland denuded by rodents, erosion, or overgrazing. In 1937 the
CCC built 91 dams throughout the state under the Soil Conservation
Service and the Division of Grazing. In April 1938 they completed a
reservoir near Granite Peak. A 357-foot pipeline carried water that
opened up a new range area west of the Mineral Mountains between
Milford and Beaver.[121] The CCC men also built the Delano Ranger
Station between 3 creeks and Puffer Lake. The station was later
moved to Beaver and is now located on the 400 block of Center
Street.

It would be very difficult to quantify the benefits Beaver County
reaped from the various CCC efforts, but it is evident that they were
involved in the building of virtually every aspect of the county's
infrastructure, recreational and cultural backdrop, and helped move
the county forward through the Depression to a point where it was
in better shape than it was before. Much of the work of the Desert
Range Branch Experiment Station was in range conservation, flood
control, public resource management, and conservation through sus-
tained yield, all issues of particular interest historically to the county.
Other projects were like much of the CCC work, simply practical
improvements of county resources. In May 1937, for instance, the
Desert Range Experiment Station CCC Spike Camp in South Pine
Valley cut 10,000 posts to be used at the range for sheep pasture, to
enclose plots, and to locate markers of sheep allotments.
Furthermore, the station modeled for county farmers and stockmen
the advantages of careful range management. The *Press* noted, "Not

only the practical minded stockmen who can see only the forage value of the most beautiful desert flower, but the aesthetic too, are among the guests at the Range. In the 55,000 acres of the Experiment Station, one may see areas of excellent forage, beautiful flowers, and an even green cover, or barren wasted desert with only the misleading green of Russian Thistle showing."[122] When the camp was eventually closed down, Milford felt the loss of this significant resource, protesting strongly the order.[123] As a result, the closure was delayed for a period of time, largely because of the lobbying efforts of the Lions Club, but was eventually closed down with the end of the CCC program.[124]

PWA/WPA and other New Deal Alphabet Agencies

The Public Works Administration hired men from Beaver to work on local civic improvement projects. Paul R. Arentz from the PWA visited the county commission on 5 February 1935 to explain the way work was conducted under the agency. He told them the government had $4.5 billion for projects over the next eighteen months. He was in Beaver County to survey what particular needs might be met by PWA programs. The principal objective of the program was to build up towns, cities, and counties, and to employ local men and teams, attempting to employ all unemployed persons in the county. Projects proposed by the commission included installation of a power plant, improvement of local streets and sidewalks, landscaping, new city halls, courthouses or schools, lining irrigation systems, and preservation of historic landmarks like Cove Fort.[125] Men hauled gravel for Beaver City streets and country roads for $3.00 a day throughout winter months. A work crew of local carpenters built "Roosevelt Memorials" or public restroom facilities. WPA recreational director for Beaver County, Stan McKnight identified an area near the Telluride plant for the development of a ski course and recreational site. The hill was described as being "not too steep but is an ideal place for the amateur to test his skill. About 7 pairs of skiies [sic] are available and every one will be given an opportunity to try their hand. It is hoped that the introduction of this sport into this section may be the foundation of a real sports program."[126]

In February 1938 work began on a ski run near the Hi Low Lake area near Clover Beds. Grading was underway for a ski run more than one mile in length that would provide slopes for beginning skiers or more advanced experienced skiers as well. An ice skating pond and hills for tobogganing and sledding were also developed. Beaver's Chamber of Commerce announced that the ski run would be opened on 6 March 1938.[127] That same year a group of skiing enthusiasts organized a local ski club to plan for future skiing projects and developments.[128] Over the next decade the ski club played a key role in encouraging further winter sports developments.[129]

In January 1939 President Roosevelt approved five new WPA projects for Utah, including in Beaver County a project to improve the state fish hatchery.[130] In 1941 Roosevelt approved an appropriation of $41,365 of WPA funds for improvements on the power plant.[131]

To regulate CWA work, a local CWA commitee for the county was appointed in November 1933 which included C.F. Harris, chair; T.L. Griffiths and Arnold Low of Beaver; D.R. McKnight of Minersville; and L.G. Clay of Milford. Theodore Bohn of Beaver served as the distribution officer. This committee functioned as the Beaver County Emergency Relief Committee headquartered on the Tolton block in Beaver City. The first allocation were 100 men whose names were drawn from the relief rolls. The principal role of the committee was to receive requests for projects from the city, county, PTA, or the board of education and other civic associations and submit them for approval to the state committee. Upon approval, they then helped organize the project itself and distributed funds allocated by the federal government.[132]

The Civil Works Administration and the Federal Emergency Relief office joined forces in December 1933 to distribute relief to 147 families or 535 individuals in Beaver County. The men who received relief under this program worked on two projects in Beaver City in December—improving the road from Fletcher Barton's into town and the Fish Hatchery road. In addition, the CWA employed 196 men from Beaver in December on various projects, with wages that varied according to the type of work—a common laborer received 50 cents an hour; timekeeper and foreman, 60 cents; a man with a team, 75 cents per hour; and blacksmiths and other skilled workers 75 cents per hour. During the last week in November 1933, the CWA payroll for projects in the county was $1,530.[133] These placements continued through the month—twenty more were employed on forest work, six sent to Delta, and fourteen to Greenriver. The payroll for the week ending 11 December was $3,945. Much of this work represented a partnership with city government which had to provide materials in certain cases for projects or other supplies.[134]

The number of men employed and the number of hours they could work fluctuated wildly over the next several months. In January 1934, for instance, thirty-four men were dropped from local civil works projects and the number of hours each could work per week was limited to fifteen. In short, this meant that the CWA payroll in Beaver County was half what it had been in December.[135] The CWA was suspended 31 March 1934 after the completion of the projects that were underway at the time—the Creek Bed road bridges, improvement of the Beaver County Jail, feeding malnourished children, and the supervising nurses and the relief medical program.[136]

The Federal Emergency Relief Administration also funneled funds into the county. In July 1934, the FERA payroll for the county for the week of 18 July was $2,310. The local committee described its purpose and method of accessing funds in an article in the *Beaver Press* dated 20 July 1934. It specified that "anyone making application for relief holds himself out as subject to a thorough investigation as to his financial resources. He does not receive relief because he is out of work, but receives it because he has exhausted all resources with which to live and make a living." Any person who applied for relief might have been put on Direct Relief Work Relief. If it was believed that the worker was squandering away his wages, he would be transfered to a program where his wages would not be given in the form of cash but in disbursement orders to be redeemed at local stores.

One typical FERA project was the curbing and guttering of the ditch just north of the Beaver High School building for three straight blocks and moving the White Way light posts back and reconnecting them—work that was superintended by city councilmen George Paice and Levi Howd, with William Goodwin as project engineer.[137] In 1935 the FERA appropriated $6,800 to improve sanitary conditions resulting from improper drainage systems and unsanitary privies and cesspools.[138]

Community Life

Throughout the Depression years, the people of Beaver County continued to raise their families and attempted to maintain community institutions that tied them together. In 1935 " a record breaking crowd gathered at the Beaver high school at 10:30 Wednesday morning to enjoy one of the best programs ever put on on Beaver's Birthday," the *Press* reported. The crowd began by singing, "Come, Come, Ye Saints" led by Professor Cannon Thomson of Beaver High. Then followed a series of readings about early pioneer life in the valley, a skit "Depicting Early Pioneer School" and a "delicious hot dinner" was provided by the four local camps of the Daughters of Utah Pioneers. The day ended, as it most likely would have in pioneer times, with a rolicking dance that ran until 12:30.[139]

There was sufficient new construction in Beaver in 1935 for one writer to describe it enthusiastically as a "building boom."[140] Several new homes were noted periodically in the paper—evidence of economic recovery.[141] Beaver City began work on a new city sewer system in November 1935, adapting in part to new growth.[142]

Active throughout the 1930s, the Beaver Chamber of Commerce contributed greatly to the building of the city's infrastructure. Meeting around a banquet table at the Meredith Cafe, twenty-three members discussed the construction of a new armory and work already underway on the sewer system. The armory would be partially funded by the state, the city, and the WPA.[143] In February 1937 the chamber discussed with George Jefferson, president of the Milford State Bank, the possibility of establishing a bank in Beaver City some time during the following year.[144] Supplementing the work of the county commission, the chamber threw its support behind a number of projects that helped Beaver meet change effectively.[145] KSUB radio station in Cedar City featured a weekly fifteen minute program on Beaver County using information provided by the chamber of commerce. Advertising the area's natural resources and built environment, it described the amenities here in glowing terms. "May we invite you to spend the week-end or regular vacation trip in

Members of the Beaver Band announce a Barn Dance. (Utah State Historical Society)

Beaver's Wonderland where Nature in all it's grandeur has created a wonderful bewitching and fascinating retreat; where we can assure you will have an outing never to be forgotten. Beaver City is surrounded by a rich farming and dairy section. The City owns its own water and electric light systems, has a $165,000 senior High School, a splendid grammar school, Carnegie Library, fine churches, and is indeed and in truth a splendid home city. Beaver welcomes the tourist and the homemaker."[146] Beaver City was also featured on KSL radio in April 1938. City councilman E.F. Mackerell told the story of the eighty-two-year history of the community, reminding his audience of the 1865 remarks of town pionner John R. Murdock, "We must be like the beaver—we must work hard and long—for here is a great country with resources everywhere about us." Mackerell noted Beaver's important scenic and mining resources as well as its key importance as the "center of the state's dairy industry."[147]

The Firmage Theater opened in Beaver in the summer of 1937—a new "De Lux" motion picture showhouse, built for $25,000. The theater, which had 400 seats, was equipped with the most up-to-date sound equipment and featured air-conditioned air in summer and

The Goddess of Liberty and her attendants. (Utah State Historical Society)

clean heated air in the winter. According to the *Press,* "Lobby appointments give the air of distinctive colorings in white, blue, beige with trimmings of stainless steel. Groups of modernistic furniture add the finishing touch."[148]

The chamber of commerce joined with the city to raise money for a race track for Beaver City at special meeting in August 1938 held at the I.O.O.F. hall. The race track project was largely completed and would cost overall an estimated $30,000. An additional $2,000 were needed to complete the grand stand, race track, and stables and stalls for horses. The track was built on the grounds of the Murdock Academy, the location of the Beaver County Fair. A race meet was held Labor Day weekend.[149]

An editorial in *The Beaver Press* in April 1944 epitomized the enthusiasm Beaver brought to the future:

> Few rural communities of Utah have natural resources and advantages to compare with those with which a beneficient Creator has endowed and surrounded Beaver City. Few towns and cities of comparable population, offer as many opportunities for expansion, and the profitable application of capital investments. . . . Sheltered from cyclones and tornadoes, floods, fogs, severe droughts and extremes in temperature, and fed by one of the most dependable and conservative small rivers in the state, admirably adapted to the production of dependable hydro-electric power, and the coolest, clearest, purest culinary water supply possible, with wonderful grazing, mineral and recreational advantages, it leaves nothing to be desired that is conducive to the comfort, convenience and well-being of homemakers and industrialists. . . . Cool attractive summer camps and trout-stocked streams, wonderful scenery and the best hunting in the world—people not only exist here—they LIVE! As a manufacturing community, we have the cheap power, water, man and woman power by people who want to make their homes here permanently; considerable surplus housing already established and available, economical transportation, an all-year desirable climate, economical fuel supply and a total absence of labor troubles. Can all these advantages long go begging to be snapped up? We think not.[150]

Beaver's Mormon congregation completed construction of a new ward chapel in December 1931. The building, designed by prominent Mormon architects Harold Burton and Theodore Burton, pulled the various activities of the church under one roof—from this point forward, Relief Society activities, the distribution of welfare for the poor, and other worship and social activities would be staged in this beautiful structure, which included classrooms on a second level and other offices and rooms in the basement.[151]

The LDS church sold the site at the northeast corner of the city part for the new federal building in 1938 for $7,500, with the stipula-

Business students at Murdock Academy. (Utah State Historical Society)

tion that the city officials beautify the lower part of the church property.[152] The new structure officially opened on 2 September 1941 and
was described by *The Beaver Press* as "a colonial design, stressing of
simplicity and design. A metal and glass cupola surmounts the roof.
The interior of the building is elaborately designed, and the modern
heating equipment has been installed."[153] The two-story black stone
Murdock Academy building was torn down in 1932 despite decades
of adapting it to new uses.[154]

Beginning with the cooperative enterprises of the nineteenth
century and continuing down through the twentieth century, volunteer activity was crucial to the development of Beaver County. Men
and women of each generation gave generously of their time, talents
and resources to build their community—the chambers of commerce, Lions Clubs, volunteer fire departments, and other entities
benefitted everyone and reflected a strong local public mindedness
and sense of connectedness.

A new volunteer fire department organized in February 1941 in
Beaver City with Walter B. Nowers as chair and Walter L. Carlton as
secretary. Charter members included all the members of the city

council and other volunteers. The group met each Thursday night at 8 P.M. in the basement of the Beaver Library.[155]

The 1940 census showed a slight decrease in the population of the county in the past decade by 152 for a total of 4,984. Most of this decrease was in Milford, which dropped by 133; both Beaver and Minersville increased in population.[156]

Between 1941 and 1943, Beaver City completed internal improvements—the hydro electric plant was completed, landscaped, and began service; Beaver City streets were repaired; and a new bridge was constructed at the Dee Stapley corner and another near the cemetery. The street in front of the court house was graveled and oiled; and the culinary water supply improved with new pipes bringing spring water to Beaver City homes without ever coming above ground.[157]

Electrical Power

Residents of Beaver City debated whether they should purchase power from Telluride Power Company or continue to supply local power with the city hydro-electric plant and build a new dam. Those in favor of a connection to Telluride emphasized that the plant's diesel engines produced power for less than half the price, and that it would put Beaver in a dangerous position financially to go further in debt to build a new dam, and that, furthermore, purchasing new equipment that would be out of date within ten years was not economically prudent either.[158] They also reminded the city that Manti was purchasing its power from Telluride and had found the arrangement to be perfectly satisfactory.[159]

In 1936 the city purchased a new diesel engine for its power plant for $21,027 raised through a bond election.[160] In 1940 the city council considered the feasibility of building a new hydro-electric plant up Beaver Canyon and upgrading the plant already up and running in town.[161] A series of public meetings was held to encourage civic involvement in the decision making process.[162] By March the city opened the bidding process for construction of a new plant, believing it would produce a more consistent supply of electricity to the city.[163] The city also applied to the Federal Power Commission for permission to construct the new plant.[164] In December 1940, Beaver

The Hotel Low in Beaver. (Utah State Historical Society)

City held a bond election in the attempt to secure $130,000 to be used to build a hydro-electric power plant at the Beaver City power site in Beaver Canyon, build a new city hall with a fire station, rehabilitate the electrical system, and other development supplemented by the rural electrification program.[165] Approved by Beaver votes 122 to 79, the bond would result in significant improvements for the area.[166]

Despite the many challenges faced along the way, including entrance into World War II, the new hydro-electric plant was completed in December 1942. Mayor Thompson described the new system in glowing terms: "The new generator plant is complete in every detail, and as fine as money can buy. It is fully automatic, insuring an even and constant flow of power and heat elements, which will be a great improvement over the system now in town and with one of the best mountain streams in this part of the state to operate from Beaver City should have one of the finest power and light system in the country."[167]

On Wednesday, 4 January 1943, Mayor Thompson turned on the switch which set the plant in motion. The older hydro and diesel engine plants were closed down, but it was planned that they would be kept in good condition for emergencies.[168] By 1943 the Telluride Power company was building connection lines—transformers and other equipment—to pick up the "dump load electricity" from the city power plant because of greater demand from small towns which depended on the company for power in times when water shortages made it difficult to generate power locally.[169] The Telluride Beaver Canyon Line would likely cost $150,000 but would service not only small towns in Beaver County but other towns in the area. It would provide an alternative independent source of power for west Beaver County which depended on Sevier County for electrical service.[170] Regardless of their efforts to upgrade service for Milford and other towns to the west of Beaver, the company experienced several major breakdowns and periods of low voltage and single phasing, all creating problems for Milford businesses.[171]

In 1999 there were two power plants operating in the county—the Sulphurdale Plant fifteen miles north of Beaver, and the Blundell Power Plant northeast of Milford.

Hospitals

Beaver City's Chamber of Commerce backed the city's efforts to develop a plan for building a hospital in town and met with the county commission on numerous occasions to discuss the matter.[172] The city sent a proposal to the WPA for support in March 1936.[173] Largely at the encouragement of Abe Murdock, Walter M. Crandall of the War Department and other army officers came to Beaver to inspect a proposed site for a 1,000-bed army hospital—for which the city proposed to donate the race track and fair grounds at Fort Cameron.[174] In 1945 the LDS church considered a proposal to build a hospital in Beaver County, splitting the costs in half with the county. Of particular concern in the debate over the issue was the lack of support given by Beaver residents to the Milford hospital.[175] Dr. L.A. Busch, Jr., of Pittsburgh bought the Milford hospital and began to remodel it not soon after. In addition, Busch purchased the practice of Dr. Owen L. Felt and planned to care for "out patients" at his offices in downtown Milford.[176]

Schools

During the Depression, it was difficult to fund schools for an entire year. In the past it had been the practice of the school board to borrow money to operate schools against tax notes, repaying the loans upon receipt of tax revenues. But under the stringencies of the Depression years, it was impossible to do so. As a result, schools were closed periodically until monies were secured to pay salaries and other school expenses.[177] For instance, in 1932 schools were held for eight months and closed during May.[178] Holding bond elections to provide more permanent funds for school operations was a frequent topic of debate. In April 1932 it was seen as a potential solution to school closure, and a bond election was scheduled for two weeks later.[179] Beaver schools closed that same week.[180] Nevertheless, Beaver County voters rallied, and a $40,000 bond was widely supported when it came to a vote, and schools were able to continue to the end of the term.[181]

Over the next few years, attendance became a critical issue for county schools because schools' budgets were in part determined by the number of students in the classroom. The policy was established that if a student missed more than fifty days he or she would receive no credit.[182] Seventy-three students graduated from Beaver High School in May in 1937, the largest graduating class ever, despite the many strains placed on education and families during the Depression years.[183] The district had enough money by 1938 to start a program of renovation and construction for local schools—including an addition on Belknap Elementary School, a new wood workshop and machine shop at Beaver High School, and a new shop and gymnasium at Milford High School.[184] School enrollment totals increased between 1938 and 1940. Nearly half of the total student population came from Beaver East and Beaver West (361 from Beaver East and 342 from Beaver West, as opposed to 398 from Milford). The school superintendent had identified fifteen additional boys and girls who were potential students but who weren't attending school. The results of the school census showed that in the county a total of 813 boys attended school, 710 girls, for a total of 1,523 students.[185] A school census conducted five years later indicated a slight drop in total number of students—to 1,407 in the county and a total of 647 from Beaver, 453 from Milford.[186]

Roads

The road between Beaver and Milford was resurfaced in 1931—graveled and oiled at the rate of 362 yards a day for about eighteen days with men working two shifts.[187] The State Road Commission and the Beaver County Commission announced a program of extensive road building to begin in 1932. Highway 91 would be the focus of much of the improvement work financed in part by the state, the federal government, and the county. The highway would be widened in places, graded, graveled, and oiled to the Millard County line. Local men would work on the project, contracted in ten-mile sections. With the completion of this work, the highway would be either oiled or paved the entire distance to Salt Lake City.[188] The Beaver County Lions Clubs backed efforts to hire unemployed county men for road construction, in this way spreading the money through the county. With the support of Senator Abe Murdock, the seriousness of the unemployment problem in the county was brought to the attention of the federal officials still considering how the work ought to be divided up and contracted out.[189] By the end of the year, $90,000 had been spent on improving twenty miles of Highway 91; ten miles of repair and improvement on the road to Puffer Lake were completed.

In 1939 the federal government appropriated $225,000 for construction of a new road eighteen miles north of Beaver between Manderfield and Pine Creek, a six-mile, safer road than the previously existing one which wound its way through Wild Cat Canyon. Ideally, all unskilled labor on the project would be done by local men, thereby bringing much needed revenue into the county.[190]

Regardless, decisions about funds coming into the county for road work were hotly contested, and Milford and Beaver were often pitted against each other as competitors for the same funds. In June 1948 the Milford Lions Club accused Beaver "interests . . . with diverting road funds which had been earmarked for Highway 21, to the re-routing of the Puffer Lake road 'for the private gain of a few individuals.'"[191] It was decided that for the three years after 1948 the

The Beaver Garage with the Low Hotel in the background. (Utah State Historical Society)

portion of Highway 21 west of Milford would be a county priority, because of the convincing argument that the entire county would benefit by the livestock and minerals trucked out of Milford to western markets.[192]

The automobile provided a new stimulus to Beaver's recreational development—making it easier for tourists to travel through Beaver County's canyons on roads constructed during the New Deal years, thus enjoying the widely varied and beautiful scenery here.[193]

Airports

Representatives from the county approached Governor Herbert B. Maw about a proposed airport to be built in Beaver, including John P. Barton, S.G. Hickman, H.D. Thompson, E.D. Joseph, and R.F. Heppler, in February 1943. The county had already secured the property and cleared the landing field, secured lumber and other building materials for a hanger, and had hauled a drilling machine to the site to begin drilling for a well, but felt that state help in the project was necessary for its success.[194] The airport project proceeded for the next

Loading a shipment of hay at the Milford airport for delivery to stranded cattle during the winter of 1948. (Courtesy Gladys Whittaker)

few years. By 1943 a two-man crew was reported operating the county road grader and caterpillar tractor on a second runway, which was like the first, approximately 6,000 feet long and 135 feet wide.[195] Once it was finished, the city chamber of commerce began efforts to locate a flight school at the site, attracting additional federal funds for the airport.[196]

In 1946 Milford's airport was given a $20,000 expenditure to upgrade the landing field, build new hangars and improve the road leading to the field. The site included a 500-foot by one-mile landing strip which would be totally paved by 1947.[197] In October 1947 the Milford city council estimated the costs of paving the strip at $55,158, $34,286 of which would be paid by the federal government.[198] The runway was oiled by August 1948, and the gravel shoulders, 200 feet on each side, were rolled and packed. The work was funded by the federal government, the State of Utah, and Milford City.[199]

Within a few years, the airport had "paid for itself" providing a safe landing field for planes in emergency situations nearby. An army transport loaded with several crewmen was guided to a safe landing at Milford by a sharp CAA operator who detected the plane's distress call over the desert to the northwest. During the heavy snows of the winter of 1948–49, the Milford airport served as the base for the "haylift" operations bringing food to sheep and cattle with national guard and air force planes. In 1954 an air force jet landed at the Milford airport because the pilot had not been able to see through a heavy fog over the Cedar City airport. The site was considered by many airline pilots to be one of the most "strategic emergency landing field between Salt Lake and Los Angeles."[200]

Milford

The railroad continued to be an important generator of jobs and income for Milford. Sixty-nine men were put on the Milford Union Pacific payroll early in 1937 in high paying jobs for a total of about $14,000 per month. This included eight train service crews of five men each, ten switch engine men, four mechanics, five car men, three dispatchers, and a night clerk for the dispatcher's office. Besides these jobs, a number of employees were added to the stations along the line to Milford earning between $200 and $350 a month.[201]

Milford experienced similarly significant progress in its built environment during the 1940s. H.S. Barrington, developer and builder, began fifteen new brick homes in the summer of 1945 near Milford's high school.[202] A number of old landmarks were torn down as Milford went through a Main Street renovation program the next year.[203] The Martin Garage and the Tanner House Hotel were each potent reminders of times gone by, their demolition a statement about movement toward the future.[204] These efforts did not go unnoticed by the rest of the state. The Ogden Standard Examiner described Milford's efforts to "improve and beautify the community, and stressed the vast resources that can be used to turn Milford into the leading city of Southern Utah."[205] This growth tested available resources, however, and in July 1946 Milford city officials put restrictions on the use of water for gardening, encouraging water users to test water nozzles, plumbing systems to insure that no water was being wasted, and to restrain from using water for any absolutely unnecessary purpose. Violators would be fined up to $50 and receive a thirty-day jail sentence.[206] A new Milford-Beaver phone line was approved by the Denver office of the Mountain States Telephone and Telegraph Company in August 1946. Responding to complaints from

Main Street in Milford. (Utah State Historical Society)

Milford long distance users, this new circuit would "relieve the situation somewhat, by providing two direct wires to Beaver, and also will
provide Minersville, Greenville, and Adamsville phone subscribers
with direct service to Beaver."[207]

Milford was made a third class city in August 1946 with a town
board president and four trustees constituting local municipal government. Town ordinances would be revised to city standards. It was
anticipated this would make it easier to regulate and encourage civic
improvements.[208] Milford businessmen began discussing the organization of a chamber of commerce in 1947 to help attract business
and resources to the area.[209] Within weeks, forty-six "progressive citizens" became charter members of the group and held their first
meeting in the I.O.O.F. Hall in Milford. They described their objectives as follows: "To encourage active participation in all things that
have to do with commercial, civic, and industrial benefit, and to
cooperate with all other organizations in worthwhile endeavors for
the public's welfare and the advancement and betterment of
Milford."[210]

Early discussions of the board of trustees included construction

Milford businesses with The Milford Hotel on the left offering a European Plan for its guests. (Utah State Historical Society)

of a new fire hall and jail, improving power and water systems and cleaning up the railroad yards.[211] The chamber of commerce took a different approach to mapping out Milford's most pressing issues, looking instead to smaller issues like cleaning up the streets. "A bigger and better Milford is okay—a fine thing," James D. Williams, chamber member, said, "but a house must have a foundation first, then the walls and roof, before exquisite furnishings can be considered. Let's try to get the city into a basis of 'sensible service' before we go in for luxuries."[212] The upgraded Milford airport was dedicated on 10 October 1948, a day celebrated with the "Flying Farmers," private pilots from across the state, army planes from Hill Field, and Utah's "Flying Mayors." A dinner for the town and the visiting dignitaries was held that night in the airport hanger.[213]

The Milford Ward built a rock meetinghouse in 1932, hauling the rock from Beaver. The Seventh-day Adventists organized a congregation in 1935. And the Nazarene church purchased the First Church of Christ, Scientist, building in 1945 for their newly organized group. The Saint Bridget Catholic Church was dedicated in Milford on 31

Members of the Milford Baseball Team. (Utah State Historical Society)

October 1948, the Feast Day of Christ the King, in the Catholic tradition. High mass was sung by Father Valine at 9:30 A.M. and Bishop
Hunt presided over the sermon, a choir of twenty men's voices came

for the dedication from the Newman Center in Salt Lake City. The property where the new church was built was bought thirty years earlier, but because of the Depression and war years, the building was not built any earlier. The building project was largely the result of the diligent efforts of Father Valine, a Dominican priest from San Francisco who was given responsibility over this area. During the construction of the church, Valine worked alongside the builders tirelessly devoted to the success of the venture.[214]

Milford farmers and stockmen met in October 1946 to form the Beaver County Rural Electrification Administration in the attempt to bring inexpensive farm power to west Beaver County. The group proposed to install a 900-horsepower hydro-electric plant at the Rocky Ford Dam near Minersville, with a two 500-horsepower standby diesel units to guarantee the power load through winter. Transmission lines and feeder lines throughout the area would also be funded and laid by the association.[215] Milford had experienced considerable problems with service provided by the Telluride Power Plant over the past several years, including low voltage, single phasing, and power outages.[216]

Fairs and Celebrations

The Beaver County Fair pulled the residents of Milford, Beaver, Minersville, and other county towns together, reminding them of what they shared instead of what made them different. In 1938 the new race track at the fair grounds was opened for the first time beginning with a parade down Beaver City's main street complete with bands, floats, and horse back riders. The rodeo grounds were brightly lit for the evening's festivities, the track graveled and oiled in preparation for the race and rodeo activities.[217] The county fair was held in Milford the next year at its new fair grounds which included as well a half-mile race track. Opening Labor Day weekend 1939, the three-day fair included various entertainments and exhibitions of Beaver County produce. Twenty-four different horse races were staged over the weeked, with awards totalling $1,515. Milford staged its first "homecoming" for the first weekend of the new fair grounds—which began with a parade Thursday morning and ended each day with a dance at the fairgrounds.[218]

In 1940 the WPA designated $12,000 for improvements on the Beaver race track at the Murdock Academy fair grounds. For the most part, these changes were beautification projects—lowering the rail around the inside of the track, installing picnic tables and shelters, landscaping, and adding other amenities.[219] At the fair that year Milford organized the celebration for Thursday, Minersville, Friday, and Beaver, Saturday. Each day included band concerts, dances in the park, and races at 2:00 in the afternoon. On Friday night at 7:30, a soft ball game between the "fat team and the lean team" of the business and professional women's club was played, and, according to one reporter, "from what the writer has witnessed during their frequent practices there should be plenty of very amusing moments and fun for all."[220] The annual horse races became a particular focal point of local fair planners.[221]

In 1949 the county fair featured tours of the Lehman Caves. Attended by the governors of Utah and Nevada, J. Bracken Lee and Vail Pittman, the program included vocal numbers and a brief commentary. A new power plant constructed at the cave provided lighting throughout the cave in its hundreds of nooks, alcoves, and mysterious spaces.[222] Early Sunday morning a caravan of more than 500 cars traveled out to the cave, including the governors' official parties, the Beaver and Milford Lions Clubs, the two city councils, the county commission, and other dignitaries.[223]

The 4th of July was yet another local favorite celebration. Typically, the day included a 6 A.M. at salute, 9:30 A.M. band concert at the Beaver City High School, and a patriotic pageant at 10 A.M. in the high school auditorium. In 1939 the pageant, written by Katherine Miller, Martha Louise Hurst, Lola White, Carlie and Kathryn Murdock, was called *My America*. Martha Louise Hurst, representing Columbia, read the narrative as the pageant proceeded with musical numbers and scenes like "The Birth of a Nation," "The Spirit of 1776," and "The Making of the Flag." Congregational singing concluded the morning festivities. Games and races held at the city park ran all afternoon: soft ball games were always a favorite county-wide activity, as were the dances that usually topped off any local celebration.[224] Minersville's American Legion organized its 4th of July celebration in 1948, including a parade at 9:30 A.M. led by a float with

A horseman and early Beaver automobile prepare for a Fourth of July parade in front of the old Beaver LDS Church. (Utah State Historical Society)

"Miss Minersville"—Shannon Banks, and Dorthy Myers as "Miss Liberty." A program and lunch followed in the school; races, sports, games and a boxing exhibition were held at the Minersville race track.[225]

An important development in preserving and documenting the history of Beaver came with the establishment of local camps of the Daughters of Utah Pioneers in the 1920s and organization of the Beaver County Company in 1931. The county company included four camps in Beaver, two in Minersville, and one in Milford. The first major project of the Beaver Company was the construction of a building in 1934 for meetings, social gatherings, and to house the collection of pioneer relics. In 1937 the Lincoln Camp in Minersville erected a monument commemorating the opening of the Lincoln Mine. The dedication of the monument on 20 March 1937 was a big affair and included speeches, costumes, a parade, sports, and an evening dance. In 1945 Margery Adams Mackerell became president of the Beaver County Camp. She established a committee to research and compile a history of the county. The 367-page volume, edited by Aird G. Merkley, was published in 1948 under the title *Monuments to Courage: A History of Beaver County.* The Daughters of Utah Pioneers also participated in the Utah Pioneer Centennial Celebration in 1947. Aird G. Merkley served as the chair of the Beaver Centennial Committee, and throughout 1947 many centennial activities were held in Beaver, Minersville, and Milford.[226]

World War II

As the United States entry into World War II seemed only a matter of time, Beaver's National Guard unit went into active service in March 1941. Beaver guardsmen underwent preparations to join other Utah groups in traveling to San Luis Obispo, California. On 17 March 1941, the men and their equipment including tanks, trucks, guns, and supplies left Beaver. The whole town came to the park in the center of Beaver City for a farewell party. Upon reaching San Luis Obispo, Beaver's soldiers were separated into other units.

At the beginning of 1940, the government announced the army draft. All young men over the age of eighteen had to register and then wait for their number to be called. Clark and Evan Patterson were the first two numbers drawn from Beaver. Evan was the first to leave. Almost every young man who qualified served for a period of time.

By December 1942, Beaver City alone had eleven commissioned officers in service and 139 young men enlisted in the armed services. By the end of 1945, nearly 700 Beaver County residents had seen military service during the war, including 339 from Beaver, 205 from Milford, 116 from Minersville, 25 from Greenville, and 11 from Adamsville. Several were wounded during combat, including Elmo James Patterson during the Japanese attack at Pearl Harbor on 7 December 1941. Local newspapers tracked where local boys were stationed and gave updates on their time in service particularly when they left to go overseas.[227]

At least twenty-two men from Beaver County died in military service during World War II, including twelve from Beaver, three from Minersville, four from Greenville, and three from Milford. Boyd

Baldwin was killed in action in the South Pacific, and William Arch Patterson during the fierce fighting on Iwo Jima. Russell V. Bakes was lost on 24 August 1944 when his plane went down in the Adriatic Sea. Milton George Smith died in a German prisoner of war camp on 19 January 1945 of wounds he received in combat prior to being taken prisoner. Warren Faux Neilsen, a bombardier, died when his plane was shot down over Holland in January 1945. Ward M. Burt was killed in action in Germany in March 1945, a few weeks before the end of fighting in Europe. Two men lost their lives in Texas. James Byron Blackner of Greenville was killed near El Paso, when a B-17 bomber which he piloted crashed. Archie Eugene Fotheringham, an aviation cadet from Beaver, was killed in a plane crash on 27 November 1943. Others died of illness, drownings, and accidents, including Alma Wayne Barton who died of a ruptured appendix, Alfred Cartwright who died of pneumonina, Elmer D. White who died from acute uremia, George Leslie Oakden who drowned at Midway Island, Joe Erickson who drowned at Hawaii, and Douglas Thompson who was killed in a weapons carrier accident on Okinawa.[228] Maurice Clothier of Minersville died after being taken captive by the Japanese on the Philippine Islands. Two other Minersville residents who died during military service were Louis Jamison and Dell Hollingshead, the latter was killed while fighting with the Marines on an island in the South Pacific. Three other Minersville men, Royal Wood, George Erickson, and Fred Potter, were also captured by the Japanese on the Philippine Islands, but they survived and returned home after the war ended in 1945.[229]

Beaver City joined the state in the Third War Loan Drive in 1943—raising more than $61,000 from county contributors. A "Bond Sale Show" raised more than $4,500 of the total by showing *The Sky is the Limit* with Fred Astaire and Jeanett Blair and staging a "Big Cash Auction" immediately after. Many Beaver businesses donated items to be auctioned off including everything from furniture to bottles of wine, rifle cartridges to silk hose, and thirty gallons of gasoline.[230]

During the war, local farmers mobilized by attempting to increase their farm productivity and planted all available cropland. Farm Mobilization Day scheduled for 12 January 1943 called for every farmer in the county to participate in forming a 1943 Farm

Plan Worksheet for Maximum War Production. According to William Peterson, director of the Extension Service, "this farm plan is the most important document farmers as a whole have ever been asked to complete. On it the farmer will indicate his maximum possible contribution to the national food goal." The worksheet also allowed the farmer to estimate his costs for livestock shelter, fencing, machinery, fertilizer labor, and so forth to meet these goals.[231] The war effort created shortages in farm labor which directly impacted output and the ability of farmers to meet these goals.[232]

On the home front, gasoline, tires, nylons, and other items were rationed. Meetings, socials, and other gatherings were curtailed in an effort to conserve gasoline. Telephones and mail were used more often for communication between communities within the county and the state.

Barbara Bradshaw remembered the day the end of the war was announced. She was working as a clerk in the rationing office in town. The fire alarm started sounding, fire trucks ran up and down main street. All the people flooded out of offices and shops onto the street shouting for joy. Soon they joined hands and moved through stores and restaurants and out onto the sidewalk in a snake dance up and down Beaver's city streets.[233]

After the war Beaver County welcomed back its young men, particularly those who had been held in Japanese prisoner of war camps. Private George Erickson was held as a prisoner after the fall of Corregidor Island, early in the war. *The Milford News* reported, "In almost constant communication with his mother and others by telephone and letter since his release from prison camp, Pfc. Erickson's return home has been slow, due to stops in San Francisco and enroute to that port."[234]

The suffering of those left behind in war torn countries was not ignored as more than 3,000 articles of clothing were collected in December 1945 for shipment to Europe.[235]

Surviving the Depression, two world wars, and other major social and economic shifts took its toil on the county, but natural disasters added to the challenges of these years as well. In January 1949, 175,000 head of sheep were snowbound and in grave danger of freezing to death because of record-breaking snow storms. In some parts of the county, families were marooned for weeks. Every available tractor, bulldozer, and piece of equipment was in almost constant use, clearing roads and searching for abandoned animals. In "Operation Airlift," two C-47s, the "flying boxcars," loaded hay at the Milford airport to feed snowbound stock west and northwest of town. The transport planes loaded between fifty and sixty bales of hay at a time, returning again and again before they completed the mission. Regardless of what sometimes seemed insurmountable obstacles, Beaver County moved into the second half of the twentieth century better equipped to deal with the challenges of the modern world.[236]

ENDNOTES

1. "Abe Murdock, 86, Dies; Former Senator From Utah," *The Washington Post,* 17 September 1979.

2. "The Death of Former Senator Abe Murdock," *The Congressional Record,* 1 October 1979.

3. "Former Beaverite Becomes Famous Thru Television," *The Beaver Press,* 25 September 1936.

4. See: Elma G. "Pem" Farnsworth, *Distant Vision—Romance and Discovery on an Invisible Frontier* (Salt Lake City, n.p., 1989); Allan Kent Powell, ed., *Utah History Encyclopedia,* (Salt Lake City: University of Utah Press, 1994); and "Acceptance and Dedication of the Statue of Philo T. Farnsworth" (Washington D.C.: Government Printing Office, 1991).

5. Patterson, "Legacy of a Great People," 145.

6. "New Warm Pool Will Open Today," *The Beaver Press,* 3 July 1931.

7. Beaver County History Committee interview with Bill Firmage, 28 January 1999

8. This summary was provided by Dell Hollingshead, whose father was a member of the 1927 basketball team

9. Bill Wood, Charles K. Jamison, and Randall M. Banks, interviewed by Jay M. Haymond, 24 February 1977, Minersville, Utah, 56.

10. Ibid., 59.

11. *The Weekly Press* (Beaver, Utah), 14 July 1922.

12. "Sheriffs Destroy 300 Gallons of Mash Made of Government Wheat," *The Beaver Press,* 3 June 1932.

13. *The Weekly Press,* 26 September 1919.

14. Arid G Merkley, editor, *Monuments to Courage: A History of Beaver*

County, (Milford, UT: Beaver County Chapter of the Daughters of Utah Pioneers, 1948), 337–38.

15. 13 *Richfield Reaper*, 30 April 1937.

16. "Rich Ore Strike on Indian Creek," *The Beaver Press*, 3 July 1931.

17. "Huge Body of Lead Ore Located in West Mt. Range," *The Beaver Press*, 10 July 1931.

18. "Beaver's Gold Fields," *The Beaver Press*, 10 July 1931.

19. "Great Future is Seen for Fortuna Plan Development," *The Beaver Press*, 21 August 1931.

20. "Fortuna Mining Company Preparing to Ship Ore from Property," *The Beaver Press*, 25 September 1931.

21. "Prospectors Rush Work in Fortuna District all Winter," *The Beaver Press*, 26 February 1932.

22. "Mining Notes," *The Beaver Press*, 17 July 1931.

23. "Milford Men Developing New Mine in the Bradshaw District," *The Beaver Press*, 21 August 1931.

24. "New Prospect Being Developed by Horn Silver," *The Beaver Press*, 4 September 1931.

25. "Plans Being Made to Reopen Sulphur Mines in this Company," *The Beaver Press*, 25 September 1931.

26. "Sulphurdale Mines Begin Operations; Machinery Arrives," *The Beaver Press*, 10 June 1932.

27. "Interest in Mining Being Evidenced," *The Beaver Press*, 20 May 1932.

28. "Reopening of Mines," *The Beaver Press*, 21 July 1933.

29. "Work Starts on Custom Rod Ore Mill in Beaver," *The Beaver Press*, 9 September 1932.

30. "Installation of Process Ore Mill Underway in Beaver," *The Beaver Press*, 16 September 1932.

31. "Ore From Fortuna Mine Gives Assay of $38.60 per Ton," *The Beaver Press*, 4 November 1932.

32. "Gold Mine Sells for $250,000," *The Beaver Press*, 5 April 1935.

33. "Important Mining Deal Consummated in Beaver," *The Beaver Press*, 10 April 1936.

34. "Car of Ore to Be Shipped from the Sheep Rock Mine," *The Beaver Press*, 9 October 1936.

35. "Star District Mining Activities," *The Beaver Press*, 26 April 1935.

36. "Rich Ore Strike," *The Beaver Press*, 3 May 1935.

37. *The Beaver Press*, 28 June 1935.

38. "Quadmetals Will Resume Operations in Near Future," *The Beaver Press*, 6 December 1935.

39. "San Francisco District is Alive with Mining Activity," *The Beaver Press*, 22 October 1937.

40. "Smelter Official is Much Impressed with Frisco Strike," *The Beaver Press*, 12 November 1937.

41. "Ray Barton Heads Bonanza Company," *The Beaver Press*, 19 November 1937.

42. "New Mining Company Receives Charter," *The Beaver Press*, 7 January 1938.

43. "Horn Silver Hits Heavy Production," *The Beaver Press*, 7 March 1940.

44. "Scheelite Adds Millions to Value of Old Hickory Mine Mill Will Be Installed," *The Beaver Press*, 5 December 1940.

45. "Tungsten Discovered in West Granite Mining District of Beaver," *The Beaver Press*, 26 February 1942.

46. "Work Resumed on Tungsten Claims in West Mountains," *The Beaver Press*, 6 August 1942.

47. "Beaver County's Tungsten Developments Move Along," *The Beaver Press*, 22 January 1943.

48. "Startling Discovery Made in Old Forgotten Mine Tunnel," *The Beaver Press*, 4 June 1943.

49. "Beaver County Tungsten Mines Are Making Surprising Showing," *The Beaver Press*, 3 March 1944.

50. "Beaver County's Minerals," *The Beaver Press*, 26 May 1944.

51. "West Mountain District Attracts Eastern Capital," *The Beaver Press*, 6 November 1943.

52. "Penn-Utah Mining Company is Formed to Develop Claims," *The Beaver Press*, 27 October 1944.

53. "Beaver County Producer Again Active," *The Milford News*, 9 August 1945.

54. "A Miner's Report of the Milford District Metal and Mineral Production During the War Years 1943–1945," *The Milford News*, 25 October 1945.

55. "Milford is Becoming Mining Capital of Southern Utah," *The Beaver Press*, 25 January 1946.

56. "Metal Producers to Construct Mill to Work Low-Grade Ores," *The Milford News*, 21 August 1947.

57. "Horn Silver Shuts Down; Lincoln Still at Work," *The Milford News*, 21 August 1947.

58. "Horn Silver to Resume Production Sept. 15; Mill Equipment on Way," *The Milford News,* 4 September 1947.

59. "Mill for Horn Silver Nearing Completion," *The Milford News,* 12 February 1948.

60. "Metal Producers Mill Adds Swing Shift; Working Horn Silver Dump and Pit Ores," *The Milford News,* 23 July 1948.

61. "Shearing Starts at Newhouse; Booking Larger Than Usual," *The Beaver Press,* 15 April 1932.

62. Alvaretta Robinson and Daisy Gillins, *They Answered the Call: A History of Minersville, Utah,* (Minersville: Minersville Centennial Committee, 1962), 137–38.

63. "Beaver County to Ship Many Turkeys," *The Beaver Press,* 11 November 1932.

64. "Brooklawn Creamery Making Extensive Improvements in Plant," *The Beaver Press,* 23 December 1932.

65. "Proposed Aid for Dairy Industry," *The Beaver Press,* 20 December 1933.

66. "Businessmen Urged to Support Newly Organzied Dairymen's Association," *The Beaver Press,* 28 January 1938.

67. "Dairymen Receive Awards from National Association," *The Beaver Press,* 10 October 1940.

68. Ibid.

69. Ibid.,102.

70. Dale L. Morgan, "Historical Sketch of Beaver County," 33.

71. "Planning Board Crops Report," *The Beaver Press,* 6 March 1941.

72. "Potato Marketing Co. Introduced Milford Valley Spuds to Nation," *The Milford News,* 3 November 1949.

73. "Boston Land Company Brings Extensive Crop Development to Milford," *The Milford News,* 7 August 1947.

74. "Milford to Ship 500 Cars of Spuds," *The Milford News,* 18 October 1945.

75. "Los Angeles Marketing Group Improves Quality of Utah Tubers," *The Milford News,* 13 September 1946.

76. Evan Patterson, "Legacy of a Great People," 108.

77. "Beaver River Water Cases Open in District Court Monday," *The Beaver Press,* 28 August 1931.

78. "Editorial, More Water—More Lights," *The Beaver Press,* 25 December 1931.

79. Bill Wood, Charles Jamison, and Randall Banks, oral interview.

80. "Minersville to Have New Water Line," *The Beaver Press*, 19 June 1936.

81. "Stresses Need for Additonal Irrigation Water," *The Beaver Press*, 10 December 1937.

82. Beaver Acquires Right to Transfer Storage Water," *The Beaver Press*, 7 August 1941.

83. "Erosion in Beaver Mountains Causing Havoc to the Range," *The Beaver Press*, 18 September 1931.

84. "Antelope Will Be Planted in County," *The Milford News*, 15 March 1945.

85. "Forest Conservation Camp to Be Established at the Tusher Ranger Station," *The Beaver Press*, 26 May 1933.

86. "Forest Men Meet With Civic Leaders," *The Beaver Press*, 28 July 1933.

87. Ibid.

88. Bill Wood, interviewed by Jay Haymond, 23 June 1978, Beaver, Utah.

89. "Many Cars of Red Cross Feed Arrive," *The Beaver Press*, 6 May 1932.

90. Ibid.

91. "Clothing and Food for Those in Need; No Cash to be Given," *The Beaver Press*, 23 December 1932.

92. "Two Government Forest Camps to be Established in Beaver County Soon," *The Beaver Press*, 12 May 1933.

93. "Beaver Canning Center Averages 158 cans per Day," *The Beaver Press*, 13 September 1935.

94. "Beaver County Office NRS Established Here," *The Beaver Press*, 10 November 1933; "Manager Jos. Manzione Reports on Employment," *The Beaver Press*, 17 November 1933.

95. "Beaver's Unemployment Situation is Improving," *The Beaver Press*, 1 December 1933.

96. "Re-Employment News: Unemployment Decreases in Beaver County," *The Beaver Press*, 13 April 1934.

97. "Are You Eligible for Relief?" *The Beaver Press*, 29 March 1935.

98. "Re-employment Office Closed," *The Beaver Press*, 8 January 1937.

99. "Bank at Beaver Closes its Door," *The Beaver Press*, 26 February 1932.

100. "Bank to Pay Ten Per Cent Dividend," *The Beaver Press*, 9 February 1934.

101. "Beaver Bank Pays Another Installment," *The Beaver Press*, 9 August 1935.

102. "Beaver Bank Pays 14 percent Additional Dividends," *The Beaver Press*, 16 October 1936.

103. "Bank Deposits Increase Thirty Thousand Per Month," *The Beaver Press*, 18 October 1945.

104. "County Ships 7 Cars of Cattle," *The Beaver Press*, 13 July 1934 and "Extensive Government Cattle Buying," *The Beaver Press*, 24 August 1934.

105. *Federal, Federal-State, State and Semi-Public Agencies with Duties or Activities which relate to Agricultural Industries in the State of Utah* (Logan: Utah State Coordinator for the Soil Conservation Service, in cooperation with Utah State Extension Service, 1938), 11.

106. "Farm Dept. Adjustment Committee Reports Progress in Beaver County," *The Beaver Press*, 28 September 1934.

107. "Rehabilitation Program Making Fine Progress in Beaver County," *The Beaver Press*, 27 August 1937.

108. "Beaver County's Outstanding Farm Problems," *The Beaver Press*, 15 December 1933.

109. "Local Groups Seek Help for Drouth Stricken Farms; County in Serious Condition," *The Beaver Press*, 13 July 1939.

110. Kenneth W. Baldridge, "Reclamation Work of the Civilian Conservation Corps, 1933- 1942," *Utah Historical Quarterly* 39 (Summer 1971).

111. *Deseret News*, 20 April 1933.

112. "CCC Army of Men Increases," *The Beaver Press*, 23 June 1933.

113. "Entertainment at CCC Camp," *The Beaver Press*, 4 August 1933.

114. "CCC Workers Begin Work on Junction Road," *The Beaver Press*, 14 July 1933.

115. "CCC Camp Established," *The Beaver Press*, 27 July 1934.

116. "Delano CCC Camp," *The Beaver Press*, 12 July 1935.

117. "CCC Camp Delano Highlights," *The Beaver Press*, 10 August 1934.

118. "Importance of CCC Shown as Projects Near Completion," *The Beaver Press*, 14 September 1934.

119. "Large Program Laid Out for Milford CCC Boys," *The Beaver Press*, 8 November 1935.

120. "Camp Supervisor Reports on CCC Activities in this Area," *The Beaver Press*, 22 November 1935.

121. *Ninth Period Report,* DG-35, 30 September 1937; *Tenth Period Report,* DG-35, 31 March 1938.

122. "Desert Range CCC Camp Notes," *The Beaver Press,* 28 May 1937.

123. "Milford Lions Protest Removal of CCC Camp," *The Beaver Press,* 21 March 1940.

124. "CCC Head Guest of Chamber Commerce Outlines Work," *The Beaver Press,* 27 June 1940.

125. Beaver County Commission Minutes, 5 February 1935.

126. "Ski Course Selected for WPA Recreation," *The Beaver Press,* 13 February 1938.

127. "Beaver Ski Fans Pick New Course," *The Beaver Press,* 25 February 1938.

128. "County Ski Club Organized," *The Beaver Press,* 20 October 1938.

129. "Ski Club Improves Sports Area," *The Milford News,* 17 January 1947.

130. "WPA Project Approved for Beaver," *The Beaver Press,* 26 January 1939.

131. "WPA Project for Beaver Power Plant Wins President Roosevelt's Signature," *The Beaver Press,* 2 October 1941.

132. "Local CWA Committee Makes a Statement," *The Beaver Press,* 12 January 1934.

133. "$3,000 CWA Payroll," *The Beaver Press,* 8 December 1933.

134. "News from the CWA," *The Beaver Press,* 22 December 1933.

135. "CWA Activities," *The Beaver Press,* 26 January 1934.

136. "CWA Work Stops March 31," *The Beaver Press,* 30 March 1934.

137. "Street Improvements," *The Beaver Press,* 18 January 1935.

138. "Sanitary Conditions in Beaver to be Improved," *The Beaver Press,* 11 January 1935.

139. Ibid.

140. "Building Boom," *The Beaver Press,* 4 October 1935.

141. "Beaver Enjoying Building Boom Greatest in Years," *The Beaver Press,* 4 October 1935.

142. "Work Begun This Week on Beaver City Sewer System," *The Beaver Press,* 15 November 1935.

143. "Beaver's Armory Needed," *The Beaver Press,* 28 March 1940.

144. "Milford Bankers Assure Local Civic Group They Will Furnish Bank Here," *The Beaver Press,* 26 February 1937.

145. "Many Problems are Discussed by Local Civic Club," *The Beaver Press,* 25 September 1936.

146. "Beaver City Being Featured Over Cedar City Station by Chamber of Commerce," *The Beaver Press*, 23 June 1938.

147. "Beaver City Featured Over KSL Broadcast Tuesday," *The Beaver Press*, 26 April 1938.

148. "Beaver's New $25,000 Theatre Will Open Tonight," *The Beaver Press*, 6 August 1937.

149. "Chamber of Commerce, City Council Meet Discuss New Race Track," *The Beaver Press*, 25 August 1938.

150. "Beaver City of the Future," *The Beaver Press*, 21 April 1944.

151. "West Ward Completes $50,000 Church," *The Beaver Press*, 25 December 1931.

152. "Beaver LDS Sell Site for Federal Building," *The Beaver Press*, 1 December 1938.

153. "Beaver's New Post Office," *The Beaver Press*, 25 September 1941.

154. "The Passing of the Murdock Academy," *The Beaver Press*, 12 August 1932.

155. "Volunteer Fire Department Organized Thursday Night," *The Beaver Press*, 27 February 1941.

156. "Official Census Shows Increase for Beaver City," *The Beaver Press*, 13 June 1940.

157. "Twenty Months Accomplishments by Beaver City," *The Beaver Press*, 29 October 1943.

158. "Statement of Telluride Proposition by McShane," *The Beaver Press*, 6 November 1931; see also "Straw Ballot Shows Decisively no Hook-up with Telluride; Preliminary Dam Work Begun," *The Beaver Press*, 9 October 1931.

159. "Manti Buys Power from Telluride," *The Beaver Press*, 27 November 1931.

160. "Beaver Buys New Diesel Engine for Power Plant," *The Beaver Press*, 30 October 1936.

161. "City Considering New Power Plant," *The Beaver Press*, 15 August 1940.

162. "Power Plant Discussed at Public Meeting," *The Beaver Press*, 12 December 1940.

163. "City Officials Open Bids on Power Plant Equipment," *The Beaver Press*, 20 March 1941.

164. "Chief Engineer Reports Progress at Beaver's New Hydro Power Plant," *The Beaver Press*, 23 October 1941.

165. "Beaver's $130,000 Bond Election," *The Beaver Press*, 19 December 1940.

166. "Bond Issue Wins Approval," *The Beaver Press*, 2 January 1941.

167. "Beaver's New Hydro-Electric Plant Ready December 20th," *The Beaver Press*, 4 December 1942.

168. "Beaver City's Fine New Hydro Electric Plant Now Operating," *The Beaver Press*, 15 January 1943.

169. "Telluride Power Nearly Ready for Connections," *The Beaver Press*, 16 July 1943.

170. "Telluride Building Beaver Canyon Line," *The Milford News*, 13 December 1946.

171. "'Unsatisfactory' Power," *The Milford News*, 12 February 1948.

172. "Chamber of Commerce 100 Per Cent in Favor of Hospital for City," *The Beaver Press*, 6 March 1936.

173. "County Hospital Idea Received," *The Beaver Press*, 13 March 1936.

174. "Beaver City Hospital Site Inspected Mon.," *The Beaver Press*, 8 January 1942.

175. "Conditional Okay is Given Hospital," *The Beaver Press*, 10 May 1945.

176. "Dr. L.A. Busch Purchases Milford Hospital," *The Beaver Press*, 13 August 1948.

177. "School Board to Call Bond Election to Prevent Closing of Beaver County Schools," *The Beaver Press*, 4 March 1932.

178. "Beaver County Schools to Run Full Eight Months; Close May 6," *The Beaver Press*, 1 April 1932.

179. "School Board Calls Election to Vote Bonds," *The Beaver Press*, 8 April 1932.

180. "Schools Forced to Close in Beaver County this Week," *The Beaver Press*, 22 April 1932.

181. "School Bond Issue Carried in County by Large Majority," and "Schools of the County Will Complete Term," *The Beaver Press*, 29 April 1932.

182. "School to Open Sept. 8, List of Student Officers and Teachers is Given," *The Beaver Press*, 28 August 1936.

183. "Seventy-Three Students to Graduate from the Beaver High School on Friday May 28," *The Beaver Press*, 21 May 1937.

184. "Work Starts on School Building," *The Beaver Press*, 29 September 1938.

185. "School Census Shows Increase in Attendance," *The Beaver Press*, 30 November 1939.

186. "Beaver County School Census," *The Milford News*, 6 December 1945.

187. "Beaver-Milford Oiled Road to be Finished Saturday," *The Beaver Press*, 7 August 1931.

188. "'91' Highway to be Oiled to Millard County," *The Beaver Press*, 24 June 1932.

189. "Beaver County Lions Clubs Unite in Demand for Road Work for Unemployed Beaver County Men," *The Beaver Press*, 15 July 1932.

190. "Work Started on Wildcat Highway Cutoff Project," *The Beaver Press*, 20 April 1939.

191. "Lions Club Charges Beaver with Diverting Funds from Highway 21," *The Milford News*, 11 June 1948.

192. "County Group Okehs Support of Highway 21," *The Milford News*, 2 July 1948.

193. "Our New Recreational Area," *The Beaver Press*, 16 November 1934.

194. "Airport Committee Solicts Aid of State Funds," *The Beaver Press*, 19 February 1943.

195. "Work Pushed on Beaver Municipal Airport Runways," *The Beaver Press*, 23 July 1943.

196. "Beaver Airport Assumes Importance Now with Flying School Assured," *The Beaver Press*, 14 April 1944.

197. "Milford to Receive $20,000 Airport Aid," *The Milford News*, 4 January 1946.

198. "Airport Runways Discussed at Special Meeting," *The Milford News*, 9 October 1947.

199. "Runway Oiling at Airport to be Completed August 11," *The Milford News*, 23 July 1948.

200. "Airport Landing Strip Gets New Surface of Heavier Mulch," *The Beaver Press*, 21 September 1956.

201. "Railroad Bringing Milford to Front," *The Beaver Press*, 5 March 1937.

202. "Work Begins on 15 Brick Houses," *The Beaver Press*, 5 July 1945.

203. See "Old Landmark is Being Torn Down," *The Milford News*, 19 April 1945; and, "Local Group Moves Toward Main Street Revamping Project," *The Milford News*, 11 January 1946.

204. "Milford's Famed Tanner House as Known Over Entire West," *The Milford News*, 25 January 1946.

205. "Milford Gets Publicity Boost in Ogden Paper," *The Milford News*, 17 May 1946.

206. "Milford Out of Water; Strict Control Measures Necessary," *The Milford News*, 12 July 1946.

207. "New Milford-Beaver Phone Line Ordered from Denver," *The Milford News*, 2 August 1946.

208. "Governor Maw to Declare Milford City," *The Milford News*, 23 August 1946.

209. "A Chamber of Commerce?" *The Milford News*, 17 January 1947.

210. "Chamber of Commerce Activated," *The Milford News*, 31 January 1947.

211. "City Starts Action on New Fire Hall and Jail," *The Milford News*, 21 March 1947.

212. "Chamber Bemoans Condition of Milford Streets," *The Milford News*, 11 April 1947.

213. "Airport Dedication Scheduled for Next Saturday, Sunday," *The Milford News*, 7 October 1948.

214. "Catholic Church to be Dedicated," *The Milford News*, 21 October 1948.

215. "South Milford Farm Group Asks REA for Electric Service Here," *The Milford News*, 11 October 1946.

216. "Farmers, Miners List Grievances in Telluride Power Hearing," *The Milford News*, 1 November 1946.

217. "County Fair Opens Today," *The Beaver Press*, 8 September 1938.

218. "Program Complete for Beaver County Fair to be Held in Milford Next Week," *The Beaver Press*, 31 August 1939.

219. "$12,000 to be Spent at Beaver Race Track," *The Beaver Press*, 22 August 1940.

220. "Beaver County Fair Next Week," *The Beaver Press*, 23 August 1940.

221. "Beaver Horse Racing Meet Promises Plenty Thrills," *The Beaver Press*, 11 August 1944.

222. "2,000 Visitors Expected at Lehman Caves for Beaver County Day," *The Milford News*, 4 August 1949.

223. "Two Chief Executives, 2,000 Citizens to Tour National Cave Monument," *The Milford News*, 11 August 1949; "Beaver County Day Draws Thousands to Lehman Caves," *The Milford News*, 18 August 1949.

224. "Throng Gathers at Beaver for Fourth of July Celebration," *The Beaver Press*, 6 July 1939.

225. "Parade, Children's Games Feature July 4 Celebration at Minersville," *The Milford News*, 9 July 1948.

226. Merkley, *Monuments to Courage,* 220, 361–67 and Robinson and Gillins, *They Answered The Call,* 255–88.

227. "Beaver Sends Greetings to 139 Men in Service," *The Beaver Press,* 23 December 1942.

228. Merkley, *Monuments to Courage,* 162, 202–3.

229. Robinson and Gillins, *They Answered the Call,* 245.

230. "Third War Loan Nears Happy Close in State, City, Nation," *The Beaver Press,* 1 October 1943.

231. "Beaver County Farms Quotas Announced for Current Year," *The Beaver Press,* 8 January 1943.

232. "Commerce Club Hears of Dire Farm Problem," *The Beaver Press,* 28 May 1943.

233. Barbara Bradshaw, oral interview by Martha Bradley, 9 August 1995, Beaver, Utah.

234. "Prisoner of Japs Now 'Back Home," *The Milford News,* 5 April 1945.

235. Merkley, *Monuments to Courage,* 133.

236. "Sheep and Cattle Men Still Face Critical Situation West of Milford," *The Beaver Press,* 3 February 1949.

CHAPTER 8

A POST WAR MOVEMENT
INTO BETTER TIMES
1950–1999

After World War II and more than a decade of economic depression, Beaver County was ready to move into better times. With a strong tradition of farming, stock raising, railroading, and mining, many county residents had to shift and try new ways of providing a living for their families, adapting to changed times and the demands of the modern world. For them, the tides of history played out locally—the deaths of young soldiers were community as well as personal, family losses. The tight-knit towns of Beaver County pulled together in the effort to meet the challenges of the post-war decades and identify new ways of reversing trends of out-migration, economic and population decline, and provide new services and amenities to local residents. Tourism, recreation, and the careful management of natural resources became principal foci of local government and businessmen. By the end of the century, Beaver once again looked to the natural environment as an important source of community identification.

298

A Demographic Profile

The daily rhythm of collective life gives unity and distinctiveness to a local population as a social organization, a community with a strong sense of identity and definition. Beaver County's demographic configuration creates a unique picture of who lived here, how groups of people interacted and earned their living, and how the community changed.

Between 1940 and 1970, population continued to decline, moving from 5,014 in 1940 to 3,800 in 1970. The census provides a look at the composition of age categories during these decades. In 1940 Beaver County's population was overwhelmingly youthful with 10 percent of the total children below the age of five. Another 23 percent of the total were between five and fourteen years old. Thirty-four percent were between the ages of sixteen and thirty-four. Middle-age men and women represented 21 percent of the county, and over the age of fifty-six there were 565, or 11 percent. The population was heavily weighted toward the young.

The loss felt by Beaver County in population between 1960 and 1970 was the largest in the state that year and was caused primarily by the out-migration of young people. The county's population in 1960 was 4,331, and in 1970 had dropped to 3,800, a change of -12.3 percent. The population was overwhelmingly racially homogeneous—3,754 Caucasian, 25 Native American, and 21 from races.[1]

During each of these decades, the non-white population of the county represented less than 1 percent of the total. Yet another interesting factor was the income range. Eleven percent of the total group had incomes in 1970 between $6,000 and $7,000; 12 percent between $10,000 and $12,000; and 10 percent between $12,000 and $15,000.. Forty percent of total incomes ranged between $10,000 and $25,000. Only a few made more than twenty-five thousand dollars (2.7 percent) and the rest made less.

Minersville declined more in population than either Beaver City or Milford. Agriculture and related industries were the prime stabilizing elements in the local economic order. Agricultural development was limited by inadequate water supplies. Population declined most in unincorporated areas, a change also reflected in residential development. Due in part to movement into municipalities, this was also a reflection on the desire for better facilities and services.

As had been true throughout the first half of the twentieth century, the tension between west Beaver County and east Beaver centered on divergent economic bases, towns vying for population and resources, and competing community systems. This played out in competition between Milford and Beaver high schools in sporting events, between city councils and chambers of commerce, or on a private level between businessmen. The county was always renegotiating, informally and sometimes with legislation, the balance between the two.

Each Beaver County town built new amenities and improved its city's infrastructure during these decades. In the 1950s Telluride supplied power to a large area that was sparsely settled and required a heavy investment for individual customers. Little industry was located in the area, and electricity was used primarily for domestic and commercial use. This type of customer did not use as much electricity as industry, and as a result Telluride's load was substantially lower than others in the Utah system which had more industrial customers. Utah Power and Light received permission in May 1958 from the United States Securities and Exchange Commission to purchase Telluride Power Company. UP & L announced its intention to maintain Telluride "for the foreseeable future" as a subsidiary of Utah Power and Light without changing rate structures or personnel.[2]

The majority of Beaver County's 4,850 residents lived in single family homes. Out of a total 2,200 residents, 1,719 or 79 percent were single family residences, 207 or 9 percent were multiple residences, and another 260 or 11 percent were mobile homes. The majority of residences, commercial and industrial institutions, and public buildings were located in the three principal cities: Beaver, Milford, and Minersville. Approximately 292 square miles are dedicated to agricultural use or 11.3 percent of the total county area.

Milford's population increased between 1939 and 1940 by 20 percent, during the same time period the number of telephones increased from 161 to 538 or an increase of 234 percent.[3] But growth was slow after the war years. After 1950 Milford increasingly turned its attention to developing a new infrastructure for the town, restoring historic properties or building new ones, and providing additional civic services and internal improvements.

New home construction made the early 1950s feel like a "building boom," as Milford expanded physically.[4]

Besides the United States Census, numerous surveys, studies, and evaluations of Beaver County have been conducted during the twentieth century which provide a demographic glimpse of local social conditions at a given moment in time. A household survey conducted for the county by the Utah Department of Employment in 1969 estimated the county's population at 3,690 (the 1970 census total was 3,713), which represents a population drop of 20 percent from 1950 (4,856) and 14 percent from 1960 (4,331 total). Of that total, 2,643 were over the age of fourteen. Of that total, 1,500 were employed and sixty-five were looking for work. In 1969 there were a total of 1,120 households, 1,244 in 1960, and 1,343 in 1950.

Interesting, as the birth rate steadily declined, the death rate increased. The county's three largest towns increased in their percentage of the total county population, and the smaller villages and periphery settlements experienced higher losses. In 1940 Milford's population represented 27.8 percent of the total; Beaver 36.1 percent; Minersville 11.4 percent; and other towns 24.8 percent. In 1970 these figures had changed slightly:, Milford 33.6 percent; Beaver 38.7 percent; and Minersville 12.7 percent. Overall population density was less than one person per square mile. Of the total population, the majority lived in incorporated municipalities or in well-defined community clusters.

The 1969 survey presents an interesting look at typical occupations and therefore the social stratification of the county during this period. Although Beaver County is primarily rural, only 10 percent of the total number of workers were farmers. Thirty-three percent of all workers were employed by the railroad, 14 percent by the government, and 19 percent worked in small businesses. One third of the total workers were women over the age of fourteen.

Limited employment opportunities, available land, and housing caused a substantial out-migration of young residents starting their family life. Recreation and tourism industries increased in importance over the next several decades. Nearly every area of Beaver

County shared the potential for expanded recreational development of some variety—vacation properties, cabins, cottages and summer homes; camping sites near fishing streams; hunting areas; natural and scenic areas, and vacation ranches. Winter sports held the best potential for attracting tourists to the area. Good terrain and weather conditions for skiing, and local availability for winter-use developments in the eastern part of the county where long winters, ample snowfall, and a large number of very cold days prevailed, made Beaver County a perfect destination ski locale.

Eighty-five percent of the population had access to public water systems; 50 percent to public sewerage systems; and electrical power was uniformly available throughout the county. Transportation routes were reputedly in good condition and adequately maintained by the county. The county library, first built in 1919 with funds donated by Andrew Carnegie, had an annual budget of $7,000. In the 1960s the library had between 5,000 and 6,000 books and subscriptions to numerous magazines. In 1966 alone the library checked out 17,566 books. According to the *Beaver Press*, "There are some families in Beaver that are such great readers, that it is difficult to keep new books and magazines in for them. They read all types of books and magazines. Some books they have read two or three times."[5]

According to the 1990 census, the typical household in Beaver included 2.95 members.[6] The median age was thirty-one years old, or six years older than the state average age of twenty-five.[7] Eighty-three percent of the work force in 1993 had graduated from high school. Because of growth of families and limited land, an increased number of farmers chose to work at least part time in second jobs to supplement their incomes. All of the adult members of one family depend in part on the income generated from the family farm—it is what binds them together as a family—but his father and his uncle also run a gas station in town. Others in the family similarly run businesses besides the farm because the farm is no longer enough to provide for them all. Total non-agricultural employment increased 9.45 percent between 1990 and 1993. Interesting, however, is the fact that agricultural prices experienced steady growth. Between 1978 and 1987, prices increased by 70 percent, primarily in livestock, poultry, and their by-products. Thirty-five percent of workers who were not doing farming worked for the government; another 28.1 percent work in trade; 12 percent in transportation-communications-public utilities; and 13.4 percent in service industries.

If standard of living is measured by local facilities, the county was well serviced by several utility companies. Milford, Minersville, and all the unincorporated areas of the county were supplied power by Utah Power and Light. Beaver City ran its own municipal electrical utility company. Mountain Fuel supplied natural gas to Beaver City, Milford, and Minersville. Public water systems provide clean healthy water; telephone service was provided by U.S. West.

County and Local Government Activities

County officials had always played a prominent role in directing the day-to-day administration of county business—distributing of land and water resources, maintaining and constructing roads, and providing county services like police and fire protection, health, and educational assistance. Many of these traditional duties were dictated by Utah state law. According to the *Utah Code,* counties are: "bodies corporate and politic."[8]

In 1972 counties were given the power to choose their own organization form, ideally, to more appropriately meet the needs of each unique situation. Beaver County maintained its three-member county commission, with members elected for four-year terms at a general election. To be considered for election, candidates needed to be inhabitants of the county. The chair presided over all commission meetings; two members had to be present for valid business.

The Beaver County Commission conducted all county business and supervised county officers and departments, which was much like running a large business. Their negotiations with federal and state agencies over location of new roads or programs which would bring needed revenue into the county were much like marketing and public relation activities of a corporation—only here the interests of the county were the core concern.

County commissioners approved and revised county budgets and met as the equivalent of a legislative body or board of trustees in the appropriation of funds for county operations. The commission was a tax levying body responsible for calculating yearly property tax rates, licensing and regulating businesses, exhibitions and recreation in the county, and making fluctuations in times of crises or great change. This body also functioned as the county board of equalization, listening to property assessment protests, making adjustments in property valuation, or submitting appeals to the State Tax Commission. Important as an employer, county officers provide a variety of services, and the county employees a number of workers for its separate functions. For instance, the county recorder, county assessors, and county treasurer insure that business transactions within the county are fair, legal and conform to national guidelines. Often contentious and thorny issues, managing sometimes scarce resources requires a sense of local issues, attitudes, and a broader understanding of law.

In unincorporated areas of the county, county government provides services such as law enforcement and fire protection. As is true in all Utah counties, the county commission regulates the election process and establishes, abolishes, or revises election districts, appoints election judges, canvasses election returns, and issues certificates of election, supervising virtually all aspects of the election process.

The county commission set county-wide policies on such issues as transportation, air quality, conservation, landfill, toxic sites, growth management, and economic development. In a county where towns are separated by such great distances, roads played a particularly important role in the movement of goods to markets, farmers to agricultural lands, and tourists through the county. By far the majority of land in the county was owned by the federal government. Of the total 1,270,891 acres of federally owned land, 1,150,078 acres were controlled by the BLM and 130,813 acres by the National Forest Service, or 77 percent of the total county land. The state owned 9 percent, and 12.6 percent was owned and managed by private or other entities.[9] Because of this, effective county government required cooperation among the separate entities and the effort to maximize limited resources. For instance, on 6 April 1964 representatives of the BLM met with the county commission to discuss the building of three new roads which, after construction, would be turned over to the county to maintain. "It was the unanimous opinion that the county and BLM should work together on the planning and location of new roads."[10] Again, on 5 April 1965: "A representative of the BLM requested permission to construct a cattle guard across one of the county's roads in the Milford Flat area. The chairman was authorized to sign an agreement with the BLM providing for the construction of the cattle guard by the BLM without cost to the county, and further providing for the construction of the cattle guard by the BLM without cost to the county if it ever becomes worn out or the road needs to be widened; otherwise the cattle guard will be maintained and repaired by the county."[11]

Beaver County purchased and sold property for construction of roads or county buildings, had the right to sue and be sued, formed contracts and purchased personal property, managed and disposed of property, levied and collected taxes as authorized by law. More than 85 percent of the land in the county was owned or administrated by governmental agencies. The principal source of revenue for Beaver County was property taxes and local option sales taxes.[12] Besides local taxes, the county benefitted from federal outlays.[13]

The way the commission raised revenues through taxes often created sectional divisions—pitting east and west county residents against each other vying for funds to support local services. For instance, in 1961 the Beaver County Commission passed a sales tax ordinance, with the intention of taxing tourists passing through town during the summer and during the deer hunt. But opponents maintained that this also penalized locals who also had to pay sales tax and were unfairly disadvantaged.[14] Answering the opposition, the county commissioners split on the issue, and commissioners Ray R. Easton and H. L. Tolley proposed that the tax stay in effect for at least one quarter and then, if Milford and Minersville chose to repeal it, they could.[15] Beaver city also adopted a local option sales tax in 1995 with the revenues to be used to finance health care facilities.

The county clerk records all proceedings of the commission and other traditional duties.[16] The County Clerk played a prominent role in election and the organization of political parties locally. He or she posted notices of elections and offices which were open for election, organized the distribution of ballots, boxes, voting booths, and all other supplies. The clerk designated the polling places for voting dis-

tricts, oversaw voter registration, prepared lists of delegates, and cer-
tified elected delegates to the party secretary and chair.

In 1960 the county commission included H.L. Tolley, Howard J.
Pryor, Ray R. Easton, and C. Victor Smith. They faced a far different
world from their predecessors a hundred years earlier—new players
including the BLM, other federal agencies, new economic forces, the
Vietnam War, and other social changes colored work even in this
county so far from the state capitol.

The Beaver County Development Committee met after the 1960s
to address the issues of out-migration and unemployment.
Supported by the 1957 Beaver County Industrial Survey Committee's
work, the committee assembled a fact sheet to submit to the federal
government as well as a plan for ways to create new job opportunities and businesses for the county.[17] The government approved the
resulting plan which allowed the county to solicit Area
Redevelopment Administration funds, or federal assistance, to create
employment in Beaver County.[18]

Twenty-five percent of the local work force was employed by government in 1970, and government expenditures affect every aspect of
the social and economic life of the area. The 1970 Beaver County
Commission, including Chair Hyrum L. Lee, George Richard
Jefferson, and Vendon Myers, began the first of a series of planning
studies that assessed Beaver County's contemporary economic,
demographic, and political system, and began planning efforts for the
future. This was done in cooperation with the city councils of Beaver
(G. Elmer Paice, mayor; Halbert T. Lund; Burton Meyers; Brent
Smith; Marvin Spendlove; and Warren Thompson), Milford (Eugene
H. Mayer, mayor; John J. Beitz; John Jiminez; Enoch Swain; Norman
Thompson; and Roy L. Young), and Minersville (Howard J. Pryor,
president; Truman Bradfield; William Gibson; Jule H. Gillins; and
Wayne Gillins). The Beaver County Planning Commission was
chaired by George A. Rich, and included members D.H. Davis, D.E.
Stapley, Wells Farrer, John Jimenez, Warren B. Johnson, and George
Richard Jefferson. Sub-committees focused on circulation and transportation issues, economic development, commerce, industry, recreation, and tourism. The County Zoning Commission addressed
planning issues in the effort to create "orderly growth and develop-

ment of the county." At first some resisted zoning ordinances, believing that the county was not large enough or densely populated enough to warrant such restrictions. One letter to the editor in the *Beaver Press* objected to zoning because he believed that it took liberty away rather than preserving it, and was a matter of expanding government control over one's private life.[19]

Senator Frank Moss announced in Beaver County that a vast land and watershed rehabilitation and flood control project had been approved by the Bureau of the Budget for Beaver and Iron counties—$944,000 in a direct grant of the $2,556,900 total cost. Other sponsoring agencies included the Utah Department of Fish and Game, the Rocky Ford Irrigation Company, Minersville Reservoir and Irrigation Company, the town of Minersville, the Beaver County Commission, and the Twin-M Soil Conservation District. According to Senator Moss, "Important rehabilitation measures needed to reverse land deterioration and to provide better use of already meager water supplies will be financed by this plan." Sample projects were constructing 18,000 feet of main channel lined with concrete, lining 97,000 feet of lateral canals, and laying pipe to more effectively control water flow.[20]

During the spring of 1962, Milford cleaned up its city streets by removing dying and unruly trees and improving curbs and gutters. Out of control trees had caused significant damage in concrete sidewalks throughout town and were being taken out altogether. The city encouraged home owners to replant new trees on their lots rather than along the curb to prevent further damage.[21]

Crews from the Utah State Parks Department worked on improvements for the Minersville Reservoir in 1965; building a boat ramp, loading docks, restroom facilities, registration booths, and other recreational facilities.[22] In addition, the State Park and Recreation Commission hired a five-man crew to care for the twenty-two state park areas near the reservoir.[23]

In 1967 the Minersville Watershed Committee began flood control work on Itsheir watershed project. First organized in 1937, the Minersville Soil Conservation District was the first district organized in Utah for flood protection projects. Two years later, a Soil Conservation Service office was established at Minersville, with

Dwight Miller as project engineer surveying and designing future projects. In October 1966, $499,057 was awarded to V.C. Mendenhall Construction Company to construct the Big Wash Debris Basin, Red Hills Debris Basin, Minersville Field Dikes, and Utopia Field Dikes. When completed, the project included nearly eight miles of dikes, 628.707 cubic yards of compacted earth fill, 229 cubic yards of grouted rock riprap, 1,978 cubic yards of loose rock riprap, and 492 linear feet of pipe.[24]

A summer storm the first week of August 1968 tested the Minersville Flood Control structure which successfully controlled the water and debris that flowed down the basin. On 29 July a storm that lasted only about forty-five minutes resulted in a peak flow of about 1,200 cfs (540,000 gallons per minute). "We'd have lost thousands of dollars in crop damage, besides extensive damage to our irrigation systems, if we hadn't had our flood control work done," Ralph Pearson, chair of the Twin-M Soil Conservation District said. Damage most likely would have been done to local homes, the school, business, and yards. According to the *Beaver County News,* 8 August 1968, one local farmer said, "Just this morning I was cussin' about the money wasted on this project—but it sure is doing a good job and worth the money now."[25]

The Sub-committee on Agriculture also studied forestry and conservation issues. Social services such as health, education, welfare, housing, utilities, and local government were also carefully evaluated for their current effectiveness. Each committee was made up of representatives from Beaver City, Adamsville, Greenville, Manderfield, North Creek, and the surrounding unincorporated areas.

Besides county services, Beaver County towns provided police and fire protection and water and sewer systems. Beaver City had one police officer and a city jail, fire, water, and sewer systems. Milford employed two officers and a part-time deputy officer, and also had fire, water, and sewer systems. Minersville had a part-time marshall and other public services. Adamsville, Greenville, Manderfield, North Creek, South Milford, and the remainder of the unincorporated area received fire and police protection from the county as well as water and sewer systems.

Beaver County's homogeneity masked social problems that called for greater attention on the part of government agencies—a high rate of alcoholism, early marriage, delinquent juvenile behavior, gambling, and other social problems were endemic to local communities. Elderly citizens depended largely on social security payments for survival and experienced a greatly reduced standard of living. Only one social organization served the elderly in the county in the 1970s. The historical tension between Milford and Beaver City which led to duplication of social service facilities—two hospitals for instance— was considered by some an inefficient use of local resources for a population of 3,713. However, Beaver County residents were self-sufficient. In 1970 only 2.66 percent were receiving public assistance.

Another concern to the county in recent decades has been the redrawing of state legislative districts which divide the county into two districts each of which includes other counties to the east and south. Under this arrangement, it is not possible to have county-wide support for one candidate and it is very difficult for candidates to the Utah House of Representatives to be elected from the county. This problem is even more severe in electing county residents to the Utah State Senate. The situation has left many county residents with a feeling of disenfranchisement, at least as far as the Utah legislature is concerned.[26]

County and city government were bolstered in their efforts by the local chambers of commerce and various fraternal organizations like the Lions Club and American Legion. The Daughters of Utah Pioneers joined with Beaver City's Chamber of Commerce to raise an information booth in the city park to distribute information about local tourist attractions.[27] A new armory building was completed in 1963, and the old American Legion hall was renovated for use as a training school for workers in the new clothing factory.[28]

Beaver had two fire districts, one encompassing the western part of the county servicing Milford and Minersville and the other the eastern part of the county that included Beaver. Each town had its own police department; the county had a sheriff's office; and the Utah Highway Patrol patroled the freeway area. The Beaver County jail had six cells and twelve beds.

In 1993 Beaver had three city parks and a nine-hole golf course. Milford had two city parks and a five-hole course. All three towns had their own city swimming pools, tennis courts, and rodeo facilities. The county fair park is located east of Milford. Beaver and Milford each have airports outside of town.

The development program of the national forests was boosted by a program of President Kennedy approving public funds to areas suffering from unemployment. Under the program, Fishlake National Forest and the Beaver Ranger District would qualify for help, and local men were being hired in November 1962.[29]

Utah Power and Light consolidated Telluride Power Company in 1963 under the jurisdiction of the Public Service Commission of Utah and the Federal Power and Security and Exchange commissions. Rate changes would reflect the same scale as maintained by Utah Power and Light throughout the area.[30] In 1966, UP & L constructed a control building at the utility company's $200,000 Cameron substation just east of Beaver. This structure was part of the $1.5 million the company was spending to provide improved facilities in its Telluride Division for west-central and southern Utah.[31]

Television came to the county in 1957 when a TV signal was located on Wild Horse Peak south of Minersville. That signal was directed primarily to the Cedar City area, and in 1958 members of the Beaver Lions Club began searching the mountain tops surrounding Beaver on foot and horseback for a suitable signal location to provide television reception to Beaver and surrounding areas. The Gillies Hill site was located, and a portable gas generator was taken to the location to power an amplifier which provided reception during the winter of 1958–59. In 1959 a road was constructed to the site and a small building was hauled to house the rebroadcasting equipment to retransmit television signals to Beaver, Milford, Minersville, Parowan, Cedar City, and Panguitch. Later a power line was built to provide a more reliable and powerful source of power than the gas-operated generator. Permanent cement block buildings were built in 1960–61. In order to help cover expenses, an assessment was made of $1.00 a month for each house with a television set. The fee remained in effect until 1985 when it was raised to $1.25 a month. The fee was voluntary and, although not all residents participated, it did help cover most expenses, with the Beaver Lions Club providing the additional funds and maintaining the entire operation until it was turned over to Beaver City for maintenance and operation in 1979.[32]

The county had two banks in 1970, two newspapers—the *Beaver Press* located in Beaver City and the *Beaver County News* in Milford—and no local television or radio stations. The county had fifty-two retail establishments ($4,826,000 total sales) and six wholesale businesses which accounted for $1,323,000 in sales.[33]

Employment and Economic Growth

During the 1980s the county continued its planning efforts with the hopes of reversing the downward trends in population and economic growth factors. Also joining for fire protection (voluntary) and law enforcement, the individual towns and unincorporated areas maximized limited resources in this way. Three public libraries—located in Beaver City, Milford, and Minersville—served the county's residents. The principal extraction industries during this decade, located in the western part of the county, included Getty Oil producing Molybdenum in the Wah Wah Mountains and Geothermal Steam in Milford; Phillips Petroleum (Geothermal Steam) in Milford; and Wiseman Ready Mix Co., and Bradshaw Pumice and Perlite in Milford. The main agricultural products were alfalfa and hay countywide and dairy products in Beaver. The number of retail businesses stayed the same and two more wholesale entities opened locally. Out of a total nonagricultural employees of 1,155, 157 worked in transportation, communication, or utilities, and 285 in trade—a significant shift. Government was by far the most important employer—with 324 workers. Another 150 worked in manufacturing and only twenty-three in mining. The highest salaries were earned by those in transportation, communication, and utilities at an average $1,566 per month; $1,268 for those in mining; and $1,136 in finance, insurance, and real estate. Government employees averaged $735 per month and manufacturing $457.[34]

A 1983 study by the Bureau of Economic Research at the University of Utah on employment patterns suggested that in 1981 the average per capita income was $6,269 (the state average was $8,322).[35] The average annual wage in 1991 was $16,032. The regional average was $12,048. Per capita income was $14,200. Estimates about numbers of individuals living below the poverty level are 13.4 percent.

Much of the growth and change during these decades was steady and measured by new construction and employment figures. Building construction activity increased during the last quarter of 1960 by 6.5 percent, according to the Bureau of Economic and Business Research of the University of Utah, primarily in housing.[36]

There was no industrial manufacturing in the county in 1967, but there was a total of 1,073 workers in a variety of other industries. Government employees numbered 292, and 238 worked in transportation industries. Local stores and other trade business employed 231 local residents. Service employees represented 121 of the total, and fifty-seven worked in mines and mining industries.[37] Unemployment in the county was at 5.6 percent, versus 4.9 statewide.[38] Workers in transportation received the highest monthly salary at an average $685; mining, $571; construction, $537 and government, $374.[39] Fifty-four percent of Beaver's income came from labor, 23 percent from proprietorship, 12 percent from property, and 10 percent from transfer payments.[40]

Because many residents in Beaver County worked family farms along with working at other jobs in industry, 1,570 residents reported agricultural activity. Although no comparable figures are available for average monthly agricultural wages, the average monthly wage for non-agricultural work was in 1969 at $467.

Union Pacific Railroad in Milford was the county's largest employer, followed by the Beaver School District, Milford Valley Memorial Hospital, and federal, state, and county offices. In private industry Farwest Garments, Inc. in Beaver (sports clothing), Essex International in Milford (producers of copper ore), and John's Apparel and Western General Dairies in Beaver were also important sources of jobs. Brooklawn Creamery and Hi-Land Dairies also located in Beaver had both been in business for several years. Hutchings Bros. Sawmill and Anderson's Sawmills in Beaver fed off the natural resources supplied by nearby forests for the base of their industries. Other extraction and production industries included Earth Sciences, Inc., in Wah Wah Springs, producers of Alunite;

Wiseman Ready Mix Co. in Milford; and Bradshaw Pumice and Perlite.

Oil and Mining

It had always been true that extraction of raw materials and mineral resources had been a crucial element of the county's economy. This continued to be true through the second half of the twentieth century. Each new find was recognized with the same enthusiasm and element of surprise. In the 1950s, according to *The Milford News*, an "oil well fever tetched" south Milford. A number of wells sunk north of town had had varying degrees of success in identifying sources of oil.[41] The El Capitan Drilling Company's "wildcat" oil well drilled in July found minor gas-oil showing at the 2,100 foot depth.[42] In August 1950 the El Capitan, out of Russell, Kansas, moved its rotary rig from the "Walt James No. 1 test well" to another location after finding no "good shows."[43]

The Metal Producers Mill opened for business three miles west of Milford on 5 June 1950. Running two shifts daily, the new ball mill had smaller crushers and other machinery than when it had closed in 1949. About twenty men were employed by the mill that was designed to process ore from the O.K. Mine, mined open-pit by the Metal Producers crews.[44] Copper concentrates were first shipped from the mill two weeks later. Mill superintendent D.C. Peacock boasted to the *News*, "We are all very happy at getting off to such a good start, and we're getting thirty percent grade of concentrate with seventy-five percent extraction on the oxidized copper ore from the old O.K. dumps. Everything is operating smoothly, and we believe we'll be able to continue operations on a twenty-four hour a day basis with no more shutdowns."[45]

The Harrington Mine, also closed since 1949, reopened in January 1951, employing twelve men. A subsidiary of the Mt. Wheeler Mines, Inc., of Pioche, Nevada, signed a twenty-year lease on the Harrington Mine near Milford and planned for a 44,000-volt power line to be extended from the Telluride Power Company to provide power for the operation.[46] After preliminary development, it was expected that ore production would start shortly.[47] The company secured a project contract from the Defense Minerals Administration for $125,240 worth of development work on the mine for a total of 2,950 feet at the 600 foot level over the next thirteen months.[48]

A group of five experienced mining and mill operators from Nevada leased Tungsten property in the Mineral Range to construct a forty to sixty ton mill in the mouth of the pass. The "Blue Star Mining Company," according to company president Lory Free was equipping the mill with $50,000 worth of heavy equipment, shipped in from California and would begin operations in late summer 1953.[49]

A uranium field was discovered in the area around the North Fork of North Creek by Louis Lessing and Tom Harris. Samples from this site assayed 63 percent; it was determined that the field was about 20 percent profitable for mining. The men drove a shaft through the property, and discovered at twelve feet a ten foot strip of commercial ore.[50] That December fifty-two separate uranium claims consolidated and incorporated the block under the name, Ubeva Mining Company. Stock in the enterprise would be sold to finance full scale production of uranium-bearing ore.[51]

The Atomic Energy Commission created incentives that encouraged uranium mining, including payments for acceptable ores—a guaranteed base price of $3.50 per pound of uranium oxide for ores assaying .20 percent; premiums based on grades above .30 percent; development allowance of fifty cents per pound of uranium oxide contained in ores assaying over .10 percent; ore haulage allowance of 6 cents per ton mile (for a maximum of 100 miles) and an initial bonus for the first 10,000 pounds of uranium produced.[52] Utah's Ubeva Uranium Company, located in Salt Lake City, sent down representatives to Beaver County to study the potential for development of new mining sites in June 1954. A group of California and Nevada investors sent R.C. Hanford, a geologist, to the area that same summer to begin a careful reconnaissance of the area as well. The Utah Apex Uranium Company and the Atlas Uranium both began operations on leased land in the Indian Creek/North Creek area and both had options to drill on other sites.[53] According to Louis Lessing, county recorder, prospecting and filing of new mining claims reached a high point in August 1954—550 new claims (largely for uranium mining) since the beginning of June.[54] As was true during the first few

The Mystery Snifter Uranium Mine in Indian Creek Canyon. (Courtesy LaVar Hollingshead)

decades of the twentieth century, outside investors drawn to the area by the county's natural resources promised to bring needed revenues as well.[55]

The uranium discoveries in the North Creek and Indian Creek areas resulted in at least two mining operations. In Indian Creek the Pole Canyon claims discovered by Louis Lessing and Tom Harris developed into the "Mystery Snifter" mine—so named because the first indication of uranium in the area was detected by a rather simple "Snifter" brand Geiger counter purchased from Sears-Roebuck by Tom Harris. According to La Var Hollingshead, who operated the mine for the first years it was in operation, as Lessing and Harris approached a old rotting log lying along the canyon floor the little Geiger counter went crazy. The prospectors immediately set about trying to discover the source of the radiation, but every time they would move away from the decaying log the counter would quiet down. Harris is reported to have exclaimed that he just could not figure out where it could be coming from, and Mr. Lessing agreed, saying "It's a mystery to me, too." It was later determined that the reason the log was radioactive was that over the years as the uranium had leached from deep in the mountain and had been carried to the surface by springs and run-off, it had been naturally attracted to the carbon deposits in the decaying log and concentrated there.

As it was, the "Mystery Snifter" operated for five years. Tons of ore were shipped from the two shafts run by La Var Hollingshead. At any given time, there were as many as fourteen men employed in the mines and another three men driving the trucks that transported the ore to Milford where it was loaded into train cars and shipped to the Vitro refinery located in the Salt Lake Valley. During the same period a smaller mine, known as the "Big Sugar," which employed an additional ten men, was also operated by Hollingshead in the North Creek area.[56]

The American Sulphur Refining Company, headquartered in Beverly Hills, California, began construction of a new plant for the refining of sulphur in October 1954. Built to the northeast of the historic mill in Sulphurdale, the new refinery used new technology to process sulphur. Representing an investment of half a million dollars, the new plant would produce 100 tons of refined crystalline sulphur daily. The product would primarily be sold for home use for fertilizers, and for use in the production of rubber and steel.[57]

Construction began on a uranium up-grading mill three miles north of Beaver about a half-mile west of Highway 91 in June 1955. According to the president of Western Hemisphere Mills, Inc., the mill would "stockpile ores from the U-Beva, and possibly other Beaver County uranium properties, so that milling can continue throughout the winter months when access to the mines is difficult."[58]

The Milford News announced in its 10 February 1955 edition that three representatives from the Atomic Energy Commission were in the county conducting preliminary tests, meeting with local officials, and making advance preparations for atomic bomb testing to be conducted that week in Nevada. They checked water and milk sources and planned to recheck them during the tests to measure increases in radiation. Also, a meeting was scheduled with area physicians to inform them about public health and safety issues during the test

LaVar Hollingshead, on the left, with two investors inside the Mystery Snifter Uranium Mine. (Courtesy LaVar Hollingshead)

periods.[59] The blast itself, early 14 February, was felt by Milford's citizens. Those who got up early enough in the morning could see the "dim glow over the southwest hills about 6:45 and heard the double concussion about 17 or 18 minutes later." Steve Clements' window shattered at the blast. In hind sight the reports after the blast are alarming, but at the time they seemed relatively insignificant to local residents. The *News* reported:

> Atomic guinea pigs, wearing the little squares of X-ray film for tests of radio-activity in the air felt "a little funny" after the blast when they began to wonder if the films were registering any fall-out, but A.E.C. officials said the only fallout reported up to nine hours after the blast was in a narrow sector crossing highway of 91–93 about 20 miles northeast of Las Vegas and extending only very lightly as far as Crystal. Highest fallout level reported was adjacent to the highway two miles south of Dry Lake in an uninhabited area. The reading was 110 milliroentgen per-hour, or the equal of an effec-

tive biological dose of about 77/100 of one roentgen a year. Official observers described the test as "a medium blast and sound." The blast reporting system observed blast at Indian Springs Air Force Base possibly strong enough to have broken large windows. Sound in the Las Vegas area was recordable only on instruments.[60]

Mineral wealth generated from nineteen organized mining districts had always been important to Beaver County. Although drilling and prospecting occasionally led to new mining activity, the decline of the mineral industry was due to several factors: the rich surface ores were depleted or gone, mining costs had increased, scarce venture capital, and low prices for metals. The Majestic Oil and Mining Co. mill and stripping operation began work on a large ore deposit about a mile from the mill. Keith Long, president of Majestic, stated that the mill was employing twenty-five men and that the mill would be operating three shifts a day, seven days a week, starting in July 1962.[61] Majestic Oil and Mining Co. was bought by Paul and Anthony Bogdanich in September 1962 with the intention of beginning open-cut copper mining five miles north of Milford in the Rocky District.[62] In 1965 discovery of high-grade lead ore south of the old slopes of the Horn Silver Mine resulted in development work by the Plata Verde Mining Company. A bulk sample of the ore yielded 41.9 ounces of silver, .075 ounces of gold, and 41.75 percent lead a ton.

The Chevron Oil Company representing the Standard Oil Company filed suit in Fifth District Court against Beaver County, challenging zoning restrictions against drilling in the sagebrush and juniper covered land near Cove Fort for commercial uses. This zoning ordinance was justified by the commission as protecting "the Beaver City businessmen who have large investments in similar services."[63]

The American Mining Company constructed a $300,000 leeching plant in Milford to handle oxide ores from the O.K. Mine at the first of 1968. Sixty local men were employed at the facility which processed ore hauled six miles from the mine in thirty-five ton dump trucks.[64]

The open-pit copper mine west of Milford—the Shield Development Company, Ltd.—was in 1970 the most important mining operation. The subsidiary of a Canadian firm was one of only a few exclusively leaching operations in the United States. This company brought substantial economic benefits to the county—direct employment for seventy men, work for trucking firms in the transportation of ores to Arizona smelters, and county property taxes. In the late 1960s, the company constructed a new facility to double its ore-processing capacity, also providing employment for construction workers and creating a new impetus to the prepared-concrete business.

Also underway in the 1970s was mining exploration to develop two mines near Minersville, blocking out deposits of lead, silver, copper, gold, and bismuth ores. Test drilling for oil near Garrison was also done in anticipation of new discoveries. Metallic mineral deposits in Beaver County, consisted of bismuth, copper, gold, iron ore, lead, manganese, mercury, molybdenum, selenium, silver, tungsten, uranium, and zinc. Non-metallic mineral deposits included alunite, barite, diatomite, fire clay, fluorspar, gem stones, nitrate, perlite, pumice, sand and gravel, silica, stone, sulphur, and volcanic grits.

The opening of the Pearl Queen Perlite Mine northeast of Milford near the Blundell Power Plant in 1996 suggests that mining will continue to be important in the county into the twenty-first century.

Red beryl was discovered in Beaver County in the late 1950s by LaMar Hodges and Lloyd Mortenson who were staking out a uranium clam in the area on the south end of the Wah Wah Mountain range southwest of Minersville. Small pieces of dark red, jewel-like stone were scattered around the area. They picked up several pieces of the stone and were able to sell them at a fair price. Several major mining companies looked at the property during the next twenty years, but none considered it worth developing. In the meantime, some surface mining was done and the gem developed a reputation for making fine jewelry. In 1975 the claim was purchased by the Harris brothers from Delta, Utah, who mined below the surface and were able to create a worldwide market for red beryl. In 1998 the mine was sold to an English conglomerate for $10 million. The Beaver County mine is the only known area in the world where gem-quality red beryl can be found.

Another rare mineral found only in Beaver County is Picasso marble, so named because it resembles the Picasso agate in color. It was discovered on Bradshaw Mountain in the Mineral Range by Steven Hodges and Larry Walker in 1980. Several hundred tons have been sold to lapidaries to be cut and polished. The most popular items are bear and bison fetishes of all sizes.

Agriculture

A 1984 article in *Newsweek* commiserated the changed appearance of American farms saying that the "country doesn't look like country anymore."[65] Farm modernization and different land policies have changed the way crops and livestock are produced. As agriculture has become increasingly mechanized and less diversified, farmland looks different. In addition, rangeland dominates much of the county. Rangeland is land covered with vegetation, predominantly native grasses, grasslike plants, or shrubs. To many, rangeland is synonymous with wide open spaces. Much of Beaver County, particularly the more arid regions, is devoted to livestock rather than crop production. Sagebrush-covered land stretches on the valley floor between the mountain ranges and serves the needs of stock raising. The Taylor Grazing Act of 1934 gave the federal government the authority to control grazing on the public domain. Today the Forest Service and the BLM control range use on public land making cooperation between county government and federal agencies on land use issues essential, The Soil Conservation Service also advised private owners on range conservation. BLM land represented in 1970 1,150,078 acres or 77.9 percent of the total land. The state controlled 9.4 percent of the total, and private owners, 12.6 percent.[66]

Regardless of market pressures and fluctuations in prices and demand, agriculture remained the economic mainstay of the county throughout these decades. Grazing and crop lands were very productive.

At the beginning of the Depression, Beaver County had a total of 395 farms, 260 of which were owned by individuals, compared to a total 238 in 1964. The average farm had between 920 acres of farmland in 1969 and 841 in 1959.[67] Of total county acreage, 14.8 percent was farmed. Seven percent of the land was harvested; the rest was used as pasture.

In terms of stock raising, between 1930 and 1964 the emphasis shifted from sheep to cattle. In 1930 the county grazed 22,783 sheep, 9,101 cattle, 582 pigs, and 9,555 chickens. In 1950 the number of sheep dipped to 1,053, with 20,306 cattle and 19,545 chickens. In 1964 the totals included 19,898 cattle, 5,615 sheep, and 8,991 chickens.[68] Also in 1964 local dairy herds produced 24,085,822 gallons of milk. Other produce included 155,167 dozen eggs, 7,666 chickens, and 54,323 pounds of wool.

In the 1950s an increasing amount of acreage was cleared of sagebrush and planted with grain, hay, and other crops. In 1952 more than 18,000 acres were under cultivation, and 5,000 acres irrigated by gravity flow from the Minersville Reservoir and another 18,000 acres irrigated by underground water brought to the surface, with wells ranging in size from thirty-five feet deep to twenty and twenty-four feet inch wells up to 500 feet deep. Sugar beets were planted in valley beginning in 1952, as well as beans, onions, and other new crops. The largest land leveling project was conducted by the Mayer and Miner work near the old Experiment Farm. There 600 acres were leveled at costs ranging from $40 to $150 per acre. The first underground steel-pipe irrigation system was laid here, as well as new wells drilled.[69]

Water

Perhaps the single most important factor impacting economic development in the county is the availability of water. To maintain and expand county economic activity, a high-quality water supply was a principal consideration. Water was used and re-used for the sustenance of forest and mountain grazing lands, hydro-electrical generation, and the base resource for pump wells in the western part of the county. Large sprinkler systems replaced historical irrigation systems, in many cases modernizing agricultural techniques, requiring considerable capital investment but long-term benefits.

Beaver County depended on the nearby mountain canyons for water. Sufficient water of high quality for domestic consumption, agriculture, industry, recreation, and wildlife was among a county's most important considerations. Water supply directly affected the economic value of the land, and has both economic and scenic value. Surface water—streams, rivers, and lakes—was the major source of water used. It was replenished by rainfall and drainage from the surrounding watershed (the land area draining into a stream or other body of water). Groundwater was the other important source of water. Most of Beaver County's drinking water came from the ground. Much of this was renewed by rain or melted snow that came down from nearby mountain ranges.

The state engineer restricted well drilling in the area south of Milford in 1952. Ground levels had receded because of the considerable ground water development in the past few years. Smaller wells for domestic and stock watering purposes could still be dug, but not for other purposes.[70]

Maintaining adequate water pressure was a persistent problem in Milford. "Keeping enough water in the storage tanks to furnish ample culinary water plus water for sprinkling lawns has been a headache for city councilmen since the early post-war years when residents started beautifying their homes, planting laws and shrubs and flower gardens," according to the Beaver County News. The city council tried a variety of different policies toward water use—watering hours, installing of a new 300,000 gallon storage tank in 1957, and drilling new wells. But with growth and changed social values and conditions, water usage varied. The Milford City Council attempted to adjust to schedules and demands of local customers. Walter Morford, city councilman, said in June 1960, "We hope that with the more liberal watering hours the residents will be using their sprinklers at sufficiently varied hours for us to maintain good pressure. If not, the next step may be restricting each home to one hose or sprinkler in use at a time. We don't know exactly what steps will be taken if the more liberal water times don't bring the results we must have."[71]

In August 1961 fifteen years of concentrated effort to develop a plan for a flood control dam in Big Wash west of Milford was started. The dam was designed to protect Milford City from flash floods in the Frisco Mountains, twenty-five miles from town. In the past, numerous floods had created extensive damage to business and residential property. In 1951 a flash flood raged through the area for five hours—storming down Main Street and through residential districts,

Puffer Lake. (Don O. Thorpe)

eventually covering the lower elevation homes and stores with a sticky, slimy mud coating. The new earth-filled dam would be fifty feet high and measure approximately 7,000 feet in length.[72]

Sewage disposal and treatment was another natural resource issue that challenged city officials. J. Donald West of Cedar City visited Milford for the Utah State Department of Health to inspect Milford sewage systems. He found a dangerous "comingling of sewer water" from a sewage disposal system that was, according to West, "offensive and hazardous at best." This had resulted, he said, because cattlemen who owned property near the plant had placed dams and lateral canals along the sewage canal which had diverted sewage into fields and polluted water systems. Furthermore, the system needed to be upgraded, modernized, and better maintained.[73]

The Utah Water Resources Board approved an appropriation for construction of the Three Creeks concrete spillway. The engineering was done by Water Resources for $25,000 and construction for $140,000. In 1977 the company repaired the Middle Kents Dam which had been condemned five years earlier. As many as 1,300 feet of twenty-four ounce galvanized pipe were laid at the head of the

Kents Lake ditch where it comes out of the south fork of the Beaver River.

The Kents Lake reservoir was located on public land administered by the Forest Service. Therefore, public and private agendas often worked at cross purposes. This was certainly true of the Kents Lake efforts to provide water to Beaver farmers. Negotiations to satisfy the needs of each group were tricky and often required significant compromise.

Primary management of water resources was a governmental concern. The Utah Water Planning Commission and the Soil Conservation Service studies of the efficient utilization of water resources and possibility of broad water movement periodically informed local leaders on the more appropriate use of local resources. For instance, in the 1970s a feasibility study was conducted in regard to regulatory storage within the Beaver River Drainage Area. Much of the water from the Beaver River was being utilized poorly, and the flow of water was inadequately managed.

The National Forests

No fences were built on forest lands after the 1930s. Land use was relatively informal—farmers grazed their cattle and sheep on the lands in the spring and summer and in the fall, particularly after the first snow storm, brought the cattle home. Sheep and cattle grazed in different areas; sheep attended by sheepherders moved in the fall to land in western Beaver County.

Although no sheep herds grazed on the Tushar Mountains, there were 1,993 cattle on the west slope of the Tushars and 1,440 on the north and east slopes. Around 6,500 are permitted in a given time at a cost of $2 a month. Cattle herds usually graze for four or more months. The Forest Service maintained the land, destroying dangerous old structures, plowing and chaining to restore forage or plant new trees, grasses and other plants. Other projects included spraying public lands to kill sage brush, conducting controlled fire burns, and developing water projects. Numerous fences were built after the 1930s—some by the Civilian Conservation Corps members working under the supervision of forest rangers and others by temporary summer employees. The fences were built to preserve the growth of grass and other plants at different elevations and to deter cattle from feeding in areas with a heavy growth of poisonous plants such as larkspur.

The forest service also headed up the Beaver Soil Conservation District first organized in the 1950s. The Beaver district was chosen by the government as a pilot district to be involved in a twenty-year program to improve all public land in the district. State and federal agencies assisted in the effort, as did the local Soil Conservation District. The original board of the district included S. Albert Smith, Fred Harris, Dan Murdock, Roy Harris, and Lavell Bradshaw. During the early years of the project, the BLM improved range land along the Mineral Range.

After 1950 the Beaver District Forest Service office built roads all over Tushar Mountain to create easier access to recreational sites and to provide access to timber for lumber companies. Ancient remains of sawmills of earlier generations speak to the same attitude of land use, seeing Beaver Mountain as a resource to be used by the inhabitants of the county.

The Utah State Board regulated wildlife hunts in these mountains, with representatives from the forest service, cattle and sheep industries, the director of Wildlife Resources, and local representatives. Beaver forest district rangers played key roles in directing land use policies and programs in the forest area.

A modern-day sawmill was started in August 1974—the Fishlake Lumber Company—by three brothers—Paul, Miles, and Tom Anderson. The original mill was a simple hand-set carriage with a conventional edging saw that sat beneath a lean-to shed. The Andersons' first logging truck was a small single axle Dodge which towed a homemade log trailer. The logs were harvested from the Fishlake National Forest and hauled onto the truck with a front end loader and unloaded by tripping the stakes by hand and letting them roll off, which risked accidents. In the 1970s the company hauled about 2,000 board feet per load and had one other employee. The timber cost less than $15.00 per thousand board feet. The company cut around 50,000 board feet a year. By 1990 the sawmill company equipment was far more sophisticated and included a Mack Tandum axle truck with a trailer and a self loader. Each load is approximately

5,000 board feet. The company employed six or seven men in the winter and ten during the logging season. Although the quality of the timber had declined, it cost $1,100 per thousand board feet. The total equipment costs rose from $15,000 in 1979 to $300,000 in 1990.

Recreation

As early as February 1950, Claude Horton, city councilman in Milford, led an effort to improve playground equipment at the Milford Elementary School. Swings, slides, teeter-totters, horizontal bars and horizontal ladders, baseball diamonds, and basketball and tennis courts were funded by the PTA, the Milford Lions Club, other city organizations and the State Board of Education. Horton also organized efforts to build a municipal swimming pool. Thirty-one volunteers joined Horton to tear down the old bathouse and excavate the old concrete pool—tearing it into chunks and hauling it away from the site. "We don't know what the pool is going to cost in actual cash," Horton said, "but we do know we're going to have a fine, modern swimming pool in operation this year. And it'll meet all state health specifications. Our kids here in Milford are as good as any kids in any other city of the state, and they are entitled to as much in the way of recreation and entertainment" as children in other county towns.[74]

Beaver opened a $40,000 swimming pool in July 1954 after nine years of fund-raising efforts by the members of the Business and Professional Women's club. Beginning in 1946, the women raised $4,867, and over the next several years they raised $20,000. In 1954 the city voted support for a bond issue for $20,000 for the city pool.[75] An early settlement two- story stone and adobe house was razed in 1954 to make room for a new super gas station on Main Street.[76] In 1956 the city set a bond election for electric system improvements in the amount of $50,000. In the previous decade, the load on the system had increased by 300 percent. The new funds would fund construction of a substation in the north part of Beaver City and a new tie line of 6,900 volts.[77]

Beaver County's proximity to mountain ranges and rich forest lands created the natural backdrop for a variety of recreational activities. For instance, in 1970 there were fifty-six camping sites in the county constructed by the forest service. When it was first set aside as forest land, the Beaver National Forest included all of the Tushar Mountain range which was about thirty-five miles long and thirty miles in width and included 19,931 acres of private land and 310,772 of public land. Much of the private land are Utah State School Sections under the control of the State Land Board.

Field and Stream magazine featured Fishlake National Forest and fishing spots throughout Beaver's nearby mountains in an article called "Southern Utah: Fishing the Crowds Haven't Found." A half-page picture of Minersville Reservoir with the caption—"Beaver is one of the best and least crowded fishing-camping areas left in the West"—reached millions of readers. The October 1969 issue of *Better Camping* magazine ran a four-page story complete with maps and pictures of the Beaver-Tushar Mountains, describing local favorite camping spots. That same month articles ran in *Westways* magazine—"Ten Hours to Beaver Canyon"—and *Sports Afield*—"12 Ways to Improve Your Score on Mule Deer."[78]

Tourism

The Beaver County Travel Council 1996 promoted Beaver County's special attraction in a pamphlet titled *Visit Scenic Beaver County.*

> From the rugged and majestic granite peaks of the Mineral Mountains to the placid waters of such areas as Puffer Lake or Three Creeks Reservoir; from pristine and tranquil meadows to wondrous and profound examples of the area's history, Beaver County is a mecca for Recreation.
>
> The County offers mountains that are a challenge to climbers while a marvel to sightseers. It offers valleys and deserts that are serene and inviting. Imagine any type of recreation a family can enjoy, and it can be found in Beaver County. Golfing, swimming, concerts, summer theater, senior citizen activities and avenues for historical wandering are but a few of the opportunities available and thriving in Beaver County.[79]

After the deprivation of the Depression and war years, Beaver County increasingly turned toward tourism as a way to attract revenue and outsiders to the county. Realizing that their best, most

Canyon Breeze Golf Course. (Don O. Thorpe)

enduring, and predictable resource was the natural beauty of this setting, local entrepreneurs and civic leaders found new ways to attract
outsiders to campgrounds, ski resorts, and fishing lakes, bringing
needed revenue and business with them.

Focusing on natural resources, lifestyle, and recreational amenities, Beaver County provided a welcome refuge from the complexi-
ties of an increasingly urban world. Once, again, the land was the key
to development and survival, the source of enjoyment and sustenance. Regulation of natural resources and development, and the
establishment of policies for land use, were directed largely by the
Beaver County Commission, which included in 1950 C.F. Gronning,
J.S. Murdock, and Ernest G. Joseph.

In 1964 local merchants and the Milford's Lion's Club attempted
to attract revenue from tourists traveling through the county after
years of depending on the railroad, mining, and agriculture for their
economy. Milford's location on Highway 21 west opened the "Circle
Route" from San Francisco through Milford to Las Vegas and Los
Angeles. They placed a sign in Cedar City that advertised that the
route through Milford was one hour shorter than that through

Beaver. The twenty-by-forty foot sign was created with "several colors and scotchlite for night viewing" and was placed about three miles north of Cedar City. Elwood Jefferson, chair of the Lion's Club, justified the financing of the sign: "It's been a long dry spell for Milford so far as tourist dollars are concerned, but now the famine is over, and with this sign showing results already, in the winter season, we're expecting a tidal wave of tourists when the travel season starts. No community in Southern Utah is more ideally situated than Milford, in relation to access to the Utah parks, the 'Circle Route,' and through traffic to Northern Utah. Our local service station operators, restaurant owners and hotel and motel owners are preparing for a big year, and they are all 'boning up' on answers to any questions tourists want to ask us."[80]

The Milford Lions attempted to facilitate business expansion into Milford. A group led by Claude Horton ordered Scotchlite mileage signs to be placed between Minersville and Cedar City in 1966 to show the distance to Milford, ideally demonstrating the convenience of traveling to this location in west Beaver County. The Lions were alarmed by the news that "12 ton Load Limit" signs were placed on the road by the State Road Commission that same year, assuming this might limit the types of industry that could locate in Milford.[81]

Beaver County was impacted by the creation of national parks that border the county. Bryce Canyon was designated as a national park in 1923 and includes 35,835 acres. Tourists traveling to Bryce frequently moved through Beaver County's forest lands and used the county's recreation facilities. It was an economic and social benefit to the county. Beaver County was located in the "golden circle" of national parks in southern Utah. It was situated sixty-eight miles from Bryce Canyon, 106 from Zion National Park, 190 from Grand Canyon North Rim, 170 from Lake Powell, and 107 from Great Basin National Park.

With the formation of the Beaver County Tourist Council in the 1980s, and the establishment of a visitor center in the city park, increasing organization planning was directed toward issues impacting tourism. Tourism was a natural way of generating new revenue for local businessmen, attracting new industry to the area and employing local men and women. According to Lucy Osborn, 3,949 visitors stopped at the Beaver City Park visitor center for information about the area. As a group, they came from thirty-seven different states and Canada. The booth was managed by Councilman Ernest Joseph and the Daughters of Utah Pioneers.[82] Recreation spots like the Elk Meadows Resort or the Blue Mountain Cattle Drive in Minersville, Utah, offered lodging, meals, and other entertaining recreational opportunities attractive to travelers eager for a western experience. The county had eleven motels and other lodging places in 1982 and fifteen in 1992.

Mt. Holly Ski Area

Increasingly in the post-war period, Beaver's mountains represented a recreational playground. In the 1970s environmentalists and developers were pitted against each other in a debate over a proposed ski development in the Tushar Mountains, seventeen miles east of Beaver. Leisure Sports, Inc., leased three square miles of heavily forested land from the state. But Wildlife Resources director Bud Phelps said in 1973 that it violated valid prior leases his division had to the same land for deer grazing. The project was located in the middle of the Fishlake National Forest, an area rich with wildlife particularly important for the deer hunt. Construction began on ski lifts, a 10,000-square-foot lodge, and other improvements in 1969. A potential benefit to the local economy, the Mt. Holly development once again focused on the paradox between protecting the environment and use of the land as a resource for economic benefit.[83] The number of visitors to Fishlake National Forest increased from 87,000 in 1966 to 219,000 in 1969.[84]

Railroad

Transportation was the principal employer—particularly the railroads. Milford had been an important transportation hub since the early 1900s as the largest cattle-shipping center west of Omaha. When the mines became depleted, agriculture and transportation became the most important industries of the area. The Union Pacific Railroad maintained a depot, shop, and switch-yard at Milford . Because of this, economic and population decline were less severe in Milford than in other parts of the county and accounted for some

The Milford Union Pacific Railroad Station. (Courtesy Gladys Whittaker)

industrial development in the city. After the termination of the Milford Roundhouse and the decrease in iron ore shipments from the Iron Mountain, the railroads declined in importance in the county. According to one study, "The importance of the railroad as an employer in Beaver County, especially Milford, can hardly be overestimated. Not only have they paid a high level of wages to a considerable portion of the work force, but the workers' retirement program and other benefits have been primary to the county's overall welfare."[85]

During the 1940s, eight passenger trains stopped in Milford every day, four west bound and four east bound. The Union Pacific Railroad provided throughout the period direct rail links through Milford between Salt Lake City and Los Angeles for both freight and passengers. However, train travel declined after World War II, and in 1964 the Union Pacific discontinued Trains 9 and 10, a change which affected about twenty Milford families—railroad employees, businessmen, and city officials. Milford mayor Ray Kizer spoke at the ICC hearings about the change in opposition to the abandonment of the service.[86] In 1968 the Union Pacific Railroad filed notice of intent to discontinue passenger trains 5 and 6 between Omaha and Los Angeles. The Milford City council, service clubs and many other groups filed protests with the Interstate Commerce Commission in Washington, D.C., because of the potential loss to local businesses.[87]

The Union Pacific defended the discontinuation because of an estimated deficit of $1 million to $1.8 million in 1967 alone. If these two lines were eliminated, they could buy freight cars and add another freight train to the line. City councilman David A. Symond expressed his belief that the Union Pacific was not doing "anything to encourage passengers to ride these trains." He mentioned a time when he rode a Streamliner that was filthy, and suggested that one way to bring back customers was to upgrade their passenger service. County agent Grant Esplin also suggested creating a program in which students from Utah State University could spend several days during the summer studying the problem and proposing solutions for improvements in local agriculture.[88]

Highways and Transportation

The completion of the first segment of Interstate 15 in Beaver County in 1960 marked the beginning of a new era in transportation in the county. However construction of the Interstate through Beaver County was not without controversy. Discussions about a proposed Interstate Defense Highway Route between Beaver and Millard County began in the Beaver County Courthouse in November 1958.[89]

Farmers opposed the location of the highway because it would cut through adjoining farm lands. They asked the Utah State Highway Department to move the highway 300 feet closer to town because they believed this would reduce the loss of agricultural land and move through commercial or residential land instead.[90] In November 1958 a crowd of 200 citizens filled the Beaver County Courthouse for a hearing about the proposed bypass. Beaver dairymen, water users, and others opposed the location of the interchange a quarter of a mile west of Beaver because they believed it would reduce valuable pasture lands. Instead, they proposed a route along Fifth West Street. Walter Kerksiek presented a petition with 500 names which requested that the highway be built east of Beaver instead of west. He also referenced a letter from U.S. Senator Abe Murdock who warned that the highway could damage surface water. Other water user groups expressed the same concern. Carlos Murdock, president of the Beaver Boosters Club, came down in favor of the Fifth West route because, he said, "Beaver had a two million dollar investment to protect on Main Street. It depends heavily on the tourist industry," he said.[91]

Beaver City resident Jim Williams did an informal count of cars that drove through town each year in August between 1955 and 1963—starting at 8:30 am and ending at 8:30 pm—in 1955, 2,496 cars passed by his home. Totals varied slightly over the years—2,398 in 1956; 2,352 in 1957; 2,920 in 1958; 2,870 in 1959; 2,359 in 1960; 3,705 for 1961; 3,445 in 1962; and 3,267 in 1963. This sampling suggests that the highway became a more important generator of local business—as travelers passed through town, they bought gas, stopped at local restaurants, or stopped at nearby stores. They were likely to stay the night in Beaver's motels or camp in the mountain parks to the east.[92]

Location of the road and interchanges relative to the town was critical in planning the route through the county, and the Beaver County Commission hotly contested the interchange question. Towns in west Beaver County wanted an interchange at the junction of U-21 and I-15, but originally Beaver wanted one at the entrance to town and one at the exit from town so that all traffic needing to get off or on would travel down Beaver's main street. But when members of the trucking industry told them they wouldn't send their trucks down Main Street, Beaver changed its request and supported the U-21 idea. The Bureau of Public Roads rejected the idea of three separate interchanges and instead projected a realignment of U-21 from the Minersville Reservoir to due east of I-15.[93]

The trucking industry threw in its support for an additional highway interchange at the junction of Interstate 15 and Highway 21; Senator Frank Moss approved the idea as well. The 800-member Colorado Motor Carriers Association believed this would facilitate long distance freight trucks to move more directly from I-15 south of Cove Fort to Denver. Moss also believed that this would improve Beaver's chances of becoming a significant trucking service center and warehousing operation. "Beaver's strategic location provides convenient access to both Los Angeles and San Francisco," Moss said. "This can mean an economic buildup for the area which would have long-term effects." Former Beaver County businessman Blayney J. Barton, who then resided on the east coast, was instrumental in lobbying for the resolution from the Colorado Motor Carriers Association and had discussed the matter with other freight carriers. Moss pointed to the significance of Utah's freeport law, saying it was also a significant factor in this discussion because it "favors cooperation with industry in this matter. The State offers to manufacturers and distributors a liberal tax exemption as a Freeport. This feature, coupled with travel times which make Beaver a day away from west coast markets, could result in Beaver becoming a strategically important terminal freight point," according to Moss.[94]

The first 8.5 miles segment of Interstate 15 in Beaver County was begun in June 1959 and was constructed for $1.7 million by Wells Cargo Construction Company of Las Vegas.[95] The section was completed by the fall of 1960 when a ribbon cutting ceremony was held 18 October 1960. Governor George Clyde officiated at the celebration, cutting a ribbon stretched across what was then described as a "super highway" and opening the road to traffic. A crowd of more than 200 individuals braved chilling winds to hear the director of State Highways C. Taylor Burton extoll the virtues of the super highway. "The big bonus of the divided highway lies in the saving of lives," He said. "This is just the "beginning of what is to be done in this area." After the next stretch was constructed for an additional cost of $2,290,000, Beaver County would have the largest number of miles of interstate in the state of Utah.[96]

The construction of Interstate Highway I-15 brought federal and state money into the county for construction—contracts for much of the work were rewarded locally, county men worked on road crews. But perhaps more important, I-15 changed the nature of interaction between tourists traveling through southern Utah and rural towns like Beaver, Milford and Minersville. Businesses at freeway exits and entrances became the most frequent contact point, diverting business from the town center and eventually changing the configuration of local business, pulling it to the periphery.[97]

While the construction of Interstate 15 drew the most attention, the extension of Highway 21 from Beaver to Minersville and Milford was also a high priority. In July 1959 a crowd of more than 2,000 southern Utah residents met at the Nevada-Utah border to dedicate Highway 21 as an all-paved route, part of the "Circle Route" from California to the Utah parks. According to the *Beaver Press,* "It is expected that oiling of the last eleven miles of gravel on the route will make it a favorite highway for Californians wishing to visit the Utah Parks and Grand Canyon, returning to their homes via a different route with no 'backtracking.'"[98] A caravan of cars left Milford at 9:30 am 12 July from Liberty Park on First West Street and proceeded to the state line dedication ceremony which began at 12:01 P.M. Beaver mayor Martell Easton was master of ceremonies and Milton Albrecht, president of the Minersville Town Board, gave the welcoming address. Miss Great Basin of Utah—Dianne Turner of Milford—and Miss Great Basin of Nevada—Alice Howell—held the ribbon across the state line as Mayor Ray Kizer of Milford and city councilman William Kaiser of Ely used the scissors.[99]

Road construction was key to tourism and was promoted with the same energy as new business development. A large crowd gathered for a hearing on Interstate 70 from Meadow Gulch to Cover Fort at the Rainbow Cafe in Richfield. Of particular interest to Beaver County, this road would help promote travel between Colorado and Utah.[100] Also in 1962 the last sixteen-mile stretch of road between Milford and Delta was completed, finishing the link on an all-paved road from Milford to Salt Lake City. The last section of the Minersville-Cedar City road, also all-paved, would be finished by the next spring. These roads provided an alternate route in the western part of the state between Salt Lake City and towns to the southwest.[101]

Beaver was the hub of Utah road work in southern Utah, with three large highway projects in various stages of planning and construction, realignment of previously existing roads like Highway 21, and improvement of roads into Beaver's canyon areas.[102] The county built a new access road from Kents Lake to Anderson Meadows where the Fish and Game Department constructed a new pond during the summer of 1956. The site was located on the South Fork of the Beaver River about four miles beyond Kents Lake. The proposed

Construction of horse stalls at the Beaver Race Track in 1978. (Courtesy J.D. Osborn)

reservoir would cost about $8,000 to build and would cover ten acres and hold sixlty-three acre feet of water. Water rights secured by the water users of Beaver Valley guaranteed the reservoir would be filled during the high water season. According to forest ranger Don Seaman, the "planned loop road will open up one of the most scenic drives in the Beaver Mountains as well as opening up some very good timber resources, and fine hunting areas."[103]

Interstate Highway 15 was by far the most significant transportation route moving north and south through Beaver Valley in the period. Impacting the way outsiders experienced Beaver County, the freeway ran to the west of Beaver City and bypassed Main Street and downtown services. Prior to the freeway bypass, there were as many as fifteen service stations along the eight block stretch of Beaver's Main Street. In 1999 there are only three. Over time, service entities—gas stations, fast food restaurants, and campgrounds—began to be built near freeway entrance and exits, thereby changing the physical character of the town, stretching it along a line oriented toward the edges of town instead of the center. Downtown businesses closed because of this effect, as the town shifted to the exigencies of modern living. Other important historical highways—State Highway 21 extending westward from Beaver City to Minersville, Milford, and into Nevada; State Highway 257, leading northward from Milford to Delta; and State Highway 153, running from Beaver eastward through the Tushar Mountains to Junction in Piute County provided a network of roads for the transportation of Beaver's citizens to their homes, places of business, or public services.

Airports

Municipal airports located at Milford and Beaver are used primarily by aircraft from Salt Lake City and St. George as well as other locations from throughout the Intermountain West. The Milford Airport is the principal landing field in the county. The construction of two small cinder block T-hangars in 1948 and the resurfacing of the mile-long landing strip in 1956 were major improvements for the airport.[104]

Milford's airport had unusual traffic during the first week of February 1962—three helicopters and an air force C-47 made emergency landings there and waited for suitable flying weather before repair crews and a new engine could be transported in. Not a large airport or landing strip for regular airlines the airport nevertheless logged 690 landings during 1961. Two hundred and sixty three of those stopped in Milford for the night—lodging in local motels and patronizing restaurants and other recreation spots. Others stopped for a few hours so passengers could go into town for a meal.[105] A severe windstorm with winds blowing at seventy miles an hour destroyed the hangers and three planes sitting on the landing field in Milford in August 1960. One Cessna 172, belonging to Don Mayer, had a smashed cowling and the radio was torn from the instrument panel as well as damage to the fuselage. The sudden winds lifted the roof off the hangar and carried it a distance before dropping it on Highway 257, scattering debris in every direction. The supporting beams crashed down on four airplanes stored within; the back wall constructed with cinder blocks was blown out altogether and strewn across the highway.[106] The Milford airport reopened in June 1968 with a grand celebration including a visit of a helicopter rescue crew from Nellis Air Force Base—the same type of helicopter used during the Vietnam war. The new facility included four T-hangers, an office lounge, and replaced the less permanent cinder block hangars that were destroyed.[107] The Lions Club served a chuck wagon breakfast and the American Legion Auxillary sold snow cones and sandwiches during the event.

Milford

Important to community identity are the traditional annual events staged by city and county leaders. Milford's annual Lions Club Labor Day race meet provided a showcase for the best horses in the county from Milford, South Milford, Minersville, Beaver, Parowan, Cedar City, and Panguitch. During the afternoon long event, the "Sentimentalists," three lovely ladies from Delta, sang in between races. The annual Jaycee Labor Day dance held in St. Bridget's Recreation Hall from nine in the evening to one in the morning was another particular favorite social activity. The pony league championship playoff baseball game and other sporting events made the Labor Day weekend a particular favorite of Milford's citizens.[108] Beaver City held competing events at the Beaver Valley Roundup— wild horses rounded up in the rugged country west of Cove Fort were used for rodeo events as well as brahma steers, calf roping, and riding a "bucking car fitted with a saddle." Sponsored by the three Beaver LDS wards, the proceeds of the roundup were set aside to light the Beaver Ball Park.[109]

The Milford Post No. 16 of the American Legion planned a "Forty-Niners Celebration" for Friday, 26 May 1950. Businesses planned to close for the afternoon which would begin with a huge parade at 1:30 P.M. Parade marshall Bud James awarded prizes to the most elaborately decorated floats. After the parade, children were invited to the park lawn by the library where various races, games and sporting events would proceed long into the evening. The season's premier baseball game, would be held at the Milford Fairgrounds and two dances were planned for adults and teenagers.[110] Kaylee Fillmore was named' 49er queen, being judged for her poise, personality, beauty, and measurements.[111] The grand prize went to the float built by the Lady Lions based on the theme—" sack from Huges Style shop." The Parowan Riding Club "Red Hill Wranglers" won second and the third place award went to the South Milford Community Club. The Milford 4-H race meet held each Labor Day was another display event for local talent.[112]

A new lighting system, the "White Way" began operating in November 1950. Mayor Delmar Kirk threw the switch from a truck platform in front of the Telluride Power Company offices in front of cheering crowds. The Legion Comic band played "There'll Be a Hot Time in the Old Town Tonight," as the lights flooded the street and the crowds let out cheers of approval.[113] The Lions Club played an important role in boosting Milford's potential for growth. "Milford used to be the liveliest town in Southern Utah—the hub around which the rest of this area revolved, and can again be Southern Utah's leading city if we all work together toward that end," they asserted enthusiastically at a gathering of businessmen and civic leaders in December 1950. The group addressed the question, How can we build our city? Gene Kirk said that the chief question was how to keep payroll money in town—Ways must be found," he said, "to make this the kind of city folks like to trade in." Roads in and out of town are key to that trade, he continued. Milford must bring tourists and pleasure drivers and "folks who are just curious to see what there is in Milford. And all of these visitors bring money with them and leave some of it here."

Mayor Delmar Kirk identified the lack of certain services—no shoe repair shop, no tin shop or other businesses. This forced people to go elsewhere for vital services where they would shop as well. Kirk also thought Milford needed a new cafe where visitors and salesmen could enjoy a good meal.[114] In 1951 the city voted on a bond issue of $15,000 for a local swimming pool and $5,000 for improvements to the water system.[115] The bond election carried by a vote of six to one.[116] Milford's children celebrated Independence Day 1951 with a full day of swimming, games in Library Park, a free show at the Firmage theater, and a dance at the Legion Open Air Pavillion. It was estimated that as many as 200 children swam that first day in the pool.[117]

The Milford Street oiling program was well underway in 1955—

Geothermal power plant at Roosevelt Hot Springs northeast of Milford.
(Courtesy Gladys Whittaker)

a total of 47,000 gallons of special road oil was mixed with 4,000 yards of selected finished gravel, spread, and rolled onto the smooth-to hard-surfaced streets. This meant that more than 80 percent of local streets were resurfaced for a total cost of $6,000. State and county personnel assisted the town with the work, providing additional equipment, expertise and labor.[118] By 1957 streets throughout the town were paved, making Milford at that time one of the few rural Utah towns with a completely paved road system.[119]

That same summer Milford erected a new building at the rear of the Mountain States Telephone and Telegraph Company of cement blocks to house the central office equipment to operate a new dial system. Cable was erected in south Milford to increase facilities and expand services.[120] The next summer Milford installed a television tower on a mountain near the Hickory Mine, site six miles west of town, and immediately started installing cable.[121] John Grimshaw announced, "We plan to keep working until we have all three Utah TV channels functioning satisfactorily, but we feel that we can safely promise good reception in the very near future on channels 5 and 2." Jay Wright, executive vice president of KSL-TV and Radio, assured a committee of county businessmen in April 1957 that they "had excellent signals on all three channels."[122] But as new buildings went up, reminders of the past disappeared. One last remnant of the mining boom days, the Palmer House on Main Street, was razed in 1957 to make room for a parking lot.[123]

Milford installed a new 126,000 gallon water storage tank sufficient for a town twice its size in 1955. Union Pacific donated the surplus tank to the city and Haven Construction of Salt Lake City moved it on special truck equipment across the Union Pacific switch tracks and main line up Center Street to its new location on the hill.[124] The city purchased a new pump and painted the tank silver to match the other storage tanks.[125] Milford's Main Street and residences in the lower areas of town had been flooded several times over the past decades—property damage always created severe problems for the town. In 1959 the United States Corps of Engineers surveyed the flood channels and recommended a flood control project. They projected that the cost of diverting the natural flood channel would be "under $400,000."

Milford played a very active part in Utah's commemoration of the Bicentennial of the American Revolution in 1776. In commemoration of the 200th anniversary of the Dominguez-Escalante Expedition that passed through Beaver County in 1776, the Milford Historical Society spearheaded a project to built a monument and ramada in the Milford Historical Park. The community raised nearly $7,000 and received a matching grant from the Utah Bicentennial Commission for the project. A day-long celebration was held on 9 October 1976 that included a parade with the arrival of a group of riders retracing the original route, a community barbecue, a dedicatory speech by Carlton Culmsee, and a performance by the Ballet Folklorico attended by over 500 people.

The Korean War

County National Guardsmen were called to active duty on 19 August 1950 as part of the activation of the Utah National Guard during the Korean War. The Korean War began in June 1950 when 90,000 North Korean troops crossed the 38th parallel separating Communist North Korea from the Republic of South Korea. The United States condemned the aggressive action, sought and won United Nations support for a police action against the invading North Korean forces, and began to mobilize the military including National Guard units for action in Korea. The North Korean troops pushed quickly south down the Korean peninsula until South Korean and United Nations forces were able to establish the Pusan defensive line in the southeastern corner of the country. On 15 September 1950 American troops stationed in Japan under the command of Douglas McArthur made a successful landing at Inchon, retook Seoul, the capitol of South Korea, and crossed the 38th parallel into North Korea. By November 1950 U.N. troops had advanced through most of North Korea and were approaching the Chinese border when Chinese Communist forces attacked, pushing the U.N. forces back to near the 38th parallel.

By the time the Communist China entered the conflict, Beaver County guardsmen were in Washington training for deployment in Korea. Following World War II the 222th Field Artillery Regiment was reorganized as the 213th Armed Field Artillery Battalion on 14

Members of the Beaver National Guard Unit during service in Korea in 1951. (Courtesy LaVar Hollingshead)

March 1947 with headquarters in Cedar City and units in Richfield, St. George, Fillmore, and Beaver. Among the men activated on 19 August 1950 were members of the Headquarters Battery in Cedar City and the Service Battery in Beaver. The Service Battery was under the command of Captain Grant Tolton and included more than fifty guardsmen from the county. Captain William W. Firmage of Beaver was assigned to Headquarters Battery, and other county residents served in other units as enlistees or draftees in the army and other branches of the armed services.

The 213th Battalion was at approximately 60 percent strength with it was activated, and at Fort Lewis, Washington, additional personnel were assigned to bring the battalion to near full strength. The training in Washington was intense.

It included familiarization fire of the small arms, firing of the 2.35 rocket launchers and grenade launchers. It included combat training which emphasized the obstacle course, combat in villages, the infiltration course, and the transition firing range. Artillery fire was the main concentration of the training. Battery and Battalion problems took up most of the time. The Battalion artillery weapons consisted of the 105 mm self-propelled Howitzer mounted on M-7 chassis. The Batteries increased their efficiency to fire and position the guns, and then learned to maneuver the Battery as part of the Battalion. To fire the guns it was necessary to go to the Yakima Artillery Firing Range which they did for two weeks in November. The total training time lasted for approximately four months to the end of December when rumors began to circulate that the Battalion was scheduled to go overseas.[126]

The rumors proved true and the battalion departed from Seattle on board the *US MTS General M. C. Meigs* on 26 January 1951 for the Far East. The ship stopped in San Francisco to take on more troops and then sailed under the Golden Gate Bridge bound for Yokohama, Japan. The day after reaching Japan, the ship departed for Pusan, Korea, where it arrived on 16 February 1951. After two months of training near Pusan, the 213th was loaded on three landing ship tanks (LSTs) and departed for Inchon on 3 April 1951. After disembarking at Inchon, the battalion marched northeastward across the Han River on the Seoul Bridge and on to positions north of Kapyong which they reached on 22 April 1951. Late that afternoon the battalion fired their first rounds in the Korean conflict. Two days later the situation became extremely tense as Chinese Communist forces from the north pushed United Nation and South Korean units back and the 213th was in danger of being overrun by the enemy forces as it provided cover fire during the withdrawal. One South Korean general gave credit to the 213th for repelling a Chinese Communist; he wrote "Without the fires of the 213th Armored Field Artillery Battalion the attack of the night before could not have been repulsed, that many Chinese had been killed by the 213th Armored field Artillery Battalion fire . . ."[127]

A month later the battalion was still in the thick of battle and won distinction when a combat patrol killed nearly 200 communist troops and captured nearly 1,000 prisoners, winning for the battalion the Presidential Distinguished Unit Citation and the Silver Star for Captain Ray E. Cox who led the patrol.[128] The citation for outstanding performance of duty and extraordinary heroism in action against the enemy by the Headquarters Battery and Battery A near

Armored weapon vehicles serviced by the Beaver National Guard unit in Korea. (Courtesy LaVar Hollingshead)

Sanghong-jong-ni, Korea, on 26 and 27 May 1951 went on to describe the action:

> During the early morning hours of 27 May, the hostile force suddenly opened fire on these two units. All available men from both batteries were immediately deployed in defensive positions. The enemy fought fiercely to break their way through the valley but, despite the necessity of hand-to-hand combat, the artillerymen held their ground which enabled their comrades to continue firing missions in support of the distant infantry. At dawn the enemy attacks abated and the men ... organized a combat patrol, using a Self-Propelled 105mm Howitzer as a tank. Driving down the valley, the friendly patrol engaged the enemy, destroying numerous machine-gun emplacements and inflicting many casualties among the hostile troops. The scattered engagements continued for several hours until the enemy finally withdrew. In the area defended, there were approximately 350 enemy dead and wounded. The retreating enemy force then attempted to climb the surrounding slopes but they were immediately subjected to an intense artillery barrage. This devastating fire caused the hostile troops to turn back and surrender to the artillery units.[129]

A few days later, the 213th Battalion moved north across the 38th Parallel into North Korea and took up defensive positions continuing to fire artillery rounds at the enemy as offensive actions ceased and diplomats met to negotiate an armistice which was finally signed in July 1953 bringing an end to the fighting. The 213th remained in action throughout 1951 when in the last months of the year most of the Utah National Guardsmen were rotated home.[130] County guardsmen served with distinction, and as the 50th anniversary of their activation for the Korean conflict approaches, the National Guard remains an important institution within the county.

The Vietnam Conflict

County newspapers are surprisingly vague about the impact of the Vietnam war on the area. Mention is made when Gary Banks was wounded in action in Vietnam in January 1968, a poignant reminder that the country was at war. While on patrol with other members of his marine company, one of his fellow soldiers stepped on a mine that killed two men and wounded the others.[131] The minutes of the county commission also are silent about the conflict that was ripping America's cities apart and causing such social disfunction throughout the country. Perhaps this was a statement about the power of traditional ways of life, and the rhythm of the rural lifestyle, but perhaps also somehow related to the respect generated by local veterans for the government, reminding young people about their responsibility to country. An interesting study conducted by the Regional Economic Information System Bureau of Economic Analysis in May 1998 enumerated the number of veterans residing in the county. In 1990 the county had 309 veterans between the ages of sixteen and sixty-four, 301 of whom were men and eight women. Of this group, 121 fought in Vietnam and survived. Obviously a significant number of local youths fought in the war, returned to their homes, and picked up their lives again. What social disruption was felt in larger cities, on college campuses, and other places was of little significance in Beaver County's towns where life continued to be focused on providing for one's family and earning a living, building a home, and forming relationships.[132] Two Beaver County soldiers were killed in Vietnam: Kim

Bird of Milford and James Low of Beaver, a warrant officer and an army helicopter pilot.

The MX Missile Project

In 1979 the United States Air Force announced plans for a new intercontinental ballistic missile system that would be deployed on a circular railroad track so that more than 200 missiles could be moved into 4,600 shelters to be constructed along the track. The air force considered sites in Nevada and Utah, and western Beaver County became a top candidate for the project.

At the end of 1980, the *Beaver County News* announced that MX was the county's top news story for the year. While government officials weighted the strategic pros and cons of the various sites, county residents considered the impacts of the influx of between 12,000 and 105,000 construction workers, the economic boon it would be for the county, the impact the project would have on county land, water, and air, and what the future of the county would be as MX would undoubtedly become a major factor in American-Soviet relations and perhaps the beginning point of a future nuclear war.[133] Construction was expected to be completed by 1994.[134]

In January 1980 the Milford City Council voted to encourage the air force to consider the area for one of the major bases. The council was not in favor of county land being used only for shelters which would provide little economic benefit, but urged that one of the major bases serving MX be built as close to Milford as possible.[135]

Utah governor Scott Matheson held a town meeting in the Milford High School auditorium on 23 February 1980 to discuss the project. The meeting indicated deeply divided opinions about MX. Wall Gregerson stated he believed that the "silent majority" in the county were not opposed to MX, but " . . . most object to the possible change in their way of life." Gregerson went on to express the concerns of many: "It could be catastrophic if Russia attacks. Russians cannot be trusted." He referred to their past actions and their presence in Afghanistan, indicating the need to support this plan to defend the United States from Soviet aggression.

Jay Hiatt lamented the fact that Milford's population was stagnant and that young people had to leave the area to find employment. He concluded, "We'd like to see some growth. If MX is it, we'll accept it and overcome the problems."

Vern Wood, speaking for the Wood and Eyre Cattle Company which ran cattle in Pine Valley, feared that MX would force them out of business because contrary to air forces promises that cattle would be permitted to graze around the clusters, it would not be possible. Furthermore, there was no extra water in the county to support the project and " . . . we'll loose one half of Beaver County to MX including antelope herds and recreation."

Dr. D.A. Synond argued that only a small minority supported the projects which included the major newspaper' editor and those " . . . who . . . expected to make big bucks." He went on to predict that "the impact of MX would be inflationary beyond belief. The impact on environment and communities would be a horror." He suggested " . . . that instead of building more war making machines, we should help the world feed themselves and make the world beautiful."[136]

If local residents were ambivalent about MX, so was the rest of the nation. Concerns of cost, actual need, and long-range impacts were debated in Congress and among military leaders. When the First Presidency of the Church of Jesus Christ of Latter-day Saints issued a statement that MX was not wanted in Utah, it became clear that the controversial project would have a difficult time ever becoming a reality.

The MX project had been proposed by Jimmy Carter, but after the election of Ronald Reagan in 1980 its status was unclear. Throughout 1981 air force planners moved forward with preliminary work on the project, making several major changes in the initial plans. However, Reagan never fully embraced the MX project and favored his own Strategic Defense Initiative which would be based in space, not in the isolated valleys of Utah and Nevada. By the end of 1981 there was little hope or concern that MX would ever become a reality.[137]

Medical and Health

Beaver County's medical and health needs continued to be a priority after World War II. In large measure, these needs were satisfied through the county health department—which includes the three county commissioners, a doctor director, and a county public nurse—and a collaboration with a multi-county regional health program. The Southwestern Planning District (a five-county area) joins Beaver with Washington, Iron, Kane, and Garfield counties in providing health care for inhabitants of the region. Beaver County had several hospital facilities and long-term care beds, primarily at Milford. Milford Valley Memorial Hospital has about fourteen general care beds and twenty long-term care. Beaver Valley Hospital at Beaver had a ten-bed capacity with no long-term beds.

In 1950 medical care provided at the small Milford hospital was restricted by the number of available full-time nurses. According to Dr. Eugene H. Davie, two registered nurses had more patients than they could properly care for. Davie offered to train girls or young women as nurses. "They would obtain," he said, "practical experience in addition to good pay at the hospital, and would be offered regular nurses lecture classes in the evening . . . They would be given a certificate, entitling them to work as a practical nurse anywhere in the country." The hospital was also short of supplies such as towels, sheets, bed pads, and other necessities, and Davie called for donations.[138]

The Milford Valley Memorial Hospital Association incorporated in 1953 with the expressed purpose to "operate, maintain, and extend or build a hospital in Milford, Utah for the purpose of promoting the health and physical welfare of the inhabitants of Milford and adjacent area." The group also planned to build a new hospital or expand the existing structure. In an important way, the group's organization expressed a commitment to keep the hospital in Milford and present a united front against efforts to pull it to the east side of the county.[139]

Plans for a new hospital in Milford were announced by the Milford Valley Memorial Hospital Association in March 1960. A strip of land 245 feet wide located between Main and 100 West streets in the southeast end of the Milford fairgrounds was secured by the city council; a survey of soil conditions, slop, and other studies preliminary to construction were begun in March as well, and Ashley T. Carpenter was hired as architect for the project. The proposed budget for the hospital construction was $350,000, including $175,000 from federal funds, another $192,500 from the county, and another 13 percent of the total cost from private funds.[140] Plans for the hospital were fine-tuned during the next several months, and a series of public hearings was held to generate support for a public bond to fund part of the project. Ideally, the hospital would service the west end of Beaver County.[141]

Milford's main businesses, clubs, and other organizations joined private individuals to raise funds for the hospital—a $160,000 bond issue, $5,000 from private donations, and smaller donations from various fund raising events. The Deer Hunters Ball, for one, raised $391.35. The Lions Club, the Lady Trainmen, Legion Auxiliary, Minersville Relief Society, ESA Sorority and the Seven Cleveretes 4-H Club all sponsored booths at a street dance sponsored by the hospital association.[142]

In December 1962, Milford received notice of approval of a federal grant of $195,294 of Hill-Burton funds for construction of a ten-bed hospital and ten-bed nursing home in Milford.[143] When completed, the Milford Valley Memorial hospital was comparable to that in Beaver, offering Xray and laboratory diagnostic services, cardiac care, and limited emergency and trauma services. The County Public Health Department provided immunizations, epidemiology, environmental health, cancer screening, WIC programs, HTN screening, and educational programs, well child assessments, school nursing services, STD program, and general health services. More than a thousand people visited the new hospital on its opening day— 6 June 1965. The Gray Ladies, Junior Red Cross Girls, and members of the Service Area Board of Trustees conducted tours of the facility and entertained guests throughout the day.[144]

Recognizing the tremendous benefit federal and state funds could provide for Beaver City if a new hospital were built there, the Beaver City Council backed efforts to plan construction of a new hospital for Beaver in October 1959, pledging to appropriate funds to be used for a "suitable" building.[145]

At a series of town meetings, local supporters of the hospital project met to discuss the implications of the county-supported hospital in Milford and the difficulty in securing federal funds for two hospitals in the county. Evan Nielsen, high school instructor, studied statistics gathered from LDS church records, 1958 income tax returns,

The Frisco Charcoal Kilns. (Courtesy Gladys Whittaker)

and a survey of local residents to determine how many families had hospital expenses the previous year. The conclusion, he suggested, was that substantial funds were being spent outside of town on medical service—money that should be spent in Beaver City instead.[146]

In 1959 the county commission helped resolve this competition by delineating the boundaries of a new Hospital Service Area, providing the way to access federal funds for a hospital in Beaver City as well as Milford.[147] Two areas in the county would therefore qualify for Hill-Burton federal funds.[148] Many members of the Beaver Hospital Committee met with the Beaver County Commission in December 1959 to petition the board for an appropriation of $15,000 to begin the hospital projects. It was clear after this point that the commission would have to juggle the two competing interests in the distribution of available resources.[149]

In 1963 voters considered a bond issue to fund $149,000 for a hospital in Service Area No. 1, the area east of Minersville Reservoir. The money, designated for construction as well as for running the hospital, was part of the total estimated cost of the facility of $253,850. Located on a site in Beaver City on the west corner of 1st North and 4th East, the building would include 745 square feet of administration space and 2,675 square feet of patient space—including ten beds and five two-bed rooms, or another 1,200 square feet, and another 625 for corridors and 210 for a day room.[150]

By April 1964 final construction plans for the Milford facility, designed by architects Carpenter and Stringham of Salt Lake City, were approved by Hill-Burton in San Francisco and accepted at the Beaver Hospital Board. Russel Mayer, chair of the board of Beaver County Service Area No. 2, said the building would be "the most modern structure Beaver County has ever known, with each room individually electrically heated, cooled by refrigeration, oxygen piped in each room, and inter-com telephone and communications extending to each room, corridor and rest area." For an estimated cost of $400,000, the structure would include ten patient rooms and wards, administration offices, recreation rooms, dining rooms, waiting rooms, a nursery, operating room, isolation ward, kitchen, laundry, and storage rooms.[151]

Progress on the Beaver City hospital project was halted while the Utah Supreme Court considered a challenge to the bond issue which would fund hospital construction in Hospital Service Area No. 1. The plaintiff, Sherman Carter, sought a declaratory judgement that Beaver County Service Area No. 1 was in violation of the bill specifying legitimate services provided by a service area—police protection, structural fire protection, culinary or irrigation water retail service and conservation, among numerous other services. Many of these services, in theory, might duplicate services offered by the county itself.[152]

During April, Beaver City voters voted nine to one in support of the hospital plan. This was the third vote, showing their willingness to help pay for the project.[153] The case, Carter vs. Beaver City, was heard by Judge Day in the county courthouse in May 1965. The court decided in favor of Beaver City and established a thirty-day time period in which protests could be filed against the decision. Construction began on the Beaver Hospital in July 1965.[154] Carter

Brothers of Cedar City built the brick building with desert coral face brick and cast stone panels.[155]

In 1998 there were two hospitals and two medical clinics in Beaver City and Milford. The Beaver Valley hospital provides the following services: x-ray, physical therapy, social services, dietary services, home health care, outpatient services, an intensive care unit, and ambulance service. The staff includes three x-ray technicians, three medical technologies, three physicians, six registered nurses, and one L.P.N.

Education

The largest problem facing the Beaver County Board of Education between 1950 and 1965 was decreasing student enrollment. Even though yearly declines were slight, they were steady. The enrollment was 1,333 in 1950, 1195 in 1952,[156] and 1,134 in 1963. In 1952 the county decreased by sixty-two students—Milford High lost no students, Milford Elementary dropped nineteen students, Minersville gained seven students, and Beaver High lost forty-one students. The next year another sixty students left the system.[157] These declines in student populations strained available support from the State Board of Education.[158] The local school board had to deal with reductions in Distribution Units (state appropriations) and had no immediate way of reducing classroom costs.

The unstable enrollment in the district caused perpetual school finance problems. According to Superintendent D.R. Pearce of the Beaver School District, "We in Beaver County are caught in the squeeze between many fixed costs and decreasing authority to provide educational opportunity to our children." As a result, the district had to cut expenditures for supplies, building maintenance, texts, and implement a more modest program. "We can no longer operate as we have done in the past by simply doubling up the children in each class."[159] A proposed three-mill property tax increase for schools was voted down in 1954, 777 to 297. Beaver, as well as seven other districts, all rural agricultural areas, voted against tax increases for school financing. In Beaver, Sanpete, and Millard counties the vote was about three to one in opposition to the idea.[160]

In the aftermath of the defeated tax increase for schools the

Beaver School Board met to consider a proposal for reducing the number of teachers in the district by four and drastic cuts in services. The Beaver County Educational Association, representing local teachers, met with the board and presented the following recommendations: (1) that teachers be given a decent raise and that the board cut programs if necessary; (2) that salary rates reflect education and experience; and (3) that the association pool contracts until a satisfactory agreement was reached.[161] Two weeks after the meeting, teachers who were members of the the Beaver County Educational Association rejected the contracts that had been recently sent and returned nearly all of them.[162] The next week the board met again to try and find another way to resolve the complicated financial situation.[163] After another meeting of the teachers association, many of the teachers voted to accept the contracts, but eighteen of the forty-nine teachers indicated that they would not return the following year.[164]

A second problem was the ratio of students to teachers—in 1950 there were 1,333 students and forty-five teachers, or a ratio of nearly thirty students per teacher. By 1964–65, with 1,204 students and fifty-four teachers, the ratio had dropped drastically to twenty-two students per teacher—well below the nationally prescribed ratio of twenty-five students per teacher. In some classes, such as the language arts program classes, 90 to 100 students attended lectures by one instructor. In other classes students met with teachers on a one-on-one basis.

The school board also struggled with issues about employment of teachers specially trained in chemistry, mathematics, and business, with fluctuating school populations. Under the "Special School" program of the State Board of Education, Beaver County was able to employ several additional instructors to maintain a satisfactory program in terms of state expectations regardless of student population.

Teacher turnover in the secondary schools was relatively high throughout the 1960s. According to one report, every other year about 50 percent of the teaching faculty changed. For instance, during the 1962–63 school year there were six new teachers at Milford High and three at Beaver High School. This raised the expense of training new teachers, and added to the costs of recruitment, while the district lost the benefit of having an experienced staff of qualified teachers.[165] Improvements were made, and since the mid-1980s the teaching faculty has been very stable.

Overall, 55.9 percent of Beaver County's educators were men. Also 55.9 percent of all teachers had bachelor's degrees, 23.7 percent had some additional training, and 20.3 percent had master's degrees or higher. As a group, these educators were relatively youthful—30.5 percent between the ages of 19–29, 28.9 percent between 30–39, 16.9 percent between 40–49, 20.3 percent between 50–59, and 3.4 over sixty. Salaries varied that same year (1970) between a typical beginning salary of $5,950 to $8,075 (typically reached after working for the school district for twelve years). A master's degree boosted one's salary an additional $600.

In 1970, 297 students were enrolled in Beaver City's Belknap Elementary and 335 in Beaver High School. Milford Elementary had 183 students and their high school 192. Minersville Elementary had 98 students and bused its students to Beaver High School. The nearest two year-state college was Dixie College located to the south in St. George and four-year college in Cedar City—Southern Utah State College. Sevier Technical College in Richfield was another educational option.

Despite these kinds of strains, the district maintained a vigorous building program, reflecting the attitude that the county's children were a primary resource and ought to be educated in the most up-to-date facilities. A survey reported that buildings throughout the county were structurally sound with the exception of the elementary schools in Minersville and Milford. They recommended restoration and modernization plans for the Beaver schools but suggested that the Milford and Minersville schools be demolished because repairs would be too costly.[166]

A delegation of seventeen Milford residents attended a school board meeting in January 1956 to request a new elementary school for Milford. The group identified a number of problems with the older structure, including drab colored walls, worn out floors, poor lighting, and other significant structural problems. They proposed that a bond issue be passed in the county to finance the building and that an engineer be hired to conduct a survey of existing school buildings in the county.[167]

The 1956 school tax levy passed with a vote of 819 to 154, reflecting significant changed sentiment and an increased awareness of the difficulties facing the county school district.[168] Beaver County voters approved a $550,000 bond issue for the construction of school buildings including a new elementary school at Milford for $365,000 and a $175,000 smaller school at Minersville. Another $600,000 were needed to remodel other county schools. It was expected that some of the money would come from the state.[169] The board hired architect L. Robert Gardner of Cedar City to design both buildings and Allred & Mitchell of Altamont as general contractors for the Milford project and the Carter Brothers of Cedar City for the Minersville school.[170]

When completed, teachers, parents, and students were satisfied with their new facility and enthusiastically described it to the *Beaver County News:* "I didn't realize what an unattractive, unsafe, undesirable building we had been using until I saw the old building empty, with no fixtures or shelves or equipment to hide the bare walls," one instructor remarked. "The new building, with modern design, features windows in both halls and exterior walls, providing an abundance of light, and adding to the cheerfulness of the general atmosphere . . . The kitchen, . . . is a dream kitchen, with three large ovens, ample cooking space on flat-topped stoves and large preparation and serving counters."[171] Class size ranged from twenty to thirty-nine students.

Local schools were affected by State Board of Education policies and responses to changing school enrollments. In 1966 the state suggested it might close the Minersville school and force the consolidation of Milford-Beaver high schools. State policy was that elementary schools had to maintain a minimum of twenty-five students per grade and secondary schools seventy-five students per grade, and that the school was obligated to provide transportation for those students in outlying areas.[172]

In response to this suggestion, Beaver's Business and Professional Women's Club sponsored a meeting with the Beaver County Board of Education on Wednesday, 12 October 1966, to discuss the consolidation issue. Parents of local students were urged to come and voice their concerns, discuss the new directive, and make their views known.[173] The reaction was overwhelmingly negative—it was clear Beaver County citizens did not want a consolidated high school and would fight it, saying there wasn't enough taxable valuation in the county to build a consolidated high school. Two hundred county residents attended the meeting, as did Leon Jennings of St. George, a member of the state board.[174] Other rural central Utah communities reacted similarly to the threat of consolidation, and Beaver County joined them in their opposition with letters, meetings, and editorials in local newspapers, voicing their almost unanimous disapproval of the concept.[175]

One of the most innovative and popular programs at Beaver High School was the students' radio station KBCS, 660 kilocycles on the radio dial, "The Voice of Beaver High School," which began its twentieth year of service in 1969. Beaver's radio station was the first in Utah to be recognized for its professional standards, when, in 1949, A.R. Adams, English instructor at the high school, purchased some war surplus equipment to start up a station. By 1950, in a two-by-four foot partitioned off space in the basement, the station began broadcasts. According to one report, "Touring artists who have been here on lyceums say the station compares favorably in every respect with professional stations. Zane G. Adler, radio and journalism instructor says, 'This is one of the most practical departments in the school because it provides on the job training for students.'"[176] The radio station helped create a sense of community in the county by broadcasting local sports events. A variety of programs ran routinely each day—newcasting: Carol Williams, Barbara Dalton, and Karma Joseph, the "Trio Time Gals" singing from 4:15–4:30; and, the "Dave Calvert Show" featuring a male quartet.

One instructor emphasized the breadth of instruction students were getting through the activity: "One real benefit which seems to receive little attention is the value of the station in teaching English to the students. The practice they get in preparing for an interview and then getting the interview into shape for broadcast is very valuable—especially since the student is often able to tape his work and hear his own voice and get to know the importance of proper usage of words and inflections."[177]

But local football and basketball games were the all-time favorite

The Philo T. Farnsworth statue on the westside of the Historic Beaver
County Courthouse (Allan Kent Powell)

radio programs on KBCS. In 1958 the Beaver Lions Club took over
sponsorship of the telephone hookups so that away games could also
be broadcasted locally.

Beaver County students held their own in national standardized tests and other evaluations. According to a study conducted by Bryce Draper, county curriculum director, Beaver County students tested above national norms in every subject. Based on the California Achievement Test Battery, scores for arithmetic, reading, reading vocabulary, and mechanics of English were relatively high. The weakest subject was spelling.[178] A 1972 evaluation found that "the instructional program in the elementary schools of Beaver School District appears to be generally sound." As far as the secondary schools were concerned, the evaluation recommended a more varied program, but found that "the curriculum offering is very good when compared with schools of similar size." An additional recommendation suggested that "the schools of Beaver School District are in the heart of one of the most beautiful and 'science rich' areas of the state. the use of the local environment as an outdoor classroom would enhance the whole education offering and provide a vehicle for the development and practice of a multitude of values and skills."[179]

In 1998 the Beaver School District managed local public schools, including by that time three elementary schools in Beaver City, Milford and Minersville, and two high schools in Beaver City and Milford. Beaver County does not have a library system but provides financial support to local municipal libraries in Beaver, Minersville, and Milford.

Religion and Fraternal Organizations

For almost a century, the principal religious activity in the county centered on LDS church congregations. But in the 1950s a Community church was organized in Beaver City. The community center in the basement of the library building was used for church services of this interdenominational union, with members of the Presbyterian, Lutheran, Baptist, Methodist and other churches joining for worship services at 7:00 P.M. Sunday evenings. Reverend Paul Davis conducted services in Beaver. He also gave services in Marysvale and Panguitch besides delivering a Community church radio broadcast every Sunday morning over radio station KSVC out of Richfield, Utah, at 11:30 A.M.[180]

Always a more diversified population than the east end of the county, Milford's Methodist congregation joined after the first worship service held in their new church building in June 1962 for a work party to paint their church, clean up the yard, and install a new roof.[181] After a procession from their old church to their new one, led by Roland Culver as marshal, Reverend Glenn R. Phillips, bishop of the Rocky Mountain Area, delivered a sermon to the congregation. Ladies of the Women's Society for Christian Service prepared and served a dinner to members of the church.[182] The old Methodist church building on Main Street was torn down in 1964 after fifty-five years to make way for a five space trailer park to be operated by the Methodist church for permanent residents.[183] The Milford LDS ward added a wing to their church building as well as remodeled the interior—building a new entrance and installing a new hot water furnace room and heating system for the building, with an intercom system and new carpets throughout.[184]

Five of Milford's churches jointed together for Thanksgiving services on 24 November 1966—the First and Second LDS Wards, the Seventh-day Adventist Church, St. Bridget's Catholic Church, and the Community Methodist Church. Jesse Long spoke at the joint service which was held at 10:00 A.M. allowing families plenty of time to return home to prepare their Thanksgiving meals.[185]

A Milford institution, Father Valine, also known as the "Doughnut Priest," was born in 1908 in the Azores off the western coast of Portugal and came to the United States with his family at the age of eight. Ordained a priest in 1929, he worked first among Portuguese parishes in California before he came to Utah in 1941. He spent six years in Logan and one year in Richfield before coming to Milford in 1948 to found St. Bridget's Catholic Church. From his base in Milford he began offering Mass in Panguitch, Beaver, Kanab, Richfield, and Grand Canyon, Bryce, and Zion National parks. According to Father Valine, "These little places had no churches and few Catholics, but I felt the need to establish a place for them so that the people would know the Church existed and was here to stay."[186] In order to raise funds for the churches Father Valine undertook several enterprises including raising alfalfa for sale to local dairymen, catering meals for special occasions, selling St. Christopher medals, and, his most famous endeavor, making doughnuts for sale to tourists and local residents into his nineties.

Construction began on a $30,000 Milford Masonic temple in May 1952. The Milford Masons of Albert Pike Lodge No. 14 had been housed in a frame structure built in 1903, also used as a skating rink, theater, dance pavilion, and Masonic hall. The new structure was a two story cinder block building, 32' by 66', with a full basement, a banquet hall, and two rest rooms. An upper story included a rest room, lobby, preparation rooms, storage rooms, and a 32' by 42' lodge room. The basement had cement block walls, glass brick windows, and glass brick decoration.

The Albert Pike Lodge No. 14 was first organized in April 1907 under a charter from the Grand Lodge of Utah. Henry Jefferson was the first "worshipful master," with Francis Kopsa, senior warden; Samuel Edward Potts, junior warden; William Henry DeWolfe, treasurer; Burnett A. Filmer, secretary; James August Ingols, senior deacon; Herbert Nichols, junior deacon; Brandt Henry Engeike, senior steward; August Thiessen, junior steward; and Alexander Boyter. About 1915 the lodge purchased the old Opera House and met in the upper story. In 1941 they commissioned plans for a new building, but didn't begin construction because of the war.[187]

Ferdinand Erickson, grand master of the Grand Lodge of Utah, Free and Accepted Masons, assisted by other grand lodge leaders, officiated at the laying of the cornerstone ceremony in May 1953. More that thirty members of the Union Pacific Masonic club of California chartered a special UP car to attend the ceremonies.[188]

Planning Issues

Over time Beaver County's master plans provide a sense of local values and goals. A particular attitude toward land use and development emerges which reflects tradition, available resources and social and cultural attitudes. In 1993 the county commission stated their planning objectives as follows:

> Land use planning is to ensure community stability. In an environment where private lands are increasingly subject to arbitrary federal and state control and where federal and state properties comprise an overwhelming majority of the County's land base, that goal can best be achieved by empowerment, by protected the property rights, integrity and independence of every citizen and by

making custom and culture an issue of local, rather than national consensus.[189]

Confronting new issues like solid waste disposal, federal and state land management plans, economic decline, the county commission recognized the need for aggressive planning and development, and most planning focused on the best utilization of Beaver County's private land, which in 1993 represented only 6.1 percent of the total land in the county. Of a total 1,660,137 acres, 1,249,120 are controlled by the BLM, 138,489 by the forest service, or a total of 1,387,589 federal acres, or 83.6 percent. The state controls another 157,787 acres or 9.5 percent, or a total 93.1 percent with the federal government. Recreation was the principal multiple use of the BLM and forest service lands. In the western part of the county, BLM lands provide opportunities for off-road vehicle use, rockhounding, hiking, biking, and other recreation activities. The state park system, in particular Minersville State Park and Reservoir, also provides a good site for fishing and boating.

The local attitude toward the BLM and other federal land management agencies might be typified by a movement that emerged during the 1980s known as the Sagebrush Rebellion. In 1979 the Nevada legislature called for state control of BLM lands. Within the year Utah followed this lead. Clearly, ranchers and farmers alike throughout rural Utah favored the idea of bringing the public domain under localized control. The idea of privatization of federal assets was popular in the rural west but failed to seize national support. Opinion about the BLM's presence and power in the county varies dramatically and depends primarily on the way one earns a living. It is sufficient to say that the federal presence has a dramatic impact on this county's economic base. The county's master plan summarizes the complexity of issues that affect county life. "With challenges posed to the County from Federal and State land management programs, few long term employment opportunities, and expansive distances between necessary services, the residents cannot absolve themselves of their civic responsibility."[190]

The county's basic planning agenda was first clearly laid out in 1970 after extensive studies of virtually every aspect of the county's business. It included goals that would impact the economy, social life, development, and the natural environment:

> To provide a system of streets, roads and highways for the movement of people and goods throughout the County, and connecting to other areas, which will assist in the development of the economy, improve safety, convenience and pleasure for people, and preserve and enhance scenic and recreational values.

> To develop sound and profitable commercial and industrial enterprises, both existing and new, which will provide local residents and visitors with goods and services of high quality at reasonable prices, and in pleasant and efficient surroundings.

> Consistent with human environmental values, to promote economic growth sufficient to provide full employment for present residents of the area, former residents who wish to return, and young people of the area as they come into the labor force, and to attract new residents to the County.

> To establish full cooperation among all municipalities and the County in providing recreational facilities and services.

> To develop recognition in all local residents that tourism is a beneficial economic and good-will industry which should be fostered and expanded.

> To develop the existing and potential agricultural assets of the County to the maximum.

> To preserve, protect and utilize the forest areas of the County for their highest and best use for the present and the future.

> To protect, enhance, and wisely use the natural resources of the County for present and future organizations, recognizing the inter-relationships between man and nature and the necessity for decisions based on long-range values over short-range interests.

> To protect, preserve and enhance human values and human lives through the establishment of a healthful environment and good health for all citizens, and to promote an environment conducive to both mental and physical well-being.

> To use to full advantage the facilities available to provide educational opportunities to all those desiring to continue developing their potential abilities; to help each person to become a contributing member of society.

> To establish a social and economic environment in which all adults who are mentally and physically capable and who are not

prohibited from doing so by care of dependent children, can earn their own livings during the whole year and are so motivated as to want to do so.

To have every family live in a safe, decent, and sanitary dwelling.

To provide a balanced program of recreational activities for all age groups within the community.

To create within the Community, understanding of the law, respect for the law, obedience to the law, revision of the law where needed for justice or clarity, and enforcement of the law fairly and uniformly.[191]

Beaver County joined with the Five County Association of Governments for regional planning and development. This group was first organized in 1957 as the Five County Organization, with the purpose of securing cooperation of the member counties to promote industry development and tourism in the area. The Five County Association of Governments was established in 1972 to "join together in a voluntary organization. . . . for the purpose of meeting at regular intervals to discuss and study area wide problems of common interest and concern, and to develop action recommendations for ratification and implementation by member governments in the area served by the region."[192] The Southwest Utah Planning District included Beaver, Garfield, Iron, Kane, and Washington counties. Also it was a part of the Color County Travel Region, which again planned for local tourism. The county is conscious of the impact of the environment on the local economy. One travel brochure proclaims: "If it involves the outdoors, you'll probably find it in Beaver County, Utah." Easy access to nearby mountains, forest lands, and deserts created a natural destination for travelers from across the country.

Planning for recreation and tourism provided an opportunity for regional planning. Each county shared the benefit of tourists moving through adjoining canyons. In addition, public agencies that organize agricultural, stock raising, and other economic industries also benefit from regional cooperation.

Partnerships with federal and state agencies facilitated the development of new programs anticipating change or planning for future development. In 1998, for instance, under the state Local

Government Comprehensive Planning Project, Beaver County received $20,000 for a review of plan consistency and update to address the county's rapid industrial growth. The county's tiered community growth approach included growth boundaries. Within the county, a council of governments was created to facilitate the plan effort and to establish formal agreements between the cities and county about resource allocation, infrastructure, and growth boundaries. Beaver and Milford cities were prepared to adopt growth boundary amendments to their general plans. In addition, the county was working toward establishing different levels of service criteria and goals.[193] Through the same program, Beaver County received funds to convert all land parcel and land-use maps to a GIS-based system.

The Circle 4 Venture

Regardless of shifting fortunes, national markets for agricultural or mineral products, the influx of newcomers, or other demographic changes, the people of Beaver County found new ways of providing support for their families, making a living, and building the community. Throughout the county's history, these efforts were marked by tension between competing forces—insiders vs. outsiders, local vs. federal interests and agendas, economic benefit vs. the preservation of a traditional efforts.

When the "Circle 4" proposed to locate a hog farming operation ten miles south of Milford, it seemed to promise economic benefits, creating new jobs, bringing needed revenue into the county, and revitalizing local agricultural efforts. Many local businessmen saw the connection between their own work and this new operation. "Circle 4" was a joint venture of four of North Carolina's largest pork producers—Smithfield Foods, Smithfield, Virginia; Murphy Family Farms, Rose Hill, North Carolina; Carroll's Foods, Virginia; and Prestige Farms, Clinton, North Carolina.

The Milford "Circle 4" complex housed 30,000 sows and a total daily population ranging 250,000 to 280,000 hogs. As many as 5,000 hogs were shipped weekly for slaughter in California, or a total population of about 600,000 per year. The complex also included a feed mill, pens and other facilities. The company planned in 1998 to expand into three more complexes along a twenty-five mile corridor, increasing their daily census to 120,000 sows and 800,000 hogs or 1.3 million hogs at a given time, or 2 million hogs per year.

Within a short period of time, the project made Beaver County the West's largest hog producing area. By the time "Circle 4" reached its long-term goal, Utah would rank eighth in the nation in hog production. The company anticipated creating 750 permanent jobs.[194] Already an important source of income to local residents, in 1998 the annual payroll was $7.5 million.[195]

When "Circle 4" first came to Beaver County, it seemed certain to offer economic prosperity, security, and unexpected benefits. It did bring much needed revenue into the county, but it also brought new challenges for local government and private citizens pitting neighbor against neighbor, locals vs. outside investors, federal vs. county and local government.

According to Mike Carter, writing for the Associated Press, Allen Mayer and his family raised alfalfa in fields south of Milford for three generations before "Circle 4" came to the county. Now each morning they are acutely aware of the gallons of hog waste fermenting in sewage lagoons nearby. The Mayers joined with fifty other Milford farm families in opposition to the company, which they described as "employing the same political tactics and environmentally questionable mass-production techniques that caused North Carolina in August to slap a moratorium on corporate hog farming, encompassing operations of all four hog producers (Smithfield Foods, Murphy Family Farms, Carroll's Foods and Prestige Farms)." "It's like the devil came to Milford," said Joey Leko, owner of the Green Diamond Ranch near the Mayer farm. "This has split this community right down the middle, so's one half won't even talk to the other."[196]

Still the economic benefit to Milford was tangible and spread throughout the area—in 1994, when construction began on the complex, mining and the railroad, long a principal employer of the town, were in decline. In more than sixteen years, the city had not issued a single building permit. In 1998, however, more than sixty buildings were being built. "Circle 4" employed more county men and women than any other business, with 300 jobs and an annual payroll in excess of $6 million.

Milford's mayor Mary Wiseman described the hog farm as "a godsend, . . . this town was dying." Patty Cherry, longtime county resident and waitress at the Hong Kong Cafe, said three of her daughters and her sons-in-law were employed by the company. A fourth daughter, who had moved out of the county, was moving back to begin work at "Circle 4." According to Cherry, "My family is together because of that farm, it seems to me that's a fair trade for a little smell."[197]

Those concerned about the environmental impact find more than just the odor objectionable. Originally the company promised to cover sewage lagoons, but in 1998 the eighty open-air lagoons held between 6 million to 27 million gallons of waste.[198] In addition to the complex problem of dealing with such an enormous amount of waste, Utah's dry, cool climate created conditions that failed to control the odor, but instead slowed down the process of bacterial decomposition. Others worried that the operation would deplete or contaminate the underground water supply and were alarmed at the company's "wholesale purchase of water rights."[199] In 1997 an accident at the farm resulted in a spill of 80,000 gallons of hog waste into a well.[200]

"Circle 4" lawyer Warren Peterson drafted in 1994 the Utah Agricultural Protection Act which prevented lawsuits in agribusiness centering on such issues as odors, creating a complicated legal situation that limited local efforts to combat huge corporate interests.

State government supported the county in its effort to accommodate the new business in the mid-1990s, considering the prospects good for creating new jobs for the county. The Utah Division of Business and Economic Development organized an informal group of professionals to meet growth-related challenges presented by the new enterprise. Members included employees of the department itself, other state and federal agencies, and local officials. This committee joined for political efforts between counties to manage and distribute resources generated from the plant in an efficient way. Les Prall, as group leader, identified resources and public programs that could better manage each new development.[201]

"Circle 4" was the best new customer for local businesses and generator of income which circulated through the economy and benefitted many. According to one report, two county commissioners had significant business dealing with the companies, as did many businesses in the county. It made good sense to do so. Nevertheless, it was a mixed blessing—and the tensions between conflicting issues and constituencies created the equivalent of a moral dilemma for the county, perhaps the most important question residents faced at the end of the twentieth century: how to bring money into the county, create more jobs, preserve the natural and historical environment, and manage new growth—in short how to maintain sustainable development.

Community Identification

Beaver County is a place based on a network of associations, long-term relationships formed in churches, in schools, in civic organizations, that created a web of friendships, a sense of connectedness that was larger than family. At the center of Beaver County's towns was the activity of its churches—LDS wards continued to bring the largest number of county men and women together for both worship and social activities—ball games, dances, theatricals, and Sunday schools created common ground and relationships that played out in the secular world as well. Congregations of Methodists, Congregationalists, and other denominations played an important role in creating a more diversified population. But perhaps the most central institution defining county-wide relationships and creating a sense of community that defied sectarian boundaries was the high schools.

Terance White in an oral interview suggested that social life was tied inextricably to high school athletic events. Here relationships were established which continued and created the base of community life. Here also was a place, a common ground, where the people of the county could come together, cheer their team on, and find a source of identification and pride.[202] White grew up in Beaver and spent the last several years at the University of Utah and said that for someone who grew up in Beaver, the pull back home is fierce. And, according to White's experience, those who grew up in Beaver had a stronger sense of connectedness to the county than newcomers. Those who were new to the area had to carve out a new niche for themselves, separate from the traditional lines of networks long

A horse race on 24 July 1979 during the Annual Beaver Lions Club Race Meet. (Courtesy J.D. Osborn)

established and perpetuated through time. For those longtime residents, newcomers presented the threat of change—unpredictable and perhaps uncontrollable.

The debate over the demolition of the old Beaver High School illustrated the tension between those who favored moving full steam toward the modern world and those for whom the high school was the symbol of tradition, an icon of community life.

The Beaver High School building expressed the influence of Frank Lloyd Wright's prairie school. The building spread out on the site with low, horizontal wings on both sides of a central mass. A pattern of windows moved across the front elevation, emphasizing the horizontality of the mass. The prominent central entrance broke up the sweeping lines of the facade and fragmented it with steps and jogs that replaced the pilasters typical of the prairie style school. Symmetrically arranged, side entrances on side walls allowed students to enter from one of three sides. Prominent grand staircases on both sides of the entrance foyer led students to upper level classrooms.

A wagon from Beaver County is in the lead during the 1997 crossing of the Mormon Trail. (Church of Jesus Christ of Latter-day Saints)

Important as a monument of past generations, the Beaver High School was demolished to make way for a new building, perhaps a fitting metaphor for the movement from the past to meet the modern world on its own terms.

Cultural events helped alleviate the tension created by change—however subtle and slow moving. Community-wide activities like the local rodeos, labor day races and 24th of July celebrations helped create bonds and maintain relationships among residents of the county.

In this way the Beaver Civic Arts program combined local history with fun activities for youth. "It's kind of unique, we've been told," BCA president Gloria Murdock told the *Deseret News* of the theater effort. "It's a totally volunteer organization."[203] During the 1991 summer, the group produced five plays that were presented in the community's civic center. The community's junior high students produced *Skinned Alive, Headin' For a Weddin,* and various musical programs. Many of the plays were written, directed, and produced by the students themselves. This devotion to the arts typified Beaver's efforts at creating community institutions that were cross-generational.

Said Murdock, "It has a lot to do with community pride. I think a lot of the adults become involved so their children can have the opportunity. It's amazing how sophisticated the young people have become with the staging and balancing. We have great support too, not only in presenting but in attending."[204]

The county's agricultural heritage is recognized in part through the Utah Century Farms and Ranches program which identifies 100-year-old farms that are still in business. This program sponsored by the Utah Department of Agriculture and Food, the Utah Farm Bureau, the Utah State University Extension Service, the Utah State Fair Board, and Brigham Young University honored three Beaver County towns, including Ronald E. Roberts's farm, Morgan/Carter Farm and Bruce Brown's farm in Beaver.

The county's architectural heritage was given national recognition with the listing of many of Beaver's nineteenth-century buildings on the National Register of Historic Places after a comprehensive survey of Beaver was completed by the Utah State Historical Society in the late 1970s and early 1980s.

Conclusion

Communities evolve and carry on attitudes, practices, traditions, and beliefs in which individuals can grow or wither. Henry Glassie writes, "Community is the product not of tradition but of personal responsibility, yours to build or destroy."[205] Daniel Kemmis argues, "If there are not habituated patterns of work, play, grieving, and celebration designed to enable people to live well in a place, then those people will have at best a limited capacity for being public with one another. Conversely, where such inhabitary practices are being nurtured, the foundation for public life is also being created or maintained."[206]

The many men and women of Beaver County who choose to live as citizens with these responsibilities are the elements of hope and sustenance in this county. For a community to be healthy, the choices we make as individuals aren't enough. Caring about the county as a whole, whether it be the shared space of our city parks or the roads that connect individuals like threads in a crazy quilt across lines of fields, creates the particular pattern that represents this county—the efforts of men and women over time who have cared enough about

The new Beaver High School. (Courtesy Richard Albrecht)

each other and their place to contribute their best to making it a better place.

One of the most important themes that run through this history is the role volunteers have played in projects of economic and political nature that have strengthened this county and helped it meet the challenges that nature, the economy, and the government have created for it. This grassroots democracy is a never-ending process, and the day it ends, genuine community life ends with it.

Chambers of commerce, Lions Clubs and American Legions, local churches, and other organizations spent countless hours making their communities more safe, more beautiful, and better places to raise families. There is a lot of theory floating around these days about "community" and its continued possibility in American culture. Some say that we've gone too far as a society in the direction of specialization or control at the top, often at the expense of those at the bottom. Yet this history of Beaver county suggests that when individuals work as members of a community, it is possible to generate new patterns of engagement, broadly shared values and approaches to new problems, and that this work is best begun in small places. It also suggests that a healthy community is well served by, and may even depend on, the elements of stability, cohesion, change, and diversity.

Today in some ways Beaver County is like a crazy quilt, with pieces, traditions, or patterns preserved from the past—vivid memories of what it took to get to this point in time. Yet distinct traditions, differentiated neighborhoods that overlap and crisscross one another in new ways, have taught new lessons. The county has always known how to come together in a crisis—the people have their own brand of public rituals. They meet together in the county courthouse or in homegrown associations. They meet because they care enough to talk to one another and listen, to take positions and argue, and out of respect and love for the preservation of their common life together to agree to live by their resolutions. In this way a common language has been spoken and preserved.

This language, best understood from the inside, has enabled the county to preserve as well forms of principle and history, to stand firm in the face of large government, and to defend themselves against the stresses and shifts of a changing economy.

ENDNOTES

1. "Beaver County Population Drops," *The Beaver County News,* 19 May 1960.

2. "UP & L Plans to Spend 2 1/2 Million Improving Telluride Power System," *The Beaver County News,* 15 May 1958.

3. "Telephones on Increase Faster than Population," *The Milford News,* 6 December 1951.

4. "Building Boom Hits Milford," *The Milford News,* 14 August 1952.

5. "Beaver's Public Library," *The Beaver Press,* 19 January 1967.

6. In 1960 this figure was 3.48 persons; in 1970 it dropped to 3.18 persons; and in 1980 it dropped again to 3.06.

7. The national median age is thirty-two.

8. *Utah Code* 17–4–1.

9. "Background for Planning, Public Facilities and Services," Mountain Area Planners, Salt Lake City, Utah, 1970.

10. Beaver County Commission minutes, 6 April 1964, Beaver County Courthouse.

11. Ibid, 5 April 1965.

12. Counties with a total taxable value of more than $100 million are authorized to impose a maximum tax rate on .0032 per dollar (0.32 percent) of taxable value, while counties with a total tax value of less than $100 million are subject to an overall limit of .0036 per dollar (0.36 per dollar (0.36 percent) of taxable value. The limits do not include property levies for (1) outstanding judgment debts, (2) special improvement districts, (3) extended services in county service areas, (4) county library disaster recovery expenses, (5) interest and bond sinking fund expenses, (6) local health departments, (7) public transit districts, (8) municipal-type services in unincorporated areas, (9) paramedic or ambulance facilities, and (10) other special exceptions listed by statue.

13. "Beaver County, Utah: Economic, Population and Housing Study," 78: Department of Agriculture, $707,846; Department of Commerce, $28,378; Department of Defense, $101,000; Department of Health, Education, and Welfare, $716,213; Department of Housing and Urban Development, $51,000; Department of Interior, $188,165; Department of Labor, $23,783; Post Office Department, $134,780; Department of Transportation, $2,991,502; Treasury Department, $171,608; Civil Service Commission, $77,181; General Services Administration, $23,813; Office of Economic Opportunity, $30,752; Railroad Retirement Board, $183,002; Selective Service System, $3,564; Small Business Administration, $281,325; and Veterans Administration, $142,949 for a total of $5,856,861.

14. "It's Time to Start Stopping," *The Beaver Press,* 11 August 1961.

15. "We Lost," *The Beaver Press,* 8 September 1961.

16. The clerk is responsible for: (1) the issuing of all marriage licenses in the county, (2) the execution of all real estate transactions approved by the commission, (3) the maintenance of a list of all persons holding notary public commissions, (4) the administration of oaths to county officials, and (5) the compilation of a master jury used by the courts to obtain a jury pool.

17. "County Development Committee Reorganizes," *The Beaver Press,* 26 September 1963.

18. "Beaver County, Okehed for ARA Financing," *The Beaver Press,* 6 February 1964.

19. "Press Time," *The Beaver Press,* 13 June 1963.

20. "Project for Beaver and Iron Counties Approved," *The Beaver Press,* 18 March 1965.

21. "Trees to be Removed from Milford Curbs," *The Beaver County News,* 1 March 1962.

22. "Work Proceeds at Minersville Reservoir on State Park Project," *The Beaver Press*, 6 May 1965.

23. See "State Park Scheduled for Minersville Reservoir," and "Minersville Reservoir Park Project Underway," *The Beaver Press*, 28 February 1963 and 21 November 1963.

24. "The Minersville Watershed Committee," *The Beaver Press*, 30 November 1967.

25. "Flood Waters Trapped; Minersville Spared Disaster," *The Beaver County News*, 8 August 1968.

26. Dell Hollingshead to the County History Committee, 28 January 1999

27. "City Park to Boast Chamber of Commerce Information Booth," *The Beaver Press*, 4 April 1963.

28. "Work on Factory Building Proceeding on Schedule," and, "Armory Dedication Set for Saturday May 18 at 7:30," *The Beaver Press*, 16 May 1963.

29. "Forest Service to Hire 30 Local Men," *The Beaver County News*, 1 November 1962.

30. "UP & L to Absorb Telluride," *The Beaver Press*, 31 January 1963.

31. "U P & L Completes Plant at Beaver," *The Beaver County News*, 26 May 1966.

32. "History of Beaver Lions Club Television," in *Beaver Lions Club 1944–1994 50th Anniversary Charter Night*, copy at the Beaver County Travel Council Office

33. "Utah! County Economic Facts—1974, Beaver County," Utah Industrial Development Information System, Bureau of Economic and Business Research, University of Utah.

34. "Utah Economic and Business Review," 39 (April-May 1979) 3,4, Bureau of Economic and Business Research, University of Utah.

35. "Profile of the Beaver/Milford Labor Market Area," Bureau of Economic and Business Research, University of Utah, 1983.

36. "Building Construction in County Shows Increase," *The Beaver County News*, 28 April 1960.

37. "Profile of the Beaver/Milford Labor Market Area," 16.

38. Ibid, 19.

39. Ibid, 20.

40. Ibid, 26.

41. "Oil Fever Hits Milford," *The Milford News*, 1 June 1950.

42. "'Wildcat' Near Here Down 3,200 Feet; Has Minor Gas-Oil Showing at 2,100-Foot Depth," *The Milford News,* 6 July 1950.

43. "Oil Well 'Dry'; El Capitan Company to Drill West of Milford-Delta Road," *The Milford News,* 10 August 1950.

44. "Metal Producers Mill Starts Work Next Monday," *The Milford News,* 1 June 1950.

45. "Local Mill to Start Shipping of Concentrates," *The Milford News,* 15 June 1950.

46. "Harrington Mine Reopens This Week; 25 Men to Be Employed at Peak," *The Milford News,* 25 January 1951.

47. "Work Resumed at Harrington Mine; Favorable Ore Bodies Contacted on Two Levels," *The Milford News,* 28 June 1951.

48. "Harrington Mines Gets Defense Minerals Administration Contract for Deep Level Development Work," *The Milford News,* 27 September 1951.

49. "Tungsten Mill to Begin Operation in Early July," *The Beaver Press,* 19 June 1953.

50. "Rich Uranium Strike At North Creek May Initiate 'Boom'," *The Beaver Press,* 9 October 1953.

51. "Uranium Claims sold by Original Discovers," *The Beaver Press,* 13 December 1953.

52. "Uranium Prospecting Takes Spotlight in Beaver Area," *The Beaver Press,* 11 June 1954.

53. "Uranium Companies Make New Strike in North Creek Area," *The Beaver Press,* 14 July 1954.

54. "Prospecting Hits New High During July," *The Beaver Press,* 13 August 1954.

55. "Hopes for Uranium Producing Mine Spurs Beaver Prospecting," *The Beaver Press,* 25 June 1954.

56. Information provided by Dell Hollingshead

57. "Activation Looms for Sulphur Deposits in Beaver County," *The Beaver Press,* 29 October 1954.

58. "Work Starts on Beaver U-Mill," *The Milford News,* 9 June 1955. By 1957, the Indian Creek Canyon uranium mine was shipping ore regularly to Salt Lake City. See, "Beaver County Uranium Mine Shipping Ore to Salt Lake: Production to be Increased After Exploration and Development is Completed," *The Beaver County News,* 20 June 1957.

59. "Atom Tests to Be Monitored in Beaver County," *The Milford News,* 10 February 1955.

60. "Atom Test Blast Felt in Milford," *The Milford News,* 25 February 1955.

61. "Mining Gets Boost in West Beaver County," *The Beaver County News,* 12 July 1962.

62. "Majestic Mill Reopens to work Cerro Verde Copper," *The Milford News,* 11 September 1962.

63. "Oil company Sues County on Zone Ordinance," *The Beaver County News,* 21 April 1966.

64. "American Mining Puts Leech Plant in Operation," *The Beaver County News,* 11 January 1968.

65. John McCormick, "The Once and Future Barn," *Newsweek,* 9 July 1984, 12.

66. Dr. Caron E. Nelson, Mountain Area Planners, University of Utah School of Business, 1967.

67. Ward J. Roylance, *Utah's Geography and Counties* (Salt Lake City: n.p., 1967), 48.

68. "Beaver County, Utah: Economic, Population and Housing Study," 69.

69. "Milford Valley Grows into Big-Time Diversified," *The Milford News,* 30 October 1952.

70. "State Engineer Closes South Milford to Further Well Drilling," *The Milford News,* 27 November 1952.

71. "Milford Still Has Problem Maintaining Water Pressure," *The Beaver County News,* 23 June 1960.

72. "Work Started on Flood Control Dam in Big Wash Near Milford," *The Beaver Press,* 25 August 1961.

73. "'Comingling' of Sewer Water Makes Milford Health Hazard," *The Beaver County News,* 20 September 1962.

74. "Work on Swimming Pool is Progressing; Crew Stymied While Awaiting Blueprints," *The Milford Times,* 23 February 1950.

75. "Beaver's $40,000 Swimming Pool to be Opened Saturday," *The Beaver Press,* 30 July 1954.

76. "Nearly 100-Year-Old Building Being Razed," *The Beaver Press,* 8 October 1954.

77. "City Sets Bond Election for Electric System Improvements," *The Beaver Press,* 9 March 1956.

78. "Beaver Valley Publicized in National Magazines," *The Beaver Press,* "Special Hunting Supplement," October 1969.

79. "Visit Scenic Beaver County, Utah," pamphlet, Beaver County Travel Council, 1996.

80. "Lions, Local Merchants Lure Tourists with New Highway Sign," *The Beaver County News,* 23 January 1964.

81. "Lions Encourage New Industry," *The Beaver County News,* 6 January 1966.

82. "City Park Has 4,000 Visitors This Summer," *The Beaver Press,* 3 October 1963.

83. *Deseret News,* 23 November 1973.

84. "Beaver County, Utah: Economic, Population and Housing Study," Prepared by the Department of Economics School of Business and Technology, Southern Utah State College, July 1970, 55.

85. Ibid.

86. "UP Trains 9, 10 will Stop Running Friday Night," *The Beaver County News,* 2 April 1964.

87. "UP Tries Again to Abandon Trains 5 & 6," *The Beaver County News,* 25 January 1968.

88. "UP Officials Meet with City Dads," *The Beaver County News,* 21 March 1968.

89. "New Federal Defense Highway Talks Set for Friday at Beaver," *The Beaver County News,* 6 November 1958.

90. "Freeway Route Change Urged for Beaver Area," *The Beaver Press,* 4 December 1959.

91. "Beaver Citizen Petition Opposes Planned Federal Highway Route," *The Beaver County News,* 13 November 1958.

92. "How Many Cars Come Thru Beaver in a Day?" *The Beaver County Press,* 31 October 1963.

93. "From the Lions Magazine," *The Beaver County News,* 2 May 1968.

94. "Interchange for Beaver," *The Beaver Press,* 20 July 1967.

95. "Commission Meeting, Ribbon Cutting Ceremony to Open Beaver Section of Interstate Highway on Tuesday," *The Beaver County News,* 13 October 1960.

96. "Ribbon Snip Opens Highway 15 Section to Interstate Automobile Traffic," *The Beaver County News,* 20 October 1961.

97. "Highway Construction Schedule Clarified," *The Beaver Press,* 5 December 1963.

98. "Thousands of Utahns to Greet Nevadans as Final Link of All-Paved Route to Coast is Opened," *The Beaver Press,* 10 July 1959.

99. "Ribbon Snip Opens Highway to Coast," *The Beaver Press,* 17 July 1959.

100. "Cove Fort Road to be Pushed at Richfield Meeting," *The Beaver County News,* 22 February 1962.

101. "Contract Let for Work on Delta Highway," *The Beaver County News,* 29 November 1962.

102. "Beaver is Hub of South Utah Road Work," *The Beaver Press,* 12 June 1959.

103. "County to Build New Access Road in Beaver Mountains," *The Beaver Press,* 15 June 1956.

104. "Airport Landing Strip Gets New Surface of Heavier Mulch," *The Beaver Press,* 21 September 1956.

105. "Milford Airport was Busy Spot This Week," *The Beaver County Press,* 1 February 1962.

106. "Freak Wind Causes Havoc at Local Airport," *The Beaver County Press,* 25 August 1960.

107. "Airport Will Be Open June 23," *The Beaver County News,* 13 June 1968.

108. "Milford Races Are Labor Day Attraction," *The Beaver County News,* 29 August 1957.

109. "Friday, Saturday Are 'Big Days' For Beaver," *The Beaver County News,* 29 August 1957.

110. "Double-Dance to Feature Annual Forty-Niner Celebration; Parade, Boxing and Games are Highlights," *The Milford News,* 18 May 1950.

111. "Mayor Kizer Garners Racing Crown From Mayor Gottfredson at American Legion 49er Celebration," *The Beaver County News,* 19 July 1958.

112. "Milford Labor Day Celebration Will Feature Horse Races, Softball, Dance," *The Milford News,* 1 September 1955.

113. "New White Way Lights in Use; Xmas Season Officially Opened," *The Milford News,* 23 November 1950.

114. "Lions Club to Sponsor 'Build Milford' Program," *The Milford News,* 14 December 1950.

115. "City to Issue Bonds for Swim Pool and Water Improvements," *The Milford News,* 1 February 1951.

116. "Bond Election for Swimming Pool, "Water Improvements, Carries 6 to 1," *The Milford News,* 29 March 1951.

117. "Milford Swim Pool Opened for Fourth; 200 Kids Enjoy Plunge," *The Milford News,* 5 July 1951.

118. "Street Paving Program Nears Completion," *The Milford News,* 12 May 1955.

119. "All Streets in City of Milford are now Paved," *The Beaver County News,* 27 June 1957.

120. "Building Under Way for Dial Phones," *The Milford News,* 2 June 1955.

121. "Televisions Installation for Milford to Start this Week," *The Beaver Press*, 10 August 1956.

122. "Public TV Gets Boost with Milford Power Installation," *The Beaver County News*, 4 April 1957.

123. "Milford's Last Landmark Being Razed," *The Beaver County News*, 25 April 1957.

124. "Milford Flood Control Project Gets Army Engineers Approval," *The Beaver Press*, 19 June 1959.

125. "New Water Tank Doubles Milford Storage Capacity," *The Milford News*, 28 July 1955.

126. Richard Campbell Roberts, "A History of the Utah National Guard," Ph.D. dissertation, University of Utah, 1973, 485–86.

127. Ibid., 488.

128. Ibid, 489.

129. Quoted in "213th Field Artillery Utah National Guard—Korean War," Supplement, *Richfield Reaper*, 15 August 1990.

130. Roberts, "The Utah National Guard," 492

131. "Gary Banks Shot by Cong Sniper in Vietnam," *The Beaver County News*, 11 January 1968.

132. "Veterans," Bureau Economic Information System Bureau of Economic Analysis, May 1998, http://govinfo.library.orst.edu/cgi-bin/usaco-list?31–001.utc.

133. *The Beaver County News*, 1 January 1981

134. Ibid, 11 January 1980.

135. Ibid 11 January 1980.

136. Ibid 28 February 1980.

137. Ibid, 10 December 1981.

138. "Drastic Shortage of Nurses Hampers Operation of Milford Hospital," *The Milford News*, 21 September 1950.

139. "Beaver County Hospital 'Belongs' to Milford Civic Organizations," *The Beaver County News*, 4 December 1958.

140. "Hospital Board Notes Progress in Building Program," *Beaver County News*, 31 March 1969.

141. "Hospital Group Explains Program at Public Meeting," *The Beaver County News*, 11 August 1960.

142. "Hospital Nearing Completion; All-Out Drive for Needed Funds is Under Way by Civic Organizations," *The Beaver County News*, 5 November 1964.

143. "Federal Grant to Help Build 10 Bed Hospital, 10 Bed Home for Senior Citizens," *The Beaver County News*, 13 December 1962.

144. "Milford Hospital Open House," *The Beaver Press*, 17 June 1965.

145. "City Council Backs Plans for Beaver Hospital," *The Beaver Press*, 9 October 1959.

146. "'Beaver's Supporting a Hospital—But it's Not in Beaver," *The Beaver County News*, 2 October 1959.

147. "County Commissioners Approve Modified Hospital Service Area," *The Beaver Press*, 11 September 1959.

148. "Two Hospital Areas Okeyed by Commissioners," *The Beaver Press*, 16 October 1959.

149. "County Commission Delays Action on Funds for Hospital," *The Beaver Press*, 11 December 1959.

150. "Press Time," *The Beaver Press*, 21 March 1963.

151. "Hospital to be Built Here," *The Beaver County News*, 30 April 1964.

152. "Supreme Court Kills Hospital Act," *The Beaver Press*, 4 March 1965.

153. "Election Shows Nine to One Want Hospital," *The Beaver Press*, 22 April 1965.

154. "Construction Starts on Beaver Hospital," *The Beaver Press*, 1 July 1965.

155. "Construction Starts on New Hospital," *The Beaver County News*, 18 June 1964.

156. "Enrollment Drops in Beaver County Schools," *The Milford News*, 17 January 1952.

157. "School Enrollment Decreases Sixty Throughout County," *The Beaver Press*, 25 September 1953.

158. 'Enrollment Drops in Beaver County Schools," *The Milford News*, 17 January 1952.

159. "Officials Issue Data on Special School Election," *The Beaver Press*, 16 April 1954.

160. "Voters Refuse Tax Increase for Additional School Funds," *Beaver Press*, 30 April 1954.

161. "Board Proposes Reductions In School Services, Teachers," *The Beaver Press*, 7 May 1954.

162. "Beaver Teachers Refuse Contracts for Next Year," *The Beaver Press*, 13 May 1954.

163. "Board of Education Calls Special Meeting on Teachers' Salaries," *The Beaver Press,* 31 May 1954.

164. "Teachers Accept Revised Salary Schedule of Board," *The Beaver Press,* 23 May 1954.

165. "County Schools Getting Better All the Time," *The Beaver County News,* 24 September 1964.

166. "Report Completed on Beaver County Schools," *The Beaver Press,* 20 April 1956.

167. "Milford Delegation Asks School Board for New Building," *The Beaver Press,* 6 January 1956.

168. "Voters Approve School Levy Increase by 5 to 1 Majority," *The Beaver Press,* 4 May 1956.

169. "Voters Okeh School Bonds," *The Beaver Press,* 21 December 1956.

170. "Contract Let for Milford School," *The Beaver Press,* 17 April 1958 and "Contract Let for Minersville School Building," *The Beaver County News,* 20 November 1958.

171. "Teachers, Students 'Thrilled' With New School Building," *The Beaver County News,* 7 January 1960.

172. "State May Close Minersville School; Force Consolidation of Milford-Beaver Highs," *Beaver County News,* 8 September 1966.

173. "Meeting in Beaver Will Discuss County School Consolidation," *Beaver County News,* 6 October 1966.

174. "School Patrons Turn Thumbs Down on Consolidation," *Beaver County News,* 13 October 1966.

175. "Consolidating Schools will Cut Out Heart of Community," *The Beaver County News,* 27 October 1966.

176. "Radio Station KBCS Marks 20th Anniversary," *The Beaver County News,* 2 October 1969.

177. Ibid.

178. "Beaver County Students Better than National Scholarship," *The Beaver Press,* 12 May 1961.

179. Utah State Board of Education, *Beaver County School District Evaluation,* 1972, 1- 2, copy at the Utah State Historical Society.

180. "Why a Community Church in Beaver?" *The Beaver Press,* 11 September 1959.

181. "Methodists Hold First Services in New Church in Milford," *The Beaver County News,* 21 June 1962.

182. "Sunday Consecration Service Will Open New Methodist Church," *The Beaver County News,* 11 October 1962.

183. "Main Street Landmark Razed," *The Beaver County News,* 2 July 1964.

184. "LDS Church Starts New Addition to Milford Chapel," *The Beaver County News,* 17 November 1966.

185. "Joint Services Scheduled by Five Milford Churches on Thanksgiving," *The Beaver County News,* 17 November 1966.

186. Quoted in Donna Davis, "Man of many missions," *Extension,* May 1988, 7

187. "Construction Starts on New $30,000 Milford Masonic Temple," *The Milford News,* 1 May 1952.

188. "Grand Master to Dedicate Milford Masonic Temple," *The Beaver Press,* 15 May 1953.

189. "Beaver County General Plan," April 1993.

190. Ibid.

191. "Planning Goals and Policies," Beaver County Master Plan Studies, 1970.

192. "Five County Association of Governments," Statement of Purpose.

193. "Local Government Planning Project," 21 October 1998, Doug Carriger, Beaver County.

194. Mick Carter, Associated Press, "Giant, Smelly Hog Farm Divides Tiny Farming Community," *Source News And Reports,* 10 November 1997.

195. "Circle 4's History," *The Spectrum,* 30 November 1997.

196. Mick Carter, "Giant, Smelly Hog Farm."

197. Ibid.

198. Solid waste settled in the primary ponds where bacteria broke the sewage down before it drained into a second lagoon in liquid form for evaporation. Usually hogs create two to three times as much sewage as human beings, and Circle 4's hogs created the equivalent of a population of 1.8 million people. Considering Utah's 2 million population this is a tremendous amount of waste.

199. Mick Carter, "Giant, Smelly Hog Farm."

200. Ibid.

201. "Utah Economic Development News," *Utah Economic Development News,* April 1996.

202. Terance White, interviewed by Martha S. Bradley, 29 September 1998, Salt Lake City, Utah.

203. *Deseret News,* 21 June, 1991.

204. Ibid.

205. Henry Glassie, *Passing the Time in Ballymenone,* (Philadelphia: University of Pennsylvania Press, 1982), 6.

206. Daniel Kemmis, *Community and the Politics of Place,* (Norman: University of Oklahoma Press, 1990), 32.

Selected Bibliography

Arrington, Leonard, *Great Basin Kingdom: An Economic History of the Latter-day Saints, 1830- 1900.* Cambridge, Massachusetts: Harvard University Press, 1958.

Arrington, Leonard J., Feramorz Y. Fox, and Dean L. May, *Building The City of God: Community and Cooperation Among the Mormons.* Salt Lake City: Deseret Book, 1976.

Belly, Keith and J. Kenneth Davies. "Minersville: The Beginnings of Lead-Silver Mining in Utah," *Utah Historical Quarterly* 51 229–51.

Betenson, Lula Parker, as told to Dora Flack. *Butch Cassidy, My Brother.* Provo: Brigham Young University Press, 1975.

Bolton, Herbert E. *Pageant in the Wilderness: The Story of the Escalante Expedition to the Interior Basin, 1776.* Salt Lake City: Utah State Historical Society, 1972.

Bonar, Linda, "Historical Houses in Beaver: An Introduction to Materials, Styles, Craftsmen," *Utah Historical Quarterly* 51:212–28.

Brooks, Juanita. *The Mountain Meadows Massacre.* Norman: University of Oklahoma Press, 1970.

Chavez, Fray Angelico, translator and Ted J. Warner, ed. *The Dominguez-*

385

Escalante Journal: Their Expedition Through Colorado, Utah, Arizona, and New Mexico in 1776. Provo: Brigham Young University, 1976.

Crampton, C. Gregory and Steven K. Madsen, *In Search of the Spanish Trail: Santa Fe to Los Angeles, 1829–1848.* Salt Lake City: Gibbs-Smith Publisher, 1993.

Ellsworth, S. George, ed. *The Journals of Addison Pratt.* Salt Lake City: University of Utah Press, 1990.

Maeser, Reinhard, *Sketches from the Life and Labors of Wilson Gates Nowers.* (Beaver: Weekly Press, 1914.

Merkley, Aird G., ed. *Monuments to Courage: A History of Beaver County.* Milford: Beaver County Chapter of the Daughters of Utah Pioneers, 1948.

Morgan, Dale L., *Jedediah Smith and the Opening of the West.* Lincoln: University of Nebraska Press, 1953.

Notarianni, Philip F. "The Frisco Charcoal Kilns," *Utah Historical Quarterly* 50: 40–46.

Patterson, Richard. *Butch Cassidy: A Biography.* Lincoln: University of Nebraska Press, 1998.

Pointer, Larry, *In Search of Butch Cassidy.* (Norman: University of Oklahoma Press, 1977.

Poulsen, Richard C., "Stone Buildings in Beaver City," *Utah Historical Quarterly* 43: 278–85.

Powell, Allan Kent, ed. *Utah History Encyclopedia.* Salt Lake City: University of Utah Press, 1994.

Robinson, Alvaretta and Daisy Gillins. *They Answered the Call: A History of Minersville, Utah.* Minersville: Minersville Centennial Committee, 1962.

Smart, Donna T. "Over the Rim to Red Rock Country: The Parley P. Pratt Exploring Company of 1849," *Utah Historical Quarterly* 62: 171–90.

Stokes, William Lee. *Geology of Utah.* Salt Lake City: Utah Museum of Natural History and Utah Geological and Mineral Survey, 1986.

Tanner, Joseph M. *A Biographical Sketch of John Riggs Murdock.* Salt Lake City: The Deseret News, 1909.

Warrum, Noble. *Utah in the World War.* Salt Lake City: Arrow Press, 1924.

Index